Assembly Language Programming for the IBM Personal Computer

DAVID J. BRADLEY

IBM Corporation

PRENTICE-HALL, INC.   Englewood Cliffs, New Jersey 07632

Library of Congress Cataloging in Publication Data

BRADLEY, DAVID J. (date)
   Assembly language programming for the IBM Personal
Computer.

   Includes index.
   1. IBM Personal Computer—Programming.   2. Assembler
language (Computer program language)   I. Title.
QA76.8.I2594B7 1984   001.64'2   83-8638
ISBN 0-13-049189-6
ISBN 0-13-049171-3 (pbk.)

Editorial/production supervision
   and interior design: Kathryn Gollin Marshak
Cover design: Photo Plus Art—Celine Brandes
Manufacturing buyer: Gordon Osbourne

IBM is a registered trademark of the International Business Machines Corporation

Printed in the United States of America

10 9 8 7

ISBN 0-13-049171-3 {P}
ISBN 0-13-049189-6 {C}

Prentice-Hall International, Inc., *London*
Prentice-Hall of Australia Pty. Limited, *Sydney*
Editora Prentice-Hall do Brasil, Ltda., *Rio de Janeiro*
Prentice-Hall Canada Inc., *Toronto*
Prentice-Hall of India Private Limited, *New Delhi*
Prentice-Hall of Japan, Inc., *Tokyo*
Prentice-Hall of Southeast Asia Pte. Ltd., *Singapore*
Whitehall Books Limited, *Wellington, New Zealand*

Contents

Preface

This book teaches you how to write assembly language programs for the
IBM Personal Computer. It also explains how to use the IBM Personal Computer
to write those programs. Finally, it shows you ways to use assembly language
programs with the rest of the system.

This is a first book in assembly language programming. Previous programming experience, in a high-level language, is desirable for the use of the book.
There is no discussion of algorithm design and programming techniques. It may be
difficult for you to use this book if you have had no previous experience in writing
BASIC or Pascal or similar programs. However, the text presents material in a
way that should allow you to begin assembly programming even if you don't know
anything about the internal workings of a computer.

The first section, comprising the first two chapters, teaches the fundamentals of computer operation. It emphasizes those functions of the computer that
aren't readily apparent when using a high-level language. This includes a
discussion of binary arithmetic and data representation. The section also deals
with the general operation of the assembler. This section may be skipped by
programmers with assembly language experience.

The second portion of the book, consisting of Chapters 3, 4, and 7, is an
explanation of the processor used in the IBM Personal Computer, the Intel 8088.
This includes a description of the 8088, its registers, and its addressing modes.
The book presents the instruction set of the 8088 together with examples showing
the use of most of the instructions. Chapter 7 is devoted to the 8087 Numeric Data

Processor. It describes the additional data types and instructions made available through the 8087. The chapter uses several examples to show the operation of the numeric coprocessor.

Where the preceding section was sufficiently broad to cover nearly all systems using the 8086/8088 processor family, the final sections are linked directly to the IBM Personal Computer. Chapters 5 and 6 deal with the creation and use of programs on the IBM machine. You'll learn how to use the assembly language "tools." These include the line editor, the assembler, and the linker, as well as an overview description of the Disk Operating System. This section describes the Disk Operating System as a program environment. Chapter 6 describes some of the special tools available as part of the Macro Assembler. This includes not only macros, but also the special data definition tools that are essential for assembly language programming.

Chapters 8, 9, and 10 cover the hardware and "microcode" portions of the IBM Personal Computer. This section emphasizes the unique aspects of the IBM Personal Computer and the application of assembly language programming to it. Of particular interest is Chapter 10, which describes the techniques of linking an assembly language program to another program or system. This chapter contains several different methods of fitting an assembly language program with another program, or making the program a permanent addition to the system.

The author was a member of the team that designed and built the IBM Personal Computer. I would like to thank all of the people in the Personal Computer organization who have helped me during the preparation of this text. Special thanks go to Dave O'Connor and Jud McCarthy, my managers during this period. Most important, I would like to thank my wife, Cynthia, for her help and encouragement.

David J. Bradley

CHAPTER

1

Introduction

Welcome to assembly language programming for the IBM Personal Computer. This book teaches you how to write assembly language programs, and it uses the IBM Personal Computer as the teaching vehicle.

ASSEMBLY LANGUAGE PROGRAMMING

Why should you be interested in assembly language programming? High-level languages such as BASIC, FORTRAN, and Pascal are commonly used today. You are probably familiar with at least one high-level language. If you're currently using an IBM Personal Computer, you know that the BASIC interpreter is part of the system unit. Why should you bother with another programming language, especially one that's going to be difficult at times? Even with today's high-powered languages, you still need assembly language because of its power and precision.

Assembly programs can be very powerful. Given programmers with equal skills and abilities, the assembly language program will be smaller in size and faster in execution than the same program written in a high-level language. This holds true for virtually all small and medium-size programs. Unfortunately, assembly language programs lose some of their power as the program size increases. That's because of the attention to detail that's necessary for an assembly program. As you'll see throughout this text, assembly language requires

1

you to decide each and every action of the computer. For a small program, this lets you optimize the program to work efficiently with the computer hardware. For a larger program, the myriad details may prevent you from doing an efficient job of the entire program, even though some individual components of the program will be very good. Clearly, assembly language programming is not the answer for all programs.

Assembly language programs are also very precise. Because assembly language allows the programmer to deal directly with the hardware, assembly programs can do things that no other program can. Certainly for I/O device programming, where the program requires control of the individual I/O device bits, assembly language programming is the only appropriate choice.

Clearly, the power and precision of assembly language programming offers advantages. But its attention to detail also causes problems. When is the correct time to use assembly language programming?

Certainly, you must use assembly language programs when there's no other way to write the program. For example, IBM programmers wrote all of the I/O device control programs for the IBM Personal Computer using assembly language routines. IBM needed the precision of assembly language to control the I/O devices and the interrupt system, where no other programming language would work. Similarly, IBM wrote the diagnostic routines, which must check every detail of the hardware, in assembly language.

You should also use assembly language when performance is a major concern. This performance may be either the execution time of a program or its final size. The FORTRAN mathematics subroutine library is an example of a program that requires good performance, both in time and space. The math routines are a part of every FORTRAN program, so they should be as small as possible. Also, those routines handle all of the math functions in a FORTRAN program, so they are used frequently. Therefore, they should execute rapidly.

What programs aren't candidates for assembly language? Well, you can write any program in assembly language, but a program of significant size is better handled in a higher-level language, such as BASIC or Pascal. These languages let you concentrate on the problem. You don't have to deal directly with the details of the hardware and the processor. A high-level language lets you step back and see the forest rather than the trees.

Obviously, then, you need to mix assembly language programs with high-level language programs. This text will concentrate on assembly language programming for those tasks for which it is well suited, such as I/O control. In fact, the final chapter deals directly with the problem of linking assembly language programs with other programming languages. These methods give you the best of both worlds. You can use assembly routines for the precise control and power when you need it, and high-level routines for the overall program. All you have to do is hook them together to make it happen.

There's a final reason for learning assembly language programming. Only by writing programs at this level of detail can you learn how the machine works at its lowest levels. If you want to know everything there is to know about a computer, you have to be familiar with its assembly language. The only way to do that is to write programs in that language. Reading the manual alone won't do the job.

IBM PERSONAL COMPUTER

Why does this text use the IBM Personal Computer as the basis for learning assembly language programming? There are several reasons. First, the IBM Personal Computer is new and powerful. As a personal computer, the IBM machine has extended capabilities, beyond those of earlier personal computers. As you'll see in more detail later, the Personal Computer uses the Intel 8088 microprocessor. This processor can do 16-bit arithmetic and address over 1 million characters of storage. These capabilities give it a power much closer to large computers than to the earlier personal computers.

Second, the IBM Personal Computer has all the development tools that you'll need to do assembly programming. Besides the assembler, IBM provides an editor, linker, and disk operating system to put it all together. There's even a debugger to help you take it all apart and then put it back together right.

Finally, the IBM Personal Computer is a good system on which to learn assembly language programming because of its availability. It is an inexpensive machine, yet still offers all the capabilities that assembly language programming requires. Even more, as a "personal" computer, the machine belongs to you, at least while you're executing your program. This means that you can try out things that you couldn't on a larger machine that you're sharing with others. You can take over the I/O attachments and program them to do interesting things. You can do anything you want with any part of the system. You can do this even if it brings the system "down." Since it's a personal machine, when there's a problem, you just turn the machine off and start all over. The only person you can interfere with is yourself. As a personal machine, it makes a great development environment.

THIS BOOK

This book introduces you to the IBM Personal Computer and its assembly language. Although the major concentration is on assembly programming, this text describes the programming aspects of the major hardware features of the machine. You'll learn how the I/O devices work and how the programs make them work correctly. You'll also learn how to write your own assembly language programs using the IBM Personal Computer. After you write these programs, this book shows you how to link them into a high-level language program or build your program into the system.

Assembly language programming is a fascinating experience, but often frustrating. This book uses examples to show you some programs that do work. These examples should get you started. But the only way you can learn about programming is to do the programs yourself. You have to make your own mistakes to learn. Good luck, and have fun.

CHAPTER

2

Computer Fundamentals

This chapter will explain the characteristics of computers. It will tell you how computers work and why they do things the way they do. Some of the concepts may be familiar to you. If you have had no previous experience with assembly language programming, many of these operations will be new.

BINARY ARITHMETIC

All computers store information using the binary system. This means that every item of information stored by the computer has only two choices. These choices are labeled "on" and "off," "true" and "false," or "1" and "0." The computer stores these values as voltage levels. Fortunately, we don't need to be concerned with the voltages, only the numbers, when writing programs. From the simple numbers 0 and 1, we can do very complicated arithmetic.

Because of the binary representation of data, computers use base 2 arithmetic to perform their computations. Base 2 arithmetic uses only the two numbers, 0 and 1. We normally use base 10, or decimal arithmetic. In base 10 arithmetic, there are 10 different numerals used, 0 through 9. Base 2 arithmetic can be thought of as the system for people with two fingers.

The limitation of only 10 numerals in base 10 arithmetic does not prevent us from representing larger numbers. We use multiple-digit numbers, where each position within the number is a different power of 10. The rightmost digit of any number is the number of units. The next digit to the left is the number of tens. The next is hundreds, and so on. The progression, from right to left, is 10^0, 10^1, 10^2, and so on. The number 2368 is really 2 thousands, 3 hundreds, 6 tens, and 8 units. Figure 2.1 shows the breakdown of the number 2368, in mathematical terms.

$$2368 = 2 \times 10^3 + 3 \times 10^2 + 6 \times 10^1 + 8 \times 10^0$$
$$= 2000 + 300 + 60 + 8$$

Figure 2.1   Decimal Representation

Base 2, or binary, arithmetic is identical, except that the positions of the number represent powers of 2 rather than powers of 10. Numbers larger than 1 are represented as multiple-digit numbers, just as numbers larger than 9 become multiple-digit numbers in base 10. Each digit of a binary number is called a bit, for Binary digIT. The position of each bit within the number corresponds to a power of 2. Figure 2.2 shows the meaning of the binary number 101101B.

$$101101B = 1 \times 2^5 + 0 \times 2^4 + 1 \times 2^3 + 1 \times 2^2 + 0 \times 2^1 + 1 \times 2^0$$
$$= 32 + 0 + 8 + 4 + 0 + 1$$
$$= 45$$

Figure 2.2   Binary Representation

We'll use the suffix "B" to indicate that a number is in binary representation. This distinguishes decimal numbers, with no suffix, from binary numbers. For example, 2368 is a decimal number, 101101B is a binary number. Most mathematics textbooks use subscripts to indicate the number system being used. We'll use the "B" since the IBM Assembler uses this character to distinguish binary numbers.

In the table of Figure 2.3, 4 bits of binary data are required to represent the largest decimal number. For larger numbers, even more bits are required. A binary number with n bits can represent a number as large as $2^n - 1$. That is, a

Decimal	Binary
1	1
2	10
3	11
4	100
5	101
6	110
7	111
8	1000
9	1001
10	1010

Figure 2.3   First 10 Integers

binary number n bits long can uniquely represent the integers from 0 to $2^n - 1$. For the 4-bit example in Figure 2.3, 15 ($2^4 - 1$) is the largest integer that can be represented.

For any particular microprocessor, there is a maximum width to the binary numbers that it can conveniently hold. For the 8088 microprocessor used in the IBM Personal Computer, the internal data operations are 16 bits wide. The maximum integer that 16 bits can represent is $2^{16} - 1$, or 65,535. However, this unsigned arithmetic allows numbers from 0 to 65,535 only. We need a variation of this scheme to indicate negative numbers.

TWO'S COMPLEMENT

To indicate both positive and negative numbers, the 8088 uses two's-complement arithmetic. In this signed arithmetic, the leftmost bit of the number indicates the sign of the integer. Positive numbers have a 0 in the most significant bit, while negative numbers have a 1. Positive numbers have the same meaning in both signed and unsigned arithmetic. Negative numbers have a different meaning. To negate a number, that is, to change its sign, the number is complemented and the result is incremented by one. In a 4-bit example, the value 5 is 0101B, while -5 is 1011B. The example in Figure 2.4 shows the method.

The example in Figure 2.5 shows that there is a single occurrence of 0 in two's-complement arithmetic. Thus, -0 equals 0. For an arbitrary n-bit number in two's-complement arithmetic, the largest value is $2^{n-1} - 1$ and the smallest is -2^{n-1}. There is a single occurrence of zero. In the 4-bit system, the largest number is 7, while the smallest is -8, as shown in Figure 2.6.

5	=	0101B
To change sign:		
Complement		1010B
Add 1		0001B
-5	=	1011B
To change sign:		
Complement		0100B
Add 1		0001B
5	=	0101B

0	=	0000B
To change sign:		
Complement		1111B
Add 1		0001B
-0	=	0000B	=	0

Figure 2.4   Two's Complement of 5   **Figure 2.5**   Zero Representation

As we'll see later, the 8088 processor can treat integers as either signed or unsigned arithmetic values. The choice is left to the assembly language programmer. However, when a program uses signed arithmetic, the 8088 processor uses two's-complement arithmetic to perform the operations.

Decimal	Binary	Decimal	Binary
7	0111	−1	1111
6	0110	−2	1110
5	0101	−3	1101
4	0100	−4	1100
3	0011	−5	1011
2	0010	−6	1010
1	0001	−7	1001
0	0000	−8	1000

Figure 2.6 Two's-Complement Numbers

HEXADECIMAL REPRESENTATION

Binary arithmetic is fine for computers, since they deal only in 1's and 0's. But human dialogue requires a more compact representation. We'll use hexadecimal data representation for our shorthand.

Hexadecimal representation of numbers is a base 16 number system. Each of the digits in a number can assume a value from 0 to 15. Each position in the number is a power of 16. Hex representation is a convenient method of writing binary information. Each hexadecimal digit corresponds to 4 bits. To convert binary to hexadecimal, group the bits into groups of 4 and read off the value as a hex digit. This gives a four-to-one compression in numerals—very convenient for human beings.

Hexadecimal arithmetic presents a slight problem, since the only single-digit numbers we have available are from 0 to 9. We will represent the numbers 10 through 15 with the first six letters of the alphabet, A through F. The equivalence table for decimal, hexadecimal, and binary is shown in Figure 2.7.

As the table shows, each hexadecimal digit corresponds directly to 4 bits of any binary number. Hexadecimal representation is normally the choice for a machine where the word size is a multiple of 4. Since the Intel 8088 has a word size of 16 bits, we will use hexadecimal notation. Each 16-bit value is represented by four hexadecimal digits. In this book, numbers written in hexadecimal notation will be indicated by the suffix "H" and binary numbers with the suffix "B."

Decimal	Binary	Hexadecimal	Decimal	Binary	Hexadecimal
0	0000	0	8	1000	8
1	0001	1	9	1001	9
2	0010	2	10	1010	A
3	0011	3	11	1011	B
4	0100	4	12	1100	C
5	0101	5	13	1101	D
6	0110	6	14	1110	E
7	0111	7	15	1111	F

Figure 2.7 Hexadecimal Numbering

Decimal numbers appear without a suffix or with the suffix "D." This representation corresponds directly to the way in which we enter numbers with the assembler. A program can use any of the three systems we have discussed (decimal, binary, and hexadecimal) to represent values for the assembler.

When writing hexadecimal numbers, it is important to make sure that the assembler understands it as a number. If you enter "FAH," it could be the hexadecimal number "FA" or it could be the variable name "FAH." The assembler assumes that a number begins with a number and that a variable begins with a letter. So "FAH" is a variable to the assembler. If we want the hex number rather than a variable, we must enter it as "0FAH," which has the desired value and begins with a number. Any hex number that begins with the values A through F must be preceded with a zero, to prevent the assembler from misunderstanding.

MACHINE LANGUAGE AND ASSEMBLY LANGUAGE

We have seen how the 0 or 1 values of the computer form a number system. We'll now look at how combinations of these same 0 and 1 values can be used to program a computer.

A computer program is a sequence of instructions. These instructions explain to the computer the job that it is to perform. This is similar to a recipe in a cookbook. In a recipe, there is a narrative that explains the actions required to create a particular dish. In a similar fashion, the computer has a sequence of instructions that tell it exactly what to do. This set of instructions is called the program. The act of developing the correct set of instructions is known as programming the computer. In our recipe analogy, the recipe is the program, and the person who wrote the recipe is the programmer. The part of the computer is played by the person cooking the meal.

The actual program that the computer executes is a bunch of 1's and 0's contained within the computer memory. This string of bits is known as machine language. Machine language is the language that the machine understands. The computer fetches these machine language instructions from memory in a well-defined manner. The computer then executes the instruction indicated by the bit configuration. This fetch–execute cycle will be explained in a later section of this chapter.

However, machine language doesn't make much sense to people. If you wanted to add two numbers in the 8088 (for example, adding the AX register to the BX register—a brief explanation of registers will follow momentarily), the instruction value is

0000001111000011B   (or 03C3H)

These two bytes tell the computer the exact operation to perform. Similarly, to subtract two numbers (subtracting the BX register from the AX register) we would have the machine language

> 0010101111000011B   (or 2BC3H)

A brief note is required here to explain what registers are, since they occur frequently in the discussion of 8088 computer fundamentals. A register is a special data storage location within the processor. The processor can access data stored in registers very quickly—much faster than data stored in memory. The registers also have special uses for some instructions. Chapter 3 will give a complete explanation of the 8088 registers.

Although machine language is really great if you are a computer, it is difficult for human programmers. Fortunately, there is an easier method than machine language programming. This method, more in tune with people than with machines, is assembly language programming.

Assembly language is a programming language that is more meaningful to programmers than machine language, yet still has the meaning of machine language. The computer reads assembly language programs and converts them into machine language, the form the computer understands. This process, called "assembling" the program, is actually a form of language translation. A computer program called an assembler performs the operation of translating the assembly language to machine language.

To show you the difference in understanding, let's look at the examples that we used above. The assembly language to add the AX register to the BX register is simply

> ADD   AX,BX

Similarly, to subtract the BX register from the AX register, we write

> SUB   AX,BX

The assembler converts these statements into the form we saw above. The computer handles the problem of converting a human-readable text file into a machine language program that the processor can execute.

Assembly language is not a language like FORTRAN, COBOL, or Pascal. These languages, and many others like them, are high-level languages. High-level languages are designed to relate directly to the problem being solved with the program. As such, they are sometimes called procedural languages, since they describe the procedure used to solve the problem. High-level languages are machine independent. A program written using the FORTRAN language for the IBM Personal Computer should run correctly, and produce the same results, when executed on the IBM System/370. The programming language is independent of the machine.

Assembly language programs, however, are directly related to the machine on which they will be executed. Assembly language is machine dependent. The assembly language for the IBM Personal Computer is radically different from the assembly language for the System/370. This is because assembly language instructions convert almost directly into machine language instructions. That is, each assembly language instruction usually translates into exactly one machine language instruction. Since the machine language for different computers is different, the assembly languages differ also.

Normally, every assembly language statement generates a machine language instruction. There are some cases in which this isn't true. This is because there are assembly language instructions that are for the assembler and are not part of the program to be executed later. They specify actions for the assembler to take. The assembler executes these instructions at the time of assembly. An example of an assembler directive (one of these assembler instructions) is

TITLE   Example Program

This instruction tells the assembler the title of the program. After the assembler translates the program, this title—"Example Program"—appears at the top of each page of the assembler printout. This instruction has meaning only to the assembler. There is no 8088 instruction that can perform that operation.

ASSEMBLY LANGUAGE SYNTAX

Before we go further, we'll discuss the syntax of assembly language statements. We need to identify the major components of assembly language so that we can use a common set of words to identify the components of the language.

An assembly language statement is composed of up to four parts. Figure 2.8 below shows a typical assembly language statement and the names of the parts.

| PART 1: | ADD | AX,BX | ; Add in the buffer length |
| Label | Opcode | Operands | Comment |

Figure 2.8   Assembly Language Syntax

The only required portion of the assembly language statement is the opcode, which is a contraction for OPeration CODE. Programmers sometimes refer to the instruction set of a machine as the set of operation codes. The opcode portion of the assembly language statement identifies the instruction for the processor to execute, in this case an ADD instruction.

The operand field contains additional information about the instruction—what values will participate in the operation, for example. The opcode determines the operand field. Each opcode requires a certain set of operands. An ADD instruction requires two operands, the two values to be added. A negate (NEG) operation requires only one operand, and some instructions, such as decimal adjust (DAA), require no operands. Chapter 4 covers these instructions and their operands.

The label and comment fields are optional for every instruction. The label field is a way of giving a name to a particular location in the memory of a computer. A unique address identifies each location, but figuring out the address for an instruction is difficult, if not impossible. The label allows a programmer-defined name to identify a particular address in storage. In technical terms, we say that the label field contains a symbolic reference to the location of the instruction. If we wish to refer to this instruction location later, we refer to it by symbolic name. We do not need to identify the absolute location at which the instruction is located. The use of labels is one of the reasons for choosing assembly language over machine language. The assembler handles the conversion of symbolic names into real addresses.

The comment field is for the convenience of the programmer. The programmer can use this area to provide additional information about the instruction. Comments need not be restricted to instructions. You can dedicate an entire line to a comment by using a semicolon as the first character of the line. This allows the programmer to include a block of information in the assembly listing, perhaps to identify the algorithm used.

Everyone has their own ideas about how programs should be commented, and you will surely develop your own. In general, you should try to include information that relates to the problem being solved. In the example above, it would have been meaningless to comment the instruction with something like "Add AX to BX." That's nothing but a rephrasing of the opcode and operands. If you're going to bother with a comment, make it something worth the effort of writing and reading.

ASSEMBLER OPERATION

Let's now look at what the assembler does in general terms. We'll explore the specifics in a later section, but we need to learn some more terms and see some actual output.

The assembler takes a program written in assembly language and converts it to machine language. The file that contains the assembly language input is called the source file. The output of the assembler is not really machine language but an intermediate representation of the program. This output file is called an object file. The data in the object file is the object code. The object code must be modified to produce true machine language. The LINK program does this for the IBM Personal Computer. This conversion step from object code to machine language is commonly called the link or the link edit. We'll see how to use the linker in a later chapter.

Besides converting the source code into object code, the assembler produces several other output files. One of these files is the listing file. It contains a listing of the actions of the assembler. The listing file contains the original source code, complete with comments. It also contains the object code output by the assembler. Figure 2.9 is an example of an assembly listing, sometimes called the print file.

```
The IBM Personal Computer Assembler 01-01-83          PAGE    1-1
Figure 2.9  Assembly Example

1                                         PAGE    ,132
2                                         TITLE   Figure 2.9  Assembly Example
3       0000                     CODE     SEGMENT
4                                         ASSUME  CS:CODE
5
6       0000  03 C3              PART1:   ADD     AX,BX         ; Add in the buffer length
7
8       0002                     CODE     ENDS
9                                         END
```

Figure 2.9   Assembly Example

Taking the example assembly statement, let's see what the assembler output is. On the right-hand side of the listing is the source statement. On the left-hand side is the information generated by the assembler. The first column contains the line number for each line in the listing. The assembler assigns these numbers to the source file. These line numbers are not necessarily related to any line numbers in the source file maintained by the editor.

The second column is the address of the instruction. The LINK program may modify this address, but it is the best guess the assembler can make during the assembly. The next column is the machine language code for the instruction. Since 8088 instructions may be 8 to 56 bits long, this field will vary in size. Also, the LINK program may change some of the information in this object code field. The linker may modify any portion of the instruction that relates to an address. Except for address fields, however, the assembly listing is a true indication of the machine code that will later be executed.

For most of the examples that follow, we'll use the assembler listing output of the program. This will allow us to see the actual code generated by the assembler.

The other output file created by the assembler is a cross-reference file. This file stores the relationships between labels and the instructions that use the labels. This information is invaluable when you try to modify the program. You can use the cross-reference data to determine all of the instructions that reference a certain location in storage. This allows a programmer to determine all of the instructions that might be affected when another section of the program changes. Chapter 5 will discuss the use of cross-reference information.

BITS, BYTES, AND WORDS

We have the name "bit" for a binary digit, a single occurrence of one of the values 0 or 1. For convenience, we will assign names to some of the combinations of bits.

A group of 8 bits is commonly called a byte. Throughout the IBM documentation and this book, we will refer to 8 bits of information as a byte. The byte deserves its special name for several reasons. The basic unit of memory is 8 bits wide. Each access to the storage of the IBM Personal Computer retrieves exactly 8 bits of information for the processor. As we'll see later, individual instructions of the 8088 can perform arithmetic or logical operations on 8-bit groups. A byte is the smallest unit of data that the 8088 can directly manipulate. The 8088 can add two 8-bit numbers in a single instruction but can't add two 4-bit numbers. The IBM Personal Computer also uses a byte for character representation. A byte can represent 256 (2^8) unique items, such as characters. In the next section we'll look at the character set of the IBM Personal Computer.

Since the byte is a single unit of memory, we must have a means for defining individual bytes in storage. In fact, the operation of the assembler is to define the contents of storage, for the execution of a program. Normally, assembly source language consists of instructions to be executed. But to place a specific value in a byte of storage, the assembler provides a special mechanism, the define byte, or DB, pseudo-instruction. DB is not an 8088 instruction. It is a command to the assembler to store specific information in memory. The pseudo-instruction

    DB   23

instructs the assembler to store the decimal value 23 into the byte of storage at the current assembly location.

    DB   1, 2, 3, 4,

stores the values 1 through 4 in four successive memory locations.

Assembly language programs use the DB operator to define data areas. In the examples above, we have placed specific values into storage. This might be a lookup table, or numeric conversion information. We'll do several examples that use defined data like that. There are also occasions when a program needs a storage location to store data during the execution of the program. At the time we assemble the program, the value of the location is unknown—indeed, the contents will be variable during the execution of the program. The instruction

    DB   ?

tells the assembler to set aside a byte of storage, but to leave the location as it is. That byte can contain any random value before an instruction stores a particular value into that byte.

We may also want to set aside a large number of locations—to establish a storage area for an array, for example. We can do this with

    DB   25 DUP(?)

which sets aside 25 bytes of storage. The keyword in this pseudo-instruction is DUP, which stands for duplicate. The value 25 is the number of times that the assembler duplicates the define byte operation. The assembler uses the value or values within the parentheses to initialize that area of storage. In this case, the value is unknown. To initialize an area with a single value, the expression

    DB   17 DUP (31)

creates 17 bytes with the value 31 in each location. Finally,

    DB   30 DUP (1,2,3,4,5)

sets aside 30 bytes with the pattern 1 through 5 in the first five bytes. The next five bytes have the values 1 through 5 stored in them, and so on. The assembler repeats the values in the parentheses until all 30 bytes have been filled.

Sometimes we will want to refer to a collection of bits smaller than a byte. A common size is 4 bits. We can represent the 10 decimal numbers in 4 bits. For this size value, we'll use the term "nybble." This term, which has gained wide usage, allows us to refer to something smaller than a "byte."

A "word" has a different meaning for a computer programmer than for an English major. In the context of computers, a word is the largest number of bits that the machine can handle as a unit. For the IBM System/370, a word is 32 bits. For the Intel 8088, a word is 16 bits. For this reason, a word is an ambiguous reference, unless the particular machine is known.

The word size of the 8088 is 16 bits. The internal data paths of the processor determine this number. The 8088 can perform arithmetic and logical operations on numbers as large as 16 bits in a single instruction. Any bigger number requires more than a single instruction. There are instructions that manipulate smaller quantities, such as the addition of two 8-bit numbers. There are a few instructions that allow single bits to be manipulated. But to add together two 32-bit numbers requires two instructions, adding 16 bits with each instruction. The largest number on which we can perform common operations such as addition is the word size of the machine.

Just as there is an assembler instruction to define a byte in memory, there is an instruction for a word in storage. The assembler operator is DW, for Define Word. The first DW statement in Figure 2.10 defines a 16-bit quantity in storage with the value 1234H. Just as with bytes, we can use the DUP operator to define large areas of word storage. Similarly, the assembler uses the ? operand to indicate unitialized areas.

```
The IBM Personal Computer Assembler 01-01-83          PAGE    1-1
Figure 2.10 Define Word Examples

 1                                           PAGE    ,132
 2                                           TITLE   Figure 2.10 Define Word Examples
 3
 4       0000  1234                          DW      1234H
 5       0002    03 [                        DW      3 DUP(5678H)
 6             5678
 7                  ]
 8
 9       0008  ????                          DW      ?
10
11                                           END
```

Figure 2.10   Define Word Examples

One of the confusing traits of the 8088 is the way it stores words in memory. In Figure 2.10, even though we have defined the word to be 1234H, the assembler stores the value in memory as 3412H, or so it seems. Let's see how this works.

Let's assume that the word of 1234H was stored in locations 100 and 101. The 8088 requires that the assembler place the value 34H in location 100, and the value 12H in location 101. The easiest way to remember this is that the assembler stores the low byte of the word (the least significant byte) at the lowest address. The assembler stores the high byte (or most significant byte) at the highest address. Figure 2.11 shows a picture of memory after the assembler stores the data. Until

Location   Value

. . .   . . .

100   34H
101   12H

. . .   . . .

Figure 2.11 Storage Representation of DW 1234H

you are accustomed to this method, it will seem that everything is in memory backward. Fortunately, unless you mix byte and word operations on the same location in storage, you won't have to worry about this apparent "switching" of bytes. A program can operate on word values without concern, and the 8088 will always straighten things out. Only if you want to access a particular byte of a word value will you have to deal with the exact method that the 8088 stores words in memory. The assembler emphasizes word structure in the program listing. It does this by displaying words in the object code as words rather than as bytes, which would appear reversed. You can identify a word since the assembler writes it as four hexadecimal characters, without spacing.

There is still another type of data structure that 8088 assembly language programs use commonly. This is the doubleword, a 32-bit data value. Programs use a doubleword value to store an address value or a very large number. To define a data area that contains a doubleword value, the assembler operator

DD   value

generates the four-byte field. The DD stands for define doubleword. Just as with the DW operator, the assembler stores the data with the least significant byte at the lowest address, and the most significant byte at the highest address. The middle two bytes are arranged in the same order. Just as with the DB and DW operators, you can use the DUP function and specify the ? operand to leave the area undefined.

There are other data structures that the assembler can generate. We'll defer the discussion of those operators until we discuss some of the features of the macro assembler and the 8087. Programs use the remaining data structures primarily for the very large numbers used with the Numeric Data Processor, or for defining their own data structures.

BIT NUMBERING

At times we will want to identify individual bits in a byte or word. To do that, we number the bits. The index, or number, assigned to each bit is the power of 2 that the bit location represents. The least significant bit is bit 0, since it represents 2^0. The most significant bit in a byte is bit 7, for 2^7. The most significant bit in a word is bit 15. Figure 2.12 shows a 16-bit word, with the individual bits numbered. This

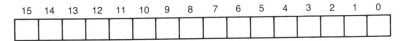

Figure 2.12 Bit Numbering

method of bit numbering is consistent with all of the IBM Personal Computer documentation.

CHARACTER SET

As we noted above, we can consider each byte of information as a character value rather than as a binary number. Each of the binary numbers from 0 through 255 may represent a particular character. Figure 2.13 displays the character set for the IBM Personal Computer. The columns of the figure correspond to the high 4 bits of the character code, while the rows correspond to the lower 4 bits of the

DECIMAL VALUE ➡		0	16	32	48	64	80	96	112
⬇	HEXA DECIMAL VALUE	0	1	2	3	4	5	6	7
0	0	BLANK (NULL)	►	BLANK (SPACE)	0	@	P	`	p
1	1	☺	◄	!	1	A	Q	a	q
2	2	☻	↕	"	2	B	R	b	r
3	3	♥	‼	#	3	C	S	c	s
4	4	♦	¶	$	4	D	T	d	t
5	5	♣	§	%	5	E	U	e	u
6	6	♠	▬	&	6	F	V	f	v
7	7	•	↨	'	7	G	W	g	w
8	8	◘	↑	(	8	H	X	h	x
9	9	○	↓	)	9	I	Y	i	y
10	A	◎	→	*	:	J	Z	j	z
11	B	♂	←	+	;	K	[	k	{
12	C	♀	∟	,	<	L	\	l	¦
13	D	♪	↔	—	=	M	]	m	}
14	E	♫	▲	.	>	N	^	n	~
15	F	☼	▼	/	?	O	_	o	△

DECIMAL VALUE ➡		128	144	160	176	192	208	224	240
⬇	HEXA DECIMAL VALUE	8	9	A	B	D	C	E	F
0	0	Ç	É	á			⌐	∝	≡
1	1	ü	Æ	í			⌐	β	±
2	2	é	FE	ó			⌐	γ	≥
3	3	â	ô	ú			⌐	π	≤
4	4	ä	ö	ñ			⌐	Σ	∫
5	5	à	ò	Ñ			⌐	σ	∫
6	6	å	û	ª			⌐	μ	÷
7	7	ç	ù	º			⌐	τ	≈
8	8	ê	ÿ	¿			⌐	Φ	°
9	9	ë	Ö	⌐			⌐	Θ	•
10	A	è	Ü	¬			⌐	Ω	•
11	B	ï	¢	½			⌐	δ	√
12	C	î	£	¼			⌐	∞	η
13	D	ì	¥	¡			⌐	∅	2
14	E	Ä	Pts	«			⌐	∈	■
15	F	Å	ƒ	»			⌐	∩	BLANK 'FF'

Figure 2.13 IBM Character Set from TRM (Courtesy of IBM; Copyright IBM 1981)

character code. Thus, location 41H is the character "A," while the character code 5EH represents the character " ˆ ."

The IBM Personal Computer character set is an extension of the ASCII (American Standard Code for Information Interchange) set of characters. In the ASCII set, the character values from 20H through 7FH represent the normal alphabetic, numeric, and punctuation characters. The character codes from 0H through 1FH are normally control characters. Figure 2.14 shows the ASCII control characters in this region. These characters have meaning when transmitted to the IBM Printer or other ASCII printers. However, as Figure 2.13 shows, these control characters will also display as graphic symbols on the screen. The IBM Personal Computer uses the control section of the ASCII table for graphics to utilize the additional capabilities of the display adapters. Since the display adapters can directly display any of the 256 codes, there is no reason to restrict any of the code points strictly to functions. IBM chose the 32 characters in the control region as those characters that would be used predominantly as display graphics and would not normally be printed. In summary, the first 32 values are control codes when transmitted to the printer, but will show as graphic symbols when transmitted to the display.

The character values from 80H through 0FFH are an extension of the ASCII character set for the IBM Personal Computer. IBM chose these characters to offer a wide range of capabilities for the computer. The sections of foreign characters, line graphics, and scientific symbols allow the IBM Personal Computer to run applications in a variety of areas.

There will be times when you want to enter the character code values into memory for later use by a program. An example might be a message that will be shown to the operator at some time during the program. Instead of looking up the code values in the table, we can enter the text string directly. The assembler allows this with the DB operator. In the operand field, instead of entering

Value	Character	Meaning
0	NUL	Null
7	BEL	Bell
9	HT	Horizontal tab
0A	LF	Line feed
0B	VT	Vertical tab
0C	FF	Form feed
0D	CR	Carriage return
0E	SO	Shift out
0F	SI	Shift in
11	DC1	Device control 1
12	DC2	Device control 2
13	DC3	Device control 3
14	DC4	Device control 4
18	CAN	Cancel
1B	ESC	Escape

Figure 2.14   IBM Control Codes

```
The IBM Personal Computer Assembler 01-01-83          PAGE    1-1
Figure 2.15 Define Byte for ASCII Text

 1                                              PAGE    ,132
 2                                              TITLE   Figure 2.15 Define Byte for ASCII Text
 3
 4      0000    54 68 69 73 20 69               DB      'This is a message',10,13
 5              73 20 61 20 6D 65
 6              73 73 61 67 65 0A
 7              0D
 8
 9                                              END
```

Figure 2.15   Define Byte for ASCII Text

numbers, we use a quoted text string. The assembler looks up the code values and enters them into storage, one byte per character. The assembler can only handle the characters in the range 20H through 0FFH. The program must enter the control characters in the range 0H to 1FH using a numeric value rather than a quoted string. This is because the text in the source file uses some of the control characters to delimit the beginning and end of source lines.

The example in Figure 2.15 generates 19 bytes of data in the program. The first 17 bytes correspond to the 17 characters in the quoted text string. The first byte is 54H, the next 68H, and so on. The last two bytes are control codes, and had to be entered as numbers. The last two bytes of the 19-byte message represent the carriage return and line feed functions. If we send this 19-byte message to the printer, it will print the text in the quotes. The control characters tell the printer to print the line and move to the next line on the paper.

COMPUTER OPERATION

The following sections explain some fundamentals of computer operation. These principles are important to an understanding of the 8088 and its operation. The information in these sections is common to all computers. Where appropriate, we'll make specific references to the 8088, although most of the 8088-specific information will appear in the next chapter.

A computer operates by fetching instructions from memory and then executing them. Each instruction goes through this two-step process. A processor register drives the fetch portion of the cycle. This register is the program counter or instruction pointer. This pointer is the "placemark" for the currently executing program. The memory location pointed to by this register contains the next instruction that the processor will fetch and execute. The processor reads the byte or bytes at that location. These bytes are interpreted by the processor and executed as an instruction. The processor increments the pointer according to the number of bytes in the instruction. The program counter now points to the next instruction in sequence. The cycle repeats in this fashion for each and every instruction. The normal flow of a program is sequential, from an instruction to the one following it.

The processor can vary the sequential fetch–execute cycle by executing an instruction that stores a new value into the insruction pointer. These instructions are transfer of control instructions, since the program execution has transferred to a new area. A jump or branch instruction is the most common way of transferring control. The jump instruction specifies the next instruction location to execute. A program loop is an example of the use of a jump instruction. The example in Figure 2.16, in 8088 assembly language, shows a value being stored into successive memory locations. The jump instruction at the end of the loop causes the instructions to repeat.

```
The IBM Personal Computer Assembler 01-01-83          PAGE    1-1
Figure 2.16  Jump Instruction

 1                                            PAGE    ,132
 2                                            TITLE   Figure 2.16  Jump Instruction
 3      0000                            CODE  SEGMENT
 4                                            ASSUME  CS:CODE
 5
 6      0000                            MEM   LABEL   BYTE
 7
 8      0000                            FIG2_16:
 9      0000  2E: C6 87 0000 R 00             MOV     MEM[BX],0
10      0006  43                              INC     BX
11      0007  EB F7                           JMP     FIG2_16
12
13      0009                            CODE  ENDS
14                                            END
```

Figure 2.16   Jump Instruction

Notice that the JMP instruction uses a label, in this case "FIG2_16," to specify the next location to be executed. This is an example of the capabilities of the assembler. Although the machine language requires the absolute address of the next instruction, the assembly language requires only a programmer-defined label. The assembler determines the absolute address and fills in the correct value for the machine language.

Jump instructions need not be unconditional, as in the example above. The 8088 has a variety of jump instructions that are executed according to a condition code. Instructions set this condition code as they are executed by the processor. The condition specified in the conditional jump instruction is compared to the condition code stored in the status register. If the conditions match, the processor jumps to the target address. If the conditions do not match, the processor ignores the jump, and the program execution continues in the normal sequential flow. Figure 2.17 changes the preceding example. The loop in this example terminates when the value in BX is equal to 1000.

```
The IBM Personal Computer Assembler 01-01-83          PAGE    1-1
Figure 2.17  Conditional Jump Instruction

 1                                            PAGE    ,132
 2                                            TITLE   Figure 2.17  Conditional Jump Instruction
 3      0000                            CODE  SEGMENT
 4                                            ASSUME  CS:CODE
 5
 6      0000                            MEM   LABEL   BYTE
 7
 8      0000                            FIG2_17:
 9      0000  2E: C6 87 0000 R 00             MOV     MEM[BX],0
10      0006  43                              INC     BX
11      0007  81 FB 03E8                      CMP     BX,1000
12      000B  75 F3                           JNE     FIG2_17
13      000D  90                              NOP
14
15      000E                            CODE  ENDS
16                                            END
```

Figure 2.17   Conditional Jump Instruction

Figure 2.17 adds a compare instruction which sets the condition codes. The conditional jump instruction (JNE for Jump if Not Equal) jumps to "FIG2_17" if the condition is true. If the condition is false, the 8088 executes the instruction following the conditional jump, in this case, the instruction NOP. The conditional jump instruction allows the program to examine the data during the program. Based on the examination, the program can take different courses of action.

SUBROUTINES

Another form of jump instruction is the subroutine jump. A sequence of instructions forms a subroutine. This code sequence performs a function that the program uses many times, and in many different places. Instead of repeating this sequence in all the places it is needed, the programmer places the instructions in a single location. This section of code becomes the subroutine.

Whenever the program requires the subroutine function, the program transfers control to the subroutine, through a subroutine jump. This jump to a subroutine is a subroutine call, or a call instruction. The subroutine call differs from the jump instruction. The call instruction saves the address of the instruction following it. This address, called the return address, is the path back to the original instructions.

Let's see how a subroutine call works. For an example, we'll be writing a program that adds together 32-bit numbers in several places. There is no 8088 instruction that will do a 32-bit addition. We can write a short sequence of 8088 instructions that will add 32-bit numbers. This section of code will become the subroutine.

The programmer writes the subroutine just like any other section of code. The subroutine is part of the assembly language program. When writing the main portion of the application program, the programmer will find occasions to add two 32-bit numbers. Instead of writing the instructions to do the addition, the program contains a subroutine call to the 32-bit add routine. The instructions in the main body of the program continue after the subroutine call. The subroutine call has the effect of a powerful 8088 instruction, since the single call does a 32-bit addition.

When this program is executed, the subroutine call instruction will not do the double-precision add, but will transfer control to the 32-bit addition subroutine. The processor executes the instructions of the subroutine, performing the addition. The last instruction of the subroutine is a special instruction for subroutines, called a return. The return instruction takes the address that was saved by the call instruction and puts it back into the instruction pointer. This causes the program to return to the instruction following the subroutine call. The subroutine call temporarily diverts the flow of the program to the subroutine code. Following the subroutine execution, control returns to main routine.

The two instructions that implement a subroutine are CALL and RETURN. The CALL instruction is the subroutine jump. A CALL saves the current value of

```
The IBM Personal Computer Assembler 01-01-83           PAGE     1-1
Figure 2.18  Subroutine Usage

 1                                                 PAGE    ,132
 2                                                 TITLE   Figure 2.18   Subroutine Usage
 3        0000                            CODE     SEGMENT
 4                                                 ASSUME  CS:CODE
 5
 6        0000  E8 0008 R                 A1:      CALL    SUBROUTINE
 7
 8        0003  40                        A2:      INC     AX
 9
10        0004  E8 0008 R                 A3:      CALL    SUBROUTINE
11
12        0007  43                        A4:      INC     BX
13
14                                        ;----- Routine continues here . . .
15
16        0008                            SUBROUTINE      PROC      NEAR
17
18        0008  B8 0000                            MOV     AX,0
19        000B  BB 0000                            MOV     BX,0
20        000E  C3                                 RET
21
22        000F                            SUBROUTINE      ENDP
23
24        000F                            CODE     ENDS
25                                                 END
```

Figure 2.18   Subroutine Usage

the instruction pointer in some special place. This saved instruction pointer value is the return address. The RETURN instruction reads this saved instruction pointer value, places it in the processor's instruction pointer, and returns control to the location following the CALL. The example of Figure 2.18 shows a subroutine being called from two different locations.

As the example program executes from the beginning, it reaches the instruction at location A1. The CALL instruction passes control to the location SUBROUTINE. As part of the CALL instruction, the processor saves the address of location A2. The subroutine is executed, and the RET (for return) instruction recovers the saved value of A2. Control returns to the main program. Later in the main program, the CALL at A3 executes, causing the subroutine to execute a second time. The processor saves the value of A4 this time. Control returns to A4 following the execution of the subroutine the second time. Notice that the same subroutine executed twice. The first time, the return was to A2 after the subroutine. The second time, the return was to A4. The power of the subroutine is its ability to be called from many different locations and return correctly to each caller.

Where is the return address saved during the subroutine execution? There are many possibilities, but the 8088 saves the value on a stack.

STACK

A stack is a data structure that is used for the temporary storage of information. A program can place information on a stack (PUSH) or remove it from the stack (POP). The stack data structure sequences the data stored in it in a special manner. At all times, the item removed (popped) from the stack is the last item placed (pushed) on the stack. The acronym for this structure is LIFO, for last in, first out. If we push two items on a stack, first A, then B, when we pop the stack the first time, B is recovered. The next pop recovers A. Information is removed from the stack in exactly the opposite order from which it was placed on the stack.

A stack can be contrasted to a queue. A queue is a normal line like that at the post office or grocery store. A queue is a first in, first out (FIFO) data structure. The first person to get into line is the first person to get out of line. A queue and a stack are very different.

A computer implements a stack with a reserved section of storage and a pointer called the stack pointer. The program uses the stack pointer to keep track of the last entry on the stack. While in the post office, the elements of the queue move as the line moves forward. Within the computer, it is much simpler to use a pointer to locate the data, and to move only the pointer when pushing or popping items. The stack pointer is incremented or decremented in response to POP or PUSH operations.

Figure 2.19 shows an example of a stack. Part (a) depicts the stack after the values A, B, and C (in that order) have been pushed onto it. The stack pointer points at the current Top Of Stack (TOS) entry, in this case C. In part (b), another item, D, has been pushed onto the stack. The PUSH operation decrements the stack pointer (SP), which now points at the new TOS, D. The stack pointer always locates the last item placed on the stack.

Figure 2.19(c) shows the stack following a POP. The POP operation has taken the value D from the stack. The POP instruction places the value removed from the stack in a specific place. If the instruction in part (c) is POP AX, the processor would put the value D into the AX register (another of those things that we'll talk about in detail in the next chapter). The POP increments the stack pointer. It now points to the new TOS, value C. Notice that items are removed from the stack in the LIFO fashion. The last item pushed onto the stack was D, and the first item removed from the stack is D.

Notice also that the value D remains in storage, but it is no longer part of the stack. Conceptually, the stack ends at the location addressed by the stack pointer. The top of the stack is below the value D.

Figure 2.19(d) shows what happens to the value D when a new item, E, is pushed onto the stack. The value E has overwritten D, and has become the new top of stack. The moral of this story is that items popped off the stack may still be in memory, but never count on it.

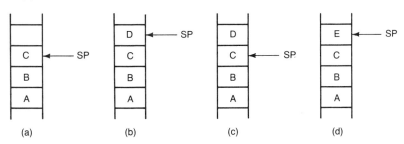

Figure 2.19 Stack Example

The examples above have used the 8088 method of stack construction. The stack pointer always points at the current top of stack. PUSH operations decrement the stack pointer, POP instructions increment it. The stack grows toward smaller memory addresses. The base of the stack is at a larger memory address than the top of stack. If we draw pictures of a stack with the lowest memory address at the top, as in Figure 2.19, the top of the stack will be at the top of the picture.

We got into a discussion of stacks because a stack is used for subroutine return addresses. How does this work?

Each CALL instruction causes a PUSH onto the stack. The CALL instruction saves the return address on the stack. The RET instruction POPs the return address from the stack into the instruction pointer. The 8088 uses a stack for return addresses because it allows nesting of subroutines. What is nesting? Figure 2.20 shows an example of nested subroutines.

Figure 2.20 is a nonsense program that we'll use as an example of subroutine nesting. Part (a) shows the stack before the program executes. As the MAIN routine executes, it calls SUBROUTINE_A. At that time, the processor saves the return address on the stack. Part (b) shows this return address, 103, as it is pushed

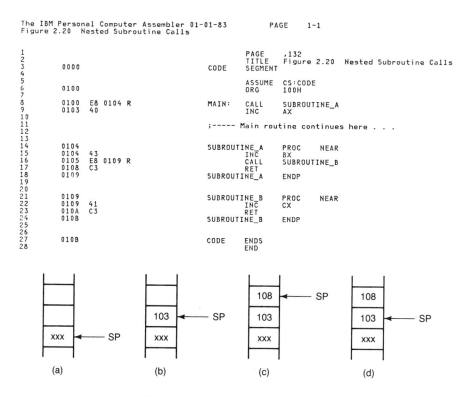

Figure 2.20 Nested Subroutine Calls

onto the stack. SUBROUTINE_A, as part of its execution, calls SUBROU-TINE_B. This call instruction saves its return address on the stack, as shown in part (c). The value 108 is the return address to SUBROUTINE_A. When SUBROUTINE_B finishes, the return instruction pops the value 108 from the stack, as shown in part (d). The processor places this value in the instruction pointer, as required by the return instruction. As the assembly listing shows, location 108 is in SUBROUTINE_A and is the location following the call to SUBROUTINE_B. SUBROUTINE_A now finishes. The return instruction pops the value 103 from the stack to the instruction pointer. Location 103 is back in the MAIN program, immediately following the call to SUBROUTINE_A.

The important thing to notice in the example of Figure 2.20 is the nesting of the subroutines. One subroutine can call another subroutine. The return instructions always go back to the correct place. The only limit to the depth of subroutine nesting (how many subroutines can call other subroutines) is the size of the stack. As long as the stack has room for another return address, another subroutine call can be nested. The LIFO structure of the stack maintains the correct ordering of return addresses.

The example program in Figure 2.20 also shows the use of another assembler pseudo-operation—PROC. The assembler uses the PROC operator to identify subroutines. As we'll see later, the assembler needs to know how far away the subroutine is, and how it should return to the caller. The operand NEAR identifies this subroutine as one located within easy reach of the calling program. We'll revisit the PROC operator when we discuss the actual operation of the CALL and JMP instructions.

INTERRUPTS

The interrupt mechanism is an important part of any computer system. As we'll see, it is also important for the IBM Personal Computer. The interrupt structure provides an efficient means for the I/O devices to communicate with the processor. We're interested in interrupts because interrupt handling is strictly in the province of assembly language programming. High-level languages do not have the facilities for dealing with interrupts at the machine level.

External devices usually cause interrupts. The interrupt signals the processor to suspend its current activity and respond to the external device. In the IBM Personal Computer, the keyboard sends an interrupt signal every time a key is pressed. The keyboard interrupt tells the processor to halt its current activity and read the character typed at the keyboard.

It's easy to see how the interrupt was named. The interrupt signal "interrupts" the current action of the processor. The interrupt is a good deal because it frees the processor from constantly monitoring the external devices. If the keyboard did not interrupt, for example, the processor would have to check the keyboard constantly to determine if a key had been pressed. Every program written for the computer would have to do the same thing and would have to do the keyboard testing very frequently in the program. But an interrupt removes that requirement. The program can execute without testing the keyboard. Whenever the keyboard has information, it signals the processor. After the processor takes care of the keyboard, it can resume the normal program execution.

The 8088 handles interrupts much like subroutines. When an interrupt occurs, it can't suspend the processor in the middle of an instruction. The 8088 first finishes executing the current instruction. The processor ignores the next sequential instruction in the program. Instead, the processor acts as if the next instruction is a subroutine call. The processor saves the address of that next instruction on the stack, and jumps to the special subroutine for interrupts. This subroutine, known as the interrupt handler, contains the instructions to deal with the interrupting device. For the keyboard, the interrupt handler reads the character and saves it for later use. After the interrupt handler deals with the device, it returns to the point of interruption. The processor fetches the return address from the stack, and program execution continues as if nothing had happened.

Since external devices cause interrupts, an interrupt can occur anytime in the execution of a program. Programs can't take any special actions to prepare for the occurrence of an interrupt. A program can't predict when the user will type a character at the keyboard. This means that the interrupt handler must not modify the values of the interrupted program. If the interrupt handler does modify any of the program values, the program won't run correctly when it regains control after the interrupt.

As part of the interrupt sequence, the 8088 saves some of the program value on the stack automatically. The interrupt handler program has the responsibility to save any other program values that the interrupt handler might modify during execution. These values are normally saved on the stack. Then, before control is returned to the interrupted program, the interrupt handler must restore the program values to the values they had at the time of the interruption. The fact that an interrupt occurred must be invisible to the executing program.

Because there can be many devices that send interrupt signals to the processor, the 8088 has a mechanism that vectors the interrupts. This means that the 8088 determines which device has interrupted, and transfers control to the correct interrupt handler for that device. The processor automatically handles the vectoring of interrupt requests. The interrupt handler does not have to determine which device interrupted before it can be serviced. This speeds up the response time to interrupts and makes interrupt programming simpler.

There are some sections of programs that can't be interrupted. Possibly a section of the program must execute very rapidly to get a specific task accomplished. Or the program might be manipulating a data area that could be changed by the interrupt handler. In either case, the program must be able to prevent, or disable, interrupts. That is, the program must be able to stop interrupts from occurring during these critical sections of the program. Following these sections the program must enable the interrupt system to allow interrupts to occur once again. A program can't disable the interrupt system for too long a time, or something may go wrong with the interrupting device. If the keyboard interrupt handler doesn't read the character before the operator types another character, the second character might be lost. The 8088 has the capability to disable all of the external interrupts. The IBM Personal Computer has a further ability to select which devices may generate an interrupt and which may not. A program can use this ability to select those critical devices and allow them to interrupt, while preventing the less critical devices. We'll discuss the methods of disabling interrupts in later chapters.

3

The 8088
Microprocessor

The 8088 is a member of a microprocessor family that includes the 8088, the 8086 microprocessor, and the 8087 Numeric Data Processor. The 8086 microprocessor is a larger brother of the 8088. It has an instruction set that is identical to the 8088. It does, however, have better performance than the 8088. This is because the data bus, the primary path between the processor and memory, is twice as large on the 8086. The 16-bit-wide data bus allows a full word of memory to be moved into the processor in a single operation. The 8-bit data bus of the 8088 requires two memory cycles to accomplish the same thing. In virtually all other respects the two processors are identical. A program written for the 8088 will execute identically, although probably faster, on the 8086. It is very difficult to write a program that can determine if it is executing on an 8088 or 8086 without consulting an external timing source.

The 8087 Numeric Data Processor (NDP) extends the instruction set of either the 8086 or 8088. This coprocessor shares instruction activity with the 8086 or 8088 master processor. The NDP executes those instructions associated with high-precision arithmetic or floating-point operations. It is possible to install an 8087 in the IBM Personal Computer. Chapter 7 will cover the 8087 NDP in more detail.

8088 PROGRAMMING MODEL

To understand the 8088, and to learn how to program it, we'll start with the internal capabilities of the processor. Within the processor there are special memory locations, called registers. These registers are available for the storage of

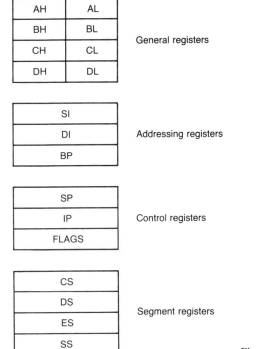

Figure 3.1   8088 Registers

data operands or memory addresses. Since registers are within the processor itself, the processor can access the data in them very quickly, much more quickly than data in memory. If a program needs rapid access to a value, keeping the value in a register speeds the execution.

Several groups of registers make up the 8088 register set. Figure 3.1 shows the registers of the 8088 and their groupings.

GENERAL REGISTERS

The first group of registers are those that are used primarily for computational activities. These general registers are all 16 bits wide, but a program may access the 8-bit high or low portions of each register individually. For example, the AX register is 16 bits wide. A program may reference the high 8 bits of the AX register as the AH register, while the low 8 bits comprise the AL register. The same is true for the BX, CX, and DX registers. A program may view this group of registers as four 16-bit registers, eight 8-bit registers, or some combination of 8- and 16-bit registers.

The primary purpose of the general register group is to hold operands. The general registers are characterized by the capability to hold either a word or a byte of data. However, the registers sometimes have special meanings assigned to them by specific instructions. Or they may have special capabilities beyond that of the rest of the group. The following paragraphs indicate some of the special uses of these general registers.

The AX register corresponds to the accumulator of earlier processors. While the 8088 has much more versatility than the earlier machines such as the 8080, particularly for arithmetic operations, it has several special-purpose functions. Intel optimized the instruction set of the 8088 for performing some operations using the AX register. For example, immediate operations are those in which one of the operands is a value contained within the instruction. Immediate operations applied to either the AX or AL register (the 16-bit and 8-bit accumulators, respectively) usually require a smaller instruction than the identical operation applied to one of the other general registers. This smaller instruction size allows a smaller program and faster execution.

The BX register serves as an addressing register as well as a computational register. When used as a 16-bit register, it can be a component in determining the operand address. The next section will outline the addressing modes of the 8088.

The 8088 instruction set uses the CX register as a counter for some instructions. These instructions use the value stored in the CX as a count which determines the number of iterations of an instruction or program segment.

The DX register serves as the accumulator extension for the multiple-precision operations of multiply and divide. Both the AX and DX registers participate in these 32-bit operations.

ADDRESSING REGISTERS

There are four 16-bit registers in the 8088 processor that can participate in operand addressing. One of these is also a general register—the BX, or base register. The other three are the Base Pointer (BP), Source Index (SI), and Destination Index (DI). A program may use the BP, SI, or DI registers as 16-bit operand registers, but the individual bytes are not accessible. Their primary purpose is to provide 16-bit values for use in generating operand addresses.

Each instruction of the 8088 specifies some operation to perform. The specific operation may require none, one, or two operands. For example, enabling the interrupts with a Set Interrupt (STI) requires no operands. The Increment (INC) instruction requires the programmer to specify a single operand, the register or memory location to be incremented. The ADD instruction must identify two operands, the values to be added. While there are some instructions that specify the location of the operand implicitly, most instructions allow the programmer to choose either a register or a memory location as the operand. If a register is to serve as the operand, the programmer only has to indicate the register's name. However, there are many different ways in which the programmer can specify the memory location that will be the operand.

The INC instruction serves as a good example. It specifies a single operand.

```
The IBM Personal Computer Assembler 12-11-82          PAGE    1-1
Figure 3.2 Operand Addressing


1                                               PAGE    ,132
2                                               TITLE   Figure 3.2 Operand Addressing
3
4      0000                          CODE       SEGMENT
5
6                                               ASSUME  CS:CODE,DS:CODE,SS:CODE
7
8      0123                                     ORG     123H
9      0123   ????                   OPND       DW      ?
10
11     0200                                     ORG     200H
12
13     0200   43                                INC     BX                ; Increment the register
14     0201   FF 06 0123 R                      INC     OPND              ; Increment the word in memory
15     0205   FF 07                             INC     WORD PTR [BX]     ; Increment the memory location
16
17     0207   FF 87 0123 R                      INC     [OPND+BX]         ; Displacement plus index
18     020B   FF 84 0123 R                      INC     [OPND+SI]
19     020F   FF 84 0123 R                      INC     OPND[SI]          ; Different method, same results
20     0213   FF 85 0123 R                      INC     OPND + [DI]
21     0217   FF 86 0123 R                      INC     [OPND] + [BP]
22
23     021B   FF 00                             INC     WORD PTR [BX + SI]    ; Base plus index
24     021D   FF 03                             INC     WORD PTR [BP] + [DI]
25
26     021F   FF 81 0123 R                      INC     [OPND + BX + DI]        ; Base + index + displacement
27     0223   FF 82 0123 R                      INC     OPND[BP][SI]
28
29     0227                          CODE       ENDS
30                                               END
```

Figure 3.2   Operand Addressing

Figure 3.2 is an assembly listing that shows several different versions of the INC instruction. The first INC instruction names the register BX as the operand. Notice that BX appears alone in the operand field of the instruction. The remaining instructions in the example name memory locations as the operand. Even though the BX register name sometimes appears, it is not the operand. It is used to determine the location of the operand.

DIRECT ADDRESSING

The simplest method of locating a memory operand is to name the memory location. The program then uses this name to refer to the memory location in the instruction. This is the method used in the instruction

        INC   OPND

The example program declares OPND as a word memory location in the assembler command

        OPND   DW   ?

When the program uses OPND as the operand, the assembler places the address of OPND into the assembled instruction. In this example you can see the address 0123 as part of the instruction's object code. Because the instruction has the address of the operand directly in it, this method is referred to as direct addressing.

ADDRESS CALCULATION

Direct addressing of memory operands has a simplicity that is appealing, but there are many cases when the program must calculate the actual memory location. The easiest case is the vector, a one-dimensional array. A FORTRAN program can create such a structure with

DIMENSION   OPND(20)

or a similar declaration in any high-level programming language. During execution, the program accesses the different elements according to an index value, such as OPND(5). Writing the corresponding program in assembly language requires that the programmer calculate where the fifth entry in the data area assigned to OPND resides. The program can then use that value for a direct address. However, if the expression is OPND(I), where the program determines I during execution, there is no way that the assembly language programmer can determine the correct direct address. The address must be calculated during the execution of the program.

The 8088 instruction set offers several ways of determining the Effective Address (EA) of an operand. These different ways of doing the address calculation are called the addressing modes. The many different modes are intended to make the job of determining the effective address of the operand easier. Through the choice of the correct address mode, the programmer can minimize the calculations required in the program.

To find the Ith entry in the array OPND, the formula is

Effective Address = base address of OPND + (I × length)

where length is the length of each entry in the array. In this example, OPND is a word array, so that each element is two bytes in length. The formula is then

EA = base address + (I × 2)

The minimum requirement to do this addressing calculation is a register that can hold the address of the operand. The program can calculate the effective address, leaving the result in one of the registers. The INC instruction can then specify which register holds the address, rather than putting the address within the instruction itself.

The program can use any of the four address registers to hold the operand address. So, in this example, the program adds 2 × I to the base address and places the result in the BX register. The corresponding vector entry would then be incremented with the instruction

INC   WORD PTR [BX]

The expression [BX] tells the assembler that the BX register contains the address of the operand, and is not the operand itself. The brackets [and] surrounding a value tell the assembler that the bracketed value is a memory

address. The assembler requires the other part of the operand expression, WORD
PTR, to tell that the operand is a WORD variable. We'll discuss the PTR operator
in greater detail later.

BASE + DISPLACEMENT ADDRESSING

Since the calculation of an operand address comprised of a base and an index is
such a common occurrence, the 8088 has addressing modes to handle the indexing
addition automatically. Instead of doing all of the calculations, the program can
determine the value of $2 \times I$ and place that in the BX register. The instruction

    INC   [OPND + BX]

calculates the effective address by adding the base address of OPND to the index
value contained in BX. This instruction accessed the same location as in the
previous case, but with fewer instructions required. Notice that the assembler did
not require the WORD PTR for this instruction. This is because the assembler
knows that OPND is a word variable. The assembler requires the PTR operator
only when it can't determine the type of the operand.

A program can use any of the four addressing registers as an index register
together with the base address. Figure 3.2 shows some of the variations possible
with a base address and an index. You can see that the assembler accepts several
different ways of writing the addressing operation. The group of five instructions
in Figure 3.2 all add the base address of OPND to the named index register.

We should note that the register does not have to hold the index value, with
the instruction providing the base address. In fact, since the BX register is named
the Base Register, it seems reasonable that we could use just the opposite
configuration. As an example of this, suppose that the program accesses many
different vectors of equal size and element length. An instructor's grade book,
using a separate vector for each set of test scores, might be such a data structure.
The program to determine the test score for the fifth student in the class for the Ith
test would have the index value already known (5), with the base address
determined during the execution of the program (the vector for the particular test).

The index register may contain either the base address of the vector, or the
index value in the vector. Because the constant value in the instruction may be
either a base value or an index value (or maybe even something else, known only
to the programmer), this value is called a displacement. It is the distance, or
displacement, from the register address to the actual location to be accessed.

BASE + INDEX + DISPLACEMENT

A program may also combine a calculated base address with a calculated index.
As Figure 3.2 shows, a program can use an addressing mode with two different
address registers. An instruction may combine either of the base registers (BX or
BP) with either of the index registers (SI or DI) to create the effective address. The

program may also specify a displacement to add to the value from the two registers. This addressing method provides the maximum in addressing flexibility, allowing the program to calculate both the base address and the index value at execution time. This capability is not always required, but it's available when necessary.

The instructor's grade book example shows an instance where a program might calculate both the base address and the vector index during the program. To determine the Ith student's score for the Jth test requires evaluating the base address for the Jth vector, and indexing in that vector to the Ith entry.

Figure 3.3 summarizes the different addressing modes available with the 8088. There are eight different possibilities. An instruction may use any of the four addressing registers with a displacement. Or, an instruction can specify any combination of a base register and an index register together with a displacement. The column identified as R/M will be explained later.

R/M	Operand Address
000	[BX + SI + DISPLACEMENT]
001	[BX + DI + DISPLACEMENT]
010	[BP + SI + DISPLACEMENT]
011	[BP + DI + DISPLACEMENT]
100	[SI + DISPLACEMENT]
101	[DI + DISPLACEMENT]
110	[BP + DISPLACEMENT]
111	[BX + DISPLACEMENT]

Figure 3.3   8088 Addressing Modes

The 8088 instruction set has optimized the displacement field for addressing to minimize the number of program bytes required. The instruction can omit the displacement field, implying a displacement of zero. If the displacement is within the range −128 to 127, a single byte suffices. When an instruction requires the full 16-bit addressing range, the displacement field can be two bytes. Thus, the displacement field can be zero, one, or two bytes in length, as required. When the displacement field is one byte, the binary number is sign-extended before the performing the addition. Sign extension means that the processor places the highest-order bit of the displacement field into the high 8 bits of the 16-bit value before performing the addition. This allows negative numbers to be represented within a single displacement byte. The best part of all this is that the assembler will determine the correct length, and assemble the correct, and shortest, instruction to do the job.

Even though the 8088 has all of this addressing power, the instruction set is designed so that the 8088 can specify only a single memory operand within any instruction. The two-operand ADD instruction must always add a register to a memory location, or a register to another register. A single instruction cannot add two memory locations in a single instruction. This means that an instruction contains only a single memory address.

MOD-R/M BYTE

How is all of this information conveyed to the 8088 in machine language? The 8088 uses the mod-r/m byte for nearly all operand addressing. Figure 3.4 shows the format of this instruction byte. The mod-r/m byte follows the operation code byte and specifies the single memory operand of the 8088 instruction. The mod-r/m byte can also name a register instead of a memory location. This single structure can handle all of the operand addressing possibilities.

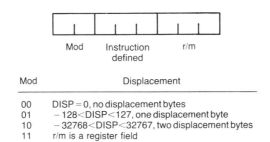

Mod	Displacement
00	DISP = 0, no displacement bytes
01	$-128 <$ DISP < 127, one displacement byte
10	$-32768 <$ DISP < 32767, two displacement bytes
11	r/m is a register field

Figure 3.4 Mod-r/m Byte

The first 2 bits of the mod-r/m byte specify the addressing mode selected. These 2 bits determine the number of displacement bytes that follow the mod-r/m byte—either zero, one, or two. The final 3 bits of the mod-r/m byte specify the form of operand addressing—the eight different combinations of base and index registers used in addressing. This field is the r/m, or register/modifier field. These 3 bits form the R/M column of Figure 3.3, which shows the possible addressing combinations. The meaning of the remaining 3 bits in the middle of the mod-r/m byte depends on the actual instruction. For the two operand instructions, like ADD, the field names the register which is the second operand. For a single operand instruction, like INC, the 3 bits usually form part of the operation code itself. The 8088 doesn't know that the instruction is an INC until it has decoded the middle 3 bits of the mod-r/m byte.

There are a couple of special cases that the mod-r/m byte also handles. If an instruction specifies a register rather than a memory location, the mode field is set to 11B to tell the 8088 that the r/m field contains a register value rather than a memory address. Finally, you might have noticed that there is no provision for direct addressing in the mechanisms of the mod-r/m byte. The 8088 treats the zero-length-displacement case of [BP + DISPLACEMENT] as the direct addressing mode. For that case, the displacement field is two bytes in length, and no register participates in the address calculation. Because of this special case, accessing the memory location pointed at by the BP register requires a one-byte displacement field with a value of zero. The same situation using the BX, SI, or DI register does not require a displacement byte. The next section will show another difference between BP and BX register addressing.

PHYSICAL ADDRESSING

All of the addressing described to this point has been concerned with generating what is called the address offset. The offset is a 16-bit value. The 8088 segments memory so that it can address more than 64K bytes of memory. This section will discuss the way the 8088 does segmentation.

Since the 8088 has a word size of 16 bits, it is natural to generate addresses that are 16 bits long. This allows for the direct addressing of 2^{16} items, or 65,536 bytes of memory. However, 64K storage locations are not enough for some programs. Therefore, Intel designed the 8088 to address 2^{20} bytes, or one megabyte of storage.

To get a 20-bit address, there must be four more address bits to go along with the 16-bit offset addresses. The extra 4 bits of address information come from the segment registers. The segment registers themselves are 16 bits wide. The 8088 combines the 16-bit address offset and the 16-bit segment register as shown in Figure 3.5. The processor extends the segment register with 4 zero bits, making it a full 20-bit value. The processor adds the offset address, the one determined through the address calculations, to the extended segment value. The 20-bit result is the pointer into actual memory.

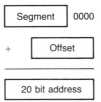

Figure 3.5   Segment–Offset Address Calculation

Each memory reference instruction can generate a 16-bit operand address. The processor really applies this offset within the defined segment. Figure 3.6 shows this way of viewing the segmentation.

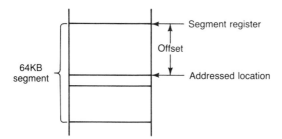

Figure 3.6   Segmentation

The beginning address of a segment always has a zero in the low 4 bits. Every sixteenth memory location has an address with this property. When designing the data layout for a program, remember that the segments must always fall on these 16-byte boundaries. These boundaries are also called paragraph boundaries.

SEGMENT REGISTERS

The 8088 has four segment registers: CS, DS, SS, and ES for Code, Data, Stack, and Extra Segment, respectively. Each of these has a normal use, but their application can be varied according to the requirements of the program.

The 8088 uses the Code Segment register to identify the segment that contains the currently executing program. The CS register combines with the Instruction Pointer to point at the current instruction. Each instruction fetch occurs at the location pointed to by the CS:IP register pair.

The combination of a segment register with an offset register to produce a physical address is written as segment:offset—CS:IP, for example. The segment value precedes the colon, the offset follows it. This notation is used both for registers and for absolute values. You can write addresses as CS:100, DS:BX, 570:100, or 630:DI.

The processor uses the Data Segment register for normal accesses to data. The operand addressing schemes we discussed in the preceding section produce a 16-bit offset. In most cases, the processor combines this offset with the DS register to form the actual memory address.

The Stack Segment register locates the system stack. All PUSH, POP, CALL, and RET instructions handle the stack data at the position defined by SS:SP. The SP register is the stack pointer, and serves as the offset into the stack segment. The Stack Segment is also the default segment whenever the addressing mode uses the BP register. This allows a program to access data on the stack using the BP register as a pointer. The next chapter contains a section on stack operations that shows how the BP addressing allows simple stack data references.

Finally, the 8088 uses the Extra Segment register for data references when more than one segment is required. A common programming operation is to copy information from one area of storage to another. If these locations aren't within the same 64K address range, it's impossible to move the data using a single segment register. With the extra segment register, a program can identify both the source and the destination segments simultaneously, as shown in Figure 3.7. The DS register locates the area providing the data, and the ES register points to the

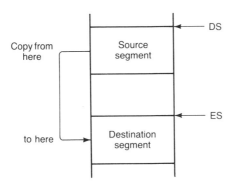

Figure 3.7 Copying from Segment to Segment

destination segment. There are some special string instructions for moving data that automatically use DS and ES as source and destination segments. The next chapter covers these instructions.

SEGMENT OVERRIDES

Each of the segment registers has the normal use indicated above. However, there are times when it's more convenient to reference data in a segment other than the data segment. An example is a small data area in a program. In most cases the program manipulates data in an area of storage pointed to by the DS register. However, there are times when the program must reference a local variable, a storage location contained in the program. To do this, the program must override the normal segment usage. Figure 3.8 shows this program organization.

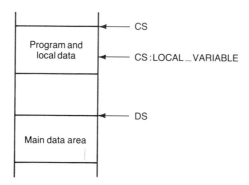

Figure 3.8 CS Override to Local Data

Instead of changing the DS register to point to the program segment, the instruction modifies the data reference to indicate that the variable resides in the Code Segment.

    INC   CS:LOCAL_VARIABLE

The "CS:" is the signal to the assembler that the data reside in the code segment. In machine language, the segment override command appears as a one-byte prefix to the normal machine language instruction. The 8088 understands this segment override prefix, and changes the normal method of address calculation. The processor uses the CS register for the physical address calculation of the data reference, rather than the DS register. A single prefix is all that is needed, since the 8088 can address at most one memory operand in an instruction.

An instruction may use any of the four segment registers for normal data references. The DS register usage is the default—that is, if the instruction specifies no other segment register, the DS is used. Remember that using the BP register in the address calculation makes the stack segment the default segment instead. An instruction may substitute any of the other three by specifying it as part of the address expression. However, there are some instructions that cannot have a segment override. These are the string instructions. The string instruction implicitly defines its segment usage and cannot be overridden. Chapter 4 will discuss the string instructions and their special uses of the segments.

SEGMENT STATEMENT

The assembler will help with the segment addressing problem. Part of the assembly language program must define the segments that make up the program. Assembly statements also tell the assembler which segment is associated with each segment register. The assembler can then determine the appropriate segment prefix if one is required. If the programmer specifies a reference to a variable in a segment not accessible with the DS register, but accessible with another segment register, the assembler generates the correct prefix. This allows the programmer to work directly with the code and data, and allows the assembler to do the work of figuring out the appropriate addressing mechanism.

Segment declarations allow the assembler to keep track of what segments are active and to detect possible errors. For example, a program can name a data variable that isn't available because there is no segment register that points to that variable's segment. The assembler will identify that as an error. This error occurs because the program has not established addressability. Although frustrating, it is better to find the error during the assembly than during the actual execution of the program.

The SEGMENT statement defines all segments. The SEGMENT statement gives each segment a name. The assembly program of Figure 3.9 shows the definition of several segments. A program may use any valid variable name as the segment name. The SEGMENT statement tells the assembler that all of the following instructions and data items will be in that segment at execution time. An

```
The IBM Personal Computer Assembler 12-11-82           PAGE    1-1
Figure 3.9  Segments

1                                              PAGE    ,132
2                                              TITLE   Figure 3.9  Segments
3
4      0000                          DATA    SEGMENT
5      0000  01                      VAR1    DB      1            ; Variable in Data segment
6      0001                          DATA    ENDS
7
8      0000                          BUFFER  SEGMENT
9      0000  02                      VAR2    DB      2            ; Variable in Buffer segment
10     0001                          BUFFER  ENDS
11
12     0000                          CODE    SEGMENT
13     0000  03                      VAR3    DB      3            ; Variable in Code segment
14
15                                           ASSUME  CS:CODE, DS:DATA, ES:BUFFER
16
17     0001  FE 06 0000 R                    INC     VAR1         ; Variable from Data
18     0005  26: FE 06 0000 R                INC     VAR2         ; Variable from Buffer
19     000A  2E: FE 06 0000 R                INC     VAR3         ; Variable from Code
20
21     000F                          CODE    ENDS
22                                           END
```

Figure 3.9 Segments

ENDS statement identifies the end of a particular segment. The ENDS statement has the segment name on it also. There must be an ENDS statement to match every SEGMENT statement. If not, the assembler will become confused and issue an error message.

ASSUME STATEMENT

After a program defines the segments, the assembler must know the segment register settings that will be in effect when the program is executed. Although the example in Figure 3.9 has only three segments, a large program could have many more. With four segment registers, a large program can address only a portion of the available segments at any one time. The assembler must know which segments will be addressed during execution. The ASSUME statement does this. The ASSUME statement identifies the segment register settings for the assembler. The programmer must associate each segment register with the segment to which it is currently pointing.

Figure 3.9 shows these segment operations. This example has three segments in it: DATA, BUFFER, and CODE. The names chosen for these segments are arbitrary. The programmer chose these names, and they have no significance to the assembler. You can, for example, call a segment CODE, and use it only for data, and vice versa. The best use, of course, is to name the segments in a way that is meaningful to the action of the program. In this example, the segments DATA and BUFFER each have a single data location within them. The segment CODE has a data location as well as three example instructions. It is unlikely that a program would define a segment with only a single storage location in it, but it will serve for this example. A program requires multiple segment definitions when it accesses data in many places within the 8088 address space. For a device control program written for the IBM Personal Computer, the program may have to reference memory in the system data area, set up an interrupt vector in low memory, and execute as a program at some arbitrary location. Each of these areas is a different segment, and must be defined in the program.

The ASSUME statement of Figure 3.9 tells the assembler to assemble the code with the understanding that the segment registers will be set as follows: the CS register contains the starting address of the CODE Segment, the DS register points to DATA, and the ES register identifies the BUFFER segment. The ASSUME means just what it says to the assembler. The assembler assembles the code with the assumption that the segment registers are set as indicated. The segment register assignments made in the ASSUME statement remain in effect during the assembly until another ASSUME specifies a new assignment. The assembler treats ASSUMEs in a sequential fashion, even though the program loops and branches around. The ASSUME statement remains in effect until the assembler sees the next ASSUME in a sequential scan of the source code. Notice that the ASSUME statement doesn't have to specify all of the segment registers.

The example does not declare the SS register. In fact, there may be times in a program when the contents of a segment register are unknown. In those cases, the ASSUME statement should name the segment NOTHING. For example, the statement

ASSUME   ES:NOTHING

tells the assembler that the program does not know what segment the extra segment register points to. Because the register is unknown, the assembler should not use it in any address calculations.

An important point to note is that the ASSUME statement does not generate any machine language instructions. It is a directive to the assembler to assume that the segment registers are set according to the information in the statement. It is up to the programmer to ensure that the segment registers are set correctly. Similarly, the assembler can't check that the ASSUME statement matches the contents of the register during execution. Because of the many paths a program might take to arrive at a particular ASSUME statement, the correctness of the statement is the programmer's responsibility. In the example, the program assumes that the segment registers have been set before this section of code executes. If they are not correct, the program will execute incorrectly, even though the assembly was correct.

The first instruction increments the value at VAR1, which is in the data segment. The assembler assumes that the DS register points to the DATA segment, according to the ASSUME statement. Since the DS register is the default segment to use for data references, the assembler doesn't generate a segment prefix override for this instruction. The four-byte machine language instruction generated by this instruction does not contain a segment prefix.

The second instruction specifies the variable VAR2, which has been defined in the segment named BUFFER. The program told the assembler that the Extra Segment register would point to the BUFFER segment. The assembler generates the four-byte machine language instruction to increment VAR2, but it precedes the instruction with the one-byte prefix that overrides the use of the DS register. The prefix byte of 26H tells the processor to use the ES register when it forms the 20-bit memory address. The assembler identifies the prefix instruction with a colon in the object code section of the listing.

The third instruction specifies VAR3 in the segment CODE. The ASSUME statement links this segment with the CS register. The assembler automatically generates the appropriate segment override prefix. In this case the prefix 2EH tells the processor to use the CS register when calculating the actual address.

At first the ASSUME statement will seem to be a curse. When writing programs for the first time, it's normal to forget the ASSUME statement. The assembler will generate a lot of error messages to help you remember. But in the long run, the ASSUME statement helps the assembly language programmer concentrate on the data structures involved in the program. The programmer must remember to establish a segment register to address the data required by the program. The assembler will relieve the burden of remembering for each instruction just where the data are residing, and which segment register must be used to get there.

A program may use the SEGMENT statement to convey information to other programs. The SEGMENT statement can specify the segment alignment in memory, the way in which it combines with other segments, and a class name. There are two segment alignments of particular interest to the IBM Personal Computer programmers. Paragraph (PARA) alignment places the segment on a paragraph boundary—a memory location divisible by 16. This means that the first byte of the segment will have an offset of 0 from the segment register. In contrast, BYTE alignment places the segment at any starting location. In this case, the segment register may or may not point at the first byte of the segment. A program may need a nonzero offset to access the first location.

The combine type parameter specifies different methods of linking segments together. This is particularly useful for modular programming. The PUBLIC declaration causes all segments with the same name to be combined as one large segment. All the CODE segments, for example, can be combined. This would join the main routine with the various subroutines in their own assembly modules. Another useful combine type is AT, which, together with an address expression, locates a segment at an absolute address. Such a declaration is necessary when dealing with data at a fixed location, such as the interrupt vectors in low storage.

A much more complete explanation of the SEGMENT statement can be found in the IBM Personal Computer Macro Assembler Reference Manual. We'll use some of these SEGMENT operations in examples later.

CONTROL REGISTERS

There are three 16-bit registers in the 8088 processor that are used primarily for control operations. These are the Stack Pointer (SP), the Instruction Pointer (IP), and the flag register. The processor uses the two pointer registers for memory addresses needed during the execution of a program. The flag register contains the condition codes that a program can use to control its execution.

Instruction Pointer

The instruction pointer is a 16-bit register that contains the offset of the next instruction. As indicated in the preceding section, the processor uses the CS register with the IP register to form the 20-bit physical address. The CS register defines the segment of the executing program while the IP determines the offset.

Because there are two registers that participate in the determination of the next instruction address, there are several different methods of changing the course of program execution. The most common occurs during normal instruction execution. As the processor fetches an instruction from memory and executes it, the IP register is incremented by the number of bytes in the instruction. The CS:IP pair now point to the next sequential instruction.

When a program alters the normal instruction flow, it executes a jump instruction. One jump instruction alters only the IP register, creating a jump within the current segment. This type of jump is called an intrasegment or NEAR jump. The specification for this jump requires only the new value of the IP register. The CS register is left unchanged. A NEAR jump can transfer control only within the current segment, so the jump distance is limited to a maximum of 64K bytes. To go to a section of the program farther away than that, the program requires a different type of jump.

The second type of jump is called an intersegment, or FAR, jump. In this jump the processor assigns new values to both the CS and IP registers. This jump allows a new program located anywhere in the address space of the 8088 to be executed. However, to execute this jump, the instruction must specify new values for both the CS and the IP registers. For a direct jump, this requires a five-byte instruction—one byte for the opcode, and two bytes each for the CS and IP registers.

Stack Pointer

The stack pointer (SP) register is a 16-bit register that identifies the offset of the current top of stack. The processor uses the stack pointer with the Stack Segment register to form the physical address. The processor uses the SS:SP register pair for all stack references, including PUSH, POP, CALL, and RETURN. The SS:SP register pair always point to the current top of stack. When an instruction pushes a word onto the stack, the SP register is decremented by two. When a word is popped from the stack, the processor increments the SP register by two. The stack grows toward smaller memory addresses. All stack operations use word values. A single byte cannot be pushed or popped on the stack.

The processor changes the SP register to reflect the actions of the stack. The SS register is not affected by any of the stack operations. The program sets the SS register independently of any PUSH or POP operation and the SS register identifies the segment in which the stack resides. This means that the system stack is limited to 64K bytes in length. As an example, if a program sets the SS register to 1000H and the SP register to 0, the first item pushed onto the stack goes at location 1000:FFFFH and 1000:FFFEH. Successive items pushed onto the stack will continue to be placed at lower and lower memory addresses until the last possible item on the stack is at 1000:0001H and 1000:0000H. If the program pushes another item onto the stack at this point, it will be placed at 1000:FFFFH and 1000:FFFEH, which is the first location used by the stack. Since the stack has now ''rolled over'' it is destroying information previously stored on the stack.

In normal usage, the stack is not 64K bytes in length. If a program establishes a stack of 512 bytes, for example, it might initialize the SS:SP pair to 1000:0200H. The first stack location is 1000:01FFH, and the last one available is 1000:0000H. If the program pushes more than 256 words on the stack, decrementing the SP register will cause the value to pass through zero, and begin placing stack information at the other end of the stack segment. When this happens the program is placing stack data in an area of memory that was not set aside for the stack, in this case, 1000:FFFFH. One of two bad things may happen. The stack may overlay program or data that should not be destroyed. Or, the stack data are going into a region of the address space that has no physical memory. Either of these can be a very difficult problem to find during the program testing, so the solution is to always leave plenty of room for the system stack. In the case of the IBM Personal Computer using the IBM Disk Operating System, a stack size of at least 128 bytes is recommended. This gives sufficient space to handle the stack requirements of the various services that DOS and the system provide, together with the normal requirements of the program.

Flag Register

The final control register is the 16-bit flag register. This register contains information that is used a bit at a time, rather than as a 16-bit number. The bits in the flag register have individual meanings to the processor. Some of the bits contain the condition code setting of the last instruction executed. The program uses these codes to modify the program execution. The program can test the condition codes in the program, and the program may choose an alternate execution path based on those values. Other bits within the flag register indicate the current operating state of the processor. Individual instructions control these bits.

The best way to explain the flag register is to describe the bits one at a time. The layout of the flag register is shown in Figure 3.10. Notice that the figure does not define every bit. Those not defined are reserved—that is, there is no definition for them at this time. They may, however, be used for some specific purpose in later versions of the processor. Because of this, a program should never rely on a value in any of these reserved bits.

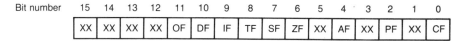

Bit number	15	14	13	12	11	10	9	8	7	6	5	4	3	2	1	0
	XX	XX	XX	XX	OF	DF	IF	TF	SF	ZF	XX	AF	XX	PF	XX	CF

Figure 3.10   Flag Register

All the flags of the lower byte of the flag register are set by arithmetic or logical operations in the processor. For example, an ADD operation sets all the flags in the low byte according to the results of the operation. With the exception of the overflow flag, all the flags in the high byte are set or reset by instructions dedicated to that purpose. The flags in the high byte reflect the processor state of the 8088 and will affect the manner in which programs execute. The flags in the low byte are condition codes, and can be interrogated by conditional jump instructions to change the order of program execution.

Sign Flag

The sign flag (SF) indicates whether the result of the last arithmetic or logical operation is positive or negative. The setting of the sign bit reflects the value of the highest bit of the last result. If the last result is negative, the sign bit is set to one. If it is positive or zero, the sign bit is cleared to zero.

Zero Flag

The zero flag (ZF) indicates that the result of the last operation was equal to zero. Programs use this flag to determine if two numbers are equal. The program subtracts the two values. The result is zero if the values are the same. The result is nonzero if the values are different.

Parity Flag

The parity flag (PF) indicates whether the number of ones in the result is even or odd. Parity is a method of checking a data value. The parity bit is an extra bit which checks the value of the other bits. A program can use the parity flag to determine whether the extra bit should be set or reset. The read/write memory of the IBM Personal Computer uses parity to check the values stored in it. That parity checking is done entirely by the system hardware, and does not affect the parity flag bit.

The parity flag is set to "1" if the result of an operation has an even number of ones. The flag is reset to "0" if the number of ones in the result is odd. The parity flag has little use in normal arithmetic and logical operations.

Carry Flag

The carry flag (CF) is the processor's link to higher-precision arithmetic. The 8088 can normally handle a maximum of 16 bits when doing arithmetic, such as an addition or subtraction. However, there are times when a program needs to manipulate numbers larger than 2^{16}. For example, to add two 32-bit numbers, the program must add the two lower parts of the numbers, and then add the two higher parts of the numbers. Figure 3.11 shows the addition of the 32-bit value 22223333H with 44445555H.

This example adds the least significant 16-bit values, producing the 16-bit result 8888H. It then adds the most significant 16-bit values to produce the result

Second Addition	First Addition
2222	3333
4444	5555
6666	8888

Figure 3.11   32-Bit Addition

6666H. The 32-bit result is 66668888H. The example requires two 16-bit additions to produce the 32-bit result. For a 48-bit number, three additions would be required, and so on. A program must break each big number into 16-bit chunks for addition.

The example above, however, was a simple one. The result of the first 16-bit addition did not affect the second addition. In the general case of addition, there is a possibility of a carry from one position to another. When the processor adds 16-bit numbers, it automatically handles the carries from one position to another. When a program adds two 32-bit numbers as in the example above, the program must remember the carry from the original 16-bit addition and used to modify the addition of the second 16-bit values. Figure 3.12 shows an addition of the numbers 22224444H with 3333EEEEH. In this example, the carry from the first addition is reflected in the second addition.

Second Addition		First Addition	
2222			4444
3333			EEEE
1	(carry from first)		
5556		1	3332

Figure 3.12   32-Bit Addition with Carry

The first 16-bit addition of 4444H with EEEEH produces a result of 13332H. Since the result is 17 bits long, it can't be stored in a 16-bit register. The carry flag of the status register holds this additional bit of arithmetic information. The second 16-bit addition adds not only the two numbers 2222H and 3333H, but also the carry flag value. There are two forms of the ADD instruction. The ADD instruction adds two 16-bit values, and produces a 17-bit result. The ADD with carry instruction (ADC) adds two 16-bit values and the carry value to produce the 17-bit result. In the example above, the first addition is an ADD, the second an ADC.

Using the carry flag to handle multiple-precision arithmetic works for both examples. In the first example, the addition of 3333H with 5555H produced a carry result of zero. When the ADC instruction adds the carry to the values 2222H and 4444H, it produces the result 6666H, the correct value. In the second example, the carry flag is set because there was a carry from the low-order addition into the high-order addition.

For even higher-precision arithmetic, a program can use the carry flag over and over in the addition process. Each 16-bit addition sets the carry flag according to the results of the addition. The program can add the next-higher significant chunk of the numbers with this carry value. In each case the carry flag contains the seventeenth bit of the previous result. The program must use this value in the addition of the next-higher portion of the number.

The carry flag also serves another, very useful purpose. When a program does subtraction, there is the possibility of borrow from one position to another. The carry flag indicates borrow from one number to another during a subtraction.

A program can subtract multiple-word integers in the same way that it adds them. It subtracts the low-order portions of the numbers, producing a 16-bit result. The subtract instruction (SUB) sets carry flag to reflect the borrow. The program performs next 16-bit subtraction with borrow. This subtract with borrow instruction (SBB) subtracts the carry flag from the result, as well as doing the normal subtraction. Like addition, a program can perform subtraction on integers of arbitrary size by using the carry flag as a borrow value.

The 8088 treats the carry flag as a true borrow. That is, if there is a borrow because of the subtraction, the processor sets the carry flag to "1." This indicates that the program should subtract the value 1 from the result of the next-higher precision subtraction. If there is no borrow, the processor resets the carry flag to "0." This indicates that the program does not need to subtract one from the next-most-significant portion of the number.

The processor sets the carry flag as a borrow indicator following a subtraction. Besides extending the processor precision, a program can use the borrow flag to determine the ordering of two numbers. If the carry flag is set, the subtrahend is greater than the minuend. If the carry flag is not set, the value subtracted is less than or equal to the value that it was subtracted from. This means that the carry flag becomes the primary indicator for determining the relative value of two numbers. After the program subtracts the two numbers, the carry flag tells which is larger. A program can test unsigned integers in this fashion, including such applications as sorting character strings. For signed numbers, the program requires additional information to determine relative magnitudes. The next chapter will discuss all the ways of testing numbers in the section "Conditional Jumps."

Auxiliary Carry Flag

You'll probably never use the auxiliary carry flag (AUX), at least directly. If you examine the conditional jump instructions of the 8088, you'll see that it's impossible to test this flag directly. The processor has an auxiliary carry flag for a very special purpose. The AUX flag allows the processor to do binary-coded-decimal (BCD) arithmetic.

BCD arithmetic is a different way of doing arithmetic than we discussed in Chapter 2. BCD arithmetic is based on the decimal system. The processor implements BCD by using 4 bits to represent a single decimal digit. Each nybble can represent the values from 0 through 9. The values OAH through OFH are never used. This means that a single byte can represent the decimal values from 0 through 99.

At first glance this method of storing numeric information seems wasteful, since BCD does not use 6 of the 16 possible states in each nybble. However, for many microprocessor applications, there is direct interaction with operator input.

Most people are conditioned to work with decimal, rather than binary or hexadecimal. Since the I/O requirements of the application may outweigh the storage or computational aspects of the application, it is convenient to maintain the information in a form that converts easily to input or output format. BCD representation fulfills this desire. BCD arithmetic also solves a representation problem that occurs in some binary systems. When an application uses floating-point numbers, there is sometimes a round-off problem because the binary numbering system does not correspond directly to the decimal system. In some instances the results of simple calculations may be incorrect in the last digit. This is sometimes referred to as the "missing pennies" problem, since it is most noticeable in accounting applications. The BCD number system is an alternative representation used for those computations.

The 8088 instruction set does not have special add or subtract instructions for BCD arithmetic. BCD arithmetic uses the normal add and subtract, just as they would be for normal binary representations. The result of adding two BCD numbers with the normal arithmetic processor may result in a number that is incorrect BCD. To fix this, the 8088 has several instructions that adjust the result to the correct BCD value. To do this conversion successfully, the processor must know if there was a carry from the lower nybble to the higher nybble in the addition. The example of Figure 3.13 shows why this is necessary.

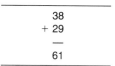

Figure 3.13 Decimal Addition

The decimal addition of 38 + 29 equals 67. But the binary addition of 38H + 29H equals 61H. If the numbers 38 and 29 represent BCD values, the program must make an adjustment following the addition. The instruction Decimal Adjust for Addition (DAA) takes a number and converts it into BCD form. In this case, the number is in BCD form—that is, both nybbles are in the range 0 through 9. However, the result is wrong. The addition sets the auxiliary carry flag in this particular addition, to indicate that there is a carry from the low-order addition (8 + 9). This flag tells the DAA instruction to add 6 to the result, producing the correct result, 67.

The processor also uses the auxiliary carry flag in correcting BCD arithmetic following subtraction with the Decimal Adjust for Subtraction (DAS) instruction. There are two other instructions that reference the AUX flag to determine the correct actions. These instructions, ASCII Adjust for Addition and ASCII Adjust for Subtraction (AAA and AAS), both perform the same type of BCD arithmetic correction as the DAA and DAS instructions. Programs use AAA and AAS with a number representation that stores each decimal number in a single byte. This representation, even more wasteful of storage space than BCD, allows a very convenient translation from ASCII to numeric and back. ASCII represents the numbers from 0 to 9 by the values 30H through 39H. Converting to or from ASCII merely involves the addition or subtraction of 30H. The next chapter will discuss the use of the decimal and ASCII adjust instructions.

Overflow Flag

The overflow flag (OF) is the only flag in the high byte of the flag register that is set by normal arithmetic operations. The remaining flags are all under the direct control of the programmer. The overflow flag is another of the arithmetic flags just like the zero and carry flags. Just as the carry flag is important for multiple-precision arithmetic, the overflow flag is vital to two's-complement arithmetic.

Two's-complement arithmetic uses the most significant bit to indicate the sign of the number. The addition unit of the processor handles both signed and unsigned numbers. Normally, the addition of signed numbers is correct. However, there are certain two's-complement numbers that, when added together, produce an incorrect result. The example in Figure 3.14, the addition of two 8-bit two's-complement numbers, shows how.

Hexadecimal	Decimal Equivalent
72H	114
+ 53H	+ 83
0C5H	197

Figure 3.14 8-Bit Addition with Overflow

If 72H and 53H are unsigned numbers, the addition is correct. If, however, the numbers are two's-complement signed numbers, the result is incorrect. The result, 0C5H, is equal to −59 in two's-complement representation. The addition of two positive numbers never results in a negative number. What has happened is that the result of the addition can't be represented in the 8-bit two's-complement range of values (127 to −128). This effect is known as overflow, since the addition has overflowed the two's-complement number range.

It is important to note that overflow and carry are two different flags, and have two different meanings. In Figure 3.14, there is no carry, because the unsigned addition gives the correct result. There is an overflow because the signed addition gives an incorrect result. It is possible for an addition to produce both a carry and an overflow, as shown in Figure 3.15.

Hexadecimal	Two's Complement	Unsigned
8EH	−114	142
0ADH	− 83	173
1 3BH	−197	315

Figure 3.15 8-Bit Addition with Carry and Overflow

Here the example is adding two negative numbers. The result, -197, is outside the range of the two's-complement representation. This is shown by the fact that the 8-bit result, 3BH, is a positive number. This example also sets the carry flag, showing that the unsigned addition produces a number greater than the maximum representable. In the case of 8-bit numbers, the maximum number is 255.

In summary, the addition operation of the processor operates identically on signed, unsigned, and BCD numbers. The carry, auxiliary carry, and overflow flags have information about the operation that allows the program to determine the correct value in the number system used. The overflow flag indicates that the result of an arithmetic operation has exceeded the range of the signed numbering system. Overflow is distinct from carry, which indicates that a carry out of the highest-order bit has occurred.

Trap Flag

The trap flag (TF) helps debug programs. This flag is not set by a processor operation. The program sets this flag, also called the trace flag or the single step flag, with a specific instruction.

When this flag is active, an interrupt occurs after every instruction. The effect is just as if an external device requested an interrupt after every instruction. The trace interrupt transfers control to the location specified by interrupt vector 4. As part of the interrupt process, the processor resets the trap flag to the inactive state. This allows the trace interrupt handler to execute without interrupting after every instruction. When the trace interrupt handler returns control to the user program, it restores the original user flag register, which still has the trace flag set. The processor executes the next user instruction, and the trap interrupt occurs again. The trace interrupt handler gets control following every instruction until the user program resets the trap flag.

The DOS debug program uses the trap flag. One of the functions of the debug program is a single step operation, which executes a single user instruction before returning control to the debug monitor. The trap flag generates that interrupt. A complete explanation of the interrupt process is given in the section "Interrupt Vectors."

Interrupt Flag

The interrupt flag (IF) controls external interrupts. During those sections of a user program where it is undesirable to allow external interrupts, the program can reset the interrupt flag. While the interrupt flag is cleared to "0," no external interrupts can occur. When the program sets the interrupt flag to "1," external devices can generate interrupts. The user program controls the interrupt flag.

The IBM Personal Computer has several methods of controlling interrupts. The interrupt flag of the status register disables all external interrupts except those caused by memory errors. For situations where a program needs to disable only some of the interrupts, there is a separate interrupt mask register. This mask register can enable and disable the individual external interrupts. Chapter 8, describing the hardware of the IBM Personal Computer, will cover the use of this register.

Direction Flag

The final flag bit in the flag register is the direction flag (DF). The 8088 instruction set contains several string instructions that operate on a large block of data. These instructions manipulate blocks of data a byte or word at a time. The index registers point to the data blocks. Following the operation on a byte or word, the processor changes the index register to point to the next element in the block.

String operations use the direction flag to indicate the direction of movement through the block of data. When the direction flag is cleared to "0," string operations increment the index register. If the direction flag is set to "1," string operations decrement the index register. The direction flag allows a single set of string operations to handle either direction, depending on the setting of the flag. In some instances it is desirable to move the string with incrementing addresses, while at other times it is best to use decrementing addresses.

As an example, suppose that a program uses the string move operation to move a block of data to a new location. If the program moves the block to a lower memory address, it clears the direction flag to increment the index registers following each move. If the move is to a higher memory address, the direction flag is set, indicating a decrement of the index registers. For most moves, it doesn't matter which way the flag is set. But if the final destination of the block overlaps the initial location and the direction flag is not set correctly, the information in the block will be destroyed during the move.

Figure 3.16 shows an example of a block move. The initial block of data is 200H bytes long, located between 300H and 4FFH. The desire is to move it to a new location, between 400H and 5FFH. The source and destination areas overlap.

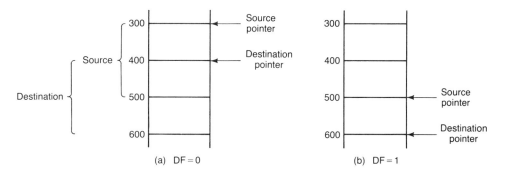

Figure 3.16 Direction Flag

In Figure 3.16(a), the example has set the source and destination pointers to the beginnings of their respective blocks. The source pointer is at 300H, the destination pointer at 400H. The example has cleared the direction flag, so that the pointers are incremented following each move. As the figure shows, after the string operation has moved 100H bytes, the source pointer moves into the destination block. This area of the destination block has already been filled with data from the move. The movement of the final 100H bytes will be incorrect, since the example has lost the original data in the block.

In part (b), the example has set the source and destination pointers to the end of their blocks. The direction flag is set, so that the pointers increment after each move. Using this method, the example moves the data correctly from the source to the destination.

The I/O programs of the IBM Personal Computer have a specific instance of direction flag usage in the display scroll routines. The I/O code uses the 8088 string move instructions to move the data within the display buffer. When the code scrolls the display up, it moves data to lower memory addresses. When it scrolls characters down on the screen, the code moves the data to higher memory addresses. In each case, the code sets or resets the direction flag according to the direction of data movement.

INTERRUPT VECTORS

Another important facet of the 8088 processor is the interrupt structure. This system component is built into the processor, and provides an efficient method to handle interrupts.

When the 8088 receives an interrupt, it determines which device is requesting service during a hardware action known as an interrupt acknowledge cycle. In the IBM Personal Computer, an interrupt controller chip, the Intel 8259, handles external interrupts. The interrupt controller is programmed to provide a one-byte number in response to the interrupt acknowledge cycle of the 8088. The number, in the range 0 to 255, is the interrupt number of the external interrupting device. For the Personal Computer, there are eight external interrupts handled by the interrupt controller, and these return interrupt values from 8 through 15.

Once the 8088 receives the interrupt number, it must pass control to the appropriate interrupt handler. The 8088 reserves the first 1024 bytes of memory for interrupt vectors. Each of the 256 possible interrupts has a four-byte region assigned to it. Interrupt 0 has the four bytes at locations 0 through 3, interrupt 1 is from location 4 through 7, and so on. Each four-byte location contains a pointer to the interrupt handler for that particular interrupt. The first two bytes contain the offset of the interrupt handler, the last two bytes are the segment. The Define Doubleword (DD) operator generates the correct values of segment and offset for this field.

Just like a subroutine call, an interrupt must save the return address on the stack. Since the interrupt handler may be anywhere in the address space of the microprocessor, the processor must handle the interrupt as a FAR call. That is, before the processor passes control to the interrupt handler, it saves both the segment and offset of the current program. Also, the return from the interrupt handler must return the machine to the exact state that it was in at the time the interrupt occurred. To help in this, the 8088 also saves the flag register on the stack. This means that every interrupt handler won't have to do the same thing. Saving the flag register also saves the current state of the interrupt enable flag. Accepting an external interrupt clears the interrupt enable flag so that the interrupt handler routine cannot be interrupted by another interrupt. The return from interrupt instruction, which restores the flag register, automatically reenables the interrupt system by restoring the interrupt flag to its condition prior to the acceptance of the interrupt.

When the interrupt occurs, the processor pushes the flag register onto the stack, followed by the CS and IP registers. The 8088 uses the interrupt number to read the pointer to the interrupt handler, and passes control to it. It is now the responsibility of the interrupt handler to save any of the registers that it modifies, and to restore them before returning control to the interrupted routine. The IRET instruction is a special return, used to return from interrupts. The IRET instruction will pop the top three words from the stack and place them in the IP, CS, and flag registers. We'll do several examples in later chapters that use the interrupt mechanism.

The programmer can use the interrupt mechanism directly without requiring external interrupts. There are instructions that cause the processor to execute as if an external interrupt occurred during that instruction. These actions are called software interrupts, since they are executed in software, but mimic the actions of an interrupt. The processor pushes the three control registers onto the stack and selects an interrupt vector using the one-byte value supplied by the program. The processor uses the stored interrupt vector in low memory as a pointer to the interrupt routine.

The software interrupts allow great flexibility in the 8088 system. For normal subroutine calls, the programmer must know where the subroutine is prior to executing the program. But if the program calls the subroutine using a software interrupt, the subroutine may be located anywhere within the address space. The calling program need not know where it is. The interrupt vector number is the only parameter required by the programmer calling the routine. The IBM control programs and operating system use this concept to great advantage. Software interrupts access the service routines of the system. The user program doesn't need to know the exact location, which might change with different releases of the support software. Also, the service routines may be replaced at any time merely by changing the four-byte vector to point to the new routine, without modifying the programs that use those routines. We'll do several examples that show the utility of this approach in Chapter 10.

CHAPTER

4

The 8088
Instruction Set

This chapter covers the instruction set of the 8088 microprocessor. The preceding chapters discussed the register layout and addressing mechanisms of the processor. In this chapter we'll explore the operations that you can do with those resources.

We'll group the 8088 instructions into several categories. The function that each instruction performs determines the groupings. This chapter is not a listing of the instructions, with each page devoted to a separate instruction. The Macro Assembler Reference Manual does that job very well. Rather, this book discusses the instruction groups, and tries to explain the best usage of the instructions. This text should give you an idea of what you can do with the instructions, rather than exactly what they do individually.

DATA MOVEMENT

By any measure, the data movement instructions are the most frequently used in the instruction set of any computer. The 8088 is no exception. Much of any data processing problem consists of moving information from one location to another. A program may do some processing on the information as it is moved, but the bulk of the work is just in the movement. This section covers the majority of the data movement instructions of the 8088. The section on string operations covers the remaining portion of data movement.

Move

The move (MOV) instruction is the basic instruction in data movement. This instruction moves one byte or word of data from a memory location to a register, from a register to a memory location, or from a register to a register. The MOV instruction can also store a value determined by the programmer into a register or memory location.

The MOV instruction is actually a family of machine language instructions with the 8088. A chart that lists the machine language variations of all the 8088 instructions is presented in Appendix A. A quick check of this chart reveals that there are seven different versions of the MOV instruction. Yet the programmer enters each of these instructions with the single operation code MOV. The assembler determines the correct machine instruction, based on the operands that the programmer supplies with the instruction. This is one of the reasons the assembler insists on typing the operands. The assembler must know what each operand is—a register, a byte memory location, a word memory location, a segment register, or something else. This typing allows the assembler to determine the correct machine language instruction. For the MOV instruction, the assembler must decide from the seven choices which is the correct form, based on the operands that the programmer supplies.

Figure 4.1 shows the different ways in which you can move data from one place to another in the 8088. Each block signifies a register or memory location. The arrows identify the data movement paths that the 8088 instruction set allows. The primary path is from memory to the registers and vice versa. Data placed in the registers can be manipulated with greater efficiency than data left in memory. The processor doesn't execute memory cycles each time the data are needed. Also, the 8088 instructions can specify only one memory operand in any

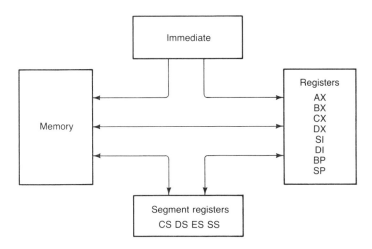

Figure 4.1   MOV Operations

instruction. Therefore, an ADD instruction requires that at least one of the operands be in a register. The 8088 doesn't have the capability of adding one memory location to another in a single instruction.

A MOV instruction may contain the new register value in the instruction. This operand form is called an immediate operand. The data are immediately available in the instruction, and no address calculation is required. You might consider this as a special addressing mode, where the operand is in a memory location in the instruction rather than in some other memory location or register. The 8088 also has immediate instructions for data manipulation as well as move operations.

Figure 4.1 also shows that an instruction can transfer immediate data directly into a register or memory location. Notice that it makes no sense to store information into an instruction, so the data flow for an immediate instruction is in only one direction.

Finally, a MOV instruction may store a segment register into either memory or a register. A MOV may also load a segment register from memory or another register. However, there is no instruction to load a segment register with immediate data. This means that it's inefficient to load a segment register with an immediate value. If a program needs to place a known value into a segment register, it must first store the value in one of the registers or a memory location. Then it can move the value into the segment register. Figure 4.2 shows how to do this.

```
The IBM Personal Computer Assembler 01-01-83          PAGE    1-1
Figure 4.2 Move instructions

 1                                         PAGE    ,132
 2                                         TITLE   Figure 4.2 Move instructions
 3          0000                    CODE   SEGMENT
 4                                         ASSUME  CS:CODE,DS:CODE
 5
 6          0000             EXWORD LABEL  WORD
 7          0000             EXBYTE LABEL  BYTE
 8
 9          0000  8B C3                    MOV     AX,BX          ; Register BX --> Register AX
10          0002  8B D8                    MOV     BX,AX          ; Register AX --> Register BX
11
12          0004  8B 0E 0000 R             MOV     CX,EXWORD      ; Memory --> Register
13          0008  89 16 0000 R             MOV     EXWORD,DX      ; Register --> Memory
14
15          000C  8A 2E 0000 R             MOV     CH,EXBYTE      ; Memory --> register (byte)
16          0010  88 36 0000 R             MOV     EXBYTE,DH      ; Register --> Memory (byte)
17
18          0014  BE 03E8                  MOV     SI,1000        ; Immediate --> Register
19          0017  B3 17                    MOV     BL,23          ; Immediate --> Register (byte)
20          0019  C7 06 0000 R 07D0        MOV     EXWORD,2000    ; Immediate --> Memory
21          001F  C6 06 0000 R 2E          MOV     EXBYTE,46      ; Immediate --> Memory (byte)
22
23          0024  A1 0000 R                MOV     AX,EXWORD      ; Memory --> Accumulator
24          0027  A0 0000 R                MOV     AL,EXBYTE      ; Memory --> Accumulator (byte)
25          002A  A3 0000 R                MOV     EXWORD,AX      ; Accumulator --> Memory
26          002D  A2 0000 R                MOV     EXBYTE,AL      ; Accumulator --> Memory (byte)
27
28          0030  8E 1E 0000 R             MOV     DS,EXWORD      ; Memory --> Segment Register
29          0034  8E D8                    MOV     DS,AX          ; Register --> Segment Register
30          0036  8C 1E 0000 R             MOV     EXWORD,DS      ; Segment Register --> Memory
31          003A  8C C0                    MOV     AX,ES          ; Segment Register --> Register
32
33                               ;-----   Immediate value to segment register
34
35          003C  B8 ---- R                MOV     AX,CODE        ; Get immediate value
36          003F  8E D8                    MOV     DS,AX          ; Value to segment register
37
38          0041                    CODE   ENDS
39                                         END
```

Figure 4.2 Move Instructions

Figure 4.2 shows an assembly listing of some of the variations possible with the MOV instruction. Notice that the single assembly operation code MOV generates a number of different machine language operation codes.

Looking at Figure 4.2, notice the syntax for the MOV instruction. The MOV operation code has two operands: the destination and the source. The instruction lists them in that order, destination followed by the source. The first instruction in the figure (MOV AX,BX) moves the contents of the BX register to the AX register. The next instruction has the opposite effect. The contents of the AX register are moved to the BX register. The MOV instruction does not modify the source operand. Thus, the instruction

    MOV   AX,BX

modifies the AX register, the destination, but does not change the BX register, the source.

None of the MOV instructions affect the status flags. Although this may seem inconvenient at times, it is the best way to handle the flag settings. As we'll see, the 8088 has instructions that can efficiently test any storage location, so a move operation isn't needed. As an example of when you don't want the flags set on a move, consider multiple-precision arithmetic. When a program does multiple-precision arithmetic, it must move portions of the operands into registers to position them for the operation. This move changes none of the flags. This allows the flags to handle the multiple-precision arithmetic.

As we mentioned earlier, there are several different forms of the move instruction in machine language. The object code in Figure 4.2 shows these different forms. If you're interested in the workings of machine language, you should compare the object code to the machine language layouts in Appendix A. This comparison can show you the workings of the different bits in the machine language. For example, you can see the immediate data values in those instructions. Fortunately, you don't have to know exactly how the assembler works to write assembly language programs.

If you wish to have the greatest possible efficiency in your programs, you should examine the object code in Figure 4.2. The number of bytes in the instruction is directly related to the amount of time it takes to execute that instruction. For example, the move instruction that takes an immediate value and places it in memory requires six bytes. The 8088 instruction set has several instructions optimized for the accumulator register, either AX or AL. Using these instructions, if appropriate, can save you time and space in a critical program.

The last two instructions of Figure 4.2 show how to place an immediate value in a segment register. Any other register, in this example the AX register, can hold the immediate value temporarily before the program moves it into the segment register.

There are other instructions that can move data around. A sample assembly in Figure 4.3 shows these instructions.

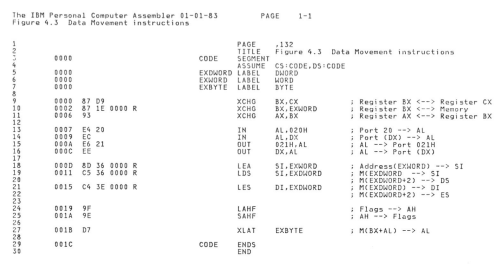

```
The IBM Personal Computer Assembler 01-01-83          PAGE   1-1
Figure 4.3  Data Movement instructions

1                                              PAGE    ,132
2                                              TITLE   Figure 4.3  Data Movement instructions
3          0000                        CODE    SEGMENT
4                                              ASSUME  CS:CODE,DS:CODE
5          0000              EXDWORD LABEL   DWORD
6          0000              EXWORD  LABEL   WORD
7          0000              EXBYTE  LABEL   BYTE
8
9          0000  87 D9                         XCHG    BX,CX        ; Register BX <--> Register CX
10         0002  87 1E 0000 R                  XCHG    BX,EXWORD    ; Register BX <--> Memory
11         0006  93                            XCHG    AX,BX        ; Register AX <--> Register BX
12
13         0007  E4 20                         IN      AL,020H      ; Port 20 --> AL
14         0009  EC                            IN      AL,DX        ; Port (DX) --> AL
15         000A  E6 21                         OUT     021H,AL      ; AL --> Port 021H
16         000C  EE                            OUT     DX,AL        ; AL --> Port (DX)
17
18         000D  8D 36 0000 R                  LEA     SI,EXWORD    ; Address(EXWORD) --> SI
19         0011  C5 36 0000 R                  LDS     SI,EXDWORD   ; M(EXDWORD  --> SI
20                                                                  ; M(EXDWORD+2) --> DS
21         0015  C4 3E 0000 R                  LES     DI,EXDWORD   ; M(EXDWORD) --> DI
22                                                                  ; M(EXDWORD+2) --> ES
23
24         0019  9F                            LAHF                 ; Flags --> AH
25         001A  9E                            SAHF                 ; AH --> Flags
26
27         001B  D7                            XLAT    EXBYTE       ; M(BX+AL) --> AL
28
29         001C                        CODE    ENDS
30                                             END
```

Figure 4.3   Data Movement Instructions

Exchange

The Exchange instruction (XCHG) is a simple exchange of two locations. The instruction can exchange two registers, or a register and a memory location. A segment register can't be one of the operands of an exchange.

The exchange instruction takes the place of three move instructions, and doesn't require a temporary storage location. If no exchange instruction existed, a program would require three moves to get the values in AX and BX exchanged. First, it would move AX to a temporary location, then move BX to AX, finally move the temporary location to BX. The XCHG performs this operation in a single instruction.

Input and Output

The 8088 has IN and OUT instructions (IN and OUT) to perform input and output operations. Every I/O device on the IBM Personal Computer has one or more registers built into it that can be manipulated by these I/O instructions. Each I/O device has an address for every register in the device. These addresses are different from the memory addresses of the system. The I/O address space is separate from the memory address space. There are a total of 2^{16}, or 65,536, I/O addresses available in the 8088. The IBM Personal Computer allocates 512 of these addresses to the System I/O Channel, for use by the various I/O adapters. Another 256 addresses are used on the System Board to control the I/O devices there.

The IN instruction transfers data from the I/O device to the AL register. The instruction can specify the address of the I/O device in two different ways. If the I/O address is in the range 0 through 255, the instruction can have the address as an immediate value. If the address is greater than 255, the instruction names the I/O address indirectly. The DX register holds the I/O address for the indirect IN instruction. The DX register can provide an indirect I/O address for all I/O devices, including those less than 256.

The OUT instruction operates in a similar manner, except that it stores the AL register in the I/O device register. The OUT instruction specifies addresses in the same way as the IN instruction.

The IN and OUT instructions can also transfer word information to and from I/O devices. For a word operation, the AX register is the source or destination. Since the 8088 has a one-byte-wide external bus, the I/O devices of the IBM Personal Computer accept only a byte of data for each I/O transfer. This means that word I/O operations aren't used on the IBM Personal Computer. However, since the 8086 has an identical instruction set, word I/O operations could be valuable on an 8086 system.

Load Effective Address

The Load Effective Address instruction (LEA) is very similar to a MOV instruction. But instead of moving the data from a memory location to a register, LEA loads the address of the data into the register. Because the 8088 instruction set can provide only a single memory address in any one instruction, the LEA instruction always specifies a register as the destination. LEA can specify the source operand in any of the addressing modes available with the mod-r/m byte.

In many cases, the LEA instruction is identical to the MOV immediate instruction. The instructions

```
MOV     BX,OFFSET EXWORD
LEA     BX,EXWORD
```

perform the identical function. The first instruction is a move immediate which uses the offset of the variable EXWORD. The OFFSET operator tells the assembler to load the BX register with the offset of the address value (all address values have a segment and an offset portion) for the variable EXWORD. The LEA instruction calculates the effective address of EXWORD and places it in BX. In this case, they are identical operations.

But if the program loaded the BX register with the address of the tenth byte in an array pointed to by the DI register, the LEA instruction would look like this:

```
LEA     BX,10[DI]
```

The 8088 would perform the address calculation using the mod-r/m byte information, just as it would for the MOV instruction. It then places the calculated offset into the BX register rather than the data at that location. There is no

comparable MOV immediate instruction that can perform the same function. Since the address is not known at assembly time, there is no way for the assembler to determine the immediate value.

Load Pointer

Since the 8088 addressing mechanism specifies both a segment and an offset for every variable, it's desirable to load all of this address information with a single instruction. The LDS and LES instructions do this job. The LDS instruction

LDS   SI,EXDWORD

loads the DS:SI register pair with the segment and offset values contained in the variable EXDWORD. LDS loads the SI register with the offset value contained at EXDWORD, and the DS register with the segment value located at EXDWORD + 2. This single LDS instruction loads two 16-bit registers with a pointer value from some location in memory. Since this instruction sets both the segment and the offset registers, the program can immediately address the object pointed to by that address. The programmer can establish the segment and offset pointer at assembly time with the DD operator. The DD operator creates a 32-bit data area. If an address expression is the operand of the DD, the two word fields contain the segment and offset of the address value, in the same format used by the LDS and LES instructions.

The LES instruction is identical to LDS, except that it loads the ES register. There are no instructions that can store the segment and offset values in a single operation. A program must store a pointer value in two word move operations rather than a single pointer store operation. This is acceptable since the program usually reads the pointer many more times than it sets the pointer. The program usually sets the pointer once during initialization, and then perhaps resets it when the system operating mode changes. In the interim, the pointer is probably accessed quite frequently. Later chapters contain some examples that both store and read the pointer values.

Flag Transfer

The 8088 instruction set has the instructions LAHF and SAHF primarily for compatibility with the 8080 instruction set. The LAHF instruction takes the low 8 bits of the flag register—those flags that are identical to the 8080 flags—and moves them into the AH register. The SAHF instruction reverses the process. The value in the AH register sets the low byte of the flag register.

If you translate a program from 8080 instructions to the 8088 instruction set, you'll need these two instructions. They are necessary to map the 8080 accumulator stack operations to the 8088 stack operations. We'll use the SAHF instruction in Chapter 7 to load a value into the flags to do some conditional branching.

Translate

The translate instruction (XLAT) converts information from one representation to another. XLAT converts the value in the AL register to another value, selected from a table pointed to by the BX register. Figure 4.4 shows schematically how the instruction executes. The BX register, together with the selected segment register, defines the starting point of a translation table in memory. The instruction adds the AL register, a value between 0 and 255, to that table address. XLAT moves the data at that location to the AL register. The XLAT instruction performs a table-lookup operation.

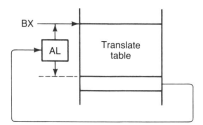

Figure 4.4   XLAT Operation

A good use of the XLAT instruction is the coding and decoding of text data. A program can implement a simple substitution cipher with this instruction. This example encrypts the 10 ASCII characters "0" through "9" for the purposes of transmission. A system might use such a technique to encode the sensitive information transmitted from one machine to another. When the data are received, another program returns the encoded characters to their original values. Figure 4.5 shows this substitution cipher.

Original	Transmitted	(b) Received	Correct
0	5	0	7
1	7	1	3
2	9	2	8
3	1	3	4
4	3	4	9
5	6	5	0
6	8	6	5
7	0	7	1
8	2	8	6
9	4	9	2
(a)		(b)	

Figure 4.5   Substitution Cipher for ASCII Numerals

Figure 4.5 has two translation tables, one for transmission, and one for reception. To transmit the value "5," the program looks up the value 5 in the transmission table (a). It finds the encoded value "6" to transmit. When that value is received, the decryption program looks up the 6 in the reception table (b) to find the real value, 5.

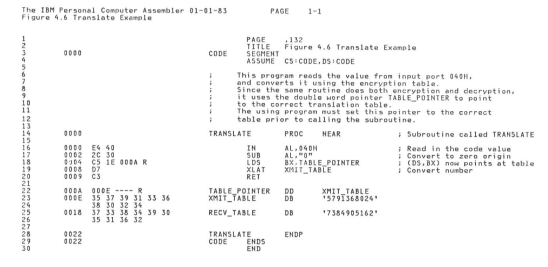

```
 1                                               PAGE    ,132
 2                                               TITLE   Figure 4.6 Translate Example
 3      0000                             CODE    SEGMENT
 4                                               ASSUME  CS:CODE,DS:CODE
 5
 6                                       ;       This program reads the value from input port 040H,
 7                                       ;       and converts it using the encryption table.
 8                                       ;       Since the same routine does both encryption and decryption,
 9                                       ;       it uses the double word pointer TABLE_POINTER to point
10                                       ;       to the correct translation table.
11                                       ;       The using program must set this pointer to the correct
12                                       ;       table prior to calling the subroutine.
13
14      0000                             TRANSLATE       PROC    NEAR              ; Subroutine called TRANSLATE
15
16      0000    E4 40                            IN      AL,040H                   ; Read in the code value
17      0002    2C 30                            SUB     AL,"0"                    ; Convert to zero origin
18      0004    C5 1E 000A R                     LDS     BX,TABLE_POINTER          ; (DS,BX) now points at table
19      0008    D7                               XLAT    XMIT_TABLE                ; Convert number
20      0009    C3                               RET
21
22      000A    000E ---- R              TABLE_POINTER   DD      XMIT_TABLE
23      000E    35 37 39 31 33 36        XMIT_TABLE      DB      '5791368024'
24              38 30 32 34
25      0018    37 33 38 34 39 30        RECV_TABLE      DB      '7384905162'
26              35 31 36 32
27
28      0022                             TRANSLATE       ENDP
29      0022                             CODE    ENDS
30                                               END
```

Figure 4.6   Translate Example

Figure 4.6 shows a subroutine that performs this encryption. The translate subroutine reads the original value from an I/O port, and returns the encoded/decoded value to the calling program in the AL register. The same subroutine does both encoding and decoding, by changing the encryption table.

The subroutine first reads the data from the input port 40H into the AL register. It subtracts the value for ASCII "0" from the data to get to zero origin. This means that the character "0" will result in a value 0 in AL, "1" will be 1, and so on. The LDS instruction loads the pointer to the correct table into the DS:BX register set. By loading this pointer from a memory location—TABLE _POINTER in this example—the subroutine can use any translation table. There are two tables in this program. One is for transmission, called XMIT_TABLE, which corresponds to Figure 4.5(a). The reception table, called RECV_TABLE, matches Figure 4.5(b). Before calling this subroutine, the main program must have stored the correct address pointer in the variable TABLE_POINTER. If the main program is receiving values, it would place the address of RECV_TABLE in the TABLE_POINTER variable. Notice that this subroutine can do almost any translation chore, since the calling program establishes the translation table.

With DS:BX pointing at the translate table, the XLAT instruction does the translation. The AL register has a value between 0 and 9. XLAT adds that value to the pointer, and loads the translated value into AL. The RET instruction returns control to the calling program.

Another common usage of the XLAT instruction is to change character representations from one machine to another. The IBM Personal Computer operates in ASCII, but most IBM machines use the EBCDIC (Extended Binary-Coded-Decimal Interchange Code) character encoding. To communicate with those machines, a program must translate the character values. The XLAT instruction is a natural for that function.

In summary, the XLAT instruction is a very powerful tool in translating byte or character information. Its very power makes it a seldom used instruction, since there are few opportunities to take advantage of it. But remember it for those occasions when it really pays off.

STACK OPERATIONS

Chapter 3 discussed how the 8088 implements a stack. The 8088 locates the stack with the SS:SP register pair. Items pushed on the stack cause the stack to grow toward lower memory addresses. The stack also serves as the storage location for subroutine return addresses. This section covers some of the instructions that directly affect the stack.

Figure 4.7 shows the assembled stack instructions. The instruction mnemonics are straightforward, with the PUSH or POP opcode followed by the register name for the operand. The only exception is the push or pop of the flag register, which uses PUSHF and POPF, respectively. Any memory location that the program can specify with the addressing modes can also be pushed or popped.

```
The IBM Personal Computer Assembler 01-01-83          PAGE     1-1
Figure 4.7 Stack operations

 1                                          PAGE      ,132
 2                                          TITLE     Figure 4.7 Stack operations
 3        0000                       CODE   SEGMENT
 4                                          ASSUME    CS:CODE,DS:CODE
 5        0000                       EXWORD LABEL     WORD
 6
 7        0000  50                          PUSH      AX              ; Push a register
 8        0001  56                          PUSH      SI
 9        0002  0E                          PUSH      CS              ; Can push segment registers
10        0003  FF 36 0000 R                PUSH      EXWORD          ; Can push memory locations
11
12        0007  8F 06 0000 R                POP       EXWORD          ; Can pop anything that pushes
13        000B  07                          POP       ES              ; Pop need not match push
14        000C  5F                          POP       DI
15        000D  5B                          POP       BX
16
17        000E  9C                          PUSHF                     ; Different mnemonic for flags
18        000F  9D                          POPF
19
20                                   ;----- Example showing paramter passing
21
22        0010  50                          PUSH      AX              ; Save 4 parameters on stack
23        0011  53                          PUSH      BX
24        0012  51                          PUSH      CX
25        0013  52                          PUSH      DX
26        0014  E8 0017 R                   CALL      SUBROUTINE      ; Transfer control
27                                   ;         ...                   ; Continue processing
28
29        0017                       SUBROUTINE      PROC      NEAR
30
31        0017  8B EC                       MOV       BP,SP           ; Establish stack address
32        0019  8B 46 02                    MOV       AX,[BP+2]       ; Get last parm (DX)
33        001C  8B 5E 04                    MOV       BX,[BP+4]       ; Get 3rd parm (CX)
34        001F  8B 4E 06                    MOV       CX,[BP+6]       ; Get 2nd parm (BX)
35        0022  8B 56 08                    MOV       DX,[BP+8]       ; Get first parm (AX)
36                                   ;         ...
37        0025  C2 0008                     RET       8               ; Return, and discard parms
38        0028                       SUBROUTINE      ENDP
39        0028                       CODE   ENDS
40                                          END
```

Figure 4.7 Stack Operations

For all stack operations with the 8088, the basic unit of information is the 16-bit word. Every item pushed onto the stack or popped from the stack is one or more words long. There are no byte operations available with push or pop instructions. If, for example, a program needed to save the AL register on the stack, it would have to push the AX register, since there is no way to save just the AL register.

The primary use of the stack is to save information temporarily. We've already seen the stack used to save a return address. A program can also save data values. If a program needs to use a register, yet also wants to save the data currently in that register, the program can push the register on the stack. The data are saved on the stack, and can be recovered later. For example, a program needs to input a value from I/O address 3DAH, but the DX register has an important data value. This code sequence

```
PUSH     DX
MOV      DX,3DAH
IN       AL,DX
POP      DX
```

saves the DX register on the stack during the time the program needs the DX register for the IN instruction.

A common usage of the stack is at the beginning of a subroutine. Usually, a subroutine tries to avoid changing any of the registers. So the subroutine, which needs registers for temporary calculations and address values, pushes all of the needed registers onto the stack before executing any subroutine code. Then, after executing the routine, the subroutine recovers the registers from the stack with POP instructions.

Remember that the stack is a LIFO data structure. The last word pushed is the first word popped. If your program has the sequence of instructions

```
PUSH     BX
PUSH     CX
. . .
POP      BX
POP      CX
```

the net effect is to exchange the values of the BX and CX registers. Just because the PUSH operation specified the BX register does not mean that a POP specifying that same register recovers the original BX contents. Another important thing is that the PUSH and POP operations must be balanced—that is, for every PUSH there must be a matching POP. Just like parentheses in an arithmetic operation, if the pushes and pops are unbalanced, the results will be incorrect. Even worse, since the 8088 stores return addresses on the stack, a mismatched push/pop operation usually results in a subroutine returning to a data value rather than to an instruction pointer value. This usually leaves the processor executing a program that the programmer never intended. So matching stack operations is a must. Be especially careful when the program has conditional jump instructions along with the stack operations. It's easy to miss one of the execution paths that may leave the stack unbalanced.

Besides saving data, a program can use the stack as a way station in some data movements. In particular, there is no move instruction that moves data from one segment register to another. Normally, setting one segment register from another requires placing the one value into an intermediate register first. This becomes a two-instruction sequence something like this:

```
MOV     AX,CS     ; Move CS value to AX
MOV     DS,AX     ; Get that value to DS
```

Each of these instructions is several bytes long, and this code sequence destroys the contents of the AX register. An alternative approach might be:

```
PUSH    CS        ; CS register to stack
POP     DS        ; Put that value in DS
```

The net effect of this sequence of code is identical. The DS register is set from the CS register. The code is only two bytes long and does not require an intermediate register. However, the two instructions take longer to execute because of the memory cycles required to read and write the data on the stack. This is a method of trading execution speed for object code size.

PARAMETER PASSING

The stack also serves as a convenient place to pass information to and from subroutines. Usually, a program passes parameters to a subroutine by placing them into the registers. However, there are instances where the number of parameters surpasses the register space available. In those cases, the program may push the parameters onto the stack before executing the CALL instruction. As we'll see in Chapter 10, the stack is the only method of passing parameters to assembly language routines from high-level languages BASIC and FORTRAN.

The subroutine can access these parameters on the stack in a very efficient method. Normally, a program can access information on the stack only by popping the data from the stack. Instead, the subroutine can use the BP register to point into the stack area. When a program passes parameters on the stack, one of the first instructions in the subroutine is

```
MOV     BP,SP
```

which sets the BP register from the current value of the stack pointer. Since the BP register is an addressing register, the subroutine can use it in address calculations. This means that all of the parameters may be accessed as displacements from the BP register setting.

The 8088 designers certainly had this parameter-passing method in mind, since the BP register uses the stack segment (SS) register as the default segment when accessing data. For all other data references, the processor normally uses the DS register. Since the stack is located in the stack segment, the SS:BP register pair very naturally addresses information on the stack.

Figure 4.7 has an example subroutine that shows the use of the BP register to access parameters passed on the stack. In this example, the main program pushes four word parameters onto the stack before the CALL. The subroutine sets the BP register to point at the data on the stack. Notice that the displacements used to access the stack data take into account the fact that the return address has also been stored on the stack, due to the CALL instruction.

In this example subroutine, the value at the current top of stack is the return address. The BP register contains the offset of that location. Two bytes away is the last parameter pushed onto the stack, the DX register. Following at two-byte intervals are the CX, BX, and AX registers, respectively. Thus, to get the parameter that was contained in the DX register, [BP+2] is the correct address, and the others follow at two-byte intervals. In this example, the value that started in the DX register goes into AX, CX into BX, and so on.

Parameter passing is not the only time that a subroutine can use the BP register for stack addressing. A subroutine might be long and involved enough that it is difficult to keep all of the necessary parameters in registers for the duration of the subroutine. Pushing those values onto the stack and setting the BP register to point to that stack area solves the problem.

Many subroutines also require some local storage for the duration of the subroutine execution. The subroutine can dynamically allocate this storage on the stack. Each time the subroutine is called, it can subtract the size of this storage area from the stack pointer. Since the stack grows toward smaller addresses, subtracting a value from the SP register is identical to pushing that many bytes of data onto the stack—except that those data areas are uninitialized. The subroutine can then use the BP register to address this storage area. When it is time to return from the subroutine call, the subroutine can add the appropriate value to the stack pointer. This returns the stack pointer to its initial value. The dynamic allocation of data means that the program uses the storage area only when required for execution, and does not reserve that storage at other times. Thus may allow a program to execute in a small memory environment when it might otherwise have been unable to do so. The best part is that the programmer does not have to design a complicated memory manager. The stack structure keeps everything in control.

The return from the Figure 4.7 subroutine shows another feature of the 8088 instruction set. The return from subroutine instruction (RET) may have an operand. This operand is a value that the processor adds to the stack pointer after it pops the return address. This example uses the value 8. This signifies that eight bytes, or four words, of data are to be removed from the stack following the return. These values are discarded, and never seen again. The effect is the same as popping the stack four times after the return. This means that the calling program does not have to pop the parameters from the stack and discard them. The return instruction has done that automatically.

This method of removing information from the stack works only for parameters that the calling program places on the stack. The subroutine must remove any dynamically allocated storage areas on the stack before executing the return. The subroutine must do this explicitly, rather than with the return instruction because the data area lies between the current top of stack and the return address.

A subroutine can return information to the calling program on the stack. If the caller pushes parameters on the stack, the subroutine can modify those values, and leave them on the stack. The calling program can pop them after the return. If the subroutine returns only one parameter, but was called with three on the stack, the RET 4 instruction does the job. The last two parameters are popped, with only the return parameter left on the stack.

When we use assembly language subroutines with high-level language programs in Chapter 10, the main program places the parameters on the stack. But these parameters will be the address of the data, not the value itself. This means that the assembly subroutine doesn't have to return parameters on the stack, and should pop all the parameters from the stack on the return.

ARITHMETIC INSTRUCTIONS

The arithmetic instructions of any processor are the ones that draw the most attention. Everyone is interested in doing arithmetic, and these are the instructions that do the job. Although they are small in number, they do the bulk of the data transformation in the processor. In actual use the arithmetic instructions are a small fraction of the total instructions executed.

The move instructions covered many of the concepts of the 8088 instruction set. There are some subtleties of operation to explore in the arithmetic instructions.

Addition

The ADD instruction performs the two's-complement addition of the specified operands. The processor places the result in the first operand, after adding the two operands together. The second operand remains unchanged. The instruction updates the flag register to reflect the result of the addition. For example, the instruction

        ADD   AX,BX

adds the contents of the BX register to the contents of the AX register, and leaves the result in the AX register. The flag register tells whether the result is zero, negative, even parity, and had a carry or overflow.

Figure 4.8 summarizes the actions of the ADD instruction. There are two forms of addition, 8-bit and 16-bit. Notice that different registers participate in the different forms of addition. The assembler ensures that the operands match. A

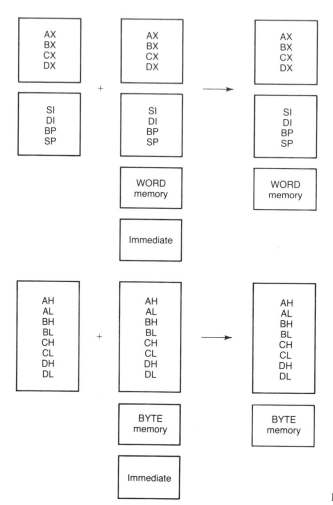

Figure 4.8 Addition Operations

byte register (for example, the CH) may not be added to a memory location that isn't a BYTE location. If a memory location is one of the operands, it may be either the destination operand or the unchanged operand. This allows an instruction to add a register to a memory location, and return the result to memory. An immediate value may also be one of the source operands. Figure 4.9 is an assembly listing of some of the arithmetic instructions.

The Add with Carry (ADC) instruction is the same as ADD, except that the carry flag is included in the addition. For every form of the ADD instruction, there is a comparable ADC instruction.

All addition instructions, both ADD and ADC, set the carry flag if there is a carry out of the high-order bit. An ADD instruction adds the two operands without reference to the carry flag. The ADC takes into account the carry flag. If

```
 1                                               PAGE     ,132
 2                                               TITLE Figure 4.9  Arithmetic Instructions
 3      0000                              CODE    SEGMENT
 4                                               ASSUME  CS:CODE,DS:CODE
 5      0000                              EXBYTE  LABEL   BYTE
 6      0000                              EXWORD  LABEL   WORD
 7
 8      0000  03 1E 0000 R                        ADD     BX,EXWORD      ; BX <- BX + [EXWORD]
 9      0004  29 0E 0000 R                        SUB     EXWORD,CX      ; [EXWORD] <- EXWORD - CX
10      0008  12 3E 0000 R                        ADC     BH,EXBYTE      ; BH <- BH + [EXBYTE] + Carry
11      000C  18 0E 0000 R                        SBB     EXBYTE,CL      ; [EXBYTE] <- [EXBYTE] - CL - Carry
12      0010  F7 1E 0000 R                        NEG     EXWORD         ; [EXWORD] <-  -[EXWORD]
13      0014  FE 06 0000 R                        INC     EXBYTE         ; [EXBYTE] <- [EXBYTE] + 1
14      0018  4E                                  DEC     SI             ; SI <- SI - 1
15
16      0019  81 C7 00C8                          ADD     DI,200         ; DI <- DI + 200
17      001D  83 EC 64                            SUB     SP,100         ; SP <- SP - 100
18      0020  83 D1 0A                            ADC     CX,10          ; CX <- CX + 10 + Carry
19      0023  83 1E 0000 R 14                     SBB     EXWORD,20      ; [EXWORD] <- [EXWORD] - 20 - Carry
20
21      0028  3B C3                               CMP     AX,BX          ; Set flags for AX - BX
22      002A  81 FE 01F4                          CMP     SI,500         ; Set flags for SI - 500
23
24      002E  F6 26 0000 R                        MUL     EXBYTE         ; AX <- AL * [EXBYTE]
25      0032  F7 EB                               IMUL    BX             ; DX:AX <- AX * BX
26      0034  F7 36 0000 R                        DIV     EXWORD         ; AX <- DX:AX / [EXWORD]
27      0038  F6 FD                               IDIV    CH             ; AL <- AX / CH
28
29      003A  27                                  DAA                    ; Decimal Adjust Addition
30      003B  2F                                  DAS                    ; Decimal Adjust Subtraction
31      003C  37                                  AAA                    ; ASCII Adjust Addition
32      003D  3F                                  AAS                    ; ASCII Adjust Subtraction
33      003E  D4 0A                               AAM                    ; ASCII Adjust Multiplication
34      0040  D5 0A                               AAD                    ; ASCII Adjust Division
35      0042  98                                  CBW                    ; AX <- Sign extend AL
36      0043  99                                  CWD                    ; DX:AX <- Sign extend AX
37
38      0044                              CODE    ENDS
39                                               END
```

Figure 4.9 Arithmetic Instructions

the carry is equal to zero, the result is equal to that of the ADD. If the carry is equal to one, the result is one more than the ADD result. Thus, a program can use the carry flag for multiple-precision operations. Figure 4.10 shows the addition of two 32-bit numbers. The example adds the 32-bit numbers VALUE1 and VALUE2, and places the result into VALUE2. Notice that one of the operands must be moved into a register. The first addition uses the ADD instruction, since

```
 1                                               PAGE     ,132
 2                                               TITLE   Figure 4.10 Multiple Precision Example
 3      0000                              CODE    SEGMENT
 4                                               ASSUME  CS:CODE,DS:CODE
 5
 6      0000  ????????                   VALUE1  DD      ?        ; 32 bit data area
 7      0004  ????????                   VALUE2  DD      ?
 8
 9                                       ;----- This code fragment adds two 32 bit numbers
10
11      0008  A1 0000 R                           MOV     AX,WORD PTR VALUE1
12      000B  01 06 0004 R                        ADD     WORD PTR VALUE2,AX       ; Perform low 16 bit addition
13      000F  A1 0002 R                           MOV     AX,WORD PTR VALUE1+2
14      0012  11 06 0006 R                        ADC     WORD PTR VALUE2+2,AX     ; High 16 bit addition
15
16                                       ;----- This code fragment subtracts two 32 bit numbers
17
18      0016  A1 0000 R                           MOV     AX, WORD PTR VALUE1
19      0019  29 06 0004 R                        SUB     WORD PTR VALUE2,AX       ; Subtract low order portion
20      001D  A1 0002 R                           MOV     AX, WORD PTR VALUE1 + 2
21      0020  19 06 0006 R                        SBB     WORD PTR VALUE2 + 2, AX  ; Subtract high order portion
22
23      0024                              CODE    ENDS
24                                               END
```

Figure 4.10 Multiple-Precision Example

the current value of the carry flag is immaterial to the addition. After the operands are positioned, the example does the second addition with the carry flag set from the previous addition, using the ADC instruction. This is also a good example of why the MOV instruction does not set any of the flags. If MOV modified the flags, the second addition would be more difficult to set up correctly.

Subtraction

The subtraction instructions (SUB and SBB) are identical to the addition instructions, except that they do subtraction rather than addition. You can modify Figure 4.8 for subtraction by changing the ''+'' sign to ''−.'' Subtraction sets the status flags according to the result of the operation, with the carry flag now representing borrow. For example, the instruction

    SUB   AX,BX

subtracts the value in the BX register from the value in the AX register, and places the result in the AX register. The status flags are changed to reflect the outcome.

   The Subtract with Borrow (SBB) instruction does multiple-precision subtraction problems. SBB includes the borrow flag as part of the subtraction. The value of the borrow flag is subtracted from the result obtained with the normal subtraction. Figure 4.10 also shows a multiple-precision subtraction, performed with the same values as the addition example. This example subtracts VALUE1 from VALUE2, placing the result in VALUE2.

Single-Operand Arithmetic

The negate (NEG) instruction is the sign reversal operator. The instruction changes the two's-complement sign of a byte or word operand. The other two single-operand instructions change the value of the operand by one. The increment (INC) instruction adds one to the operand, while the decrement (DEC) subtracts one from the operand. Increment and decrement can step an address pointer through a range of storage locations. They can also implement a loop counter. Each pass through the loop decrements the counter. When the value hits zero, the loop is done.

   All of these single-operand instructions may have either a byte or a word location as the operand. The assembler needs help if one of these instructions specifies a memory location using one of the indirect addressing modes, such as [BX+SI]. The assembler needs to know the size of the memory operand, so it can use the correct operation code. The instruction can use the BYTE PTR or WORD PTR modifiers to describe the operand.

   All three instructions modify the status register the same way that the arithmetic instructions do. Add one, subtract one, and subtract from zero, are identical to INC, DEC, and NEG, respectively. The single operand instructions are more efficient.

Compare

The compare instruction (CMP) compares two values by subtracting them. CMP discards the result, but sets the status flags according to the result. The instruction modifies only the flags. A program can use the compare instruction in the way as the subtract instruction. There is, however, no compare with the borrow instruction.

Multiple-precision compare functions take a little more effort than comparing bytes or words. In fact, it's much simpler to use the subtract instruction rather than the compare instruction. Figure 4.11 shows the comparison of a pair of 32-bit memory values, using the AX register as a temporary storage area. This comparison determines which of the numbers is larger. The program sets the condition codes as its result. The carry flag determines which of the numbers is larger. If the carry flag is "1," then VALUE2 is larger.

The second program in Figure 4.11 tests two 32-bit numbers for equal. Notice that the program saves the low-order result and later combines it with the high-order result. This determines if the result is identically zero. The next section describes the OR instruction, but essentially it combines the two values such that the final value is zero if and only if both of the values combined were equal to zero. The zero flag returns the result of this comparison subroutine. If the zero bit equals "1," the numbers are equal.

```
The IBM Personal Computer Assembler 01-01-83          PAGE    1-1
Figure 4.11 Multiprecision Compares


1                                          PAGE    ,132
2                                          TITLE   Figure 4.11 Multiprecision Compares
3       0000                        CODE   SEGMENT
4                                          ASSUME  CS:CODE,DS:CODE
5
6       0000  ????????             VALUE1 DD      ?       ; 32 bit operand
7       0004  ????????             VALUE2 DD      ?
8
9       0008                       FIG4_11 PROC   NEAR
10
11                                 ;----- This subroutine compares two 32 bit numbers for unequal
12
13      0008                       COMPARE_UNEQUAL:
14      0008  A1 0000 R                    MOV     AX,WORD PTR VALUE1
15      000B  2B 06 0004 R                 SUB     AX,WORD PTR VALUE2      ; Subtract low order portion
16      000F  A1 0002 R                    MOV     AX,WORD PTR VALUE1+2
17      0012  1B 06 0006 R                 SBB     AX,WORD PTR VALUE2+2    ; Subtract the high 16 bits
18      0016  C3                           RET                            ; Return with flags set
19
20                                 ;----- This subroutine will compare two 32 bit numbers for equal
21
22      0017                       COMPARE_EQUAL:
23      0017  A1 0000 R                    MOV     AX,WORD PTR VALUE1
24      001A  2B 06 0004 R                 SUB     AX,WORD PTR VALUE2      ; Subtract low 16 bits
25      001E  8B D8                        MOV     BX,AX                  ; Save the low order result
26      0020  A1 0002 R                    MOV     AX,WORD PTR VALUE1+2
27      0023  2B 06 0006 R                 SUB     AX,WORD PTR VALUE2+2    ; Subtract the high 16 bits
28      0027  0B C1                        OR      AX,CX                  ; Combine the two numbers
29      0029  C3                           RET                            ; Zero flag indicates equal
30
31      002A                       FIG4_11 ENDP
32
33      002A                       CODE    ENDS
34                                         END
```

Figure 4.11   Multiprecision Compares

Decimal Adjust

A program uses the same set of arithmetic instructions to manipulate binary-coded-decimal (BCD) numbers as it does for two's-complement numbers. However, the result of the arithmetic may produce a result which is incorrect for BCD representation. The decimal adjust instructions correct the result after the two's-complement arithmetic.

Decimal Adjust for Addition (DAA) and Decimal Adjust for Subtraction (DAS) are used for packed BCD operations only. In packed BCD, there are two decimal digits packed into each byte of data. DAA and DAS operate only on byte data in the AL register. With these limitations built into the instructions, there are no operands with either DAA or DAS.

Figure 4.12 shows two examples. The first example adds two packed BCD numbers. Both of the BCD numbers are two decimal digits, so they are represented in a single byte. The example adds these numbers, leaving the result in AL. The DAA instruction immediately afterward corrects the result of the addition and converts it to packed BCD form. Following the DAA instruction, the value in the AL register is a valid packed BCD number, in the range 0 to 99. If the

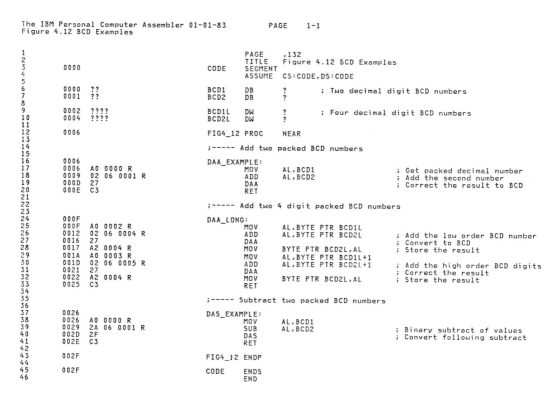

```
The IBM Personal Computer Assembler 01-01-83        PAGE    1-1
Figure 4.12 BCD Examples

1                                          PAGE    ,132
2                                          TITLE   Figure 4.12 BCD Examples
3           0000                    CODE    SEGMENT
4                                          ASSUME  CS:CODE,DS:CODE
5
6           0000  ??               BCD1    DB      ?        ; Two decimal digit BCD numbers
7           0001  ??               BCD2    DB      ?
8
9           0002  ????             BCD1L   DW      ?        ; Four decimal digit BCD numbers
10          0004  ????             BCD2L   DW      ?
11
12          0006              FIG4_12 PROC    NEAR
13
14                            ;----- Add two packed BCD numbers
15
16          0006              DAA_EXAMPLE:
17          0006  A0 0000 R            MOV     AL,BCD1         ; Get packed decimal number
18          0009  02 06 0001 R         ADD     AL,BCD2         ; Add the second number
19          000D  27                   DAA                     ; Correct the result to BCD
20          000E  C3                   RET
21
22                            ;----- Add two 4 digit packed BCD numbers
23
24          000F              DAA_LONG:
25          000F  A0 0002 R            MOV     AL,BYTE PTR BCD1L
26          0012  02 06 0004 R         ADD     AL,BYTE PTR BCD2L   ; Add the low order BCD number
27          0016  27                   DAA                        ; Convert to BCD
28          0017  A2 0004 R            MOV     BYTE PTR BCD2L,AL   ; Store the result
29          001A  A0 0003 R            MOV     AL,BYTE PTR BCD1L+1
30          001D  02 06 0005 R         ADD     AL,BYTE PTR BCD2L+1 ; Add the high order BCD digits
31          0021  27                   DAA                        ; Correct the result
32          0022  A2 0004 R            MOV     BYTE PTR BCD2L,AL   ; Store the result
33          0025  C3                   RET
34
35                            ;----- Subtract two packed BCD numbers
36
37          0026              DAS_EXAMPLE:
38          0026  A0 0000 R            MOV     AL,BCD1
39          0029  2A 06 0001 R         SUB     AL,BCD2         ; Binary subtract of values
40          002D  2F                   DAS                     ; Convert following subtract
41          002E  C3                   RET
42
43          002F              FIG4_12 ENDP
44
45          002F              CODE    ENDS
46                                    END
```

Figure 4.12   BCD Examples

result was less than 100, the AL register contains the answer, and the carry flag is "0." If the result is in the range 100 to 198, the AL register has the two lowest-order decimal digits, and the carry flag is set to indicate the carry.

The DAA instruction sets the flag register correctly. If the addition results in a value in the range 100 to 198, the carry flag indicates the carry out of the high-order decimal position. Similarly, a zero result leaves the zero flag set. For packed BCD operations, the sign and overflow flags have no meaning, although the sign flag is set if the high-order bit of the AL register is set. The DAA instruction specifically uses the auxiliary carry to determine the correction. Following the DAA, the auxiliary carry flag is indeterminate.

The second example in Figure 4.12 shows a multiple-precision BCD addition. This is very similar to multiple-precision binary arithmetic, except for the DAA instruction following each byte addition. Because of the limitations of the DAA instruction, the example cannot add the two packed decimal words as words and then apply the correction. Only byte arithmetic is allowed on packed BCD variables.

Finally, Figure 4.12 shows the use of the DAS instruction. It is just like binary subtraction, except that the DAS instruction must follow the subtraction. Here again, only byte operations are allowed.

ASCII Adjust: Addition and Subtraction

The ASCII adjust instructions are very similar to the decimal adjust instructions. They follow addition or subtraction operations on unpacked BCD numbers. Where a program uses the decimal adjust instructions (DAA & DAS) with packed BCD representation, it uses ASCII adjust for unpacked BCD numbers. In unpacked BCD numbers, a single byte represents the decimal numbers between 0 and 9. The number scheme is referred to as ASCII decimal because of the ease with which a program can convert the numbers to and from ASCII representation (add or subtract 30H, respectively).

After the addition of two unpacked decimal numbers, a program executes the ASCII Adjust for Addition (AAA) instruction, which converts the result to the correct unpacked representation. The rules for addition are identical to those for packed decimal. Since the addition of two unpacked decimal numbers may result in a number greater than 9, the AAA and AAS instructions require more than the AL register. For AAA, the low digit of the corrected result remains in AL. If the decimal addition resulted in a carry from the low digit, the AAA instruction increments the AH register by one. If that happens, AAA sets the auxiliary carry and carry flags to one. Otherwise, it resets them to zero. The other flags are undefined following the adjust instruction. The ASCII adjust instructions differ from the decimal instructions in that they affect the value in the AH register as well as setting the carry flag when there is a carry from the low-order digit.

A program uses ASCII Adjust for Subtraction (AAS) following the subtraction of one unpacked decimal number from another. The result of the byte operation must be placed in the AL register. The result of the ASCII adjust instruction remains in the AL register. If the subtraction results in a borrow, AAS decrements the AH register, and sets the carry and auxiliary carry flags. Otherwise, the flags are reset. The other flags are undefined following the instruction.

Multiply

The 8088 microprocessor is significantly more powerful than the 8-bit machines that preceded it. One of the reasons for the increased power is the addition of multiply and divide instructions to the processor instruction set. Previous microprocessors had to rely on assembly language programs using addition and subtraction to perform the multiply and divide operations.

There are two forms of the multiply instruction. Multiply (MUL) multiplies two unsigned integers to produce an unsigned result. The Integer Multiply (IMUL) instruction multiplies signed integers. The integer multiply takes the two's-complement numbers as the operands, and produces a result that has the correct sign and magnitude.

Both multiply instructions work on either byte or word operands. However, the range of options for the operands is much more limited than it is for add and subtract. Figure 4.13 summarizes the multiply operations. To multiply 8 bits by 8 bits, one operand must be the AL register, and the result is always the AX register. The result of the multiply may be up to 16 bits in length (the maximum value would be $255 \times 255 = 65,025$). To multiply 16 bits by 16 bits, one operand must be the AX register. The result, which may be up to 32 bits long (the maximum value is $65,535 \times 65,535 < 2^{32}$) is placed in a pair of registers. The DX register contains the high 16 bits of the result, while the AX holds the least significant portion. Notice that multiply does not allow an immediate operand.

The flag register settings are somewhat different for multiply than they are for the other arithmetic operations. The only two flags with valid meaning are the carry and overflow flags. They are also set differently for the two instructions.

Unsigned multiplication (MUL) sets both flags if the top half of the result is nonzero. If two bytes are multiplied, setting the carry and overflow flags indicates that the result is greater than 255, and cannot be contained in a single byte. For a word multiplication, the flags are set if the result is greater than 65,535.

Signed integer multiplication (IMUL) sets the carry and overflow flags according to the same criteria—that is, the flags are set if the result cannot be represented in the low half of the result. However, since the number is signed, the task is not as simple as comparing the top half with zero. IMUL sets the flags if the top half of the result is not the sign extension of the low half of the result. This means that if the result is positive, the test is the same as that for MUL—it sets the flags if the top half of the result is nonzero (but the most significant bit is zero, indicating a positive result). If the result is negative, IMUL sets the flags if the top half of the result is not all ones (but the most significant bit is a one, indicating the

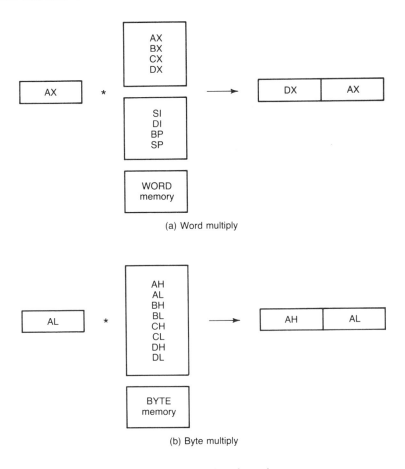

(a) Word multiply

(b) Byte multiply

Figure 4.13 Multiply Operations

negative result). For example, a byte multiply with a negative result sets the flags if the result is less than −128, since, that's the smallest number representable in a single byte. Another example, a word multiply with a positive result sets the flags if the result is greater than 32,767, the largest number representable in a single word.

ASCII Adjust: Multiply

When a program multiplies two unpacked decimal numbers, the result in the AL register is a binary number. Since the largest unpacked BCD number is 9, the maximum result of unpacked BCD multiplication is 81. However, this result is not a valid unpacked BCD representation of the number. The ASCII Adjust for Multiply (AAM) instruction converts the binary result into an unpacked decimal result. The action of AAM is to place the most significant decimal digit into the AH register, and leave the least significant decimal digit in the AL register. For example, if a program multiplies the values 6 and 7, the result in AL is 2AH, the AAM instruction converts the result, leaving 04H in the AH register, and 02H in the AL register—or the unpacked decimal number 42 in AH:AL.

The AAM instruction generates the unpacked decimal result by dividing the number in the AL register by 10. It places the quotient in the AH register, leaving the remainder in the AL register. AAM sets the sign and zero flags according to the result in the AL register. Since the result is unpacked decimal, the sign is always positive, and the zero flag is set only if the original number is a multiple of 10—that is, the least significant decimal digit is equal to zero. AAM leaves the remaining flags undefined. The carry flag does not come into play since the multiplication of two unpacked decimal numbers never produces a result that exceeds the two-decimal-digit representation available.

A program may also use the AAM instruction at any time to divide a binary number in the AL register by 10. As such, it might be considered a special case of the divide instruction, where the single byte value in the AL register is divided by 10. The quotient is placed in AH, the remainder in AL.

Divide

The 8088 instruction set contains division as part of the arithmetic functions. As with multiplication, there are two forms of the division—one for unsigned binary numbers, the other for signed two's-complement numbers (DIV and IDIV, respectively). Either form of division may be applied to byte or word operands.

The divide (DIV) instruction performs an unsigned division of the dividend and produces both a quotient and a remainder. Like multiply, the operands must appear in specific locations. Also like multiply, one of the values is twice the size of the normal operand. For division, the dividend is a double-length operand. Byte operations divide a 16-bit dividend by an 8-bit divisor. Division produces two results. Division places the quotient in the AL register, the remainder in the AH register. This placement of operands makes the division instruction the complement of multiply. This means that multiplying the AL register by a byte operand, and then dividing the AX register by the same operand, returns AL to its original state. The AH register would be set to zero, since there is no remainder. Figure 4.14 shows the schematic of the divide operation.

The word operation divides a 32-bit dividend by a 16-bit divisor. The dividend is in the DX:AX register pair, with DX holding the most significant portion, and AX holding the least significant. Word division places the quotient in the AX and the remainder in DX. Here again the multiply and divide operations are complementary. Multiplying AX by a word value, and then dividing it by the same value, returns AX to its original value. Here the DX register becomes zero since there is no remainder.

None of the status flags are defined following a division instruction. However, a significant error condition can occur during a division. If the quotient is

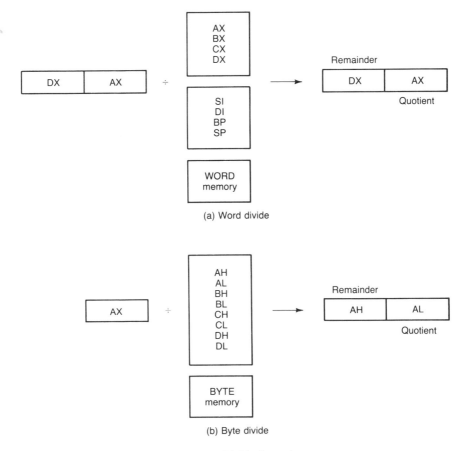

Figure 4.14 Divide Operations

greater than can fit in the result register, the processor can't give the correct result. For a byte division the quotient must be less than 256, and less than 65,536 for a word operation. The process does not set any status flags to signal this error. Instead, the processor executes a software interrupt, the level 0 interrupt. As with all software interrupts, this divide-by-zero interrupt saves the flags, code segment register, and instruction pointer on the stack. The processor transfers control to the location indicated by the pointer at location 0. The divide-by-zero routine should take the appropriate action to handle the error condition. (Interrupt 0 is called divide by zero even though a division by a number other than zero can trigger it. Intel documentation calls it divide by zero, but more appropriately it would be called the division overflow interrupt.)

The signed integer division (IDIV) differs from the DIV instruction only in that it takes into account the sign of the two operands. If the result is positive, the actions are as described for the DIV instruction, except that the maximum value of the quotient is 127 or 32,767, for byte or word operations, respectively. If the result is negative, the quotient is truncated, and the remainder has the same sign as the dividend. The minimum quotients for negative results are -128 and $-32,768$ for byte and word operations. Figure 4.15 shows four sample divisions, and the results obtained from them.

Dividend (AX)	Divisor (mod-r/m)	Quotient (AL)	Remainder (AH)
7	2	3	1
7	-2	-3	1
-7	2	-3	-1
-7	-2	3	-1

Figure 4.15 Signed Division Examples

The examples above are byte operand divisions, with the dividend in the AX register, and the divisor specified by the mod-r/m addressing byte. The division places the quotients in the AL register, with the remainder in the AH. Notice that the sign of the remainder is always the same as the dividend. The quotient value is always truncated toward zero.

ASCII Adjust: Division

Just like the other arithmetic operations, division has an instruction to manage ASCII unpacked decimal numbers. However, unlike the others, the program must execute the ASCII Adjust for Division (AAD) instruction prior to the division. The AAD instruction takes the two-digit unpacked decimal number in the AX register (most significant digit in AH) and converts it to a binary number in the AL register, leaving a zero in AH. This sets AX with an appropriate value for division by a single-digit unpacked decimal number. AAD sets the condition codes according to the result in the AL register. The parity, sign, and zero flags reflect the AL value, while the others are unknown.

Following the division, the quotient may not be a single-digit unpacked decimal number. That's because there is no divide overflow signaled in this case. The worst case is the division of 99 by 1, producing a quotient of 99. The number is less than the maximum for both DIV and IDIV, so there is no divide overflow. However, this number is greater than the maximum unpacked decimal number, which is 9. There are two methods of dealing with this. First, a test can follow every AAD–DIV sequence to detect a quotient greater than 9, and take the appropriate overflow handling. Or the program can use an AAM instruction following the division to convert the quotient into a two-digit unpacked decimal number. However, the program must save the remainder elsewhere before executing the AAM, since AAM destroys the AH register. This alternative generates a two-digit decimal result from the division of a two-digit value by a single-digit number. If the unpacked decimal number used as a divisor is zero, however, the division will invoke the divide-by-zero interrupt, indicating divide overflow.

Convert

When a program does signed integer division, there is a problem if the dividend is a byte operand. It is certainly valid to divide a byte value by a byte value, but the divide instruction requires the dividend in the AX register. For signed division, the AX value must be the correct two's-complement version of the number. The Convert Byte to Word (CBW) instruction handles this task by taking the number in AL and sign-extending it into the AH register. Thus, if the value in AL is positive, it fills AH with zeros. If AL is negative, it sets AH to all 1's. CBW sets AX as the 16-bit value with the same value as the original byte in AL. For word division, the Convert Word to Doubleword (CWD) instruction performs the identical function. CWD sign-extends the word in AX into the DX register. These two instructions extend operands prior to doing signed integer division.

For unsigned integer division in the same circumstances, there is no sign to extend in the high-order portion of the dividend. The correct action in those circumstances is to fill the AH (or DX) register with all zeros prior to the division. There are many instructions that can do that job, including the MOV immediate instructions, or a simple

        SUB   AH,AH

which guarantees that the AH register is zero.

ARITHMETIC EXAMPLE

To illustrate many of the functions that we have discussed in the preceding sections, let's do an arithmetic problem in assembly language. The example is simple, but uses many of the instructions. The problem is to calculate the quotient of two arithmetic expressions, where some of the values are constant, and others are variables. The values are all 16-bit signed integers.

The formula to calculate is

$$X = \frac{A \times 2 + B \times C}{D - 3}$$

The assembly language routine of Figure 4.16 solves this problem. The routine first does the two multiplications. Since the 8088 always places the result of a 16-bit multiply in the DX:AX register pair, the example moves the result of the first multiply into the BX:CX register pair before doing the second multiplication. When both multiplies are complete, the routine performs the numerator addition. Since the multiplies produced 32-bit results, the routine requires a multiple

```
The IBM Personal Computer Assembler 01-01-83       PAGE    1-1
Figure 4.16 Arithmetic Example

 1                                             PAGE    ,132
 2                                             TITLE   Figure 4.16 Arithmetic Example
 3                                      ;------------------------------------------------
 4                                      ;
 5                                      ; This example calculates the formula
 6                                      ;
 7                                      ;           A * 2  +  B * C
 8                                      ;   X  =    ---------------
 9                                      ;              D  -  3
10                                      ;
11                                      ; All variables are 16 bit signed integers.
12                                      ;------------------------------------------------
13
14      0000                            CODE    SEGMENT
15                                              ASSUME  CS:CODE,DS:CODE
16
17      0000  ????                      X       DW      ?              ; Storage for variables
18      0002  ????                      A       DW      ?
19      0004  ????                      B       DW      ?
20      0006  ????                      C       DW      ?
21      0008  ????                      D       DW      ?
22
23      000A                            FIG4_16 PROC    NEAR
24
25      000A  B8 0002                           MOV     AX,2           ; Set up the constant
26      000D  F7 2E 0002 R                       IMUL    A              ; DX:AX = A * 2
27      0011  8B DA                             MOV     BX,DX
28      0013  8B C8                             MOV     CX,AX          ; BX:CX = A * 2
29      0015  A1 0004 R                          MOV     AX,B
30      0018  F7 2E 0006 R                       IMUL    C              ; DX:AX = B * C
31      001C  03 C1                             ADD     AX,CX
32      001E  13 D3                             ADC     DX,BX          ; DX:AX = A * 2 + B * C
33      0020  8B 0E 0008 R                       MOV     CX,D
34      0024  83 E9 03                          SUB     CX,3           ; CX = D - 3
35      0027  F7 F9                             IDIV    CX             ; AX = (A*2 + B*C)/(D-3) Quotient
36      0029  A3 0000 R                          MOV     X,AX           ; Store the result
37      002C  C3                                RET
38
39      002D                            FIG4_16 ENDP
40      002D                            CODE    ENDS
41                                              END
```

Figure 4.16   Arithmetic Example

precision add. This addition leaves the result in DX:AX. The example calculates
the denominator in the CX register, and then divides it into the numerator. The
program stores the quotient from AX into the result variable X. This problem
ignores the remainder.

LOGICAL INSTRUCTIONS

The next class of instructions is the logical operators. These instructions
transform data, like the arithmetic operations, but they do so in a nonarithmetic
manner. While the add and subtract instructions are related to grade school
arithmetic, the logical instructions work with the one and zero values that a
computer uses. In general, these instructions allow a program to do bit-level
operations.

The four main logical functions are AND, OR, Exclusive OR (XOR), and
NOT. There are other logical functions that are composites of these four, but the
8088 does not have instructions for them. These four logical instructions operate
directly on the zero and one values of binary representation.

The NOT function is the simplest. This instruction is based on the true/false
definition of one and zero. NOT TRUE is FALSE and NOT FALSE is TRUE.

The NOT function complements all the bits in the data value. Another way of looking at it is that NOT is equivalent to subtracting the data from a value of all ones. Figure 4.17 shows the function of the NOT operator on a single bit.

Value	NOT (Value)
0	1
1	0

Figure 4.17   NOT Operation

The remaining three logical functions are all functions of two operands. Figure 4.18 shows the results of the three functions on a pair of bits.

X	Y	X AND Y	X OR Y	X XOR Y
0	0	0	0	0
0	1	0	1	1
1	0	0	1	1
1	1	1	1	0

Figure 4.18   Logical Operations

The figure shows the result of each of the operators on a single pair of bits. Since the 8088 operates on byte or word operands, the 8088 replicates the results of the table at each bit position in the operand. For example, a byte AND operation ANDs the values in bit 0 of both operands to produce the result, placed in bit 0 of the destination. The instruction repeats the AND function for bits 1 through 7. The result is the bit-by-bit AND function of the individual bit positions in the operands.

The AND function is "1" only if both operands are "1." In true/false terminology, the result is true only if both X and Y are true. The OR function gives a "1" result if either of the operands is a "1." The result is true if either X or Y is true. The OR operation is sometimes called the Inclusive OR, to distinguish it from the remaining operator, Exclusive OR. The result of X XOR Y is equal to "1" only if one operand is "1" and the other is "0." If both are "0," or both are "1," the result is "0." The Exclusive OR function corresponds closely to addition with the carry ignored.

Figure 4.19 shows the 8088 logical instructions. The NOT instruction, with a single operand, has a form almost identical to that of the Negate (NEG) instruction. The remaining logical instructions mimic the syntax of addition and subtraction.

When the 8088 does a logical operation, it sets the flags according to the result. Since the operation is not arithmetic, it always sets the carry and overflow flags set to "0." Logical operations leave the auxiliary carry flag undefined, while the other flags (sign, zero, and parity) correctly reflect the result of the operation. The exception is the NOT operator, which does not affect any of the flags.

```
 1                                          PAGE    ,132
 2                                          TITLE   Figure 4.19 Logical Instructions
 3     0000                           CODE   SEGMENT
 4                                          ASSUME  CS:CODE,DS:CODE
 5     0000                    EXBYTE  LABEL   BYTE
 6     0000                    EXWORD  LABEL   WORD
 7
 8     0000  22 06 0000 R             AND     AL,EXBYTE                ; AL <- AL AND [EXBYTE]
 9     0004  81 E3 9FEF               AND     BX,1001111111101111B     ; BX <- BX AND 9FEFH
10     0008  80 26 0000 R 03          AND     EXBYTE,00000011B         ; [EXBYTE] <- [EXBYTE] AND 3
11
12     000D  08 2E 0000 R             OR      EXBYTE,CH                ; [EXBYTE] <- [EXBYTE] OR CH
13     0011  0B 16 0000 R             OR      DX,EXWORD                ; DX <- DX OR [EXWORD]
14     0015  0D FFF9                  OR      AX,0FFF9H                ; AX <- AX OR 0FFF9H
15
16     0018  33 1E 0000 R             XOR     BX,EXWORD                ; BX <- BX XOR [EXWORD[
17     001C  30 1E 0000 R             XOR     EXBYTE,BL                ; [EXBYTE] <- [EXBYTE] XOR BL
18     0020  34 EF                    XOR     AL,0EFH                  ; AL <- AL XOR 0EFH
19
20     0022  F7 D1                    NOT     CX                       ; CX <- NOT CX
21     0024  F6 16 0000 R             NOT     EXBYTE                   ; [EXBYTE] <- NOT [EXBYTE]
22
23     0028  F7 06 0000 R 0003        TEST    EXWORD,0003H             ; Set flags for [EXWORD] AND 3
24     002E  84 E0                    TEST    AH,AL                    ; Set flags for AH AND AL
25     0030  A9 0002                  TEST    AX,02H                   ; Set flags for AX AND 2
26
27     0033  D1 C1                    ROL     CX,1                     ; Left rotate one position
28     0035  D3 0E 0000 R             ROR     EXWORD,CL                ; Right rotate variable amount
29
30     0039  D0 16 0000 R             RCL     EXBYTE,1                 ; Left rotate one position
31     003D  D3 DB                    RCR     BX,CL                    ; Right rotate variable amount
32
33     003F  D1 E0                    SHL     AX,1                     ; Left shift one position
34     0041  D1 E0                    SAL     AX,1                     ; Identical instruction
35
36     0043  D3 EB                    SHR     BX,CL                    ; Right shift variable amount
37     0045  D0 3E 0000 R             SAR     EXBYTE,1                 ; Right arithmetic shift
38
39     0049                    CODE   ENDS
40                                    END
```

Figure 4.19   Logical Instructions

The primary use of the logical operators is bit manipulation in the 8088. The smallest unit of data that the 8088 can work on is a byte. None of the arithmetic operations can isolate or change a single bit directly. The logical instructions allow a program to handle individual bits.

Why are single-bit operations of interest? Many times a program must store information that is a true/false indicator. The bit might indicate that the printer is busy, the shift key is depressed, or program initialization has been performed. In such instances it is a waste of computer storage to allocate an 8-bit byte to store that single piece of information. The program can combine a number of these bits in a single byte if the program has a method of isolating the individual bits for testing and setting. This combination of single-bit flags is very prevalent in I/O devices, which have hardware devices that respond to different addresses. It is much simpler for an I/O device to have multiple bits at a single address than to detect multiple addresses.

The logical instructions can isolate single bits in a byte or word so that they can be set, reset, or tested. The instructions use a mask value to isolate the bits. The instruction applies the mask value bit by bit to the data value. To set a single bit, use the OR instruction. The mask value is all zeros, with a one at the bit location to set. The OR of the mask value and the operand sets a "1" at the selected bit, and leaves all other bits of the result unchanged. Similarly, the AND operator can reset a single bit. Set the mask value with all ones except the bit location to reset. That location always goes to "0," while the others remain unchanged.

Programmers do not use the Exclusive OR function as frequently as AND and OR, but it does have a use. The XOR instruction can complement a single bit with a data area. Set the XOR mask so that the bit to complement is a "1" and all others are "0." When the XOR is done, the bits matched with zeros remain unchanged. The bits matched with ones are complemented. If the original value is a "0," "1" XOR "0" gives "1," the complement of "0." If the original value is a "1," "1" XOR "1" gives "0," the complement of "1." The three logical operators allow a program to set, reset, or complement single bits in a data area.

The final instruction in the logical operators is the TEST instruction. This operation is identical to AND, except that it doesn't change the destination. It sets the flag values according to the result. Thus, TEST is to AND as CMP is to SUB. The instruction tests a particular bit, or set of bits, within a byte or word.

How does the test instruction work? Suppose that a program wishes to test the least significant bit of a byte, bit 0. The program creates a mask value of 01H, either in a register, or as an immediate value. The TEST (or AND) instruction produces a result that is guaranteed to be "0" in all locations except bit 0. The value of bit 0 reflects the value of the original. If the original bit is "0," bit 0 remains zero. If it is a one, it remains a one. More important, the result of the operation, as set in the status flags, indicates the state of that bit. If the bit is a one, the result is nonzero, and the zero flag is cleared. If the bit is a "0," the result is zero, and the zero flag is set. Thus, a program can test a single bit by TESTing or ANDing it with a mask value that has a one only in the bit location to examine. The flag register reflects the state of that single bit. The TEST instruction examines that single bit without destroying the information in the other bits, since the instruction does not modify the destination.

SHIFT AND ROTATE INSTRUCTIONS

The remaining logical instructions in Figure 4.19 perform the shifting of data. A shift operation moves all of the bits in a data area, either to the right or the left. An example is a church pew, with both men and women seated in it. As a new person arrives at church and slides in at the end of the pew, all of the other people in the pew slide over one position. If the pew is full, the person at the end falls out as everyone slides over. A shift instruction does exactly the same type of thing, where you can think of men and women as the ones and zeros.

The picture of Figure 4.20 shows the eight different shift and rotate instructions available. Within these instructions there are also variations. First, we will examine those things that the instructions have in common.

Like the other logical instructions, the shift and rotates operate on either byte or word data. Every instruction specifies a single operand. This operand may be

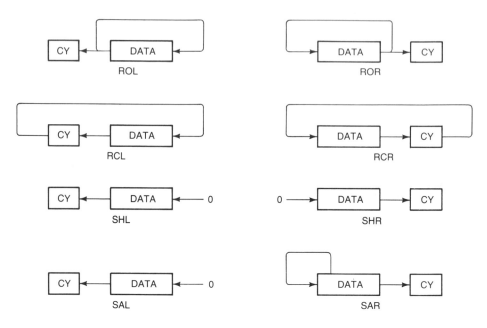

Figure 4.20   Shift Operations

either a register or a memory location. All of these instructions use the mod-r/m byte to specify the single operand.

All of the shift/rotate instructions specify a shift count. That is, the program specifies the number of bits to be shifted in the instruction. This value is the shift count. The most common value is one. This count moves the bits in the operand one location. However, an instruction may specify an arbitrary shift count by storing that value in the CL register prior to the shift. If the instruction indicates that the shift count is to come from the CL register, the value of that register determines the number of times the bits are shifted. The number in CL may be anything from 0 through 255, but in practice, values of 0 through 16 are reasonable. A value of 0 causes no shifting, while any value greater than 16 moves more bits than the operand contains.

One other thing in common with all of the shift instructions is the setting of the carry flag. The bit that falls off the end has a special place. The shift/rotate instructions place the last value shifted out of the operand into the carry flag. If the shift was for a single bit, the bit at the far end becomes the new carry value. For a multiple-bit shift, the bit shifted into the carry comes from within the operand. The carry flag is significant when used for multiple-precision operations. Since a shift operand may be at most 16 bits, a program can manage a larger data value with multiple shifts and the carry flag. The program breaks up the operand into 16-bit chunks, and shifts each part a single bit at a time. The program uses the carry flag to communicate the shifted out information to the next portion of the shift.

The top four instructions in Figure 4.20 are rotate instructions. The figure contains schematic representations of the operation for each instruction. The rotates, as the pictures show, take the bit that comes out one end and stick it back in the front end. The Rotate Left (ROL) and Rotate Right (ROR) instructions differ only in the direction of data movement. Similarly, Rotate Left with Carry (RCL) and Rotate Right with Carry (RCR) are mirror images of each other. ROL and RCL differ in the treatment of the carry flag. A byte ROL operation rotates 8 bits of data according to the shift count. The byte RCL instruction treats the data as 9 bits wide, with the carry flag acting as the ninth bit. A word ROL rotates 16 bits, a word RCL rotates 17 bits.

The shift instructions, at the bottom of Figure 4.20, do not bring the shifted out bits back around into the operand. They go to the carry flag and nowhere else. The shift type determines the value shifted into the operand. For a logical shift, the value shifted into the operand is always a "0." An arithmetic shift chooses the input bit to preserve the sign of the operand.

Why is a shift called arithmetic, when it's included in the section on logical operations? Shifting a number by one bit position is equivalent to multiplying or dividing that number by 2. In the decimal, or base 10, number system, adding a zero to the end of a number multiplies it by 10. In binary arithmetic, adding a 0 to the end multiplies it by 2. Since the computer can't add another bit to the end of an operand, a shift operation does the same thing. A left-shift operation moves all the bits to the left one position, and puts a zero into the low-order bit position. Thus, a left shift multiplies the number by 2. If the shift value is greater than one, the number is multiplied by 2 raised to the shift count power. For example, a left shift of 3 bits is equivalent to multiplying by 8.

Shifting a number to the right is the same as dividing by 2. The shifted operand is the quotient, and the carry flag is the remainder. If the shift count is greater than one, the operand is still the quotient, but the remainder is discarded. Thus, shift operations make very effective ways of multiplying and dividing by powers of 2. In fact, the shift/multiply capability makes it a good choice at times as a substitute for multiply, even when the multiplicand is not a power of 2.

The problem with arithmetic shifts occurs when a negative number is right-shifted to divide by 2. If the instruction shifts a "0" into the highest bit position, the result becomes positive, with an absolute value one-half that of original number. The Shift Arithmetic Right (SAR) instruction solves this problem by retaining the high-order bit position while shifting all of the other bits. Thus, a negative number stays negative, while a positive number stays positive. The problem doesn't occur for a left shift, since the sign bit is at the left end of the operand. Because of this, the Shift Logical Left (SLL) and Shift Arithmetic Left (SAL) instructions are identical.

Because of the arithmetic nature of the shift/rotate instructions, they all affect the overflow flag as well as the carry flag. The overflow flag is undefined for shift counts greater than one. But for shift values of one, a shift/rotate instruction sets the overflow flag if the sign of the number changes as a result. If the high-order bit has not changed, the overflow bit is cleared to "0." Thus, the overflow flag indicates whether the multiply or divide implicit in the shift/rotate operation has produced a valid two's-complement result.

Two examples of shift/rotate instructions are given in Figure 4.21. The first example shows a value multiplied through the use of shift-left instructions. This example does a multiply by 9, which isn't a power of 2. The example shifts the data left by three positions to multiply it by 8. The routine then adds that value to the original data to give a result equal to the original number times 9.

The disadvantages of this method are obvious. It requires many more instructions than a simple multiply—which would go something like this:

```
PUSH      DX
MOV       DX,9
IMUL      DX
POP       DX
```

Also, the shift multiply by 9 produces a 16-bit result rather than the 32-bit result of the IMUL instruction.

However, a program may desire the shift multiply in some instances. Its primary advantage is its speed of execution. The IMUL instruction takes a great deal of time, whereas shift instructions execute rather rapidly. For the example of Figure 4.21, the shifting method executes about 25% faster. Not a tremendous gain, but it could be crucial if an application depended on multiplying integers by

```
The IBM Personal Computer Assembler 01-01-83          PAGE    1-1
Figure 4.21 Shift Examples

 1                                        PAGE    ,132
 2                                        TITLE   Figure 4.21 Shift Examples
 3            0000                  CODE   SEGMENT
 4                                        ASSUME  CS:CODE,DS:CODE
 5
 6                                 ;--------------------------------------------
 7                                 ; This routine takes the number in AX
 8                                 ; multiplies it by 9, without using the
 9                                 ; multiply instruction.
10                                 ;--------------------------------------------
11
12            0000                  MUL9   PROC    NEAR
13
14            0000  51                     PUSH    CX         ; Save the CX register on the stack
15            0001  50                     PUSH    AX         ; Temporary save of AX
16            0002  B1 03                  MOV     CL,3       ; Will shift by 3 positions
17            0004  D3 F8                  SAR     AX,CL      ; Multiply AX by 8
18            0006  8B C8                  MOV     CX,AX      ; AX*8 in CX
19            0008  58                     POP     AX         ; Original AX value
20            0009  03 C1                  ADD     AX,CX      ; AX now has 9 times original value
21            000B  59                     POP     CX         ; Recover the original CX value
22            000C  C3                     RET
23            000D                  MUL9   ENDP
24
25                                 ;--------------------------------------------
26                                 ; This program fragment isolates the bit
27                                 ; in the AX register specified by the number
28                                 ; in CL.
29                                 ;--------------------------------------------
30
31            000D  53                     PUSH    BX         ; Save BX on stack
32            000E  BB 0001                MOV     BX,1       ; Put a one in Bit 0 position
33            0011  D3 C3                  ROL     BX,CL      ; Move the mask bit
34            0013  23 C3                  AND     AX,BX      ; AND isolates the selected bit
35            0015  5B                     POP     BX         ; Recover BX value
36
37            0016                  CODE   ENDS
38                                        END
```

Figure 4.21   Shift Examples

9. Multiplying by a power of 2 would produce even greater gains in execution speed.

The second example of Figure 4.21 shows the variable shift count used to determine a bit selection. This code fragment assumes that the information in the AX register is bit significant, and the CL register indicates the bit to select from AX. If CL equals 8, bit 8 is selected in AX. The routine shifts the mask value in the BX register into position, based on the bit value in the CL register. The AND instruction isolates the selected bit.

For this example to work successfully, however, the number in CL must be in the range 0 through 15. The example could use an AND instruction to isolate the low 4 bits of the shift value in the CL register. AND CL,OFH guarantees the number in CL to be between 0 and 15. You could further modify this example to select more than one bit from the word. You could select a nybble from the 16-bit word by changing the original mask value in the BX register.

STRING INSTRUCTIONS

One of the areas that received special attention in the 8088 instruction set is string handling. A common data type is a string of characters or numbers that a program manipulates as a group. The program moves the string from one place to another, compares it to other strings, and searches it for specific values. Character strings are a common type of string data. The program represents each word, sentence, or other structure by a string of characters in storage. Text editing functions, as an example, make heavy use of search and move functions. The string instructions of the 8088 accomplish these operations with a minimum of programming effort, and a minimum of execution time.

First, let's discuss the concepts of string manipulation. A program can do string operations on either byte or word data. Individual elements of the strings may be either 8 or 16 bits. Also, the string instructions do not use the addressing modes that the rest of the data-handling instructions do. In fact, the string instructions are very precise in their addressing, with no variation allowed. String instructions address the operands with either the DS:SI or ES:DI register combination. Source operands use DS:SI, destination operands use ES:DI— hence the names source index and destination index registers. All of the string instructions have a built-in update of the address following an operation. Many chunks of data compose a string, but the string instructions can operate on only one element at a time. This makes it is necessary for the program to work through the string, one element at a time. The automatic increment or decrement allows rapid processing of string data. The Direction Flag in the status register controls the direction of string manipulation. When the direction flag is set to "1," the addresses decrement, while they increment if the flag is cleared to "0." The size of the operand determines the amount of the increment/decrement. Byte string instructions change the address by one after each string operation, while word string instructions change the address by two. This leaves the pointer aimed at the next element in the string following the operation.

Load and Store

The assembly listing in Figure 4.22 shows the different string instructions. The Load String (LODS) and Store String (STOS) are the simplest of the string instructions. If the program specifies a byte operand for the LODS instruction, LODS loads the AL register loaded from the byte pointed to by the DS:SI register pair. It then changes the SI register by one. It increments or decrements depending on the setting of the direction flag. If LODS specifies a word operand, it loads the AX register and changes SI by two. The STOS instruction is just the opposite, with the byte in AL or the word in AX stored into the memory location. For stores, the ES:DI register pair specifies the location. The store instruction modifies the DI register, by either one or two, depending on the type of operand.

The programmer may specify the LODS instruction, and indeed, all of the string instructions, in several ways to the assembler. The programmer may specify the type of operand as part of the operation code, or the assembler can determine the type of string element based on the operand presented in the instruction. As Figure 4.22 shows, the instruction

    LODS   EXBYTE

generates the load string instruction for byte strings, as does the instruction

    LODSB

```
The IBM Personal Computer Assembler 01-01-83      PAGE    1-1
Figure 4.22  String Instructions

1                                        PAGE    ,132
2                                        TITLE   Figure 4.22  String Instructions
3        0000                            CODE    SEGMENT
4                                        ASSUME  CS:CODE,DS:CODE,ES:CODE
5        0000            EXBYTE   LABEL   BYTE
6        0000            EXWORD   LABEL   WORD
7        0000            EXBYTE1  LABEL   BYTE
8        0000            EXWORD1  LABEL   WORD
9
10       0000  AC                 LODS    EXBYTE          ; Load AL from DS:SI
11       0001  AD                 LODS    EXWORD          ; Load AX from DS:SI
12       0002  AC                 LODSB                   ; Load AL from DS:SI
13       0003  AA                 STOS    EXBYTE          ; Store to ES:DI from AL
14       0004  AB                 STOS    EXWORD          ; Store to ES:DI from AX
15       0005  AB                 STOSW                   ; Same as above
16       0006  F3/ AA             REP     STOSB           ; Store AL at ES:DI for CX times
17
18       0008  A4                 MOVS    EXBYTE1,EXBYTE  ; Move byte [ES:DI] <- [DS:SI]
19       0009  A5                 MOVS    EXWORD1,EXWORD  ; Move word [ES:DI] <- [DS:SI]
20       000A  A4                 MOVSB                   ; Move byte [ES:DI] <- [DS:SI]
21
22       000B  F3/ A5             REP     MOVSW           ; Move words CX times
23
24       000D  AE                 SCAS    EXBYTE1         ; Test AL w th [ES:DI]
25       000E  F3/ AE             REPE    SCASB           ; Test AL with [ES:DI] while =
26       0010  F2/ AF             REPNE   SCASW           ; Test AX with [ES:DI] while <>
27
28       0012  A7                 CMPS    EXWORD,EXWORD1  ; Compare word [DS:SI] to [ES:DI]
29       0013  F3/ A7             REPE    CMPSW           ; Compare words while equal and CX <> 0
30       0015  F2/ A6             REPNE   CMPSB           ; Compare bytes while not equal, CX <> 0
31
32       0017            CODE     ENDS
33                                END
```

Figure 4.22   String Instructions

In the first case, the assembler determines that the referenced string is composed of bytes, since EXBYTE is a BYTE variable. In the second case, the programmer directly specifies that this would be a byte. The assembler requires no operand field. Programmers use the second form in many cases because there is no variable name associated with the string. The program locates the string dynamically in storage, and there is no fixed location, and, consequently, no variable name for it. The STOS instruction is similar. To specifiy a word string, rather than a byte string, the opcode is LODSW or STOSW to specify the word string directly. The assembler must know whether the instruction is for a byte or word string, since the machine language instruction is different for different types. This machine language difference determines the value to change the index register.

The instruction must specify an operand when using the generic LODS or STOS instruction. If the program has no covenient label for the string, it can use the LODSB or STOSB form. The advantage of using the generic LODS form, and naming an operand is that the assembler checks not only the type of the operand, but also its addressability. Since the LODS instruction accesses only items in the DS segment, the ASSUME statement must match the segment location of the named variable. Similarly, the assembler checks the STOS generic form for addressing in the ES segment. Either form is acceptable to the assembler, but you should use the generic form to allow the assembler to do the best possible job of checking the program for errors before execution.

REP Prefix

There is another special usage for the string instructions. There is an instruction prefix specifically for the string instructions. This prefix, like the segment override prefixes used to generate special segment addressing, precedes the normal instruction and modifies its actions. However, this instruction prefix turns a string instruction into a loop. The prefix is REP, which stands for Repeat. The 8088 uses this prefix in conjunction with the CX register, which specifies the number of times to repeat the instruction.

The STOSB instruction is an example. The instruction

```
REP     STOSB
```

is a special form of the store byte instruction. The STOSB instruction repeats until the CX register is decremented to zero. The STOSB writes the byte in AL into storage at the location pointed to by ES:DI, and increments/decrements DI by one—just as the normal STOSB instruction. The REP prefix decrements CX, and if it is not zero, repeats the entire instruction. The store string continues until CX reaches zero.

This capability turns the STOS instruction into a fill instruction. The program places the fill value in AL, the byte count in CX, the address of the block in ES:DI, and clears the direction flag. The REP STOSB instruction then fills the block with the value from the AL register. Figure 4.23 shows this code fragment.

```
 1                                              PAGE      ,132
 ::                                             TITLE     Figure 4.23  Block Fill
 3        0000                        CODE      SEGMENT
 4                                              ASSUME    CS:CODE,DS:CODE,ES:CODE
 5
 ::                                     ;----------------------------------------
 7                                     ; This example fills the data area
 8                                     ; BYTE_BLOCK with the value 01H
 9                                     ;----------------------------------------
10
11        0000  BF 000B R                       MOV       DI,OFFSET BYTE_BLOCK   ; Address of data area
12        0003  B9 0032 90                      MOV       CX,BYTE_BLOCK_LENGTH   ; Number of bytes to fill
13        0007  B0 01                           MOV       AL,01H                 ; Fill character
14        0009  F3/ AA                REP       STOS      BYTE_BLOCK             ; Fill the block
15
16        000B     32 [             BYTE_BLOCK  DB        50 DUP(?)
17                     ??
18                 ]
19
20      = 0032                       BYTE_BLOCK_LENGTH     EQU       $-BYTE_BLOCK
21
22        003D                        CODE      ENDS
::3                                             END
```

Figure 4.23   Block Fill

The REP prefix doesn't make sense with the LODS instruction. Loading a continuous string of data into the accumulator gives the program no chance to deal with the data as they are loaded. The REP instruction will prove valuable with the other string instructions.

Move String

It might be tempting to use the LODS and STOS instructions to move data from one location to another, but there is another string instruction to do just that, Move String (MOVS). This instruction is like a combination of the LODS and STOS instructions. It takes data from [DS:SI], places it at [ES:DI], and changes both SI and DI to point to the next location in each string. MOVS does it all in a single instruction, and does not load the data into the accumulator during the move. MOVS does the combination of LODS and STOS faster, and with fewer side effects.

The MOVS instruction specifies two memory operands. Together with another string instruction (CMPS), it is the only 8088 instruction that can deal with two memory operands. All other instructions require one of the two operands to be in a processor register. As with the LODS and STOS instructions, the MOVS string operation works with either byte or word strings. Since the string instructions strictly determine addressing, the operands specified by the programmer are used only to determine the type of string. The instruction must specify both operands, and they both must be the same types. Or the programmer may specify the type of move as part of the operation code, as MOVSB for byte strings or MOVSW for word strings. If the program uses the generic form, MOVS, the assembler checks the variables for the correct segment addressability as well as determining their type.

Combining the MOVS instruction with the REP prefix makes a very powerful block move instruction. With the count in CX, and the direction flag indicating the direction of movement, the REP MOVS instruction moves data from one region to another very rapidly. Once the processor starts the REP MOVS instruction, it moves the data at the fastest possible rate. It doesn't have to fetch any other instructions during the move, so the only thing going on is data movement.

The setting of the direction flag is crucial to the correct operation of the REP MOVS instruction. We discussed the various settings for the direction flag in Chapter 3, specifically for the string move operation. A program must adhere to the guidelines in that discussion, especially when the source and destination areas overlap.

Scan and Compare

Programs can use the two remaining string instructions to compare string information. The first is Scan String, SCAS. This instruction compares the value in AL or AX with the memory operand pointed to by ES:DI. SCAS sets the zero, carry, and overflow flags to indicate the result of comparing the accumulator and the memory location. Of course, SCAS modifies the DI register to move on to the next operand in the string.

The SCAS instruction cannot use the normal REP prefix to scan a long string of information. Just as REP LODS makes no sense, a REP SCAS instruction does not allow the program to test each comparison. Instead, there are two variations of the REP prefix, Repeat while Equal (REPE) and Repeat while Not Equal (REPNE). As with the normal REP prefix, the program loads the CX register with the length of the string. If REPE is specified, the instruction executes until AL (or AX) does not match the memory location, or until CX equals zero, whichever comes first. As long as the accumulator matches the memory location, SCAS continues. The REPNE instruction is just the opposite. The scan continues until the accumulator matches the value in the register.

The combination of SCAS and REPNE allows a program to do a rapid table search. To look up an entry in the table, the program must search every location in the table for a match against the argument. Figure 4.24 shows how the SCAS instruction performs this function. The AL register holds the match argument. The table SCAN_TABLE contains the values to search for a match, and the CX register has the length of the table. The REPNE SCASB instruction scans the table until the accumulator is matched. At this point the DI register points to the byte in the table just following the one that matched. You can determine the offset of the matching value by subtracting one from DI at the label FOUND. The program can use this offset information to access another table, or tables, that indicate the response to these input data. An important thing to note is the JE instruction following the scan instruction. There are two ways in which control can pass to that instruction: the byte in the string matches the AL register, and the REPNE condition no longer holds; or the count in the CX register reached zero without a match in the table. Some programming situations ensure that the second condition never occurs. However, most programs must make allowances for

```
The IBM Personal Computer Assembler 01-01-83        PAGE    1-1
Figure 4.24  Table Scan

 1                                                PAGE    ,132
 2                                                TITLE   Figure 4.24  Table Scan
 3      0000                              CODE    SEGMENT
 4                                                ASSUME  CS:CODE,DS:CODE,ES:CODE
 5
 6                                        ;-------------------------------------
 7                                        ; This example scans a table of values until
 8                                        ; the value in the AL register matches the table
 9                                        ; entry.
10                                        ;-------------------------------------
11
12      0000  BF 000B R                   MOV    DI,OFFSET SCAN_TABLE     ; Address of table
13      0003  B9 000A 90                  MOV    CX,SCAN_TABLE_LENGTH     ; Length of scan table
14      0007  F2/ AE              REPNE   SCASB                          ; Scan until match found
15      0009  74 00                       JE     FOUND                   ; If equal, then match
16                                        ; ...                         ; Otherwise no match found
17      000B                      FOUND:
18                                        ;----- Program continues here . . .
19
20
21      000B  51 57 45 52 54 59  SCAN_TABLE        DB      'QWERTYUIOP'
22            55 49 4F 50
23    = 000A                      SCAN_TABLE_LENGTH EQU     $-SCAN_TABLE
24
25      0015                      CODE    ENDS
26                                        END
```

Figure 4.24   Table Scan

incorrect input data. After the scan instruction, the program will jump to the label FOUND if the scan instruction set the zero (or equal) flag. This is the guarantee that a match was found. If the CX register has reached zero, the last scan iteration would have cleared the zero flag, indicating that no match was found.

The final string instruction is Compare Strings (CMPS). Like the Scan String, it is a comparison operation. Like the MOVS instruction, it works with two memory operands. CMPS compares the string at DS:SI to the string at ES:DI, and sets the flags accordingly. Like SCAS, you can't use the REP prefix with it, but you can use REPE and REPNE with great facility.

Figure 4.25 shows an example using the CMPS instruction. This example compares a five-character input string against a table of character strings. The program attempts to match the input string with an entry in the table. The output,

```
The IBM Personal Computer Assembler 01-01-83        PAGE    1-1
Figure 4.25  String Compare

 1                                                PAGE    ,132
 2                                                TITLE   Figure 4.25  String Compare
 3      0000                              CODE    SEGMENT
 4                                                ASSUME  CS:CODE,DS:CODE,ES:CODE
 5
 6                                        ;-------------------------------------
 7                                        ; This example compares a five character
 8                                        ; string against a table of five character strings.
 9                                        ; The routine exits when it finds a match.
10                                        ;-------------------------------------
11
12      0000                      FIG4_25 PROC    NEAR
13      0000  BE 001B R                   MOV    SI,OFFSET ARGUMENT       ; Address of search parameter
14      0003  BF 0020 R                   MOV    DI,OFFSET COMPARE_TABLE  ; Table to be searched
15      0006  BB 0000                     MOV    BX,0                     ; BX will count table entries
16      0009                      COMPARE_LOOP:
17      0009  56                          PUSH   SI                       ; Save arg pointer
18      000A  57                          PUSH   DI                       ; Save table pointer
19      000B  B9 0005                     MOV    CX,5                     ; Compare 5 bytes
20      000E  F3/ A6              REPE    CMPS   ARGUMENT,COMPARE_TABLE   ; Compare the values
21      0010  5F                          POP    DI                       ; Recover pointers
```

Figure 4.25   String Compare

```
22    0011  5E                          POP    SI
23    0012  74 06                       JE     FOUND            ; Match has occurred
24    0014  83 C7 05                    ADD    DI,5             ; Move to next table entry
25    0017  43                          INC    BX               ; Adjust index to next
26    0018  EB EF                       JMP    COMPARE_LOOP     ; Go back and try again
27
28    001A                 FOUND:
29    001A  C3                          RET
30    001B                 FIG4_25 ENDP
31
32    001B  41 42 43 44 45  ARGUMENT       DB      'ABCDE'
33    0020                  COMPARE_TABLE  LABEL   BYTE
34    0020  51 57 45 52 54 50             DB      'QWERT','POIUY','ASDFG','LKJHG'
35          4F 49 55 59 41 53
36          44 46 47 4C 4B 4A
37          48 47
38    0034  5A 58 43 56 42 4D             DB      'ZXCVB','MNBVC','VWXYZ','ABCDE'
39          4E 42 56 43 56 57
40          58 59 5A 41 42 43
41          44 45
42
43    0048                 CODE    ENDS
44                                 END
```

Figure 4.25 *Continued*

in the BX register, is the index number of the string when it is found. The program uses the REPE prefix, so that the Compare String instruction executes until one of the characters in the argument does not match one of the characters in the table. If all five characters match, the routine has found the correct entry. The JE instruction (which means Jump if Equal) tests the result of the CMPS instruction. If the compare ended because of a character mismatch, the zero flag indicates a not-equal condition. If, however, the CMPS instruction ended because the CX count was zero, the zero flag would indicate the match and the program would jump to FOUND. You should note that this example lacks some of the necessities that would make it into a good program. For example, it doesn't handle the case when the input string doesn't match any of the entries. Any good programmer will tell you that you always have to handle the exception conditions.

TRANSFER OF CONTROL INSTRUCTIONS

The transfer of control instructions are used to send the program executing in a different section of instructions. Included in this set are both call and jump instructions. A call instruction invokes a subroutine, while a jump instruction transfers control to the named location without saving a return address. The conditional jump instructions allow the computer to think. Conditional instructions can test the outcome of a previous operation, and modify the flow of the program based on that result. If conditional jump instructions did not exist, computer programming would be much simpler, but also much less productive.

The first thing to discuss with the transfer of control instructions are the addressing methods used to identify the target location. Although the destination of a jump instruction is a memory location, just like a data reference, programs use jump instructions in a different way from data references. Because of this, there are better ways to address the jump target.

Near and Far

A jump instruction modifies the Instruction Pointer (IP) register and possibly the Code Segment (CS) register. These registers indicate the next instruction to be executed. In this context, a jump instruction is a special form of MOVing data into a register or pair of registers. Indeed, some computers handle the jump instructions in exactly that manner. However, the methods used to load the CS:IP registers in the 8088 are much different from the methods used for the other registers.

We must review some definitions before proceeding. If a jump instruction modifies only the IP register, it is an intrasegment jump, since the jump takes place within the segment. It is also be called a NEAR jump. If the jump modifies the CS register, it is an intersegment, or FAR, jump.

The attributes NEAR and FAR are part of the assembler operation. Any program label in the assembly has the attribute of either NEAR or FAR, just as data values have attributes such as BYTE or WORD. Several of the examples in this chapter have procedures which have used NEAR as an attribute on the PROC statement. This means that the label associated with that PROC (the name of the procedure) has the attribute NEAR. The assembler uses this information to determine what kind of jump or call instruction to generate when going to that location. Since most procedures are subroutines, the NEAR or FAR attribute of the PROC also determines the type of return instruction generated for the subroutine. A CALL to a FAR procedure saves both the CS and IP values, while a CALL to a NEAR subroutine leaves only the IP value on the stack. The return instruction must specify which way control came to the routine, so that the subroutine can return to the correct location.

Jump Addressing

If the instruction contains the target address of the jump or call as part of the instruction (as do the data in an Immediate instruction), it is a direct jump. If the instruction has the address in a register or storage location, it is an indirect jump, since the instruction requires fetching the address fetched from some intermediate location. The program cannot branch directly to the desired location, but must go there indirectly.

There are two methods of calculating the target address of the jump. If the instruction specifies an address value, it is an absolute jump. That is, it is a jump to an absolute address. The instruction may specify the target location as being a certain distance from the current location. This method, similar to the offset used with indexed addressing, is a relative jump.

An advantage to relative jumps is that a program most often jumps to a location nearby. A jump instruction can use a one-byte displacement value. If the displacement is treated as a two's-complement number, the two-byte relative jump instruction (one byte for the opcode and one byte for the displacement) can jump 127 bytes forward or 128 bytes backward within the program. The 8088 processor has two kinds of relative jumps: one has a one-byte displacement, the other has a two-byte displacement.

In the 8088 processer, all of the conditional jumps use a one-byte displacement. Sometimes this is inconvenient, as when a conditional jump is to a location 150 bytes away. In those cases, the program must use a pair of jumps, a conditional jump and an unconditional jump. We'll show an example of this method later. Normally, the one-byte displacements for conditional jumps in the 8088 minimizes the amount of code required to implement any particular function.

When calculating the displacement for a relative jump, the 8088 bases the displacement on the value of the Instruction Pointer following the execution of the instruction. Figure 4.26 shows several examples of relative jump instructions. If the location immediately following the jump is the target, the displacement is zero. To jump to itself, the displacement is -2. With a two-byte displacement, the jump can be anywhere within the range $-32,768$ to $32,767$ bytes away from the IP at the end of the jump instruction.

Unconditional Transfers

An unconditional instruction is one that transfers control every time it executes. In contrast, a conditional instruction tests the current state of the machine to determine whether or not to transfer control. There are two types of unconditional transfer of control instructions—jumps and calls.

All CALL instructions are unconditional. Figure 4.27 shows the different CALL instructions. The intrasegment, or NEAR, call specifies a new value for the IP and saves the old IP value on the stack as the return address. The intersegment, or FAR, call establishes a new segment and offset for program execution and saves both CS and IP on the stack. The near direct CALL is a

```
The IBM Personal Computer Assembler 01-01-83        PAGE    1-1
Figure 4.26  Relative Jumps

 1                                          PAGE    ,132
 2                                          TITLE   Figure 4.26  Relative Jumps
 3
 4      0000                        CODE    SEGMENT
 5                                          ASSUME  CS:CODE
 6
 7                                  ;----- This example shows the code offsets for relative jumps
 8
 9      0000                        START:
10      0000   EB FE                        JMP     START            ; Jump to itself
11      0002   EB 00                        JMP     SHORT LABEL_ONE  ; Jump to next location
12      0004                        LABEL_ONE:
13      0004   EB 01 90                     JMP     LABEL_TWO        ; Forward jump w/o SHORT
14      0007                        LABEL_TWO:
15      0007   E9 0200 R                    JMP     LABEL_THREE      ; Long jump to far away
16
17                                  ;. . . Use ORG to simulate far away
18
19      0200                                ORG     200H
20      0200                        LABEL_THREE:
21
22      0200                        CODE    ENDS
23                                          END
```

Figure 4.26 Relative Jumps

```
The IBM Personal Computer Assembler  01-01-83        PAGE    1-1
Figure 4.27  Call Instructions

 1                                         PAGE     ,132
 2                                         TITLE    Figure 4.27   Call Instructions
 3
 4        0000                     FAR_SEG SEGMENT
 5                                         ASSUME   CS:FAR_SEG
 6        0000                     FAR_LABEL        PROC     FAR
 7        0000  CB                          RET
 8        0001                     FAR_LABEL        ENDP
 9        0001                     FAR_SEG ENDS
10
11        0000                     CODE    SEGMENT
12                                         ASSUME   CS:CODE
13
14        0000  0000 ---- R        INDIRECT_FAR     DD       FAR_LABEL
15        0004  0018 R             INDIRECT_NEAR    DW       NEAR_LABEL
16
17        0006  E8 0018 R                  CALL     NEAR_LABEL        ; Relative call
18        0009  9A 0000 ---- R             CALL     FAR_LABEL         ; Absolute call
19
20        000E  2E: FF 16 0004 R           CALL     INDIRECT_NEAR     ; Indirect near call
21        0013  2E: FF 1E 0000 R           CALL     INDIRECT_FAR      ; Indirect far call
22
23        0018                     NEAR_LABEL       PROC     NEAR
24        0018  C3                          RET
25        0019                     NEAR_LABEL       ENDP
26        0019                     CODE    ENDS
27
28                                         END
```

Figure 4.27   Call Instructions

relative jump, using a two-byte displacement field. The other call instructions are all absolute jumps. The direct FAR CALL requires a four-byte operand field, to specify the new values for both the CS and the IP registers. The indirect jumps use the mod-r/m address byte to specify a register or memory operand. That operand contains the subroutine address. NEAR indirect calls load the word operand into the IP. FAR calls load the doubleword memory operand into CS:IP. It loads the first word into IP and the second word into CS. If the instruction specifies a register as the operand for an indirect intersegment call, the result is unpredictable. The 8088 takes the new CS value from somewhere unknown. It is wisest not to attempt this variation of the instruction.

Matching the CALL instructions are the return instructions (RET). All returns are indirect jumps, since they take their address from the top of stack location. An intrasegment return pops a single word from the stack and places it into the IP, while an intersegment return pops two words from the stack, placing the word from the lower address into IP, and the word from the higher address into CS.

Programs may modify both NEAR and FAR returns by specifying a byte-count parameter. The instruction adds this value to the Stack Pointer after popping the return address(es) from the stack. This instruction allows the subroutine to remove parameters from the stack without individual pop instructions. This accentuates the stack as a vehicle for passing parameters to subroutines. We discussed this concept in greater detail earlier in this chapter in the section "Stack Operations."

The unconditional jump instructions (JMP) are identical to the CALL instructions in their addressing capabilities. There is an additional jump instruction, one that specifies a single byte displacement for a near relative jump. There is no corresponding CALL instruction because subroutine jumps are very seldom to neighboring locations. The same methods of generating addresses apply to the jump instructions as to the calls.

A note about code optimization and the way the assembler works. As the assembler is making its first pass through the code and assigning addresses to the instructions, it must make a decision whether to use the two- or three-byte variation of the JMP instruction. If the jump is backward, that is, to a location that the assembler has already seen, the assembler can determine the correct displacement. The assembler then knows if the jump is within the range of the short displacement. However, if the jump is forward, to a label that the assembler has not yet seen, the assembler must assume that it will be farther than 128 bytes away. The assembler then generates the long form of the jump instruction. The assembler must choose the worst case since it can't back up and increase the size of an instruction later. The assembler replaces the three-byte jump with a two-byte jump and a single-byte no operation (NOP) instruction if it later finds that the jump is within the short range. Since the short jump executes somewhat faster, this is an execution time savings, but still leaves the object code larger than necessary.

If the assembly language programmer knows that a forward jump instruction is to a location in the range of the short jump, it can be communicated to the assembler like this:

```
JMP    SHORT LABEL
```

The attribute SHORT tells the assembler to generate the SHORT form of the jump instruction, even though it can't see the label yet. If the programmer makes a mistake, and the jump really shouldn't be a short one, the assembler issues an error message. Figure 4.26 has an example of the SHORT operator.

Figure 4.28 shows how a program can implement a branch table using the indirect jump instruction. This example selects between a number of routines, based on the value of the argument in the AL register. A similar program could CALL an indexed subroutine. This is the assembly language implementation of the CASE statement found in some high-level languages.

Conditional Jumps

The conditional jumps fall into two categories: flag testing, which tests the results of a previous arithmetic or logical operation; and loop testing, which controls the iteration of a section of code. All of the conditional jumps have a one-byte displacement. If a conditional jump is to a location more than 128 bytes away, a different construct must be used. As an example, suppose that the program needs to execute the label ZERO if the zero flag is set. This label is more than 128 bytes away. The code to handle this occurrence looks something like this:

```
JNZ    CONTINUE
JMP    ZERO
CONTINUE:
```

```
The IBM Personal Computer Assembler 01-01-83          PAGE    1-1
Figure 4.28  Branch Table

 1                                          PAGE    ,132
 2                                          TITLE   Figure 4.28  Branch Table
 3
 4      0000                        CODE    SEGMENT
 5                                          ASSUME  CS:CODE
 6
 7                                  ;--------------------------------------------
 8                                  ; This example branches to a routine
 9                                  ;  based on the value in the AL register.
10                                  ;  The AL value is the index into the
11                                  ;  routines that can execute.
12                                  ;--------------------------------------------
13
14      0000  2A FF                         SUB     BH,BH                 ; Zero to BH register
15      0002  8A D8                         MOV     BL,AL                 ; Index value into BX
16      0004  D1 E3                         SHL     BX,1                  ; * 2 for word index
17      0006  2E: FF A7 000B R              JMP     CS:[BX + BRANCH_TABLE]  ; Indirect branch
18
19      000B                        BRANCH_TABLE    LABEL    WORD
20      000B  0011 R                         DW      ROUTINE_ONE
21      000D  0011 R                         DW      ROUTINE_TWO
22      000F  0011 R                         DW      ROUTINE_THREE
23                                  ; . . .
24
25      0011                        ROUTINE_ONE     LABEL    NEAR
26      0011                        ROUTINE_TWO     LABEL    NEAR
27      0011                        ROUTINE_THREE   LABEL    NEAR
28
29      0011                        CODE    ENDS
30                                          END
```

Figure 4.28   Branch Table

The program uses a conditional jump for the opposite condition. An unconditional jump instruction, which can use a displacement as large as 32,768 bytes, gets to the label ZERO, while the nonzero condition uses the label CONTINUE. If minimizing the size of a program is a goal, you should avoid this method, since it turns a conditional jump instruction into a five-byte code sequence. Sometimes restructuring the code will bring the target of the jump in the range. However, don't go overboard trying to minimize the code. In almost all cases, it really doesn't matter how big the program is, just as long as it fits. If you're trying to make something fit into a fixed-size ROM module, this might be a concern, but usually the effort of changing the program is not worth the benefit.

Condition Code Tests

The first group of conditional jump instructions test the current setting of the flag register. The instruction then jumps or not, based on the condition codes. The conditional jumps do not set the flags in any way. They only test the current setting of the flags. The previous arithmetic or logical instruction has set the flags. In the examples that follow, we will normally assume that the compare (CMP) instruction has set the flags.

Figure 4.29 shows the conditional jump instructions and the flags that they test. The figure lists the conditional instructions as the rows, and shows the five status flags as the columns. An X in any position indicates that the instruction does not test that flag. A ''0'' means that the flag must be zero for the condition to be true and the jump to be taken. A ''1'' indicates that the flag must be set to a one for the jump to be taken. Some of the table entries show a formula that must be satisfied for the jump to be taken. These are for the arithmetic jumps, and we'll discuss them in more detail later.

Figure 4.29 further divides the conditional jumps into three sections: those that directly test one of the flags, those that make an unsigned arithmetic comparison, and those that make a signed arithmetic comparison.

Figure 4.29(a) shows the individual flag tests. A conditional jump can test each of the five flags directly for either a zero or one. The figure shows the test of the carry flag in the unsigned arithmetic section, since it also has an arithmetic meaning. Notice that many of the conditional jump instructions have more than one mnemonic for the instruction, even though they perform the same test. For example, the test of the zero flag is JZ, for Jump if Zero. However, the instruction JE, for Jump if Equal, also generates the same instruction. This code sequence shows the reason:

```
CMP     AX,BX
JE      LABEL
```

The CMP instruction subtracts BX from AX, setting the flags according to the result. Since the result is zero if the two operands are equal, the zero flag indicates equality. Similarly, JNZ (Jump if Not Zero) is identical to JNE (Jump if Not Equal). JP (Jump if Parity) is the same as JPE (Jump if Parity Even), and JNP (Jump if No Parity) is the same as JPO (Jump if Parity Odd).

Conditional Instructions	OF	CY	Flags Z	P	S	Comments
JE/JZ	X	X	1	X	X	
JP/JPE	X	X	X	1	X	
JO	1	X	X	X	X	
JS	X	X	X	X	1	
JNE/JNZ	X	X	0	X	X	
JNP/JPO	X	X	X	0	X	
JNO	0	X	X	X	X	
JNS	X	X	X	X	0	
			(a)			
JL/JNGE	a	X	X	X	b	a NEQ b
JLE/JNG	a	X	1	X	b	Z OR (A NEQ B)
JNL/JGE	a	X	X	X	b	a = b
JNLE/JG	a	X	0	X	b	(NOT Z) AND (a=b)
			(b)			
JB/JNAE/JC	X	1	X	X	X	
JBE/JNA	X	1	1	X	X	CY OR Z
JNB/JAE/JN	X	0	X	X	X	
JNBE/JA	X	0	0	X	X	(NOT CY) AND (NOT Z)
			(c)			

Figure 4.29 Conditional Jump Flag Testing. (a) Flag Testing; (b) Signed Arithmetic; (c) Unsigned Arithmetic.

Signed arithmetic comparisons use the next group of conditional instructions, as shown in Figure 4.29(b). There are four conditions that can be tested: less than, less than or equal, greater than, and greater than or equal. The other four mnemonics are the negations of these statements. The assembler uses less than and greater than for signed arithmetic. In the next section we'll see that the assembler uses above and below for unsigned arithmetic comparisons.

You can understand arithmetic comparisons if you use them together with the CMP instruction. For example,

```
CMP     AX,BX
JL      LABEL
```

The jump will be taken if AX is less than BX. You can read the combination of the compare instruction and the conditional test together as a single statement. The destination operand comes first, then the conditional operator, followed by the source operand. Here's another example:

```
CMP     CX,WORD_IN_MEMORY
JNLE    LABEL
```

You should read this as "Jump if CX is not less than or equal to the contents of the memory location WORD_IN_MEMORY." You can use this technique to determine the meaning of any of the arithmetic jump instructions, whether signed or unsigned.

As Figure 4.29(b) shows, the signed arithmetic comparisons do not directly test a single flag. In fact, each of the instructions tests some combination of the overflow, sign, and possibly the zero flag. For example, JL, Jump if Less, requires that the sign and overflow flags have differing values. If they have the same value, the first operand was not less than the second one. Let's look at this operation in a little more detail, to understand the operation of the signed arithmetic comparisons.

When two signed numbers are compared, there are four combinations of the sign and overflow flags. We'll look at each of the four to determine what happened, and what the relationship of the operands was to produce that result. In each case we'll assume that the operation setting the flags was a CMP instruction, which subtracted the two operands.

$$\text{Sign} = 0, \qquad \text{Overflow} = 0$$

$S = 0$ indicates that the result of the subtraction was positive. $O = 0$ means that no overflow occurred, so the two's-complement result is correct. Subtracting two numbers and getting a positive result means that the first number is the larger of the two, and therefore the relationship is greater than. However, subtracting two equal numbers also leaves a positive result, so the $S = 0$, $O = 0$ condition indicates greater than or equal.

$$S = 1, \qquad O = 0$$

In this case, O = 0 means that the result is correct, and S = 1 means that the result is negative. To get a negative result the larger number must have been subtracted from the smaller one, so the relationship is less than.

   S = 0,   O = 1

Here the O = 1 means that the result is incorrect—that is, it has gone beyond the capabilities of the number system. This means that the addition of two positive values has yielded a negative result, or vice versa. For the purposes of this comparison, it means that the sign of the result is incorrect. Therefore, the result of this comparison is identical to that of S = 1, O = 0, which indicates less than.

   S = 1,   O = 1

Again, the O = 1 indicates that the sign result is incorrect. Therefore, the subtraction must have resulted in a very large positive number, so the relationship is greater than.

   The zero flag also comes into the equation for some of the comparisons. For example, JLE (Jump if Less than or Equal) is true if either the condition for less than (sign and overflow not the same) or the condition for zero (zero flag equals one) is true. These three flags allow the 8088 to test all of the possible combinations of signed numbers.

   The final section of the table, Figure 4.29(c), shows the conditions tested for unsigned arithmetic. As with signed arithmetic, there are four possible relations between the two operands that the processor can test. The assembler uses the words above and below for comparison, to indicate unsigned arithmetic. It was probably the view of the instruction set designers that programs would use unsigned arithmetic for address calculations, since there are no negative address-es. Above and below indicate positioning within the memory space, while greater than and less than indicate ordering of signed numbers. The important thing to note is that the instruction specified in the assembly language program is the one executed, irrespective of the type of operands compared. For example, a program compares two signed numbers, and uses the JA (Jump if Above) instruction. The processor executes the conditional jump depending on the relationship of the two numbers, considered as if they were unsigned numbers. It is up to the programmer to use the correct conditional instruction.

   The 8088 considers only two flags when determining the relationship of two unsigned numbers. The carry flag indicates which of the numbers is larger. A comparison sets the carry flag if the first operand is below the second. It clears the carry if the first operand is either above or equal to the second operand. The zero flag determines which of these is correct.

   You read unsigned comparisons in the same way as signed comparisons. For example,

   CMP   AX,BX
   JA   LABEL

The program jumps to LABEL if AX is above BX. The conditional jump is always taken if the stated relationship exists between the first operand and the second operand of the preceding compare instruction.

Loop Control

There are several conditional jump instructions intended to control the looping of a computer program. Since the program loop is frequently used, efficient control of the loop is desirable. Figure 4.30 shows four instructions designed to make program loops easy in 8088 assembly language.

Just as string instructions use the CX register as a counter, the LOOP instructions use CX as a loop counter. All of these instructions treat the CX register implicitly as the counter for the number of iterations of a loop. The LOOP instruction is the simplest. The LOOP instruction decrements CX and transfers control to the label if CX is not equal to zero. If subtracting one from CX results in zero, LOOP does not jump, and executes the next sequential instruction.

The sequence of code below shows the normal use of the LOOP instruction.

```
        MOV     CX,LOOP_COUNT
BEGIN_LOOP:
        ;... Body of Loop
        LOOP        BEGIN_LOOP
```

The program places the number of loop iterations into the CX register prior to executing the loop. The body of the loop executes, followed by the LOOP instruction. LOOP decrements the count by one, corresponding to the single

```
The IBM Personal Computer Assembler 01-01-83         PAGE    1-1
Figure 4.30  Loop Instructions

 1                                         PAGE    ,132
 2                                         TITLE   Figure 4.30  Loop Instructions
 3
 4      0000                       CODE    SEGMENT
 5                                         ASSUME  CS:CODE
 6
 7                             ;----------------------------------
 8                             ; This example shows the loop instructions.
 9                             ;  The instructions here do not form an
10                             ;  executable program.
11                             ;----------------------------------
12
13      0000  E3 06                     JCXZ    END_OF_LOOP     ; No loop if CX already zero
14
15      0002               BEGIN_LOOP:
16
17                             ; . . . . Body of Loop
18
19      0002  E2 FE                     LOOP    BEGIN_LOOP      ; Jump until CX is zero
20
21                             ; . . . . Or, if testing a condition
22
23      0004  E, FC                     LOOPE   BEGIN_LOOP      ; Jump if equal and CX not zero
24
25                             ; . . . . Or
26
27      0006  E0 FA                     LOOPNE  BEGIN_LOOP      ; Jump if not equal and CX not zero
28
29      0008               END_OF_LOOP:
30
31      0008               CODE    ENDS
32                                 END
```

Figure 4.30 Loop Instructions

execution of the loop just performed. If the count in CX is now zero, the program continues with the next instruction. If, however, the count is not zero, control returns to the beginning of the loop to make another pass through the body of the loop. The body of the loop is executed as many times as the number initially loaded in the CX register. One important note, however, is that if the code in the loop modifies the CX register, the number of loop iterations won't match the initial value.

The method above works equally well for loop control whether the number of loops is known at assembly time (as in the example above, where LOOP_COUNT was an immediate value) or the number of loops is determined during execution. However, if the computed number turns out to be zero, the loop executes 65,536 times. When the 8088 executes the first LOOP instruction, it decrements CX from 0 to 0FFFFH, and since CX is nonzero, it repeats the loop. Thus, handling a zero loop count is a special case.

The JCXZ (Jump if CX is Zero) instruction handles this special case. This instruction tests the current contents of the CX register, and jumps if the value is zero. The instruction does not test the condition flags, nor does it affect them. The following example is identical to the preceding one, except that it loads the CX register from a memory location whose contents are calculated during execution. Since it's possible that the loop count might be zero, the example uses the JCXZ instruction to test for skipping the loop entirely.

```
          MOV     CX,LOOP_COUNT_WORD
          JCXZ    END_OF_LOOP
BEGIN_LOOP:
          ; . . . Body of Loop
          LOOP         BEGIN_LOOP
END_OF_LOOP:
```

A program does not need to use the JCXZ instruction in every loop with a calculated loop count. If the programmer knows that zero will never be a count value, the test is unnecessary. However, experience usually indicates that the value that can "never" happen is usually the first one to occur once you execute the program.

The remaining two LOOP instructions provide even greater control of program loops. These instructions are similar to the REPE and REPNE instruction prefixes. While the LOOP instruction exits only when the CX register reaches zero, the LOOPE (Loop while Equal) instruction exits if the zero flag is not set, or if the CX register has reached zero. This allows a dual test for the termination of a loop. The program can set CX to the maximum number of iterations for the loop, and can test the zero flag at the end of each loop for the loop terminating condition. The LOOPNE (Loop while Not Equal) instruction performs the complementary test on the zero flag. The loop terminates if the CX register has reached zero, or if the zero flag is set.

The following example shows the use of the LOOPNE instruction. This example adds two lists of numbers in order to find a pair of entries that add to exactly 100. Because each iteration of the loop adds the numbers before testing, it isn't feasible to use the REPNE CMPSB instruction.

The example assumes that DS:SI and ES:DI have been initialized to point to the lists.

```
        MOV     CX,MAX_LOOP_COUNT ; Maximum number of passes
    BEGIN_LOOP:
        LODSB                      ; Get the number from list one
        ADD     AL,ES:[DI]         ; Add from the second list
        INC     DI                 ; Point to next in second list
        CMP     AL,100             ; Test for match with desired value
    LOOPNE      BEGIN_LOOP         ; Again if no match and more values
        JE      MATCH_FOUND        ; Branch here to determine loop end
```

PROCESSOR CONTROL INSTRUCTIONS

The remaining instructions in the 8088 repertoire control the operation of the processor. Many of the instructions set or reset some of the indicators in the status register.

Flag Setting

There are three instructions that can directly control the state of the carry flag. The STC, CLC, and CMC instructions can set, reset, or complement the carry flag, respectively. The carry flag is the only condition code flag to receive all of this attention. This is primarily because of the importance of the carry flag in multiple-precision arithmetic operations. The carry flag is crucial for intermediate steps in any multiple-word arithmetic operation. The ability to set or clear the carry flag can help with the loop processing of multiple-precision arithmetic. Figure 4.31 is an example of the use of the CLC instruction. The loop within the example adds the individual bytes of two 10-digit packed BCD numbers. The routine executes the loop five times, since it handles two digits with each iteration. The carry flag communicates the carry information from one loop to the next. The CLC instruction clears the carry before the first loop to ensure that there is no carry into the first addition. The carry flag is also important in rotate instructions, where it becomes the ninth or seventeenth bit of the register during the shift operation.

Two of the processor state flags have instructions that manipulate them. A program can set or clear the interrupt mask with the STI and CLI instructions, respectively. The STI instruction enables the interrupt system of the 8088, allowing it to acknowledge external interrupts. The CLI instruction disables the external interrupt system.

```
The IBM Personal Computer Assembler 01-01-83        PAGE    1-1
Figure 4.31  Multiple Precision BCD

 1                                            PAGE    ,132
 2                                            TITLE   Figure 4.31  Multiple Precision BCD
 3
 4      0000                          CODE    SEGMENT
 5                                            ASSUME  CS:CODE, DS:CODE
 6
 7      = 0005                        NUMBER_LENGTH  EQU    5                 ; 5 byte BCD numbers
 8      0000    05 [                  NUMBER_ONE     DB     NUMBER_LENGTH DUP (?)
 9                  ??
10               ]
11
12      0005    05 [                  NUMBER_TWO     DB     NUMBER_LENGTH DUP (?)
13                  ??
14               ]
15
16
17                                    ;--------------------------------
18                                    ; This routine adds the packed BCD number
19                                    ;  location NUMBER_ONE to the packed BCD number
20                                    ;  in location NUMBER_TWO, and leaves the result
21                                    ;  in NUMBER_TWO.
22                                    ;--------------------------------
23
24      000A                          START_ADD:
25      000A    B9 0005                       MOV     CX,NUMBER_LENGTH         ; Determine # bytes to add
26
27                                    ;----- Set index registers to point at least significant bytes
28
29      000D    BE 0004 R                     MOV     SI,OFFSET NUMBER_ONE + NUMBER_LENGTH - 1
30      0010    BF 0009 R                     MOV     DI,OFFSET NUMBER_TWO + NUMBER_LENGTH - 1
31
32      0013    F8                            CLC                             ; Start with no carry
33
34      0014                          ADD_LOOP:
35      0014    8A 04                         MOV     AL,[SI]                 ; Get ONE value
36      0016    02 05                         ADD     AL,[DI]                 ; Add the TWO value
37      0018    27                            DAA                             ; BCD adjust
38      0019    88 05                         MOV     [DI],AL                 ; Store the result
39      001B    9C                            PUSHF                           ; Save the carry flag
40      001C    4E                            DEC     SI                      ; Point to next byte of ONE
41      001D    4F                            DEC     DI                      ; Point to next byte of TWO
42      001E    9D                            POPF                            ; Get back the flags
43      001F    E2 F3                         LOOP    ADD_LOOP                ; Do next highest byte
44
45      0021                          CODE    ENDS
46                                            END
```

Figure 4.31   Multiple-Precision BCD

A program can set or reset the direction flag using the STD or CLD instructions, for Set Direction and Clear Direction. The CLD instruction clears the direction flag, and causes the string instructions to move in an ascending sequence through memory. STD sets the flag, and causes the string instructions to decrement the address pointer after each operation.

Special Instructions

The NOP instruction is the least powerful of the 8088 instructions. It does nothing—a NO Operation. A careful examination of the machine codes for this instruction reveals that it is really an XCHG instruction. Specifically, it is

> XCHG   AX,AX

which, as you might imagine, is the equivalent of doing nothing. Although the NOP instruction doesn't do anything, there are instances when it is desirable to use it, just to take up time. A short loop intended to take a certain amount of time to execute can use NOPs to fill out the body of the loop to get the exact execution time (although a loop is not the best way to kill time, unless it is a very short interval). The developers of the IBM Personal Computer required NOPs in several places to satisfy some hardware timings. A program cannot access the timer counter device, for example, more often than once every microsecond. Two successive IN instructions violate this timing requirement, so several NOPs are between the IN instructions.

The HLT (Halt) instruction does just that. The processor halts following the execution of that instruction. If interrupts are disabled when the processor halts, the computer has just become a vegetable. The only recourse is to turn the power off and back on to regain control. However, if the interrupts are enabled when the processor halts, the interrupts will be accepted and control passed to the interrupt handler. Following the IRET of the interrupt controller, the program begins executing at the location following the HLT instruction. A program can use the HLT instruction with multitasking systems to terminate the currently active task, but it is seldom the best way to do it. The Personal Computer developers use the halt instruction only when a catastrophic hardware failure has occurred and further execution is unwise.

The LOCK instruction is actually an instruction prefix, like the segment overrides or the REP prefix. It is intended for a multiprocessing system, where there may be several processors accessing the same memory locations. The LOCK prefix causes the 8088 to assert control lines to gain exclusive access to the memory for the duration of the prefixed instruction. The best example of this is setting/testing a flag in a shared memory.

```
        MOV        AL, 1
LOCK   XCHG        AL, FLAG_BYTE
        CMP        AL, 1
```

In this example, the FLAG_BYTE contains either a zero or one indicator. A processor sets the flag to one when it enters a guarded region of the program, where it is performing system operations that only one processor at a time can do. Before it enters the guarded region, the processor must test to see if any other processor is already executing there. If so, it must wait before it enters; otherwise, it may enter the region. This example makes this test and ensures that no other processor enters the region. The example uses the LOCK prefix with the XCHG instruction. The LOCK gives the processor exclusive use of the memory for the duration of the XCHG instruction, which is a read of the memory location, followed by a write of the same location. The XCHG writes the "1" in the AL register into FLAG_BYTE, while it moves the current contents into AL. Now if AL is a one, there is already another processor in the guarded region, and the testing processor must wait. If the AL register is a zero, the processor may enter the guarded region, and the XCHG has set FLAG_BYTE to one so that no other processor may enter. The LOCK prefix has prevented any other processor from testing the flag byte during the brief interval between the testing and the setting of the flag location.

Unfortunately, this discussion of the LOCK prefix is academic. The IBM

Personal Computer does not implement the hardware signals necessary for LOCK operation.

The WAIT instruction stops the execution of the processor, similar to the HLT instruction. But with the WAIT, execution resumes when an external input to the 8088, the TEST pin, becomes active. If the TEST pin is active when the WAIT instruction is executed, there is no cessation of instruction activity. If the TEST pin is inactive, the processor waits until the TEST pin becomes active. The 8088 uses this instruction in conjunction with the ESC instruction to provide access to the 8087 Numeric Data Processor.

The ESC (Escape) instruction provides expansion capability to the 8088 instruction set, without modifying the processor. The ESC instruction contains an address mode field, and can specify a memory location through the normal addressing modes of the 8088. However, the processor does nothing except read that location and throw away the data.

The ESC instruction allows another processor, or coprocessor as it is called, to monitor the execution of the 8088. The ESC instruction activates the coprocessor, which it executes as its own. If the coprocessor requires any memory address, the 8088 provides the address during the dummy read. The coprocessor can then access data at that address in the manner it requires. The full power of this ESC instruction will be apparent in Chapter 7, which discusses the 8087 Numeric Data Processor, a coprocessor to the 8088.

CHAPTER

5

Using DOS
And The Assembler

This chapter handles the "nuts-and-bolts" training necessary to assemble and execute programs. The preceding chapters explained the operation of the 8088. Now it's time to put that training to the test. Only by actually writing and executing a program successfully can you have a true appreciation of the 8088 instruction set.

In this chapter we discuss the four main phases of program preparation: editing, assembling, link editing, and debugging. Each of these phases is accomplished with a different program and a different set of procedures. All of these programs execute under the umbrella of the Disk Operating System (DOS). Three of these programs are part of the DOS package, which you can license from the same dealer that supplies that IBM Personal Computer hardware. The assembler is a separate item, but available from the same source. This text deals exclusively with IBM program products.

DISK OPERATING SYSTEM

Since we'll be working with the Disk Operating System for program preparation and execution, we'll start with a discussion of what DOS is and what it can do. The Disk Operating System provides the environment in which other programs execute. In large machines, the operating system is the program that controls the execution of the machine. Most large computers have multiple users, all compet-

108

ing for the resources of the machine. The operating system is the referee that decides which user may use which resource at what time. The operating system prevents the users from interfering with one another. The operating system also offers a set of services that relieve the user from having to deal with the difficulties of the hardware. These services keep the user from messing up the hardware by doing operations which destroy the data or programs of other users. Most large machine operating systems are constructed so that a user program may not directly interact with the computer hardware. The needs of many users preclude the individual freedoms of programs.

For small computers, like the IBM Personal Computer, the operating system serves a different purpose. Personal computers are used by a single person at a time. Scheduling the resources of the machine is handled by some external means—whoever is sitting at the keyboard has everything at his or her fingertips. At the program level, there is no prohibition against performing any sequence of instructions. The program can harm only the individual currently using the machine, and then only in the sense the program or data might be lost.

The purpose of the IBM Personal Computer DOS is to provide an operating environment and a set of services for users. The user may be a programmer, or it may be some other application program. For example, when you sit down at the keyboard and begin to work with the system, you are a user of DOS. But when the editor saves a file on the diskette or fixed disk, the editor uses DOS. The editor is using the services of DOS to save the file, rather than including the programs to do that job in the editor.

The primary service of the Disk Operating System on the IBM Personal Computer is to provide a file system and an execution environment for programs. The file system is the method by which data are saved and restored on the diskette or fixed disk. If all of the application programs use the DOS to save information, they can share the information. Each application does not have to redo the job of writing the file system code.

FILE SYSTEM

Each diskette used on the IBM Personal Computer can store 160K to 360K bytes of data. A fixed disk can store over 10 million bytes. The problem of storage management is apparent. With all of this storage capacity, there must be some way of keeping everything sorted out. As a DOS user, you are interested in a collection of data as a single entity—for example, an assembly language program. You don't want to be concerned with the location of those data on the diskette. The mapping of the data to physical locations on the diskette is the job of the system.

The basic unit of data storage is a file. A file is a collection of data which are related in some manner. The owner, or creator, of a file gives it a name. All references to that data can use the name to locate the data. Referencing the data doesn't require the program to know anything about the physical location of the data.

A file is made up of records. Each record is a single unit of data, but not necessarily a single byte. The best way to understand files and records is to recall what they mean in an office environment.

A file is a large cabinet or folder that holds lots of papers. The file folder usually has a name on it—the file name. In the file folder are the individual records. For example, a teacher's file folder may contain the tests taken by the students. Each test in the file is a record. The instructor has collected and stored the records with a meaningful name, such as "FIRST TEST." The teacher locates an individual test by first finding the correct file and then searching the file for the correct record.

Now how does this relate to files in a computer? The file is a collection of related data, and each file has a name. The records are in the file. The programmer determines the size and content of the records. The DOS does not control record format. It merely stores the records in the file. The DOS views a record as a collection of bytes in the file. The programmer defines the significance of the bytes in the record.

Let's look at an assembly language program as an example of a computer file. The program has a name, and that name becomes the file name. The file is made up of records, where each record is a single assembly language statement. Each record has a layout that is meaningful to the assembler, but not to DOS. The different areas in each record are fields. The DOS doesn't care how the records are divided into fields. That job is left to the application, in this case, the assembler.

FILE NAMES

While we're talking about file names, we should discuss how DOS lets you name files. There are two parts in each DOS file name. The first part of the file name may be one to eight characters long. This is the part that the user specifies, the "name" of the file. The second portion, known as the extension, is one to three characters long. The application program usually specifies this part, the "type" of file. A period (".") separates the name and the extension. For example, "COMMAND.COM" has a name COMMAND and an extension COM.

Sometimes the user can specify the extension of the file name. However, DOS or an application program use the file name extension to indicate the type of file. For "COMMAND.COM" the .COM indicates a command file. The assembler has an input file and up to three output files. The input file extension is .ASM for assembly file, and the output extensions are .OBJ, .LST, and .CRF for object, listing, and cross-reference files, respectively. In many instances the application programs require that the files have a certain extension.

DIRECTORY

Since the diskette can hold a great deal of information, it would be wasteful to dedicate a complete diskette to a single file. The operating system manages the method of storing multiple files on the fixed disk or diskette.

A storage device can hold more than one file because DOS builds a directory of the contents. The directory is like a table of contents. The directory lists each of the files on the disk or diskette. Besides the file name, DOS also includes other necessary and helpful information. The directory contains the pointers necessary to find the actual location of the data on the device. A convenient feature of the directory is the time stamp of each file. Whenever a program creates or updates a file, DOS records the date and time. This is helpful when you're dealing with multiple copies of some information and must find the most recent version.

The diskette directory manages the problem of multiple files on a single disk or diskette. But DOS can deal with only one drive at a time. If your system has more than one disk or diskette drive, you must tell DOS in which drive the file is located. The diskette drive name becomes a prefix for the file name. For example, COMMAND.COM in drive A has a fully qualified name of A:COMMAND.COM.

COMMAND PROCESSOR

Besides the file system, DOS provides an environment to execute application programs. The first part of DOS that the user sees is the command processor. This is the part of DOS that responds to user commands and starts the execution of application programs.

When the IBM Personal Computer is first turned on, it has very little intelligence: a great deal of strength perhaps, but not much ability to do anything with it. The read-only memory (ROM) in the machine contains routines which test the system components (Power-On Self-Test or POST) and initialize the input/output devices for action. The remainder of the ROM Basic Input/Output System (BIOS) provides a set of services to help the assembly language programmer access the hardware devices without reference to the specifics of the hardware implementation. All of this is nice, but it doesn't provide an environment for the execution of serious application programs.

The DOS takes care of this. After POST initializes the system, it loads DOS into memory from the DOS diskette or the fixed disk. This process is known as "booting" the system. The phrase is taken from the saying, "lifting yourself by your own bootstraps." The first action of DOS is to load in the minimum amount of code necessary to load in the rest of DOS. Hence, DOS lifts itself in through its own bootstraps. DOS ends the bootstrap procedure by displaying the copyright notice and title. Among other things, this title indicates the current DOS level. At times the DOS level is important, since each new version of DOS means additional function in the system.

After the bootstrap operation, DOS is ready to accept commands from the system operator (except for a special case we'll discuss later). At this point the command processor is in control. DOS has loaded the command processor, the file system and other utilities, and they're all ready to go. The command processor indicates that it's in control with the prompt

A>

This prompt has two meanings. The ">" symbol signals that the command line interpreter is awaiting a command. The "A" indicates the default diskette drive. DOS can keep track of the files on a single diskette only. If more than one disk or diskette will be in use at the same time, the user must indicate which drive DOS should use. The IBM Personal Computer identifies drives by letters of the alphabet. A system with two diskette drives has an A: drive and a B: drive. The fixed disk is normally the C: drive. (The drives are usually named with a colon following them.) The default drive contains the files that DOS uses unless the operator tells it differently. To access a file on the default drive, DOS only needs the file name. To access a file on any other drive, DOS must be told the drive name as well as the file name.

DOS perform actions only in response to commands from the user. All DOS commands begin as an input in response to the ">" prompt. The system user enters the command name, and the command line interpreter handles the request. How the interpreter handles the request depends on the command entered by the user. There are built-in, or resident, commands, which are always available. Or the command may invoke a nonresident, or transient, operation. These commands require a particular diskette file before they can be executed.

The built-in commands maintain the file system. These commands are resident in DOS because they are frequently used to manage the diskette data. When the user enters, the command line interpreter passes control to the routine in DOS. The routine performs the function, according to the specifications of that command, and returns control to DOS. Figure 5.1 lists the resident commands of the Disk Operating System.

An example resident command is DIR. This command displays the directory

Command	Action
COPY	Copy a file from one location to another
DATE	Display/modify the current date
DIR	List the directory of a diskette
ERASE	Remove a file from the diskette
PAUSE	System wait until key is entered
REM	Enter a remark
RENAME	Change the name of a diskette file
TIME	Display/modify the current time
TYPE	Display the contents of a file

Figure 5.1   DOS Resident Commands

```
A>dir
COMMAND     COM      4959     4-06-82    12:00p
FORMAT      COM      3816     4-06-82    12:00p
CHKDSK      COM      1720     4-06-82    12:00p
SYS         COM       605     4-06-82    12:00p
DISKCOPY    COM      2008     4-06-82    12:00p
DISKCOMP    COM      1640     4-06-82    12:00p
COMP        COM      1649     4-06-82    12:00p
EXE2BIN     EXE      1280     4-06-82    12:00p
MODE        COM      2509     4-06-82    12:00p
EDLIN       COM      2392     4-06-82    12;00p
DEBUG       COM      5999     4-06-82    12:00p
LINK        EXE     41856     4-06-82    12:00p
BASIC       COM     11136     1-01-80     4:43a
BASICA      COM     16512     1-01-80     4:55a
ART         BAS      1920     4-06-82    12:00p
SAMPLES     BAS      2432     4-06-82    12:00p
MORTGAGE    BAS      6272     4-06-82    12:00p
COLORBAR    BAS      1536     4-06-82    12:00p
CALENDAR    BAS      3840     4-06-82    12:00p
MUSIC       BAS      8704     4-06-82    12:00p
DONKEY      BAS      3584     4-06-82    12:00p
CIRCLE      BAS      1664     4-06-82    12:00p
PIECHART    BAS      2304     4-06-82    12:00p
SPACE       BAS      1920     4-06-82    12:00p
BALL        BAS      2048     4-06-82    12:00p
COMM        BAS      4352     4-06-82    12:00p
           26 File(s)
```

Figure 5.2   Diskette Directory

of a diskette. Figure 5.2 shows the output of the directory command. Notice that the directory command shows the name and extension of every file on the diskette. The length of the file in bytes, and the date and time when it was created, are all displayed. Since DOS must read the directory of a diskette in order to load any program, the directory command is a built-in function.

If the user enters a nonresident command, the command interpreter attempts to load the desired command from the disk or diskette. In this instance, the interpreter acts as a program loader. The interpreter assumes that the command name is the name of a file. It searches the directory for a file with a name matching the command, and loads that file. The interpreter then passes control to that program, so it can do whatever it's supposed to do.

The command processor won't load just any file. The file name extension must be either .COM or .EXE. These are command files and execution files, respectively. The final product of the assemble and link operation is an .EXE file. This means that it is possible for you to write your own DOS command. If you have written, assembled, and linked an assembly language program, and leave that program on the diskette, you may load and execute it just as any other DOS program. It's this capability that lets you write programs to execute with the DOS.

There is a difference between .COM and .EXE files. They have slightly different structures and get control in different ways. Even though .EXE files are the normal output of the link step, there are reasons for using .COM files at times. In a later section we'll discuss the differences between the files, and how to convert an .EXE file into a .COM file.

Let's now look at an example of a transient command. The Macro Assembler is a good example. To invoke the assembler, you enter the command

        A>ASM

If you look at the directory of the assembler diskette, you'll see that there is a file named ASM.EXE. This file is the assembler. In response to the ASM command, the command processor searches the diskette in drive A: (the default diskette). When it finds the file ASM.EXE, it loads the assembler and passes control to it. The assembler is now in control of the system. Hopefully, it will return control to the command processor when it has completed the assembly. Notice that the assembler file is an .EXE file, so the command processor can load it.

If the assembler is not on the diskette in the A: drive, the user can specify the drive with

        A>B:ASM

The prefix B: tells DOS that the file is on the diskette in the B: drive. A file is completely specified by identifying not only the file name, but also the drive on which it resides. The file name alone is sufficient for a file on the default drive. To assemble a file on the B: drive with the assembler on the A: drive, this is the command:

        A>ASM   B:FILE.ASM

This command specifies both the program ASM, on the default drive, and the source file FILE.ASM, on the B: drive.

You can do this a different way. You can make the B: drive the default drive, and specify the command like this:

        A>B:
        B>A:ASM   FILE.ASM

The command B: tells DOS to switch to B: as the default drive. Notice that the prompt changes to B>, indicating that B: is the default drive. The command in this example is identical to the one above.

The command line interpreter can also execute a file with an extension of .BAT, known as a batch file. This file type is quite different than the .COM or .EXE files. A .BAT file does not contain machine language code for execution. The batch file contains text commands that the command processor interprets. The .BAT file contains DOS commands, each of which is executed in turn. One way to think of a .BAT file is that it replaces the keyboard input. Instead of entering commands from the keyboard, the batch file holds the commands. When DOS has executed the contents of the .BAT file, it goes to the keyboard for the next command. This makes the batch file a very convenient way to handle repetitive tasks. Once the batch file has been created, invoking it with a single command replaces all of the other command input.

There is a special batch file, named AUTOEXEC.BAT. DOS executes this file, if it exists, immediately after DOS is loaded. DOS passes control immediately to the batch file commands. This lets a diskette automatically go to a desired user program. Suppose that you had written an application program that used DOS functions. (In this case, we usually say that the program was written to "run under DOS.") By creating an AUTOEXEC.BAT file that starts the application program, the application operator will never need to know how the command line interpreter works. The first thing the user knows is that the application is in control.

DOS FUNCTIONS

The command line interpreter provides a mechanism to get your assembly language program into execution. Once it's running, DOS also provides access to the file system, through the DOS functions. This section shows what these functions are, and how a program can use them. Appendix D of the Disk Operating System Reference Manual contains a complete description of these functions.

A program executes a DOS function through a software interrupt. By using an interrupt, a program can call the routine without knowing its location. The programmer specifies the desired interrupt. During the DOS initialization, it sets the interrupt vectors for the DOS functions to point to the correct routines. Thus, as different versions of DOS are distributed, it is unnecessary to modify your program. Figure 5.3 shows the DOS interrupt vectors.

Several of the interrupts are actually for user routines. Interrupts 22H, 23H, and 24H are pointers to routines that can be in your program. These vectors

Interrupt	Operation
20H	Program end
21H	Function request (see Figure 5.5)
22H	End address
23H	CTRL-BREAK address
24H	Critical error handler
25H	Absolute disk read
26H	Absolute disk write
27H	End but stay resident

Figure 5.3 DOS Interrupts

identify the program to execute when the named condition occurs. For example, DOS executes an interrupt 23H when the CTRL-BREAK key is depressed. This keystroke normally signals a break in program execution. DOS sets these three interrupts to the normal DOS handling of each condition. If a program needs to treat these differently, it can change the interrupt vector.

As an example, let's look at interrupt 24H, the critical error handler. Whenever DOS detects an error, it invokes this interrupt. Normally, this vector points to a DOS routine that prints an error message on the display. For a diskette error, DOS displays a diskette error message. The user has the option of retrying, aborting, or ignoring the operation that caused the error. For this example, we'll assume that you're writing a program to format diskettes. This is an operation that physically locates the tracks and sectors on the diskette media. As part of the format operation, you'll test the diskette for problem areas before you use it. This is known as verifying the diskette. Since it is possible for a diskette to have a bad spot or two, and still be usable, you'll mark the bad spots in a special way so that you won't use them inadvertently later.

The format program replaces the critical error handler. You don't want DOS to write an error message for the user. Rather, you want the program to handle the verify error, and mark this as a bad spot on the diskette. To do this, you replace the interrupt vector at location 00090H (24H × 4) with a pointer to the error-handling routine. When DOS detects a diskette error, the routine can mark that location as a bad spot, without any user indication of the problem.

DOS interrupts 25H and 26H link together two portions of DOS. The file structure implementation of DOS actually has two ingredients. One is the code that links directly to the hardware, known as IBMBIO.COM. The other implements the file system, known as IBMDOS.COM. When the file system part of DOS communicates to the BIO (Basic I/O) part of DOS, it uses these two interrupts. Although available for your use, their primary purpose is to separate the two sections of DOS. Interrupt 25H does an absolute disk read, while interrupt 26H does an absolute disk write. At this level the interface deals with definite locations on the diskette, and not records within a file.

The interrupts 20H and 27H provide a mechanism for returning control to DOS following the execution of a program. Interrupt 20H is the normal exit. Interrupt 27H is interesting in that it ends the program but doesn't return the memory used by the program back to DOS. Whatever is left in the program area remains there until the power is turned off or the system is reset. This function is valuable when you want to provide a new interrupt handler or similar function that must remain as part of the system. In Chapter 10 we'll provide an example that uses the INT 27H exit to extend the system.

A caution on the use of DOS interrupts 20H and 27H. They work best when executed in a .COM file. The format of an .EXE file is sufficiently different that these DOS functions require a little more effort. In the next section we'll discuss the differences between .COM and .EXE files, and why the exit interrupts operate differently.

Interrupt 21H is the DOS function interrupt. This interrupt gives access to the DOS I/O structure. Figure 5.4 shows the possible functions using this interrupt. A program selects the function by setting the AH register to the correct value prior to issuing the interrupt 21H.

The parameters for these functions are given in Appendix D of the DOS

Value in AH	Function
0	Program end
1	Keyboard input
2	Display output
3	Auxiliary input (asynchronous communications)
4	Auxiliary output
5	Printer output
6	Direct console I/O
7	Direct console input without echo
8	Console input without echo
9	Print string
0AH	Buffered keyboard input
0BH	Check keyboard status
0CH	Clear keyboard buffer and do function # in AL
0DH	Disk reset
0EH	Select disk
0FH	Open file
10H	Close file
11H	Search for first entry
12H	Search for next entry
13H	Delete file
14H	Sequential read
15H	Sequential write
16H	Create file
17H	Rename file
19H	Current disk
1AH	Set disk transfer address
1BH	Allocation table address
21H	Random read
22H	Random write
23H	File size
24H	Set random record field
25H	Set interrupt vector
26H	Create a new program segment
27H	Random block read
28H	Random block write
29H	Parse filename
2AH	Get date
2BH	Set date
2CH	Get time
2DH	Set time

Figure 5.4 DOS Interrupt 21H Functions

manual. Rather than discussing each of these functions in detail, we'll do an example that uses some of them. In particular, the example uses the DOS diskette functions.

FILE CONTROL BLOCK

Before we can do that example, however, we need to consider a DOS data structure that is an essential part of the file system—the File Control Block (FCB). This structure is used for all file operations.

The File Control Block is the communication method between the user program and the DOS functions. Every file action refers to the FCB. Figure 5.5 shows the layout of the standard FCB. There is a variation of the FCB, known as the extended FCB, that is used in special situations. It is used to "hide" a file. A hidden file is write-protected. This means that a program cannot modify the file without first changing the FCB for the file. A hidden file does not appear in directory listings. Hiding a file is a simple method of protecting a file from a clumsy user. Our examples deal strictly with the standard FCB.

The fields of the FCB cover the file attributes. Drive number, file name, and extension form the identifier for the file. File size and date are file attributes that we have seen on the directory listing. The remaining fields—current block number, record size, relative record number, and random record number—position the file for reading and writing. The record size determines the size, in bytes, of the user-defined record. All reads and writes of the file take place on a

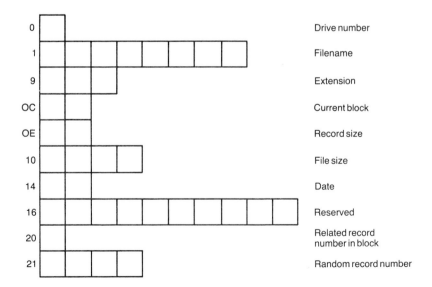

0	Drive number
1	Filename
9	Extension
OC	Current block
OE	Record size
10	File size
14	Date
16	Reserved
20	Related record number in block
21	Random record number

Figure 5.5 File Control Block

record boundary. The record size determines the amount of data handled by each operation.

There are two methods of positioning a file for record access. The first method, sequential, treats the records in order. The current block number and relative record number identify the next record to be accessed. As a program does a read or write operation, DOS increments the relative record number to point to the next record. Sequential operations proceed from the beginning to the end of a file. An assembly language program file is an example of a sequential file. The assembler reads records from beginning to end.

A program may also access a file as a random file. Random does not mean that a record is chosen randomly. Rather, it means that the program may select any record in the file as the next record. Another term for random file is direct file. The program can directly access any record.

A program can treat a file in either manner. For sequential operations, DOS automatically updates the relative record number field in the FCB. The program must supply a record number for random access of the file. A random file is the file system equivalent of a vector. Just as the program must supply an index to locate any element in a vector, the program must supply a record number to access a record in a random file.

We are now ready to look at the DOS functions and FCB in an example. Figure 5.6 is a long program that does little. The purpose of the program is to show the functions of DOS interrupt 21H and the use of the FCB. However, the operations performed in this program can be applied to a real problem.

```
The IBM Personal Computer Assembler 01-01-83            PAGE    1-1
Figure 5.6  DOS Function Example


1                                                PAGE    ,132
2                                                TITLE   Figure 5.6  DOS Function Example
3       0000                          CODE    SEGMENT
4       005C                                  ORG     05CH                              ; First FCB location
5       005C                          FCB     LABEL   BYTE                              ; Block label
6       005C   ??                     FCB_DRIVE       DB      ?                          ; Drive number
7       005D       08 [               FCB_NAME        DB      8 DUP(?)                   ; Name
8                      ??
9                          ]
10
11      0065       03 [               FCB_EXT         DB      3 DUP(?)                   ; Extension
12                     ??
13                         ]
14
15      0068   ????                   FCB_BLOCK       DW      ?                          ; Current block number
16      006A   ????                   FCB_RECORD_SIZE DW      ?                          ; Record size
17      006C   ????????               FCB_FILE_SIZE   DD      ?                          ; Total size of file
18      0070   ????                   FCB_DATE        DW      ?                          ; Date created
19      0072       0A [               FCB_RESV        DB      10 DUP(?)                  ; Reserved for DOS use
20                     ??
21                         ]
22
23      007C   ??                     FCB_CURRENT_RECORD  DB      ?                      ; Current record number
24      007D   ????????               FCB_RANDOM_RECORD   DD      ?                      ; Random record number
25      0090                                  ORG     090H
26      0090                          DISK_TRANSFER_ADDRESS    LABEL   BYTE             ; Data buffer area
27      0100                                  ORG     100H
28                                            ASSUME  CS:CODE, DS:CODE, ES:CODE
29      0100   E9 01B8 R                       JMP     PROGRAM_START                     ; Jump around messages
30
31      = 0020                         RECORD_SIZE     EQU     32                        ; Size of records
32      0103   03 00 00 00 00          KEYBOARD_BUFFER DB      3,0,0,0,0                 ; For buffered input
33      0108   46 69 6C 65 20 61       FILE_ERROR_MSG  DB      'File already exists',10,13,'$'
34             6C 72 65 61 64 79
35             20 65 78 69 73 74
36             73 0A 0D 24
37      011E   55 6E 61 62 6C 65       BAD_OPEN_MSG    DB      'Unable to open file',10,13,'$'
```

Figure 5.6   DOS Function Example

```
38              20 74 6F 20 6F 70
39              65 6E 20 66 69 6C
40              65 0A 0D 24
41      0134    45 72 72 6F 72 20    BAD_WRITE_MSG    DB      'Error in writing to file',10,13,'$'
42              69 6E 20 77 72 69
43              74 69 6E 67 20 74
44              6F 20 66 69 6C 65
45              0A 0D 24
46      014F    45 72 72 6F 72 20    BAD_READ_MSG     DB      'Error in reading file',10,13,'$'
47              69 6E 20 72 65 61
48              64 69 6E 67 20 66
49              69 6C 65 0A 0D 24
50      0167    45 72 72 6F 72 20    BAD_CLOSE_MSG    DB      'Error in closing file',10,13,'$'
51              69 6E 20 63 6C 6F
52              73 69 6E 67 20 66
53              69 6C 65 0A 0D 24
54      017F    54 77 6F 20 63 68    INPUT_BAD_MSG    DB      'Two character input required',10,13,'$'
55              61 72 61 63 74 65
56              72 20 69 6E 70 75
57              74 20 72 65 71 75
58              69 72 65 64 0A 0D
59              24
60      019E    45 6E 74 72 79 20    CHAR_BAD_MSG     DB      'Entry must be char|char',10,13,'$'
61              6D 75 73 74 20 62
62              65 20 63 68 61 72
63              7C 63 68 61 72 0A
64              0D 24
65
66                                   ;----- Set Disk Transfer Address
67
68      01B8                         PROGRAM_START:
69      01B8    B4 1A                        MOV     AH,1AH                          ; Set disk transfer address
70      01BA    BA 0090 R                    MOV     DX,OFFSET DISK_TRANSFER_ADDRESS
71      01BD    CD 21                        INT     21H
72
73                                   ;----- Search for similar file
74
75      01BF    B4 11                        MOV     AH,11H                          ; Do a search for entry
76      01C1    BA 005C R                    MOV     DX,OFFSET FCB                   ;   to see if a file with
77      01C4    CD 21                        INT     21H                            ;   this name already exists
78      01C6    0A C0                        OR      AL,AL
79      01C8    75 09                        JNZ     NO_FILE                        ; Jump if this is new name
80      01CA    BA 0108 R                    MOV     DX,OFFSET FILE_ERROR_MSG       ; Identical file error msg
81      01CD                         ERROR_EXIT:
82      01CD    B4 09                        MOV     AH,9                           ; This routine will display
83      01CF    CD 21                        INT     21H                            ;   the string and exit
84      01D1    CD 20                        INT     20H                            ;   from the program
85
86                                   ;----- Create the file
87
88      01D3                         NO_FILE:
89      01D3    B4 16                        MOV     AH,16H                         ; Create the file
90      01D5    BA 005C R                    MOV     DX,OFFSET FCB
91      01D8    CD 21                        INT     21H
92      01DA    0A C0                        OR      AL,AL                          ; Test for success
93      01DC    74 05                        JZ      CREATE_OK
94      01DE    BA 011E R                    MOV     DX,OFFSET BAD_OPEN_MSG         ; Create failed error msg
95      01E1    EB EA                        JMP     ERROR_EXIT
96
97                                   ;----- Set up the FCB parameters
98
99      01E3                         CREATE_OK:
100     01E3    C6 06 007C R 00              MOV     FCB_CURRENT_RECORD,0           ; Initialize current record
101     01E8    C7 06 007D R 0000            MOV     WORD PTR FCB_RANDOM_RECORD,0   ;   and random record fields
102     01EE    C7 06 007F R 0000            MOV     WORD PTR FCB_RANDOM_RECORD+2,0
103     01F4    C7 06 006A R 0020            MOV     WORD PTR FCB_RECORD_SIZE,RECORD_SIZE   ; Set record size
104
105                                  ;----- Write out the original file
106                                                                                 ; This loop will write
107     01FA    B0 41                        MOV     AL,'A'                         ;   out the letters
108     01FC                         CHARACTER_LOOP:                                ;   of the alphabet
109     01FC    BF 0090 R                    MOV     DI,OFFSET DISK_TRANSFER_ADDRESS
110     01FF    B9 0020                      MOV     CX,RECORD_SIZE
111     0202    F3/ AA                       REP     STOSB                          ; Fill data area with chars
112     0204    50                           PUSH    AX                             ; Save the character
113     0205    BA 005C R                    MOV     DX,OFFSET FCB
114     0208    B4 15                        MOV     AH,15H                         ; Sequential write of this
115     020A    CD 21                        INT     21H                            ;   character block
116     020C    0A C0                        OR      AL,AL                          ; Test for successful write
117     020E    58                           POP     AX                             ; Recover character
118     020F    74 05                        JZ      WRITE_OK
119     0211    BA 0134 R                    MOV     DX,OFFSET BAD_WRITE_MSG        ; Write failed error msg
120     0214    EB B7                        JMP     ERROR_EXIT
121     0216                         WRITE_OK:
122     0216    FE C0                        INC     AL                             ; Move to next character
123     0218    3C 5B                        CMP     AL,'Z'+1                       ; Wrote last character?
124     021A    75 E0                        JNE     CHARACTER_LOOP                 ; Write the next character
125
126                                  ;-----Inquiry/update section
127
128     021C                         KEYBOARD_LOOP:                                 ; This loop will accept
129     021C    BA 0103 R                    MOV     DX,OFFSET KEYBOARD_BUFFER      ;   input and modify the
130     021F    B4 0A                        MOV     AH,0AH                         ;   file
131     0221    CD 21                        INT     21H                            ; Buffered keyboard input
```

Figure 5.6 *Continued*

```
132   0223  80 3E 0104 R 02          CMP     KEYBOARD_BUFFER+1,2        ; Were two characters read?
133   0228  74 09                    JE      KEY_INPUT_OK
134   022A  BA 017F R                MOV     DX,OFFSET INPUT_BAD_MSG    ; Input error msg
135   022D                   KEYBOARD_ERROR:
136   022D  B4 09                    MOV     AH,9
137   022F  CD 21                    INT     21H                        ; Print bad input message
138   0231  EB E9                    JMP     KEYBOARD_LOOP              ; Go back for more kb input
139   0233                   KEY_INPUT_OK:
140   0233  BA 019E R                MOV     DX,OFFSET CHAR_BAD_MSG     ; Set up pointer in case
141   0236  A0 0105 R                MOV     AL,KEYBOARD_BUFFER+2       ; Get first keystroke
142   0239  3C 24                    CMP     AL,'$'                     ; Test for exit character
143   023B  75 03                    JNE     CHANGE_RECORD             ; Change record if not
144   023D  EB 55 90                 JMP     PROGRAM_EXIT
145
146                         ;----- Read the old record
147
148   0240                   CHANGE_RECORD:
149   0240  3C 41                    CMP     AL,'A'                     ; Test character to be in
150   0242  7C E9                    JL      KEYBOARD_ERROR            ;   range 'A' - 'Z'
151   0244  3C 5A                    CMP     AL,'Z'
152   0246  77 E5                    JA      KEYBOARD_ERROR
153   0248  2A E4                    SUB     AH,AH                      ; Convert the character to
154   024A  2C 41                    SUB     AL,'A'                     ;   a record index
155   024C  A3 007D R                MOV     WORD PTR FCB_RANDOM_RECORD,AX ; Store in FCB
156   024F  BA 005C R                MOV     DX,OFFSET FCB
157   0252  B4 21                    MOV     AH,21H                     ; Random read of the record
158   0254  CD 21                    INT     21H
159   0256  0A C0                    OR      AL,AL                      ; Test for error
160   0258  74 06                    JE      RANDOM_READ_OK
161   025A  BA 014F R                MOV     DX,OFFSET BAD_READ_MSG     ; Read failed error msg
162   025D  E9 01CD R                JMP     ERROR_EXIT
163
164                         ;----- Display the old record
165
166   0260                   RANDOM_READ_OK:
167   0260  C6 06 00B0 R 0A          MOV     DISK_TRANSFER_ADDRESS+32,10 ; Put in carriage return,
168   0265  C6 06 00B1 R 0D          MOV     DISK_TRANSFER_ADDRESS+33,13 ;   line feed and string
169   026A  C6 06 00B2 R 24          MOV     DISK_TRANSFER_ADDRESS+34,'$' ;   terminator
170   026F  B4 09                    MOV     AH,9
171   0271  BA 0090 R                MOV     DX,OFFSET DISK_TRANSFER_ADDRESS
172   0274  CD 21                    INT     21H                        ; Display the record
173
174                         ;----- Update the record
175
176   0276  A0 0106 R                MOV     AL,KEYBOARD_BUFFER+3       ; Get the replacement
177   0279  B9 001F                  MOV     CX,RECORD_SIZE-1          ;   character
178   027C  BF 0091 R                MOV     DI,OFFSET DISK_TRANSFER_ADDRESS+1
179   027F  F3/ AA                   REP     STOSB                      ; Fill last 31 positions
180   0281  B4 22                    MOV     AH,22H
181   0283  BA 005C R                MOV     DX,OFFSET FCB
182   0286  CD 21                    INT     21H                        ; Random write new record
183   0288  0A C0                    OR      AL,AL                      ; Test for error
184   028A  74 06                    JZ      RANDOM_WRITE_OK
185   028C  BA 0134 R                MOV     DX,OFFSET BAD_WRITE_MSG    ; Write failed error message
186   028F  E9 01CD R                JMP     ERROR_EXIT
187   0292                   RANDOM_WRITE_OK:
188   0292  EB 88                    JMP     KEYBOARD_LOOP             ; Go back for another record
189
190                         ;----- End the program
191
192   0294                   PROGRAM_EXIT:
193   0294  B4 10                    MOV     AH,10H                     ; Close the file
194   0296  BA 005C R                MOV     DX,OFFSET FCB
195   0299  CD 21                    INT     21H
196   029B  0A C0                    OR      AL,AL                      ; Test for error
197   029D  74 06                    JZ      CLOSE_OK
198   029F  BA 0167 R                MOV     DX,OFFSET BAD_CLOSE_MSG    ; Close failed error msg
199   02A2  E9 01CD R                JMP     ERROR_EXIT
200   02A5                   CLOSE_OK:
201   02A5  CD 20                    INT     20H                        ; Exit to DOS
202   02A7             CODE    ENDS
203                            END
```

Figure 5.6 *Continued*

The example program consists of two sections. In the first part, it creates a file. The file contains 26 records of 32 bytes each. Each record has a single letter of the alphabet. Record 1 is "AAAA . . . A," record 2 is "BBBB . . . B," and so on. The file creation uses sequential techniques.

The second part of the example treats the file as a random file. In response to a user keyboard input, the program reads and displays one of the 26 records. The keyboard input also edits the record. The program changes the final 31 characters of the record to the value entered from the keyboard. The program exits when a "$" is entered from the keyboard.

This example simulates an inquiry data base. The first part creates the data base. The second phase handles random inquiries into the data base and editing of the data. Any real data base program would be much more complex than the example here, but the example shows the major file functions.

The program of Figure 5.6 is a .COM file. In the next section we'll talk about the differences between this file and the .EXE file. The use of a .COM file here allows us to use INT 20H for exit. For a .COM file, the program must begin at offset 100H in the segment. The first 100H bytes of the program segment are called the Program Segment Prefix (PSP), and contain some special fields for the use of the assembly language program.

The FCB is offset 05CH in the segment. The program uses this seemingly arbitrary location for a good reason. The DOS command line interpreter fills in this FCB. When the user invokes the program by entering its name, DOS parses the remainder of the command line for file names. It places the first file name following the command into an FCB at location 05CH. If a second file name appears on the command line, it is placed in an FCB at offset 06CH. Since this example deals with only one file, only the FCB at 05CH is used. The syntax for starting this program is

    A>FIG5-6 TEST.FIL

FIG5-6 is the name of the program. It actually appears on the diskette as FIG5-6.COM. The file TEST.FIL is the file that the program creates and later modifies. The command line interpreter takes the file name "TEST.FIL" and places it in the correct position in the FCB at 05CH. By making the file name a command line parameter, this program can create and modify any file. If we had chosen to include the file name as part of the assembly input, we could have worked with only a single file.

At offset 05CH the program has the structure of the FCB laid out. The label FCB identifies the first location. Each of the fields in the FCB has its own label and size, so that the program can treat them individually. For example, to set the record size, the program modifies the variable FCB_RECORD_SIZE.

At offset 080H there is another special field of the PSP. This area, 128 bytes large, is the default location for the Disk Transfer Area (DTA). DOS uses the DTA as the buffer area for file records. Whenever DOS reads or writes a record, it uses the DTA buffer. DOS initializes the DTA to offset 080H of the program segment. The program may change it by using function 1AH of interrupt 21H. If the record size is greater than 128 bytes, it must be changed. This example moves the Disk Transfer Area offset 90H in the segment. This is necessary because the FCB at 05CH extends through location 80H. If the default DTA were used, the file transfer would destroy the last byte of the FCB. Since this byte contains a value for the random record number, and this program uses random I/O, it is necessary to avoid this collision.

The first instruction of the program, at offset 100H, is a jump to the real beginning of the program. This may seem inefficient, but the assembler does a much better job of assembly if all data areas appear before the instructions that reference them. In fact, the program may have errors if it makes forward data references. For safety's sake, the data area appears at the beginning of the program.

The first section of the program sets the Disk Transfer Area. This program uses the buffer at offset 90H. Since the record size is only 32 bytes, there is plenty of room before the beginning of the program.

Next, the code uses an interrupt 21H function to search for a file with the name in the FCB. Note that DS:DX points to the FCB, as they will for every file operation. If DOS finds a file with a matching name, the program exits with an error message, rather than destroying the already existing file. This example will work only on a new file, and can't use one that already exists. This test ensures that the program doesn't destroy an existing file. Of course, if this were a real program, we would probably arrange it to work with both new and existing files.

At NO_FILE, the program creates the file. Because the command processor set up the FCB, this program didn't have to fix it up before the create function. If the operation fails for some reason, such as no directory space or no room on the diskette, the program exits with a different error message.

Whenever DOS accesses a file, the program must first open the file. The open operation establishes a link between the operating system and the user program. During the open, DOS searches the diskette directory, finds the file (or perhaps not, an error condition), and sets the field of the FCB relating to file size. Once DOS has opened the file, it doesn't need to search the directory every time it accesses the file. DOS retains the file linkage information in the FCB until it "closes" the file. With the terms "open" and "close" you can see again the influence of traditional paper handling. The file folder must be opened before the records can be read. The file folder is closed before it is put away back in the cabinet.

This example opens the file by creating it. If the file had already existed, an open function (AH=0FH) would have established the link. After this example successfully opens the file, it changes some of the fields in the FCB. In particular, it must set the record size to 32 bytes, since DOS sets a default record size of 128 bytes.

The CHARACTER_LOOP section of the code writes the 26 records to the file. A REP STOSB fills the DTA buffer with the character for that record. A sequential write function (AH=0AH) writes the individual records. The program checks for errors also.

At KEYBOARD_LOOP, the nature of the program changes from creation to inquiry/update. The example uses buffered keyboard input provided by DOS. This function lets the user enter the two-character string and edit the input if necessary. The two-character input must be terminated with a return key. The program checks the input for validity, and rejects it with an error message if it doesn't meet the input requirements.

If the user enters a "$," the program jumps to the exit. However, for a character between "A" and "Z," the program reads the record corresponding to that character. The record is displayed, showing the current contents. The code fills the final 31 bytes of the buffer with the second character entered at the keyboard. It writes the modified record using a random write.

The final section of the program closes the file. Just as the file open established the link between DOS and the user program, the close function severs that link. An important reason for closing a file is to make sure that DOS writes all of the modified records onto the diskette. During normal program execution, DOS may leave the last several records in a buffer. This speeds execution since DOS doesn't need to write the diskette for every record. The close function writes out the contents of the buffer to the diskette.

The example of Figure 5.6 shows the basic components of file access using DOS. The program does nothing useful, but to flesh it out would require many more instructions. Those instructions would show very little in DOS function usage. An important thing to notice in this example is the necessity of checking for errors following every DOS operation. While DOS handles media errors, using interrupt 24H, the application must handle problems such as identical file names or out of space on the diskette. The error philosophy in the example is very simple—write a message and exit. In real programs, the error handling is more complex and much more necessary. The loss of valuable data must be avoided.

Finally, if you execute the example program, you probably won't be very happy with the user considerations. There is no prompt for user input, the error messages are cryptic, and some of the messages end up writing on top of the previous message, obliterating it. The program requires more work before it would be usable by someone who didn't write the program or study the code very carefully.

.COM AND .EXE FILES

The preceding example was a .COM file. However, the natural output of the assembly/link process is an .EXE file. Why bother with .COM if .EXE is easier?

Each of the file types has its advantages. We need to understand the differences between them to make a reasonable decision about which to choose in each instance.

The primary difference between .COM and .EXE files is the object file format on the diskette. Both file types are machine language programs. The .COM file is ready to run. DOS can load it directly from the diskette into memory. DOS then passes control to offset 100H in the segment set aside for the program. The .EXE file is not immediately ready to run. The object file on the diskette has a header field. This header contains information created by the linker. The most noticeable of this is relocation information. While a .COM file is code segment relocatable, the .EXE file may be relocated in many different segments. This limits the .COM file to a maximum size of 64K bytes, unless the program loads the other segments in the program. An .EXE file may contain multiple segments that are dynamically relocated in the program space.

What is relocatability? When a program is assembled, it is located at a specific place in memory. As we have seen, the assembler automatically starts each segment at offset 0. In the assembly listings, there are "R" symbols next to some addresses. This indicates that the address is relocatable. If the program is moved so that it starts at a location other than offset 0, that location must be modified. Normally, the linker handles the relocation. But some addresses can't be relocated until the program is loaded. An .EXE file contains the data that identify those locations.

The .COM file is not relocatable. It does not have relocation information in a program header. Instead, the .COM program must be "code segment relocatable." This means that the program is always loaded at the same offset, while the code segment may be modified. All offsets in the program remain the same. It also requires that the programmer ensure that any segment register arithmetic (such as setting an immediate value into a segment register) is always referenced to the current code segment register. For example, to set the DS register to the current code segment value, the correct program sequence is

```
PUSH    CS
POP     DS
```

It is sometimes tempting to write the following code to do the same job, assuming that the instruction segment is named "CODE," as in Figure 5.6.

```
MOV     AX,CODE
MOV     DS,AX
```

This example doesn't work correctly in a .COM program. The segment value for the segment CODE isn't known at assembly or link time. It's only known when the program is loaded. Since the .COM file can't tell the loader where all these segment references occur (the relocation information), the program will execute incorrectly.

The setting of the segment registers and stack location differs between the two file types. For a .COM file, DOS sets the CS, DS, ES, and SS registers to the segment in which it loads the program. It sets the SP register to point to the last available memory location in the segment. Thus, the program takes up the first part of the segment, and the stack the last part.

The .EXE file header specifies the values for the CS, IP, SS, and SP registers. DOS sets the DS and ES registers to point to the segment in which it loads the program. The CS register points to the segment identified as the one containing the starting location of the program. While a .COM program must start at offset 100H of the program segment, an .EXE program may specify a different starting location. The assembly END statement may contain an address value, as shown here:

```
END     START_LOCATION
```

This tells the assembler/linker to pass control to START_LOCATION when the program is loaded.

Both file types use the Program Segment Prefix (PSP). This is the first 100H bytes of the segment in which the program is loaded. This area contains the special fields that we saw in Figure 5.6. For an .EXE file, the DS and ES registers point to that data area, while CS and SS are set by the assembly/link steps. For the .COM file, all the registers point to the PSP. This gives both types immediate access to the data in the PSP.

The advantage of the .COM file is that the CS register identifies the PSP. In an .EXE file, the CS register does not. The DOS program exits, interrupts 20H and 27H, require that the CS register point to the PSP when the interrupt is executed. With an .EXE file, this is difficult to do. Fortunately, the following instruction sequence allows an .EXE program to exit back to DOS.

```
PROGRAM       PROC    FAR
              PUSH    DS          ; Save segment of PSP
              MOV     AX,0
              PUSH    AX          ; Save offset of 0 on stack
              . . .
              RET
PROGRAM       ENDP
```

Offset 0 of the PSP contains an INT 20H instruction. The PUSH of DS and a 0 establishes a far return address to offset 0 of the PSP. When the program executes the return, it goes to the INT 20H instruction. But the CS register now has the value of the PSP, and the INT 20H returns control to DOS.

There is no comparable way to do an interrupt 27H function—exit to DOS but leave the program resident. Although there are ways to get the CS register set correctly before doing the INT 27H, it is usually easier to structure the program as a .COM file.

Finally, the .COM file requires less diskette space than an .EXE file with the same program. Since the .COM file has no program header, the space for it is not required. When we discuss the DEBUG program in the next section, we'll cover a method that lets you convert an .EXE file to a .COM file.

CREATING AN ASSEMBLY LANGUAGE PROGRAM

There are several steps on the path from the idea to an executing program. This section discusses those steps related to creating an assembly language program for the IBM Personal Computer. This section discusses the line editor, the assembler, the linker, and the debugger. The editor creates the assembly language source programs. The assembler converts the source language to object code, which is very similar to machine language. The linker changes the object code into an .EXE file, ready for execution. Finally, the debug program can help find the errors in the program.

DOS LINE EDITOR

The line editor creates text files. The contents of a text file are in ASCII representation. The editor lets you type in the text you want in the file. When you need to modify the text later, you use the editor again.

The Line Editor (EDLIN) is part of the IBM Personal Computer Disk Operating System. The file EDLIN.COM is a transient command—that is, it is loaded into memory only when requested. To run the editor, the command is

A>EDLIN FILE.ASM

where FILE.ASM is the text file to be edited. FILE.ASM may already exist, as it will if you modify an existing program. If FILE.ASM does not already exist, EDLIN creates it. When the editing is complete, the finished results are placed in the file FILE.ASM. If EDLIN didn't create FILE.ASM for this editing session, it renames the old version of FILE.ASM to FILE.BAK (for backup). By creating a backup, you can recover from any major errors in editing the file by using the backup file. You discard the file with editing errors, and rename the .BAK file to the .ASM file. This is the safety net for editing.

EDLIN is a line-oriented editor. It handles each line of text separately. This is in contrast to a full screen editor, which displays a section of the edited file on the screen. In a full screen editor, such as the IBM Personal Editor, you move the cursor to any location on the screen, and modify the text there. With EDLIN, you edit only a single line of the text file at a time. If you intend to do any serious assembly language programming, you should use a full-screen text editor. IBM offers a very good full-screen editor as the Personal Editor. The examples in this book were prepared using that editor. This book discusses only EDLIN, since it's distributed with DOS. But because EDLIN isn't the best choice, we'll cover EDLIN with only a brief mention of the commands, and an example. You should refer to the DOS manual for a complete explanation of the EDLIN commands.

Figure 5.7 summarizes the EDLIN commands. As we go through the example, we'll refer to these commands.

Figure 5.8 shows two example editing sessions using EDLIN. The first part

Action	Syntax
Append lines	[n] A
Delete lines	[line] [,line] D
Edit line	[line]
End edit	E
Insert lines	[line] I
List lines	[line] [,line] L
Quit edit	Q
Replace text	[line] [,line] [?] Rstring [<F6>string]
Search text	[line] [,line] [?] Sstring
Write lines	[n] W

Figure 5.7   EDLIN Commands (Courtesy of IBM; Copyright IBM 1981)

```
A>EDLIN FIG5-8.ASM
New file
*I
        1:*         PAGE      ,132
        2:*CODE     SEGMENT
        3:*         ASSUME    CS:CODE
        4:*
        5:*START:   PROC      NEAR
        6:*         MOV       AX,CODE
        7:*         MOV       DS,AX
        8:*         RET
        9:*START    ENDP
       10:*END
       11:*^C
*E
A>
A>EDLIN FIG5-8.ASM
End of input file
*L
        1:*         PAGE      ,132
        2: CODE     SEGMENT
        3:          ASSUME    CS:CODE
        4:
        5: START:   PROC      NEAR
        6:          MOV       AX,CODE
        7:          MOV       DS,AX
        8:          RET
        9:
       10: START    ENDP
       11: END
*3
        3:*         ASSUME    CS:CODE
        3:*         ASSUME    CS:CODE,DS:CODE
*5
        5:*START:             PROC      NEAR
        5:*START    PROC      NEAR
*6
        6:*         MOV       AX,CODE
        6:*         MOV       AX,CS
*9I
        9:*
       10:*^C
*L
        1:          PAGE,132
        2: CODE     SEGMENT
        3:          ASSUME    CS:CODE,DS:CODE
        4:
        5: START    PROC      NEAR
        6:          MOV       AX,CS
```

Figure 5.8 EDLIN Example

```
           7:          MOV      DS,AX
           8:          RET
           9:
          10:*START    ENDP
          11: END
   *E
   A>
```

Figure 5.8 *Continued*

creates a file called FIG5-8.ASM. The "New file" indicates that the file did not already exist. The symbol "*" is the EDLIN prompt. Whenever this symbol appears, you may enter any of the commands from Figure 5.7. The "I" command lets you insert text into the file. EDLIN displays the line numbers of each line as you enter the text. Control-C (^C on the listing) terminates the insert portion. The "E" ends the editing session, saves the file, and returns control to DOS.

The second part of Figure 5.8 edits the file created in the first part. You invoke the editor with the same command line, but the phrase "End of input file" indicates that the file already exists. The "L" command lists the file as it currently exists. The example uses single line editing commands to modify several of the lines. Entering a "3" displays the third line, and leaves it available for editing. DOS has a set of line editing commands built in, and Figure 5.9 shows them. You can use these editing operations in EDLIN, or anytime DOS is handling the keyboard input. In particular, you can use these commands for the command processor input.

Let's go back to the example in Figure 5.8. After displaying the line with its line number, you can edit the line with the DOS commands. The F3 key redisplays the line and allows you to enter the changes at the end. Line 5 editing shows the use of the DEL key to remove the ":" from the label. Line 6 editing uses the → key (cursor right) to position the cursor following the ",". The new value, "CS," is then typed in, replacing the "CODE." The example does an insert preceding line 9—a blank line for appearance. The example lists the file again so that you can see the editing changes. The End edit command returns control to DOS.

There are other things you can do with EDLIN and the DOS editing

```
   DEL—Delete the next character in the retained line
   ESC—Cancel any editing on the retained line
   F1 or ->—Copy one character from retained line
   F2—Copy all characters up to a specified character
   F3—Copy all remaining characters to the screen
   F4—Skip all characters to a specified character
   F5—Accept edited line for continued editing
   INS—Insert characters into line (until insert hit again)
```

Figure 5.9 DOS Editing Keys, (Courtesy of IBM; Copyright IBM 1981)

commands. The best way to learn them is to look through the DOS manual and then try lots of them. However, you should consider a full-screen editor for serious programming work.

ASSEMBLER AND MACRO ASSEMBLER

Now that you've created the source file, it's time to use the assembler. There are two versions of the assembler. The full version is the Macro Assembler, or MASM.EXE on the assembler diskette. There is also a smaller version of the assembler, without macro capability, called the Assembler, or ASM.EXE. MASM requires 96K bytes of storage to run effectively, while ASM can execute with only 64K bytes. These sizes have nothing to do with the size of the source program. They refer to the amount of storage required to assemble the program, not to execute the final program. A user program that may require only 4K bytes to execute needs a machine with at least 64K to develop the program.

The input to the assembler is the source file created by EDLIN or a similar editor. The source file is an ASCII text file. The assembler produces up to three output files. The object file is the machine language version of the program. The object file is not quite ready to execute, but it's close to the actual machine language. The listing file is an ASCII text file which contains the source information as well as assembler-generated information. The examples in this book are assembler listing files. Finally, the assembler may produce a cross-reference file. This file, which is neither a machine language nor a text file, contains information about the usage of symbols and labels in the assembly program. Like the object file, the cross-reference file requires further processing before you can use it.

The assembler is started with a DOS command. Either

    A>ASM

or

    A>MASM

starts the assembler. ASM starts the small assembler; MASM invokes the macro assembler. After the assembler starts executing, it asks questions to determine which files to use in this assembly. Figure 5.10 shows the sequence of commands that gets the assembler started.

Following the command ASM, DOS loads the assembler into storage. The assembler displays the copyright message and begins asking questions. If you have a system with a single diskette drive, you can remove the assembler diskette at this time, and insert the data diskette. The assembler prompts for the file to be assembled. You only have to enter the file name, not the .ASM extension. The assembler also asks for the names of the output files. The assembler gives the object file the same name as the source, with an .OBJ extension, unless you

```
A>ASM
The IBM Personal Computer Assembler
Version 1.00 (C)Copyright IBM Corp 1981

Source filename [.ASM]: B:FIG5-10
Object filename [FIG5-10.OBJ] B:
Source listing   [NUL.LST] B:
Cross reference [NUL.CRF] B:

Warning Severe
Errors   Errors
0        0

A>DIR B:FIG5-10.*
FIG5-10   ASM        44      1-01-83   12:00a
FIG5-10   LST        426     1-01-83   12:00a
FIG5-10   OBJ        40      1-01-83   12:00a
FIG5-10   CRF        19      1-01-83   12:00a

A>
A>B:
B>A:ASM FIG5-10,,,;
The IBM Personal Computer Assembler
Version 1.00 (C) Copyright IBM Corp 1981

Warning  Severe
Errors   Errors
0        0

B>
```

Figure 5.10   Assembler Execution

choose a different name. The "B:" response in this example tells the assembler to place the object file on the B: drive. Similar responses to the listing and cross-reference prompts tell the assembler to put those files on the B: drive. Following the assembly, the directory listing shows the files, all on the B: drive, that the assembly created.

The prompts all have defaults, and they are indicated in the brackets. If you respond with a return to any of these prompts, the assembler uses the default value. The default value for the listing and the cross-reference files is NUL. The NUL file is a special file in DOS. Anything written to the NUL file is thrown away and can't be recovered. The NUL file is a WOF (write-only file).

If the assembler detects any errors during the assembly, it writes them on the listing file. It also shows them on the display. This allows you to respond directly to any errors detected. You don't have to scan the listing file for the errors. If you execute the small assembler, ASM, it reports errors with only an error number. The macro assembler, MASM, shows the error number and the error message. The smaller size of the assembler doesn't leave room for the text error message.

The second portion of Figure 5.10 shows a simpler method of invoking the macro assembler. This method is convenient when the system you are using has two diskette drives. Place the assembler diskette in the A: drive, the data diskette containing the source file in the B: drive. Set the B: drive as the default drive. Invoke the assembler with the A:ASM command. The rest of the command, FIG5-10,,,; tells the assembler all of the information that it requested in the prompts of the previous example. FIG5-10 names the file to assemble, while the successive commas tell the assembler to generate object, listing, and cross-reference files according to the standard naming conventions. This method of assembling produces results identical to those of the first example.

There are many variations in the way that you can give the file names to the assembler. The two examples here show two extremes. The first example specified every file name in response to a prompt. In the second, no prompting was necessary. The Macro Assembler reference manual describes, in much more detail, the different variations possible with the ASM (or the MASM) command.

When the assembly completes, the output files are ready for use. The object file is an input for the next step in the creation of executable machine language. This is the LINK step, covered in the next section.

The listing file is the combination of the source file and a readable version of the machine language. You can display this file with the DOS TYPE command, such as

   A>TYPE B:FIG5-11.LST

The TYPE command takes the contents of the file and sends them to the display. You can print the file at the same time by depressing Control-PRTSC before issuing the TYPE command. The Control PRTSC tells DOS to transmit everything to both the screen and to the printer. The result is that the listing appears on both the screen and on the printer. You should specify that the listing be created 132 columns wide. You do this with the assembler PAGE command, which you can see in nearly all of the example programs. The command

   PAGE   ,132

tells the assembler to make the listing file 132 characters wide. You must also set the printer column width before printing. You can do this with the DOS MODE command.

   A>MODE LPT1:132

This command sets the IBM Printer into the 132-column mode. This prints the listing file without the line wrapping that you'll see on the display.

Symbol Table

The listing file contains additional information that has not been shown in the book thus far. Following the listing of the program, the symbol table appears. An

```
The IBM Personal Computer Assembler 01-01-83            PAGE    Symbols-1
Figure 5.6  DOS Function Example


Segments and groups:

                    N a m e                Size   align   combine class

CODE . . . . . . . . . . . . .             02A7   PARA    NONE

Symbols:

                    N a m e                Type   Value   Attr

BAD_CLOSE_MSG. . . . . . . . . .           L BYTE 0167    CODE
BAD_OPEN_MSG . . . . . . . . . .           L BYTE 011E    CODE
BAD_READ_MSG . . . . . . . . . .           L BYTE 014F    CODE
BAD_WRITE_MSG. . . . . . . . . .           L BYTE 0134    CODE
CHANGE_RECORD. . . . . . . . . .           L NEAR 0240    CODE
CHARACTER_LOOP . . . . . . . . .           L NEAR 01FC    CODE
CHAR_BAD_MSG . . . . . . . . . .           L BYTE 019E    CODE
CLOSE_OK . . . . . . . . . . . .           L NEAR 02A5    CODE
CREATE_OK. . . . . . . . . . . .           L NEAR 01E3    CODE
DISK_TRANSFER_ADDRESS. . . . . .           L BYTE 0090    CODE
ERROR_EXIT . . . . . . . . . . .           L NEAR 01CD    CODE
FCB. . . . . . . . . . . . . . .           L BYTE 005C    CODE
FCB_BLOCK. . . . . . . . . . . .           L WORD 0068    CODE
FCB_CURRENT_RECORD . . . . . . .           L BYTE 007C    CODE
FCB_DATE . . . . . . . . . . . .           L WORD 0070    CODE
FCB_DRIVE. . . . . . . . . . . .           L BYTE 005C    CODE
FCB_EXT. . . . . . . . . . . . .           L BYTE 0065    CODE   Length =0003
FCB_FILE_SIZE. . . . . . . . . .           L DWORD 006C   CODE
FCB_NAME . . . . . . . . . . . .           L BYTE 005D    CODE   Length =0008
FCB_RANDOM_RECORD. . . . . . . .           L DWORD 007D   CODE
FCB_RECORD_SIZE. . . . . . . . .           L WORD 006A    CODE
FCB_RESV . . . . . . . . . . . .           L BYTE 0072    CODE   Length =000A
FILE_ERROR_MSG . . . . . . . . .           L BYTE 0108    CODE
INPUT_BAD_MSG. . . . . . . . . .           L BYTE 017F    CODE
KEYBOARD_BUFFER. . . . . . . . .           L BYTE 0103    CODE
KEYBOARD_ERROR . . . . . . . . .           L NEAR 022D    CODE
KEYBOARD_LOOP. . . . . . . . . .           L NEAR 021C    CODE
KEY_INPUT_OK . . . . . . . . . .           L NEAR 0233    CODE
NO_FILE. . . . . . . . . . . . .           L NEAR 01D3    CODE
PROGRAM_EXIT . . . . . . . . . .           L NEAR 0294    CODE
PROGRAM_START. . . . . . . . . .           L NEAR 01B8    CODE
RANDOM_READ_OK . . . . . . . . .           L NEAR 0260    CODE
RANDOM_WRITE_OK. . . . . . . . .           L NEAR 0292    CODE
RECORD_SIZE. . . . . . . . . . .           Number 0020
WRITE_OK . . . . . . . . . . . .           L NEAR 0216    CODE

Warning Severe
Errors  Errors
0       0
```

Figure 5.11   Symbol Table for Figure 5.6 Program

example is shown in Figure 5.11. This is the symbol table for the program of Figure 5.6. The symbol table shows all of the symbols defined in the program. Also, it identifies the attributes of each. Since the assembler is strongly typed, it maintains this information and presents it in the listing file for your use. Symbols are identified as labels, variables, or numbers. The tables give values when known. For any data structure, it also displays the length.

Cross-Reference

The cross-reference file produced by the assembler is not quite ready for use. You must execute the CREF program to change the .CRF file into an ASCII text file. You invoke the CREF program just like the assembler, except that you specify only two files: the input file, with a .CRF extension, and an output file, with a .REF extension. If you enter the DOS command A>CREF, you are prompted for the two filenames. Alternatively, the command A>CREF B:FIG5-10,B: takes as input the file B:FIG5-10.CRF and produces the output file B:FIG5-10.REF. As

```
Figure 5.6  DOS Function Example

Symbol Cross Reference                        (# is definition)       Cref-1

BAD_CLOSE_MSG. . . . . . . . . .      50#    169
BAD_OPEN_MSG . . . . . . . . . .      37#     86
BAD_READ_MSG . . . . . . . . . .      46#    141
BAD_WRITE_MSG. . . . . . . . . .      41#    105    159

CHANGE_RECORD. . . . . . . . . .     126    128#
CHARACTER_LOOP . . . . . . . . .      94#   110
CHAR_BAD_MSG . . . . . . . . . .      60#   123
CLOSE_OK . . . . . . . . . . . .     168    171#
CODE . . . . . . . . . . . . . .       3#    28     28     28    173
CREATE_OK. . . . . . . . . . . .      85     88#

DISK_TRANSFER_ADDRESS. . . . . .      26#    68     95    144    145    146    148    152

ERROR_EXIT . . . . . . . . . . .      76#    87    106    142    160    170

FCB. . . . . . . . . . . . . . .       5#    71     82     99    136    155    165
FCB_BLOCK. . . . . . . . . . . .      15#
FCB_CURRENT_RECORD . . . . . . .      23#    89
FCB_DATE . . . . . . . . . . . .      18#
FCB_DRIVE. . . . . . . . . . . .       6#
FCB_EXT. . . . . . . . . . . . .      11#
FCB_FILE_SIZE. . . . . . . . . .      17#
FCB_NAME . . . . . . . . . . . .       7#
FCB_RANDOM_RECORD. . . . . . . .      24#    90     91    135
FCB_RECORD_SIZE. . . . . . . . .      16#    92
FCB_RESV . . . . . . . . . . . .      19#
FILE_ERROR_MSG . . . . . . . . .      33#    75

INPUT_BAD_MSG. . . . . . . . . .      54#   117

KEYBOARD_BUFFER. . . . . . . . .      32#   112    115    124    150
KEYBOARD_ERROR . . . . . . . . .     118#   130    132
KEYBOARD_LOOP. . . . . . . . . .     111#   121    162
KEY_INPUT_OK . . . . . . . . . .     116    122#

NO_FILE. . . . . . . . . . . . .      74     80#

PROGRAM_EXIT . . . . . . . . . .     127    163#
PROGRAM_START. . . . . . . . . .      29     66#

RANDOM_READ_OK . . . . . . . . .     140    143#
RANDOM_WRITE_OK. . . . . . . . .     158    161#
RECORD_SIZE. . . . . . . . . . .      31#    92     96    151
WRITE_OK . . . . . . . . . . . .     104    107#
```

Figure 5.12   Cross-Reference for Figure 5.6 Program

with the assembler, there are other variations that are described in the Macro Assembler Reference Manual.

Figure 5.12 shows the output of the cross-reference processor. This particular cross-reference map is from the program of Figure 5.6. The left column contains all of the symbol and variable names defined in the program. Across from each symbol is a series of integers. Each integer identifies the line number in which that symbol appears. If the line number is followed by a "#," the symbol is defined in that line number. If the "#" does not appear, the symbol is referenced in that line.

How can you use the cross-reference listing? The cross-reference lets you determine the user of each particular symbol. For example, if a variable is being set with an incorrect value, the cross-reference listing identifies every instruction that references that symbol by name. This should help identify the instructions that are causing the problem. Or perhaps you are modifying an existing program. This program was written by someone else, or written by you so long ago that you've forgotten how it works. If you want to change one of the subroutines, you must know what portions of the program are using that subroutine. The cross-reference listing shows every CALL instruction (or any other instruction, for that matter) that references that symbol. If you examine these calling locations, you can determine if the change is acceptable to all callers of the subroutine. The cross-reference makes the job of determining all of the referencing locations much simpler.

LINKER

The output of the assembler is not ready to execute. The object code produced by the assembler must be "linked" before it can be executed.

The LINK (LINK.EXE) program distributed on the DOS diskette actually performs two separate functions. It can link together many different object modules into a single program. The linker also builds an executable load module from the assembler object module. We'll examine these functions separately.

Multiple Modules

As the name indicates, the primary purpose of the LINK program is to "link," or join, several object modules into a single executable module. All of the examples so far have been single module programs. That is, all of the function was in a single source module. However, it is not always possible, or desirable, to do this.

There are several reasons why a program may be broken down into several modules. The first is size. A very large program becomes very unwieldy, difficult to edit, and time consuming to assemble. Suppose that you make a mistake on a single line of a 5000-line assembly language program. You have to edit the entire program to change that one line. You then have to assemble the entire 5000-line program, which takes a fair amount of time. After a relatively short LINK step, the program is ready to run.

Suppose that instead of a 5000-line program, you break the program up into 10 program modules, each of which is about 500 lines long. To edit a single line, you only have a 500-line source file to edit. The assembly of the 500-line program is much more rapid than that of the 5000-line program. The LINK step is still relatively quick, certainly when compared to the assembly of the large program. Trimming the size of the individual modules lets the edit/assembly process proceed more quickly.

Another reason for breaking the program into smaller modules is ownership. For a large programming project, there is usually more than one person engaged in the effort. If there is a single source file, the individual programmers have to take turns working on it. This approach quickly becomes unwieldy.

The final reason for making modular programs is reusability. When you write a program, you probably use a number of subroutines. If you have done a good job, each of these subroutines performs a specific function, with a well-documented input and output specification. The time will come, later, when you are writing another program. You'll want to use that same subroutine as part of the new program. If that subroutine is a separate program module, there is no problem linking it into the new program. If you haven't made it into a separate module, you'll have to edit it out of the original routine and insert it into the new program. After you try this once or twice, you'll probably wish there were an easier way.

To break a program up into modules requires that you, the programmer, do several things. You must carefully design your program, breaking it up into smaller components. You must define the parameters for both input and output of these smaller routines. Finally, you must be able to communicate between the program modules. The first two jobs are a basic part of programming, and we won't discuss them here. The last job is part of the assembler and linker, and we'll look at how it works.

If you have designed a program as several modules, the primary, or main, program must be able to call these subroutines. The CALL instruction does the job. It has a single operand, the label of the subroutine. In all of the examples so far, that subroutine has been part of the same program module, so the assembler knew exactly what address the subroutine would have at execution time. This lets the assembler determine the correct offset value for the address field of the instruction.

We now have the situation where the assembly of the subroutine is done separately from the assembly of the CALL instruction. This means that the assembler can't determine the correct address for the call. Since the assemblies of the subroutine and the main routine are done separately, there is no way that the assembler can figure out the correct value. However, the LINK program can handle this job. The link step does the address resolution. All of the program modules are part of the input to the LINK program, so that the linker knows where every subroutine will end up. The linker can then resolve those addresses that the assembler couldn't.

EXTRN and PUBLIC

The linker, however, can't do it all by itself. The programmer must tell the assembler which routines are accessed in another program module. This is done with a PUBLIC statement, telling the assembler that this symbol is available to other programs. Also, the programmer tells the assembler which labels are external to this program module. The assembly language statement to do this is EXTRN, for external. This statement declares the label to be external to the current assembly, so the assembler can handle the label correctly. The assembler flags this instruction so that the linker can find it later and insert the correct address.

The EXTRN statement serves two purposes. It tells the assembler that the named label is external to the current assembly. Now the assembler could assume that any label that it can't find during the assembly is external. This would work, but if you ever misspelled a label name, the assembler would assume that it was an external label, and there would be no error message. This defers the error message to the LINK step. At that point, you would learn about the misspelling. For most people, this is much later than they'd like to hear about it, especially something as simple as a misspelling. So the assembler indicates an error for any label that it can't match up.

The second reason for the EXTRN statement is to tell the assembler what kind of label it is. The assembler is strongly typed, so it needs to know what every symbol is. This lets it generate the correct instructions. For a data value, the EXTRN statement can indicate a byte, word, doubleword, or other type of construction. If the label is for a subroutine or some other program label, the label can be either NEAR or FAR, depending on which segment the label is in. The EXTRN statement requires that the programmer indicate what kind of label it is. Since the assembler also manages the segment addressing of the program, the EXTRN statement indicates which segment the symbol appears in. Instead of making this part of the EXTRN syntax, it is determined by the placement of the EXTRN statement. The assembler assumes an external symbol to be in the segment in which the EXTRN statement for that symbol appears.

Figure 5.13 is a sample assembly program, showing the use of the EXTRN statement. In this example, there are two labels external to the program. There is a byte-size data variable, OUTPUT_CHARACTER. The ":BYTE" following the variable name is the way you specify the variable attribute. The program label, OUTPUT_ROUTINE, is labeled NEAR to show that it is in the same segment. The program in Figure 5.13 references these names and the assembler knows the

```
The IBM Personal Computer Assembler 01-01-83        PAGE    1-1
Figure 5.13  Main routine

 1                                             PAGE    ,132
 2                                             TITLE   Figure 5.13  Main routine
 3
 4       0000                          STACK   SEGMENT STACK
 5       0000      40 [                         DW      64 DUP(?)                    ; Allocate space for the stack
 6                      ????
 7                           ]
 8
 9       0080                          STACK   ENDS
10
11       0000                          CODE    SEGMENT PUBLIC
12
13                                             EXTRN   OUTPUT_ROUTINE:NEAR, OUTPUT_CHARACTER:BYTE
14
15                                             ASSUME  CS:CODE
16
17       0000                          START   PROC    FAR
18
19       0000   1E                             PUSH    DS                           ; Segment of return address
20       0001   B8 0000                        MOV     AX,0                         ; Establish return address
21       0004   50                             PUSH    AX                           ; Offset of return
22       0005   FC                             CLD                                  ; Ensure correct direction
23       0006   8C C8                          MOV     AX,CS                        ; Establish segment addressing
24       0008   8E D8                          MOV     DS,AX
25                                             ASSUME  DS:CODE                      ; Indicate new segment addressing
26       000A   BE 001C R                      MOV     SI,OFFSET MESSAGE            ; Address of message string
27       000D                         LOOP:
28       000D   AC                             LODSB                               ; Get the next byte of the message
29       000E   A2 0000 E                       MOV     OUTPUT_CHARACTER,AL         ; Store in memory location
30       0011   E8 0000 E                       CALL    OUTPUT_ROUTINE              ; Output the character
31       0014   80 3E 0000 E 0A                CMP     OUTPUT_CHARACTER,10          ; Look for ending character
32       0019   75 F2                          JNE     LOOP                         ; Loop if not
33
34       001B   CB                             RET                                  ; Return to DOS
35
36       001C   54 68 69 73 20 69    MESSAGE DB       'This is a test',13,10
37              73 20 61 20 74 65
38              73 74 0D 0A
39
40       002C                         START   ENDP
41       002C                         CODE    ENDS
42                                             END     START
```

Figure 5.13 Main Routine

```
The IBM Personal Computer Assembler 01-01-83              PAGE   1-1
Figure 5.14  Output subroutine

 1                                            PAGE    ,132
 2                                            TITLE   Figure 5.14  Output subroutine
 3
 4      0000                          CODE    SEGMENT PUBLIC
 5
 6                                            ASSUME  CS:CODE,DS:CODE ; This must be true when called
 7
 8                                            PUBLIC  OUTPUT_CHARACTER,OUTPUT_ROUTINE
 9
10      0000  ??                      OUTPUT_CHARACTER        DB      ?
11
12      0001                          OUTPUT_ROUTINE PROC    NEAR
13
14      0001  A0 0000 R                       MOV     AL,OUTPUT_CHARACTER     ; Get character to output
15      0004  B4 0E                           MOV     AH,14                   ; BIOS function
16      0006  BB 0000                         MOV     BX,0                    ; Set active page
17      0009  BA 0000                         MOV     DX,0                    ; BIOS parameters
18      000C  CD 10                           INT     10H                     ; Display routine
19      000E  C3                              RET                             ; Return to caller
20
21      000F                          OUTPUT_ROUTINE  ENDP
22      000F                          CODE    ENDS
23                                            END
```

Figure 5.14   Output Subroutine

correct instruction to generate. If the EXTRN statement wasn't there, the assembler would indicate errors. In the assembly listing you can see the "E" next to the address field of the instructions referencing the external symbols.

We now have to handle the other side of the problem. How does the linker know where the external symbols are located? Figure 5.14 shows the subroutine referenced in Figure 5.13. Those variables and program labels that another program can reference are declared PUBLIC. This means that any other program module may access those values. Any other variables and program labels in the program that are not named as PUBLIC can't be referenced by other programs. While this may seem inconvenient, there would be a different problem if all labels were PUBLIC. It would mean that every label in every module that you might link together must be unique. That is, you could never use the same name twice, even in separate modules. This might severely hamper the reusability of some subroutines, since they might be used years later. Remembering all the label names and ensuring that none were repeated would be a difficult task. Notice that the PUBLIC statement doesn't require attributes for the symbols. The normal assembler statements take care of that.

The LINK program matches up all the external symbols with their corresponding PUBLIC declarations. The linker then places the correct values into the instructions that reference external values. Each of those fields in the assembly listing with an "E" next to it is handled.

The linker also combines any segments with the same name. In our examples of Figures 5.13 and 5.14, the main routine and the subroutine are both in the segment named CODE. Since the EXTRN statement in the main routine said that the subroutine OUTPUT_ROUTINE was NEAR, it had better be in the same segment. The PUBLIC attribute on the SEGMENT statement tells the linker that the segment can be combined with other segments that have the same name. This lets the linker combine the two program modules into the same segment for execution.

There is another segment in Figure 5.13 that we should discuss. This program executes as an .EXE program. When DOS passes control to an .EXE program, it establishes a stack for the program. The stack information comes from the linker, which places it in the header of the .EXE file. It is up to the programmer to provide for that stack. If the programmer doesn't, the linker gives a warning. This won't stop the program from executing in normal circumstances. However, it does leave the program with the default stack, which may be the wrong size or in the wrong place. The segment named STACK in Figure 5.13 takes care of this need. Naming it STACK and setting its attribute as STACK signals the intention to set up this area as the stack. The linker also makes sure that the Stack Pointer is set correctly when control goes to the program.

Link Operation

Let's now trace the steps that combined these program modules into a single executable module. You assemble the programs using the commands covered in the preceding section:

    B>A:MASM FIG5-13,,,;
    B>A:MASM FIG5-14,,,;

This produces the two object modules, FIG5-13.OBJ and FIG5-14.OBJ. You invoke the LINK program to combine the modules. Figure 5.15 shows the actions that start the LINK.

This example assumes that the DOS diskette is in drive A: and that the data diskette is in drive B:, and drive B: is the default drive. Once started, the LINK program prompts the user for the object files to link. You enter the filenames without the OBJ extension. If you're linking more than one module, enter the names with ''+'' signs separating them. This example links the modules FIG5-13 and FIG5-14.

The modules are linked together in the same order that they are input to the LINK program. In this case, the code in FIG5-13 precedes the code in FIG5-14. Specifying the names in the reverse order would have similarly reversed their

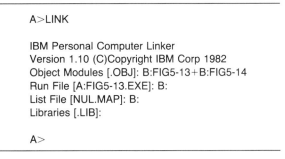

```
A>LINK

IBM Personal Computer Linker
Version 1.10 (C)Copyright IBM Corp 1982
Object Modules [.OBJ]: B:FIG5-13+B:FIG5-14
Run File [A:FIG5-13.EXE]: B:
List File [NUL.MAP]: B:
Libraries [.LIB]:

A>
```

Figure 5.15 Linker Execution

order in the code. Normally, there is no reason to place the code in a particular order. The one exception to this is the entry point for the program. After this example, we'll talk about how to manage the entry point.

The next prompt from the linker asks for the name of the execution or run file. The default name is the filename for the first object module, with an extension of .EXE. You may change the filename by entering a different name, but you can't change the .EXE extension.

The next prompt asks for a filename to store the link map. You may choose any filename for this file, but the default produces no map. In this example, the entry B: tells the linker to put a link map on drive B:. The linker chose the name FIG5-13.MAP for the file. Figure 5.16 shows the file FIG5-13.MAP produced by this link operation. We'll come back to it in a moment.

The final prompt by the linker asks for any program libraries to include as part of the link. For some high-level language programming, you may need to name the run-time library in this step. For our assembly language programs, there is no need to specify a library.

Link Map

Figure 5.16 shows the link map output from the link step. With this simple example, there isn't a great deal to look at. There is a separate line for each segment in the execution file. Going across the line are the starting and ending addresses for each of the segments, as they will be loaded into storage. Notice that the CODE segment has a length of 3CH. This is equal to the combined lengths of the CODE segments in the two program modules. The other segment in our example is the STACK segment, 80H bytes in size.

There are several things to notice about the addresses in the link map. First, they are all 20-bit addresses and start at location 0. Since DOS will load the program at some location other than 0, the loader will relocate these values. However, their relative positioning remains the same. The other thing to notice about the segments is that they aren't placed into storage right after one another. Although the CODE segment is only 3CH long, the STACK segment is at 40H. Segments must be on paragraph boundaries for the offset addresses to remain correct. Paragraph boundaries let the segment registers point directly to the first location of a segment. So the linker has placed the STACK segment on the first paragraph boundary following the end of the CODE segment. In this case, with CODE ending at 3BH, the next location divisible by 16 is 40H.

Start	Stop	Length	Name	Class
00000H	0003EH	003FH	CODE	
00040H	000BFH	0080H	STACK	

Program entry point at 0000:0000

Figure 5.16   Link Map for Figures 5.13 and 5.14

You may have noticed that the combined length of the CODE segments in the two routines is not really 3CH. In lieu of any other specification, the linker has placed the beginning of each section of the CODE segment on a paragraph boundary. The first module, FIG5-13, has a length of 2BH. The linker put the next module, FIG5-14, at the next paragraph boundary, in this case 30H. The 0CH length of the second module gives the total CODE segment length of 03CH. Paragraph alignment is the default combination of the assembler and linker. The assembler SEGMENT can change this alignment to either BYTE or WORD if so desired. BYTE alignment packs the program modules together in the segment. This is the most space efficient method of combining modules. However, the paragraph alignment guarantees that there won't be any segment addressing problems during execution. If a program does address arithmetic and hasn't been aligned on a paragraph boundary, it's possible for errors to occur.

The last portion of the link map shows the entry point for the execution file. This address, like the others, is relative to the beginning of the execution module and is relocated by the loader. There are several ways to indicate the starting address for an .EXE program. One way is to let the program begin executing with the first byte of the program module. For this to work, you must be careful that the first byte of the first segment in the run file is the first instruction that you want executed. The better way to specify the entry point is to name the entry point in the END statement of the main routine. In Figure 5.13, the last statement of the program is

    END   START

where START is the label of the first instruction to execute. Since we linked the modules together in order, that also happens to be the first instruction in the program. However, if we were to link the modules in the opposite order, the entry point would still be correctly located. Try it and see.

In any link operation there should be only one END statement with a starting location. Notice that FIG5-14 does not have an entry point named on its END statement. If there is more than one entry point named, the linker usually takes the last one named. It is better to do it right than to take the chance that the linker will pick the wrong one. Remember that this method of specifying the entry point for a program works only for an .EXE file. A .COM program always begins execution at offset 100H in the program segment.

DEBUG

The DEBUG program gives you a method of working with a machine language program to find errors. The DEBUG routine lets you work through the program a step at a time, and look at what's going on. DEBUG is another program that comes as part of the DOS diskette. You load it just as any other program. You communicate with DEBUG using the keyboard and display. DEBUG prompts with a ''—'' whenever it is expecting some action from you.

Instead of listing the commands for DEBUG, we'll use the debugger to examine the operation of the program we just wrote in Figures 5.13 and 5.14. Figure 5.17 shows the listing from that session.

```
B>A:DEBUG FIG5-13.EXE
-R

AX=0000  BX=0000  CX=003F  DX=0000  SP=0080  BP=0000  SI=0000  DI=0000
DS=04B5  ES=04B5  SS=04C9  CS=04C5  IP=0000   NV UP DI PL NZ NA PO NC
04C5:0000 1E             PUSH    DS

-U

04C5:0000 1E             PUSH    DS
04C5:0001 B80000         MOV     AX,0000
04C5:0004 50             PUSH    AX
04C5:0005 FC             CLD
04C5:0006 8CC8           MOV     AX,CS
04C5:0008 8ED8           MOV     DS,AX
04C5:000A BE1C00         MOV     SI,001C
04C5:000D AC             LODSB
04C5:000E A23000         MOV     [0030],AL
04C5:0011 E81D00         CALL    0031
04C5:0014 803E30000A     CMP     B,[0030],0A
04C5:0019 75F2           JNZ     000D
04C5:001B CB             RET     L
04C5:001C 54             PUSH    SP
04C5:001D 68             DB      68
04C5:001E 69             DB      69
04C5:001F 7320           JNC     0041

-D4C5:0

04C5:0000  1E B8 00 00 50 FC 8C C8-8E D8 BE 1C 00 AC A2 30   .8..P|.H.X>..,"0
04C5:0010  00 E8 1D 00 80 3E 30 00-0A 75 F2 CB 54 68 69 73   .h...>0..urKThis
04C5:0020  20 69 73 20 61 20 74 65-73 74 0D 0A 00 00 00 00    is a test......
04C5:0030  00 A0 30 00 B4 0E BB 00-00 BA 00 00 CD 10 C3 00   . 0.4.;..:..M.C.
04C5:0040  00 00 00 00 00 00 00 00-00 00 00 00 00 00 00 00   ................
04C5:0050  00 00 00 00 00 00 00 00-00 00 00 00 00 00 00 00   ................
04C5:0060  00 00 00 00 00 00 00 00-00 00 00 00 00 00 00 00   ................
04C5:0070  00 00 00 00 00 00 00 00-00 00 00 00 00 00 00 00   ................

-RAX
AX 0000
:1234

-E 4C5:21
04C5:0021  69.     73.      20.     61.20   20.

-G 3C

AX=0E54  BX=0000  CX=003F  DX=0000  SP=007A  BP=0000  SI=001D  DI=0000
DS=04C5  ES=04B5  SS=04C9  CS=04C5  IP=003C   NV UP DI PL NZ NA PO NC
04C5:003C CD10           INT     10
-T

AX=0E54  BX=0000  CX=003F  DX=0000  SP=0074  BP=0000  SI=001D  DI=0000
DS=04C5  ES=04B5  SS=04C9  CS=F000  IP=F065   NV UP DI PL NZ NA PO NC
F000:F065 FB             STI
-T

AX=0E54  BX=0000  CX=003F  DX=0000  SP=0074  BP=0000  SI=001D  DI=0000
DS=04C5  ES=04B5  SS=04C9  CS=F000  IP=F066   NV UP EI PL ZR NA PE NC
F000:F066 FC             CLD
-G 4C5:3E

T
AX=0754  BX=0000  CX=003F  DX=0000  SP=007A  BP=0000  SI=001D  DI=0000
DS=04C5  ES=04B5  SS=04C9  CS=04C5  IP=003E   NV UP DI PL NZ NA PO NC
04C5:003E C3             RET
-G

his is    test

Program terminated normally
-R

AX=0754  BX=0000  CX=003F  DX=0000  SP=007A  BP=0000  SI=001D  DI=0000
DS=04C5  ES=04B5  SS=04C9  CS=04C5  IP=003E   NV UP DI PL NZ NA PO NC
04C5:003E C3             RET
-Q

B>
```

Figure 5.17   Debug Listing for Figures 5.13 and 5.14

This example invokes the DEBUG routine and also names the program to work with, in this case, FIG5-13.EXE. After DEBUG loads, it brings in the program. The debug routine is in control and shows the symbol "—" to indicate that it's awaiting input. Nothing happens with the program until you tell it to.

The "R" command displays the registers as they are when the program FIG5-13 is loaded and gains control. All are self-explanatory, except perhaps the flag values. Instead of showing the flag register in hexadecimal notation. DEBUG shows the individual flags. NV indicates No oVerflow, UP is the direction flag, and so on. The final line of the register display is the next instruction to be executed. At location 4C5:0000 is a PUSH DS instruction.

We should pause briefly in the discussion of the DEBUG routine to examine the information displayed in the registers. The registers are set as they will be when the program FIG5-13 is given control from the command line processor. Note that CS:IP points to the first instruction, as indicated on the END statement of the assembly. The DS and ES registers point to the Program Segment Prefix. Finally, SS:SP locates the STACK segment. This register setting will be contrasted to the settings for a .COM file later in this section.

To see more of the instructions, "U," for unassemble, displays the next 20 or so instructions. This is helpful when debugging code that you don't have a listing for. Unassembling the code lets you see the instructions. This may help you save printer paper and time when you've modified a program slightly. Your listing no longer quite matches the program in memory. Unassembling the program helps you determine the correct address for each instruction.

However, the DEBUG unassembly has several failings when compared with a listing. There are no comments (which may be essential to understanding the program), and the memory locations are identified only by address, not by variable name. For example, the instruction at 4C5:000E appears in Figure 5.13 as

    MOV   OUTPUT_CHARACTER,AL

while in the unassembled listing it shows as

    MOV   [0030],AL

These are the same instruction. The variable name OUTPUT_CHARACTER is more meaningful than the memory location [0030] to the programmer doing the debugging. But the DEBUG program doesn't know the variable names and must rely on the actual addresses.

The DEBUG program also doesn't produce the same assembly mnemonics that are accepted by the assembler. This means that some of the instructions don't look the same. The instruction at 4C5:0014 unassembles as

    CMP   B,[0030],0A

but the instruction in Figure 5.13 is

    CMP   OUTPUT_CHARACTER,10

The unassembler works only in hex, for both input and output. So that's where the 0A comes from. We already figured out why we get [0030] rather than OUT-PUT_CHARACTER. But what's the "B,"?

The assembler has typed variables. That is, the variables are known to be byte, word, or other kinds of variables during the assembly operation. So when the programmer enters an immediate instruction that references memory, the assembler knows how big the memory location is. For this example, OUT-PUT_CHARACTER is known to be a byte variable. But the DEBUG progam has no idea how big the variable at location [0030] is. But the unassembler does know that instruction transfers a single byte of immediate data to location [0030]. So the "B," means that the immediate operation is a byte move. To get the same effect in the assembler, the instruction would be

    CMP   BYTE PTR [0030],10

You can view the "B," as shorthand notation for BYTE PTR. Similarly, "W," is used for WORD PTR, "L" to indicate a long or far return, and so on.

As part of the unassemble instruction, the object code for that instruction is displayed. At location 4C5:001C you can see some instructions that don't appear in Figure 5.13. This is the data area holding the message string "This is a test." However, the unassemble command doesn't know when the instructions stop and where the data begin. So it treats everything as an instruction. (By the way, should your program branch to this data area, this is the sequence of instructions that would execute.)

The display, "D," command can display data areas. The display is broken into two parts. There is a hexadecimal listing of the memory locations, followed by the ASCII representation of the memory locations. The instructions don't make any sense, but the data area shows up very clearly. If you have nothing better to do someday, you might try to write a program where the instructions form the ASCII characters for your initials.

The debugger can modify the registers and memory locations. Entering "R" followed by a register name displays that register and gives you an opportunity to modify the value. Entering a return leaves it unchanged, while entering a new value changes it.

You can also modify memory locations. The "E," for edit, lets you modify memory. DEBUG displays the values at the individual locations, followed by a ".". You may change the location by entering a new value, hit the space bar to move to the next location, or enter a return to return to the debug command prompt. In this example, the first three locations are unchanged. Location 04C5:0024 was changed from 61H to 20H. Since this is the data area, the message we'll see displayed will differ from the message that was assembled.

All of the instructions that reference memory locations accept an address as part of the command. The "E" command shows the address entered, as did the display command. The unassemble command could likewise have used an address. You may enter the address as segment and offset, or simply as an offset. If you use only an offset DEBUG picks the appropriate segment register. For "U" it uses the CS segment. For "D" and "E" the DS register points to the default segment.

It's now time to try executing this program. We could just start the program and see what happens. But we don't need the DEBUG program to do that. The debugger allows us to set stopping points in the program, known as "breakpoints." By setting breakpoints in the program, we can force the program to give control back to DEBUG. This gives us another opportunity to examine the registers and memory to monitor the progress of the program.

The go command, "G," transfers control from DEBUG to the program. Instruction execution begins at the location pointed to by the CS:IP register pair (just as in the real processor). Execution continues in the tested program until it executes a breakpoint. In this example, we have set a breakpoint at location 3CH. Since only the offset was specified, DEBUG uses the CS value for the segment. A look at the listing of Figure 5.14 shows that offset 3CH is the INT 10H instruction. This particular place was chosen in the example since this a point where control is transferred to a ROM BIOS routine. Examining the program at this point ensures that we have set the registers correctly before executing the BIOS routine.

When the breakpoint is encountered, control returns to DEBUG. It displays the registers, together with the next instruction, just as with the "R" command. DEBUG is back in control, and you can enter any of the commands.

There are limitations to the use of breakpoints. The breakpoint is actually implemented as the 0CCH operation code. This instruction causes an INT 3. The software interrupt gives control back to DEBUG. Since an instruction returns control to DEBUG, the breakpoint must be at the beginning of an instruction. If the breakpoint is somewhere else, DEBUG won't regain control, and the program will execute an instruction that is different from the one intended. For example, if we had specified "-G 3D," the instruction at 3CH would have been an INT 0CCH, and the program would have gone off somewhere unknown.

As long as the breakpoint is placed with care, all will go well. The "G" command lets you set up to 10 breakpoints. Once any of them is encountered, all of the breakpoints are reset to their original value. A Go command without any breakpoints never encounters any of the previously entered breakpoints, because they have all been removed. If you start execution and your program halts or goes into an infinite loop, there will probably be no way to get control back without using System Reset (CTL-ALT-DEL), which means that you'll have to start all over. You should be careful when starting an unknown program.

If you want to make a permanent breakpoint, use "E" to change the first byte of an instruction to 0CCH. This breakpoint is there forever, or at least until you change it. You might want to use such a breakpoint at the entry point of an error-handling routine. During the debugging stage, you probably want to look carefully at the errors encountered, rather than letting the program handle them.

There is another thing to remember about the breakpoint. It won't work if you try to set a breakpoint in read-only memory. Since you can't write into ROM, the 0CCH instruction is never placed into memory.

The next DEBUG command is "T." The trace command executes a single instruction of the program. There are several iterations of the "T" command in this example. You can see that the program is executing the first instructions of the ROM BIOS routine pointed to by INT 10H. The ROM BIOS routine is, as its name implies, located in ROM. The trace command makes it possible to "break" the program while it's executing in ROM.

The trace command works by setting the trace bit in the flag register before passing control to the user program. This flag bit causes an interrupt (INT 1) following the execution of every instruction. The INT 1 vector returns control to DEBUG. The INT 1 actions automatically reset the trace bit. This means that DEBUG doesn't get interrupted after each of its instructions. The trace command is an excellent way to work your way through a difficult section of code. DEBUG shows each instruction, together with the registers just prior to the execution of that instruction. Since the operation uses interrupts rather than breakpoint instructions, you can even trace through ROM.

Back to the example. The "-G 4C5:3E" command allows the ROM BIOS subroutine to complete execution. Notice that the program has written the "T" to the display. The ROM BIOS routine at interrupt 10H writes characters to the display. This is the first character of the message. Since we're now reasonably certain that the program executes correctly, entering "G" without breakpoints lets the program run to completion.

Since this example was an .EXE file, INT 20H could not be used to return control to DOS. Instead, the routine pushed the DS register and a 0 value. The FAR return instruction at the end of the main routine returns control to DOS. DEBUG recognizes this, and captures the state of the machine at the end of the tested program. If this were a .COM program, the INT 20H would likewise have brought DEBUG back in control. Having now tired of this example, we can exit from DEBUG back to DOS with the quit, "Q," command.

CONVERTING FROM .EXE TO .COM

As part of the DOS diskette, there is a utility called EXE2BIN. This program converts a program from the .EXE representation to the .COM type. However, the EXE2BIN program does not work with all programs. Here is a method using the DEBUG program that converts any program into a .COM file.

Figure 5.18 shows the program that we'll convert. This program does exactly the same function as the preceding example. That is, it prints "This is a test" on the display. But for this program, DOS function 9 of INT 21H displays the string.

Notice that the program has been written as a .COM file. The tipoff is the

```
The IBM Personal Computer Assembler 01-01-83          PAGE   1-1
Figure 5.18  .EXE to .COM Example

 1                                              PAGE     ,132
 2                                              TITLE    Figure 5.18  .EXE to .COM Example
 3       0000                         CODE      SEGMENT
 4       0100                                   ORG      100H
 5                                              ASSUME   CS:CODE, DS:CODE
 6
 7       0100  BA 0109 R                         MOV      DX,OFFSET MESSAGE
 8       0103  B4 09                             MOV      AH,9                 ; DOS Display string
 9       0105  CD 21                             INT      21H                  ; Print the string
10       0107  CD 20                             INT      20H                  ; Return to DOS
11
12       0109  54 68 69 73 20 69     MESSAGE DB          'This is a test',10,13,'$'
13             73 20 61 20 74 65
14             73 74 0A 0D 24
15       011A                         CODE      ENDS
16                                              END
```

Figure 5.18   .EXE-to-.COM Example

ORG 100H statement preceding the first instruction. The remainder of the program must be code segment relocatable. That was no trick for this simple program, but you should keep this in mind when writing a program that you'll convert to .COM.

You assemble and link the program in the normal fashion. Prior to starting the DEBUG routine, however, rename the .EXE file to a .COM file. You must do this because the DEBUG program doesn't let you write an .EXE file. Figure 5.19 shows the sequence of steps to follow. The example issues the DEBUG

```
B>A:ASM FIG5-18,,,;
The IBM Personal Computer Assembler
Version 1.00 (C)Copyright IBM Corp 1981

Warning Severe
Errors  Errors
0       0

B>A:LINK FIG5-18,,,;
IBM Personal Computer Linker
Version 1.10 (C)Copyright IBM Corp 1982

 Warning: No STACK segment
There was 1 error detected.

B>RENAME FIG5-18.EXE FIG5-18.COM

B>A:DEBUG
-NFIG5-18.COM
-L
-M 400 1000 100

-U100 10F
06D7:0100 BA0901        MOV     DX,0109
06D7:0103 B409          MOV     AH,09
06D7:0105 CD21          INT     21
06D7:0107 CD20          INT     20
06D7:0109 54            PUSH    SP
06D7:010A 68            DB      68
06D7:010B 69            DB      69
06D7:010C 7320          JNC     012E
06D7:010E 69            DB      69
06D7:010F 7320          JNC     0131
-D100

06D7:0100  BA 09 01 B4 09 CD 21 CD-20 54 68 69 73 20 69 73   :..4.M!M This is
06D7:0110  20 61 20 74 65 73 74 0A-0D 24 00 00 00 00 00 00   a test..$......
06D7:0120  00 00 00 00 00 00 00 00-00 00 00 00 00 00 00 00   ................
06D7:0130  00 00 00 00 00 00 00 00-00 00 00 00 00 00 00 00   ................
06D7:0140  00 00 00 00 00 00 00 00-00 00 00 00 00 00 00 00   ................
06D7:0150  00 00 00 00 00 00 00 00-00 00 00 00 00 00 00 00   ................
06D7:0160  00 00 00 00 00 00 00 00-00 00 00 00 00 00 00 00   ................
06D7:0170  00 00 00 00 00 00 00 00-00 00 00 00 00 00 00 00   ................
```

Figure 5.19   .EXE to .COM Example

```
-RCX
 CX 0380
 :120

-W

Writing 0120 bytes
-Q

B>DEBUG FIG5-18.COM
-R

AX=0000  BX=0000  CX=0120  DX=0000  SP=FFF0  BP=0000  SI=0000  DI=0000
DS=04B5  ES=04B5  SS=04B5  CS=04B5  IP=0100   NV UP DI PL NZ NA PO NC
04B5:0100 BA0901          MOV     DX,0109

-Q

B>FIG5-18
This is a test
```

Figure 5.19 *Continued*

command, without the file name. You could specify FIG5-18.COM on this line, but by not doing so, we can demonstrate some other DEBUG functions. The "N" command in DEBUG lets you name a file. The "L" command then loads that file into storage. When the file name is on the DEBUG command line, it performs the same function as the "N" and "L" commands.

With the file now loaded, you'll find the program actually loaded at offset 400H. The "M" command moves the block of memory from 400H to 100H. The length of 1000H was chosen just to make sure that it was big enough for the program. The program is now in the .COM file format, and can be written back to the diskette. Before doing so, however, you modify the CX register to show the actual length of the program. For all DEBUG diskette file reads and writes, the CX register contains the length of the file. Since the .COM file is now much shorter than the .EXE file, we can save diskette space by making CX the correct value for the program. The "W" command writes the file back on diskette. This,

Command	Description
D	Display memory contents
E	Change memory contents
F	Fill a block of memory
G	Execute the program
H	Hexadecimal add and subtract
I	Read and display an input port
L	Load from diskette
M	Move a memory block
N	Establish a file name
O	Output a value to a port
Q	Quit debugging
R	Display registers
S	Search for a particular byte string
T	Execute a single instruction
U	Unassemble a block of code
W	Write data to the diskette

Figure 5.20 DEBUG Commands

by the way, is another advantage of using .COM files. DEBUG won't write an .EXE file to the diskette, since the header information is no longer in memory. DEBUG can write a .COM file to the diskette. If you're debugging a program, and want to modify a byte or two rather than reassembling the program (this is called "patching" the program), you can do it. Just modify the program, make sure that CX is set correctly, and "W" saves it on diskette.

Finally, let's exit DEBUG and come back with the fresh version of FIG5-18.COM. Looking at the registers here shows the register setup for a .COM file. Contrast this to the register setup for the .EXE file shown in Figure 5.17. These differences should help to point out some of the differences between .COM and .EXE files.

There are other commands available with the DEBUG program. Figure 5.20 shows the command set for DEBUG. The DOS manual describes all of the commands in detail.

CHAPTER

6

Features
Of The Macro
Assembler

This chapter will explain some of the features of the IBM Macro Assembler. Although we have covered all of the 8088 processor instructions, there are other instructions that are part of the assembler. We have already discussed some of these pseudo-instructions, like the data definition operators such as DB and DW. This chapter introduces more powerful assembler operations. The common thread linking these features is that you can use them to make the job of writing assembly language programs simpler and easier.

We'll cover two major areas in this chapter. The first is the macro operation of the macro assembler. Macros are a powerful instruction-generating tool. An understanding of macros will be necessary for Chapter 7, which discusses the 8087 Numeric Data Processor. The second area deals with data structures. We have previously discussed data definition together with the data types. Here we'll define data structures that are made up of collections of bytes and words. This section covers segments, structures, and records for data definition.

MACROS

A macro is a programming tool that allows you to create your own assembler operations. In reality, a macro is a text-substitution mechanism. The macro processor lets you define a new operation code for the processor. As part of the definition, you tell the assembler the text for this operation code. When the assembler encounters this newly defined operation code, the assembler refers back to the saved definition of the macro. It places the text from that definition into the assembly. For example, a program can define an often repeated sequence of instructions as a macro. Whenever those instructions are to appear in the program, the programmer can use the macro operation code instead.

There are two distinct steps in using a macro. In the first step, the program defines the macro. The programmer gives the macro a name and a definition. The definition consists of the assembler operations and instructions that are generated whenever that macro name appears. The second step is the invocation of the macro. This occurs when the assembler encounters the macro name used as an operation code. The assembler substitutes the defined instructions in place of the macro name

Let's take an example from the 8087 instructions that we'll cover in Chapter 7. There is a problem with writing programs that use the instructions for the 8087 Numeric Data Processor. The Macro Assembler does not include the 8087 opcodes. To use the 8087, you must form the 8087 instructions using either Define Byte operators or the WAIT and ESC opcodes. The best way to do this is with a set of macros, which allow you to write 8087 instructions. A program can then specify the 8087 instructions even though they aren't part of the assembler.

A macro is used most commonly in assembly language programming. Although there is no reason why a high-level language can't use a macro processor, they aren't frequently found. The IBM Personal Computer Macro Assembler provides a macro capability. As we have noticed, there are two versions of the assembler. The small assembler, ASM, does not support macro capability. The full-size assembler, MASM, allows all of the macro operations discussed in this section. To use MASM, your personal computer must have at least 96K bytes of memory.

A very simple macro you can use for an 8087 operation code is the FENI macro. The 8088 Macro Assembler does not recognize the FENI operation code, which is really an instruction directed toward the 8087. Figure 6.1 shows the two steps in the macro process: the definition of the FENI macro and its later invocation. Figure 6.1 contains two parts: part (a) is the source file for the program, while part (b) contains the assembly listing of the program. Figure 6.1 lists the two portions separately to show you which portions are written by the programmer and which are generated by the macro processor.

A program defines a macro with the MACRO operation code. In Figure 6.1, the macro definition looks like

```
FENI    MACRO
;----- Body of the macro
        ENDM
```

The MACRO statement is a pseudo-operation code. This particular pseudo-op tells the assembler that a macro is being defined. The name field of the operation is the name that the program gives to the macro, in this case FENI. The instructions

```
          PAGE    ,132
          TITLE   Figure 6.1  Macro Definition

FENI      MACRO
          DB      0DBH,0E0H
          ENDM

CODE      SEGMENT
          ASSUME  CS:CODE

          FENI
CODE      ENDS
          END
```

Figure 6.1(a) Source File for Program

```
The IBM Personal Computer MACRO Assembler 01-01-83          PAGE    1-1
Figure 6.1  Macro Definition

 1                                              PAGE    ,132
 2                                              TITLE   Figure 6.1  Macro Definition
 3
 4                               FENI           MACRO
 5                                              DB      0DBH,0E0H
 6                                              ENDM
 7
 8        0000                   CODE           SEGMENT
 9                                              ASSUME  CS:CODE
10
11                                              FENI
12        0000  DB E0                +          DB      0DBH,0E0H
13
14        0002                   CODE           ENDS
15                                              END
```

FIgure 6.1(b) Assembly Listing for Program

Figure 6.1 Macro Definition. (a) Source File for Program; (b) Assembly Listing for Program.

(or assembler actions) to be substituted for the macro name follow this header line. Finally, the ENDM operation code tells the assembler that this is the end of the macro. The text between the MACRO statement and the ENDM statement is called the body of the macro. In Figure 6.1, the body of the FENI macro is a Define Byte operator. Since there is no 8088 instruction that matches the FENI instruction, the machine language code for the FENI must be built from DB operators.

An important thing to notice is that there is no machine language code generated during the definition of a macro. You can tell that because the address and data columns of the assembly listing are blank. When the assembler first sees the macro definition, it stores the definition away for later use. Later, the program of Figure 6.1 invokes the FENI macro. The assembly language programmer uses the macro name FENI as if it were an assembly language operation code, just like CLD or DAA. The assembler refers to its saved definition of the FENI macro. The assembler takes the text from the body of the macro and places it into the assembly at this point. The ''+'' sign appearing to the left of the DB statement in the assembly listing is an indication that the macro processor has inserted this line of code. Also, you can compare the source listing to the assembly listing. You'll see that the source file shows only the FENI operation code. The assembly listing shows the FENI operation code with the body of the FENI macro following it. In this case, the body of the macro is the DB line.

This simple example shows the power of the macro processor. We needed an operation code named "FENI" that was not supported by the assembler. Without the macro processing capability, a programmer would code the

    DB   0DBH,0E0H

operation for every FENI operation. With macros, we may define the FENI macro, and use it as an operation code forever after in that assembly. There are two good reasons for using macros like this. First, it's easier to write the program. Second, it's much more meaningful to read FENI than to read DB 0DBH, 0E0H.

You can compare a macro to a subroutine. A subroutine is a section of code that is defined in a single location of the program. The program can pass control to the subroutine from anywhere within the program. Using a subroutine saves programmer time and program space. Instead of repeating the instructions of a subroutine each time it is needed, you call the subroutine. The subroutine performs the defined function and control returns to the caller.

Similarly, the assembly program defines a macro at a single location. Once it is defined, you can invoke (or "call") the macro from anywhere in the assembly. Using a macro saves programmer time and source file space. Instead of repeating the instructions of a macro each time they should appear, you invoke the macro. The assembler generates the defined instructions and continues processing the next operation code in the assembly.

The difference between the macro and the subroutine is the time at which they are used. A macro is a text-processing operation. A macro is defined and "executed" at assembly time. The execution of a macro is the replacement of the macro name with the text of the macro body. A subroutine, however, is defined during the assembly, but is not executed until the program is executed. We say that a macro is executed during the assembly, while a subroutine is executed during the execution of the program.

The best way to distinguish between a macro and a subroutine is to remember when their effect is felt. In fact, a macro processor is not necessarily part of a programming language. Suppose that you were a lawyer, and wrote up lots of wills for people. Since the wills are quite often very similar, you could define a set of "will macros" that would contain the common sections of the wills that you write. The first section of the will would be unique, naming the parties in the will. The remainder of the will would be made up of various will macros that fill in the common portions of the will. When the "will processor" is executed, the output is a text document. The macros expand to write out the common parts of the will. You only have to fill in the unique portions between the macros.

If macros and subroutines are so similar in most respects, why use a macro rather than a subroutine? Well, in many cases it is possible to use either. You may define a sequence of instructions as either a macro or as a subroutine. When you require that sequence of instructions in the program, you can call the macro, or you can call the subroutine. Which you do depends on your definition of the sequence of instructions. Time and space considerations determine the trade-off.

In most cases, using a macro results in a program that is bigger. That is, it takes more bytes of object code to realize the same function. The code using macros is faster in execution. There is no overhead of executing a subroutine call and return each time the code sequence is repeated. For the minimum-size program, you should use a subroutine. For a maximum-speed program, you use a macro.

The FENI macro of Figure 6.1 is an obvious choice for a macro. Not only does the code execute faster as a macro than as a subroutine, but it is also smaller. The CALL instruction, for a NEAR subroutine, requires three bytes. The FENI macro requires only two. For the 8087 macros, it would require more bytes of object code to support the 8087 through subroutine calls than it would to use macros. Speed of execution is also best using macros.

MACRO ARGUMENTS

There is a feature of subroutines that is also included in macro processing. It is possible to modify the actions of a macro through the use of arguments. Just as the arguments to a subroutine can modify the execution of the subroutine, the arguments of a macro determine the actual instructions that are generated. Just as a subroutine without arguments has relatively few uses, so does a macro without arguments.

Let's take another simple example. We have determined that our program adds a different constant value to a specific memory location in many places in the program. Rather than write the instruction

        ADD   MEMORY_BYTE,5

or

        ADD   MEMORY_BYTE,7

many different times, we would like to use a macro for that instruction. However, the constant value is different in each use of the instruction. So we make the constant value an argument to the macro. Figure 6.2 shows the definition and invocation of the ADDBYTE macro. The example uses the symbol CONSTANT in the macro definition as an argument to the macro. Any symbols appearing in the operand field of the MACRO statement are treated as arguments. At the time the macro is defined, the symbol CONSTANT has no meaning. It merely serves as a placeholder in the text of the macro. Later, when the macro is invoked, the text processing of the macro substitutes the defined value of the argument for the symbol used during the definition of the macro.

It is important to notice that the macro argument is a text argument. Since the macro processor is really a text processor, it doesn't know numbers from letters, and vice versa. This allows the macro call to use a symbol rather than a number. Any meaning associated with the character string is placed there by the assembler, not the macro processor. The macro processor substitutes the text string of

```
The IBM Personal Computer MACRO Assembler 01-01-83            PAGE    1-1
Figure 6.2  Macro Argument

 1                                              PAGE     ,132
 2                                              TITLE    Figure 6.2  Macro Argument
 3
 4                                    ADDBYTE MACRO    CONSTANT
 5                                            ADD      MEMORY_BYTE,CONSTANT
 6                                            ENDM
 7
 8     0000                           CODE    SEGMENT
 9                                            ASSUME  CS:CODE
10
11     0000   ??                      MEMORY_BYTE      DB      ?
12
13     = 0004                         FOUR             EQU     4              ; Symbol for constant
14
15                                            ADDBYTE          2
16     0001   2E: 80 06 0000 R 02    +         ADD     MEMORY_BYTE,2
17                                            ADDBYTE          4
18     0007   2E: 80 06 0000 R 04    +         ADD     MEMORY_BYTE,4
19                                            ADDBYTE          FOUR
20     000D   2E: 80 06 0000 R 04    +         ADD     MEMORY_BYTE,FOUR
21
22     0013                           CODE    ENDS
23                                            END
```

Figure 6.2 Macro Argument

the macro call for the symbol used in the macro definition. Thus, a program can use the equated value "FOUR" just as readily as the constant value "4."

The ability to use symbols as arguments to a macro is crucial for our next example macro. This macro, one of the 8087 instructions, requires an argument that almost certainly is a symbol in normal use. The macro, FLDCW, is an 8087 instruction that specifies a memory location. Since we have referred to most memory locations symbolically in our assemblies, we want to continue this practice with our 8087 mnemonics.

Figure 6.3 shows the FLDCW macro and several invocations of it. Notice that FLDCW uses the symbol "SOURCE" as an argument. SOURCE is the address from which the 8087 loads the control word. FLDCW uses the 8088 ESC instruction to generate the required machine language. However, the ESC instruction requires an address value to determine the mod-r/m byte for the

```
The IBM Personal Computer MACRO Assembler 01-01-83            PAGE    1-1
Figure 6.3  FLDCW Macro

 1                                              PAGE     ,132
 2                                              TITLE    Figure 6.3  FLDCW Macro
 3
 4                                    FLDCW   MACRO    SOURCE
 5                                            DB       09BH
 6                                            ESC      0DH,SOURCE
 7                                            ENDM
 8
 9     0000                           CODE    SEGMENT
10                                            ASSUME  CS:CODE
11
12     0000   ????                    MEMORY_LOCATION DW      ?
13
14                                            FLDCW    MEMORY_LOCATION
15     0002   9B                     +         DB      09BH
16     0003   2E: D9 2E 0000 R       +         ESC     0DH,MEMORY_LOCATION
17                                            FLDCW    ES:[DI]
18     0008   9B                     +         DB      09BH
19     0009   26: D9 2D              +         ESC     0DH,ES:[DI]
20                                            FLDCW    MEMORY_LOCATION[BX+SI]
21     000C   9B                     +         DB      09BH
22     000D   2E: D9 A8 0000 R       +         ESC     0DH,MEMORY_LOCATION[BX+SI]
23
24     0012                           CODE    ENDS
25                                            END
```

Figure 6.3 FLDCW Macro

instruction. The macro uses the argument SOURCE to do just that. This arrangement of the FLDCW macro allows a very natural programming method. Just as you would write

        INC   MEMORY_LOCATION

you can write the 8087 instruction

        FLDCW MEMORY_LOCATION

Not only does this work for a symbolic memory location, it also works for the other addressing modes. Figure 6.3 contains several examples of base and index address methods to determine the memory operand. Since the macro processor handles the argument as a chunk of text, the argument can be made up of any text string you desire.

You may define a macro with more than one argument. The only limitation to the number of arguments you can have with a macro is the number of symbols that you can fit on a single assembly line. The macro processor treats everything following the MACRO statement as an argument. You use commas to separate the symbols during the macro definition. A MACRO statement with three arguments looks like this:

        EXAMPLE MACRO ARG1, ARG2, ARG3

Similarly, when you call a macro, you must specify a value for every argument of the macro. If you should omit an argument, the assembler substitutes a text string of zero length. Sometimes this is desirable, but often it produces an incorrect assembly. If there is more than a single argument to a macro, the commas in the invocation of the macro separate the argument text. This is exactly the same way you would specify multiple parameters in any 8088 instruction, so it should come naturally to you. An invocation of our three-argument macro above might be

        EXAMPLE 5, [BX], MEMORY_BYTE

Our next example will show you several possibilities of multiple arguments.

CONDITIONAL ASSEMBLY

So far in our discussion of macros, they have mimicked subroutines, both in their operation and in their use of arguments. The next thing we need is conditional processing. Just as a subroutine has the ability to change its execution based on the conditions at the time of execution, the macro should be able to change its code generation based on the conditions at the time of assembly.

The IBM Macro Assembler can do conditional assembly. In fact, conditional assembly is not necessarily part of macro processing. A program can use conditional assembly anywhere in the assembly source. However, conditional assembly most frequently occurs in macros. Only the Macro Assembler, MASM, supports conditional assembly on the IBM Personal Computer.

As with macros, conditional assembly occurs during the assembly, not during the execution of the program. Conditional assembly allows the programmer to "program" the assembler into assembling different sequences of code. The assembler determines what to assemble using a parameter known during the assembly. While a program can use this capability any time during the assembly, we'll examine it primarily, as it affects the assembly of macros.

Figure 6.4 shows a conditional assembly during the expansion of the 8087 instruction macro FIDIVR. This macro requires conditional assembly because of the typing of variables in the assembler. You can apply the instruction mnemonic FIDIVR to two different types of operands, as we'll see in Chapter 7. The operand can be either a two- or a four-byte integer. We would like the assembler to determine the correct machine language based on the type of operand. The ADD instruction, as we have seen, really has several forms, based on the operands supplied to the assembler. The assembler determines the correct form of ADD based on those operands. We want to be able to do the same thing with the FIDIVR instruction. But now the macro processor must determine the kind of operand and generate the correct instruction.

The FIDIVR instruction can have one of two different operands, and depending on that operand, the resulting instruction is different. So our macro expansion for FIDIVR should reflect the correct operand. Two things allow this: conditional assembly and the TYPE operator.

The assembler has an operator, called TYPE, that returns a value equal to the

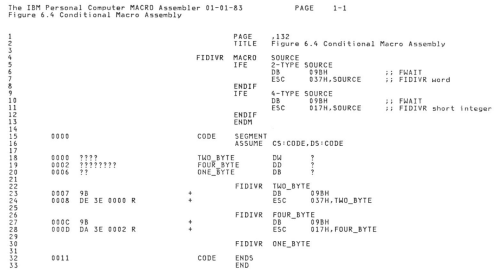

```
The IBM Personal Computer MACRO Assembler 01-01-83          PAGE    1-1
Figure 6.4 Conditional Macro Assembly

 1                                        PAGE    ,132
 2                                        TITLE   Figure 6.4 Conditional Macro Assembly
 3
 4                              FIDIVR  MACRO   SOURCE
 5                                      IFE     2-TYPE SOURCE
 6                                        DB      09BH              ;; FWAIT
 7                                        ESC     037H,SOURCE       ;; FIDIVR word
 8                                      ENDIF
 9                                      IFE     4-TYPE SOURCE
10                                        DB      09BH              ;; FWAIT
11                                        ESC     017H,SOURCE       ;; FIDIVR short integer
12                                      ENDIF
13                                      ENDM
14
15      0000                    CODE    SEGMENT
16                                      ASSUME  CS:CODE,DS:CODE
17
18      0000   ????             TWO_BYTE        DW      ?
19      0002   ????????         FOUR_BYTE       DD      ?
20      0006   ??               ONE_BYTE        DB      ?
21
22                                      FIDIVR  TWO_BYTE
23      0007   9B               +        DB      09BH
24      0008   DE 3E 0000 R     +        ESC     037H,TWO_BYTE
25
26                                      FIDIVR  FOUR_BYTE
27      000C   9B               +        DB      09BH
28      000D   DA 3E 0002 R     +        ESC     017H,FOUR_BYTE
29
30                                      FIDIVR  ONE_BYTE
31
32      0011                    CODE    ENDS
33                                      END
```

Figure 6.4 Conditional Macro Assembly

size of the operand. For the FIDIVR example, we expect the operand to be either a two- or a four-byte integer. Therefore, the TYPE of the operand will be either two or four.

The expression

```
IFE     2-TYPE SOURCE
```

in the FIDIVR macro tests the TYPE of the operand SOURCE. The arithmetic expression 2-TYPE SOURCE evaluates to 0 if the operand SOURCE is a two-byte integer and is a nonzero value for any other type of operand. The IFE (Assemble if Equal) statement tells the assembler to assemble the expressions following the IFE statement if the operand field of the IFE statement is equal to zero. Thus, the IFE evaluates as true if the operand SOURCE is a two-byte integer. If the IFE expression evaluates as true, all the expressions following the IFE statement are assembled until an ENDIF statement is encountered. For this example, this means that the code

```
DB      09BH
ESC     37H,SOURCE
```

is assembled if the operand SOURCE is a two-byte integer. The first macro invocation in Figure 6.4 shows the macro using a two-byte integer as the operand. Thus, the assembler chooses the ESC 37H option for the macro expansion.

Since the FIDIVR instruction has two options, corresponding to the two different operands, the macro uses a second IFE clause for the other condition. When the operand is a four-byte integer, the macro generates the ESC 17H code. The macro expansions in Figure 6.4 show the two different code expansions.

Notice that the last macro invocation in Figure 6.4 has an operand which doesn't meet either of the criteria. Since neither of the IFE statements evaluate as true, neither of them are assembled. In this case, the macro processor doesn't generate any text.

There are different tests that the assembler can make with the IF clause. The table in Figure 6.5 illustrates these different tests. The general format of the IF statement is

```
IFxx    expression
. . .
ELSE
. . .
ENDIF
```

The assembler handles the code following the IFxx statement if the condition evaluates as true. The code assembled following an IF statement is terminated with either an ELSE statement or an ENDIF statement. The ELSE statement is optional. If it appears, the code following it is assembled if the condition of the IF statement is not met. The ENDIF statement ends the conditional assembly, and must appear.

IF Operation		Assemble Code If:
IF	expression	Expression is not equal to 0
IFE	expression	Expression is equal to 0
IFDEF	symbol	Symbol has been declared external
IFNDEF	symbol	Symbol has not been declared external
IFB	<argument>	Argument is blank
IFNB	<argument>	Argument is not blank
IFIDN	<arg1>,<arg2>	String arg1 is identical to string arg2
IFDIF	<arg1>,<arg2>	String arg1 is different than string arg2
IF1		The assembler is in pass 1
IF2		The assembler is in pass 2

Figure 6.5   IF Expressions for Conditional Assembly

Let's look at another example to see several other uses of conditional assembly. This example, Figure 6.6, shows the use of another IF clause, IFB. It also shows the use of nested conditionals. The macro here is FLD, the load instruction for the 8087. This instruction requires several conditions in its assembly since it can exist in the following forms:

```
FLD
FLD       1
FLD       short_real
FLD       long_real
FLD       temporary_real
```

The operand field of the FLD macro may be either blank, constant, a four-byte variable, an eight-byte variable, or a ten-byte variable. The FLD macro must determine which of these is the case and generate the correct code. (Chapter 7 explains all of these data types in great detail.)

The IFB expression determines whether or not the operand is present. If the operand isn't present, the assembler generates the correct code for that case since the IFB evaluates as true. The first macro call shows this, which generates the code

```
DB     09BH,0D9H,0C1H
```

The EXITM statement contained in this section of the IF clause is the command to exit the macro. Whenever the assembler encounters this statement while expanding a macro, it terminates the macro expansion, just as if the statement had been ENDM. For this macro, it makes the assembler skip the remaining portion of the macro. Exiting the macro in this manner also causes the warning message "Open conditionals: 1" to appear in the assembly listing. This message alerts you that the assembler did not encounter the ENDIF statement that matches the conditional IF statement. This occurs because you exited the macro early. Although this isn't desirable, it does no damage. If the EXITM statement isn't in a conditional clause, no warning appears.

The EXITM is necessary in this macro because the assembler tests all

```
The IBM Personal Computer MACRO Assembler 01-01-83          PAGE    1-1
Figure 6.6  Nested Conditional Assembly

 1                                         PAGE    ,132
 2                                         TITLE   Figure 6.6  Nested Conditional Assembly
 3
 4                                 FLD     MACRO   SOURCE
 5                                         IFB     <SOURCE>
 6                                         DB      09BH,0D9H,0C1H            ;; FLD ST(1)
 7                                         EXITM
 8                                         ELSE
 9                                         IFE     TYPE SOURCE
10                                         DB      09BH,0D9H,0C0H+SOURCE   ;; FLD ST(i)
11                                         ENDIF
12                                         IFE     4 - TYPE SOURCE
13                                         DB      09BH
14                                         ESC     8,SOURCE             ;; FLD short_real
15                                         ENDIF
16                                         IFE     8 - TYPE SOURCE
17                                         DB      09BH
18                                         ESC     40,SOURCE            ;; FLD long_real
19                                         ENDIF
20                                         IFE     10 - TYPE SOURCE
21                                         DB      09BH
22                                         ESC     01DH,SOURCE          ;; FLD temporary_real
23                                         ENDIF
24                                         ENDIF
25                                         ENDM
26
27      0000                       CODE    SEGMENT
28                                         ASSUME  CS:CODE, DS:CODE
29
30      0000 ????????              FOUR_BYTE   DD      ?
31      0004 ????????????????      EIGHT_BYTE  DQ      ?
32      000C ????????????????????  TEN_BYTE    DT      ?
33      ??
34
35                                         FLD
36      0016 9B D9 C1           +          DB      09BH,0D9H,0C1H
37                                         FLD     1
38      0019 9B D9 C1           +          DB      09BH,0D9H,0C0H+1
39                                         FLD     FOUR_BYTE
40      001C 9B                 +          DB      09BH
41      001D D9 06 0000 R       +          ESC     8,FOUR_BYTE
42                                         FLD     EIGHT_BYTE
43      0021 9B                 +          DB      09BH
44      0022 DD 06 0004 R       +          ESC     40,EIGHT_BYTE
45                                         FLD     TEN_BYTE
46      0026 9B                 +          DB      09BH
47      0027 DB 2E 000C R       +          ESC     01DH,TEN_BYTE
48
49      002B                       CODE    ENDS
50                                         END
Open conditionals: 1
```

Figure 6.6 Nested Conditional Assembly

conditional statements, even if they won't assemble. In this case, if the operand SOURCE is blank, the ELSE clause prevents any of the other FLD cases from being generated. However, the assembler goes ahead and evaluates the

IFE   TYPE SOURCE

statement even though it can't generate any code. If SOURCE is blank, the assembler generates a syntax error. You can ignore the error, but it goes against our principles to accept an assembly with error messages. The use of the EXITM, however, generates a warning message "Open conditionals." Although this warning is not desirable, it is the lesser of the two evils.

Notice that the FLD macro uses the ELSE clause to indicate that the assembler should execute the expressions for evaluating the operand field only if the operand field is not blank. The IF statements using the TYPE operator determine which type of operand has been used for this macro invocation. Although it isn't mentioned in the Macro Assembler Reference Manual, the TYPE operator returns a 0 value if the operand is a constant rather than a symbol. This macro chose this approach for workability rather than elegance.

REPEAT MACROS

The Macro Assembler has some special macro forms when you want to repeat the same section of code several times. These macro expressions are REPT, IRP, and IRPC. Each of these expressions acts as a macro in itself, generating the code following it until the assembler encounters the ENDM statement.

To simply repeat a sequence of instructions, you use the REPT macro.

```
REPT      expression
;. . . REPT macro body
ENDM
```

duplicates the code in the macro body. The value of the expression determines the number of times the text is repeated.

You may use different arguments for each repetition with the IRP macro.

```
IRP       dummy,<list>
;. . .IRP macro body
ENDM
```

goes through the body of the macro once for every item in the list. Each time through the macro body, the assembler replaces the parameter "dummy" with the next item on the list. Items on the list must be numeric expressions.

If you want to use character values in the list, use the IRPC macro.

```
IRPC      dummy,string
;. . .IRPC macro body
ENDM
```

goes through the body of the macro once for every character in the string. The dummy parameter is replaced with the next item in the string each time through. Figure 6.7 shows an example of each of these repeat functions.

```
The IBM Personal Computer MACRO Assembler 01-01-83          PAGE    1-1
Figure 6.7  Repeat Macros

 1                                        PAGE    ,132
 2                                        TITLE   Figure 6.7  Repeat Macros
 3
 4      0000                      CODE    SEGMENT
 5                                        ASSUME  CS:CODE, DS:CODE
 6
 7                                        REPT    3               ; Repeat the code 3 times
 8                                        INC     AX
 9                                        ENDM
10      0000  40                +         INC     AX
11      0001  40                +         INC     AX
12      0002  40                +         INC     AX
13
14                                        IRP     VALUE,<5,10,15,20>
15                                        ADD     AX,VALUE
16                                        ENDM
17      0003  05 0005           +         ADD     AX,5
18      0006  05 000A           +         ADD     AX,10
19      0009  05 000F           +         ADD     AX,15
20      000C  05 0014           +         ADD     AX,20
21
22                                        IRPC    CHAR,ABCD
```

Figure 6.7   Repeat Macros

```
23                                             ADD      AX,CHAR&X
24                                             ENDM
25        000F   03 C0            +            ADD      AX,AX
26        0011   03 C3            +            ADD      AX,BX
27        0013   03 C1            +            ADD      AX,CX
28        0015   03 C2            +            ADD      AX,DX
29
30        0017                         CODE    ENDS
31                                             END
```

Figure 6.7   *Continued*

MACRO OPERATORS

The IRPC example in Figure 6.7 also shows how to use the "&" symbol. This macro operator joins two items together. In this example, the "&" operator joins the parameter CHAR to the constant text "X." As you can see, this forms a valid register name.

Another valuable macro function is the LOCAL statement. The LOCAL statement defines a label which is used only in the macro. This label must be unique for each invocation of the macro. Suppose that you want to write a macro that requires a section of code like this:

```
AAAAA:    ADD      AL,[BX]
          INC      BX
          LOOP     AAAAA
```

The first time you invoke this macro everything works fine. However, the second time you use this macro in the same assembly, the label AAAAA appears for the second time. The assembler can't allow two labels with the same name in the same assembly, and marks this as an error.

If you declare the label AAAAA as LOCAL in the macro, the problem is solved. The assembler substitutes its own unique name for each occurrence of the

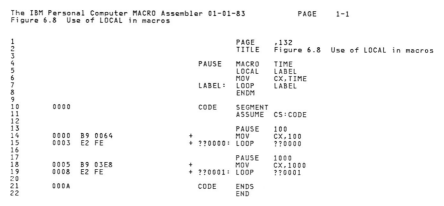

```
The IBM Personal Computer MACRO Assembler 01-01-83          PAGE    1-1
Figure 6.8  Use of LOCAL in macros

 1                                             PAGE     ,132
 2                                             TITLE    Figure 6.8  Use of LOCAL in macros
 3
 4                                    PAUSE    MACRO    TIME
 5                                             LOCAL    LABEL
 6                                             MOV      CX,TIME
 7                                    LABEL:   LOOP     LABEL
 8                                             ENDM
 9
10        0000                        CODE     SEGMENT
11                                             ASSUME   CS:CODE
12
13                                             PAUSE    100
14        0000  B9 0064          +             MOV      CX,100
15        0003  E2 FE            + ??0000:     LOOP     ??0000
16
17                                             PAUSE    1000
18        0005  B9 03E8          +             MOV      CX,1000
19        0008  E2 FE            + ??0001:     LOOP     ??0001
20
21        000A                         CODE    ENDS
22                                             END
```

Figure 6.8   Use of LOCAL in Macros

Symbol	Meaning
;;	Comment for use in macro definition only
&	Concatenate text with parameter
!	Enter next character literally
%	Convert the following expression to a value

Figure 6.9 Macro Symbols

label AAAAA. The first time the assembler sees a LOCAL symbol, it gives it the name "??0000." The next occurrence becomes "??0001," and so on. Each label is unique in the assembly, so there won't be any errors. Figure 6.8 shows the use of the LOCAL statement. This macro, PAUSE, sets up a loop count and then loops using the local label. This macro lets a program pause for a variable amount of time. If you need LOCAL in a macro, it must appear as the first statement in the macro, immediately following the MACRO statement.

There are some special symbols that help you manipulate macros and their parameters. The table in Figure 6.9 shows you the four symbols together with their meanings.

Figure 6.10 is an assembly listing of a program that uses these symbols. We have already seen the use of ";;" in some of the 8087 macros. This special comment field identifier tells the macro processor to delete the comment field during the macro expansion. This lets you put comments in a macro without having them appear in every expansion of the macro. We also saw the use of "&" in Figure 6.7.

The "!" symbol lets you include any symbol as the next character. You'll need this operation if you want to include one of the special macro symbols such as "%" in the macro and not have it cause a macro operation. Finally, the "%" operator converts a symbol into the number which it currently represents. You can use this feature to number things during macro generation. In our example, the macro numbers messages according to the number represented by VALUE.

```
The IBM Personal Computer MACRO Assembler 01-01-83          PAGE    1-1
Figure 6.10 Macro Special Characters


1                                      PAGE    ,132
2                                      TITLE   Figure 6.10 Macro Special Characters
3
4       = 0000                 VALUE   EQU     0
5
6                              EXAMPLE MACRO   PARAMETER
7                                      DB      'MSG&PARAMETER'          ;; Comment appears only in definition
8                                      INC     AX
9                                      ENDM
10
11
12      0000                   CODE    SEGMENT
13                                     ASSUME  CS:CODE
14
15                                     EXAMPLE %VALUE
16      0000  4D 53 47 30        +     DB      'MSG0'
17      0004  40                 +     INC     AX
18
19      0005                   CODE    ENDS
20                                     END
```

Figure 6.10 Macro Special Characters

INCLUDE STATEMENT

The INCLUDE assembler statement inserts text into the assembly from another file. The INCLUDE operation is particularly applicable to the set of macros, such as a set of 8087 macros, for example. The 8087 macros represent all of the 8087 instructions. You need to include that set of macros, or some subset of them, in every assembly that uses the 8087. However, it is a nuisance to get a copy of those macros into every source file. Besides, the macros take up so much room that the source code would quickly fill your diskette if you attempted to put a copy of the macros in every file.

The INCLUDE function of the assembler handles the problem. The statement

    INCLUDE   filename

takes the contents of the named file and includes it as part of the assembly. The assembler inserts the file contents at the location of the INCLUDE statement. The INCLUDE statement is a natural for use with macro libraries, such as the 8087 macros. You place the INCLUDE statement at the beginning of the program, and every 8087 instruction in the program assembles correctly.

Similarly, you can use the INCLUDE statement to bring in other sections of code. If you want to break your program up into small source files, but assemble it as one file, the main source file can consist of INCLUDEs for all of the smaller source files. However, for the reasons we discussed in Chapter 5, assembling small modules and linking them together with LINK is probably a better approach in most cases.

Another possibility for an INCLUDE file is a data structure. You may be using a particular data structure in several programs. You can maintain the data structure definition as a separate file, and access it using the INCLUDE statement in every program that requires it. Later in this chapter we'll discuss the ways that a program can set up and use data structures.

If the INCLUDEd file is a macro file, there is no reason for it to appear in the assembly listing each time you assemble the program. You can use the IF1 conditional to delete the macros from the listing, but still make them available for code generation. The assembly sequence

    IF1
    INCLUDE   87MAC.LIB
    ENDIF

includes the file 87MAC.LIB during the first pass of the assembler. It is during the first pass that the assembler expands all the macros into their final form. Since the assembler doesn't need the macro definitions during the second pass, the program should include them only for the first pass. This speeds up the assembly, since the macro file isn't read during the second pass. The assembler doesn't print the

```
            PAGE    ,132
            TITLE    Figure 6.11 8087 Macro INCLUDE

IF1
INCLUDE 87MAC.LIB
ENDIF

CODE     SEGMENT
         ASSUME   CS:CODE, DS:CODE

TWO_BYTE         DW      ?

         FENI
         FIDIVR  TWO_BYTE
         FLD

CODE     ENDS
         END
```

Figure 6.11(a) Source Instructions

```
The IBM Personal Computer MACRO Assembler 01-01-83              PAGE    1-1
Figure 6.11 8087 Macro INCLUDE

 1                                              PAGE    ,132
 2                                              TITLE    Figure 6.11 8087 Macro INCLUDE
 3
 4                                      ENDIF
 5
 6      0000                            CODE    SEGMENT
 7                                              ASSUME   CS:CODE, DS:CODE
 8
 9      0000  ????                      TWO_BYTE         DW      ?
10
11                                              FENI
12      0002  9B DB E0         +                DB      09BH,0DBH,0E0H
13                                      FIDIVR  TWO_BYTE
14      0005  9B               +                DB      09BH
15      0006  DE 3E 0000 R     +                ESC     037H,TWO_BYTE
16                                      FLD
17      000A  9B D9 C1         +                DB      09BH,0D9H,0C1H
18
19      000D                            CODE    ENDS
20                                              END
Open conditionals: 1
```

Figure 6.11(b) Assembly Listing

Figure 6.11   8087 Macro INCLUDE. (a) Source instructions; (b) Assembly Listing.

macro file since it creates the listing file during the second pass. Figure 6.11 shows this use of the IF1 . . . INCLUDE . . . ENDIF for the 8087 macros. This figure contains both the source and listing files for the program. The assembler handles the 8087 instructions correctly without a listing of the macros that define them.

SEGMENTS

We looked at the SEGMENT statement previously. Now we have a chance to examine it more closely, and see what other things it can do.

In most of the example programs that we have used so far, there has been a single SEGMENT statement. Since the program code must be in some segment, we have to name one. Since the assembler must be able to determine the segment addressing, the single ASSUME statement in the programs identifies the only segment of the program. In a case like this, we aren't using the segmentation capabilities of the 8088 to their fullest, and in many instances, it isn't necessary to do so. If a program and its data area reside within the same 64K address region, there's no reason to exercise the segmentation capabilities of the processor.

There are instances in which a program must use more than a single segment statement. Several of the DOS examples in Chapter 5 showed one such usage. In those examples, the program defined a STACK segment. The segment name was immaterial, but the class of the segment, as indicated on the SEGMENT statement, had to be STACK. This is because the .EXE file requires a stack area set aside for the execution of the program. If the program didn't establish a STACK segment, the DOS loader would leave the stack initialized at some location that might be inappropriate. In that case, the program would probably not run very well.

Another use of the SEGMENT statement is to locate data at some particular place in the machine. As we have seen with DOS, it's best if the program is code segment relocatable. In that way we don't care where DOS loads the program. But there will be instances when the actual location of the code or data is important. In those cases we can use the AT directive of the SEGMENT statement to locate the data.

To see the value of the AT directive, we'll look at an example. This example uses the ROM BIOS of the Personal Computer as the starting point. Although assembly language is a very powerful programming tool, it is also a difficult tool to work with, particularly for large programs. Therefore, you choose assembly language because it has attributes which make it desirable for a particular job. For the IBM Personal Computer, assembly language programming is the best language for the jobs that ROM BIOS performs. We can characterize these applications by a requirement to control an I/O device, which usually requires bit significant operations. The ability to manipulate precisely located memory locations and I/O ports are all part of this programming. Assembly language programming is also used in cases where you require the minimum code size or the best possible execution speed. All of these are characteristics of the ROM BIOS.

This example utilizes a part of ROM BIOS. In a later chapter we'll discuss just how to go about replacing parts of the ROM BIOS. For this case, however, we're interested in accessing the data structures that ROM BIOS uses. If you examine the assembly language listing of the ROM BIOS (which is given in Appendix A of the Technical Reference Manual for the IBM Personal Computer), you'll see that it locates the DATA segment at segment 40H or absolute address 400H. The program in Figure 6.12 accesses the data in the ROM BIOS data area for a specific purpose. There is a variable, KB_FLAG, in the DATA segment that indicates the current state of the shift keys. One of the complaints often made about the IBM keyboard is that you can't tell whether you are in CAPS LOCK state or not. The program of Figure 6.12 reads the CAPS LOCK data bit and displays it at the upper right corner of the color/graphics display screen. Although this program doesn't do it, we'll assume that when you actually use this section of code, the upper right corner of the screen is set aside for this indicator.

The DATA segment of Figure 6.12 shows how the programmer can transfer absolute address information to the program. The DATA SEGMENT statement uses the AT directive to locate the segment unconditionally at paragraph 40H.

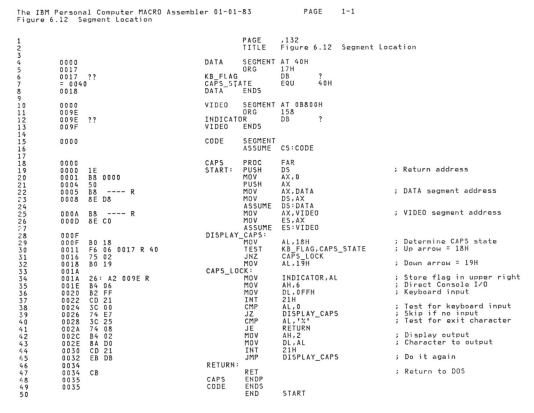

```
 1                                          PAGE    ,132
 2                                          TITLE   Figure 6.12  Segment Location
 3
 4       0000                       DATA    SEGMENT AT 40H
 5       0017                               ORG     17H
 6       0017  ??                   KB_FLAG         DB      ?
 7     = 0040                        CAPS_STATE      EQU     40H
 8       0018                       DATA    ENDS
 9
10       0000                       VIDEO   SEGMENT AT 0B800H
11       009E                               ORG     158
12       009E  ??                   INDICATOR       DB      ?
13       009F                       VIDEO   ENDS
14
15       0000                       CODE    SEGMENT
16                                          ASSUME  CS:CODE
17
18       0000                       CAPS    PROC    FAR
19       0000  1E                   START:  PUSH    DS              ; Return address
20       0001  B8 0000                      MOV     AX,0
21       0004  50                           PUSH    AX
22       0005  B8 ---- R                    MOV     AX,DATA         ; DATA segment address
23       0008  8E D8                        MOV     DS,AX
24                                          ASSUME  DS:DATA
25       000A  B8 ---- R                    MOV     AX,VIDEO        ; VIDEO segment address
26       000D  8E C0                        MOV     ES,AX
27                                          ASSUME  ES:VIDEO
28       000F                       DISPLAY_CAPS:
29       000F  B0 18                        MOV     AL,18H          ; Determine CAPS state
30       0011  F6 06 0017 R 40              TEST    KB_FLAG,CAPS_STATE ; Up arrow = 18H
31       0016  75 02                        JNZ     CAPS_LOCK
32       0018  B0 19                        MOV     AL,19H          ; Down arrow = 19H
33       001A                       CAPS_LOCK:
34       001A  26: A2 009E R                MOV     INDICATOR,AL    ; Store flag in upper right
35       001E  B4 06                        MOV     AH,6            ; Direct Console I/O
36       0020  B2 FF                        MOV     DL,0FFH         ; Keyboard input
37       0022  CD 21                        INT     21H
38       0024  3C 00                        CMP     AL,0
39       0026  74 E7                        JZ      DISPLAY_CAPS    ; Test for keyboard input
40       0028  3C 25                        CMP     AL,'%'          ; Skip if no input
41       002A  74 08                        JE      RETURN          ; Test for exit character
42       002C  B4 02                        MOV     AH,2            ; Display output
43       002E  8A D0                        MOV     DL,AL           ; Character to output
44       0030  CD 21                        INT     21H
45       0032  EB DB                        JMP     DISPLAY_CAPS    ; Do it again
46       0034                       RETURN:
47       0034  CB                           RET                     ; Return to DOS
48       0035                       CAPS    ENDP
49       0035                       CODE    ENDS
50       0035                               END     START
```

Figure 6.12   Segment Location

Looking further at the ROM BIOS listing shows us that the variable KB_FLAG is at offset 17H in the DATA segment. The ORG 17H in the program locates the offset of that variable for the assembly. Finally, the EQU for CAPS_STATE comes directly from the ROM BIOS listing. This bit location indicates the current state of the CAPS LOCK toggle.

There is another SEGMENT statement in Figure 6.12. This is the VIDEO segment, located at 0B800H. This is the segment address for the display buffer for the color/graphics display adapter. We need this address to store the indicator on the display. If we want to put the character in the upper right corner, assuming an 80-character screen, the correct offset for the character is 158 decimal. Chapter 8 describes the programming attributes of the hardware device, so you'll have to take it on faith for now.

The first portion of the program establishes the segment addressing required in the program. The DS register points to the DATA segment, ES to the VIDEO segment. Even though the program declares the segments as absolute using the AT declaration, the assembler still indicates them as relocatable, with the ''R'' attribute. However, the LINK program places the correct values into these data fields.

The program tests the KB_FLAG, allowing the assembler to generate the correct offset—17H. The example uses the down-arrow symbol to indicate normal case, the up arrow to signify CAPS LOCK. The program reads keyboard input using the DOS function, displaying the character if one is entered. The example arbitrarily chose the symbol '%' to terminate the program. If the user enters any other character, the program displays the character and returns for more.

If you should enter and execute this program, you will see the up or down arrow displayed in the upper right corner of the color/graphics display. If the color display is in 40-character mode when this program is executed, the arrow indicator appears on the second line from the top. If you want to run this program with the monochrome display adapter, change the VIDEO segment to 0B000H, the location of the monochrome display buffer.

When you execute this program using the color/graphics adapter in the 80-character mode, you'll see a great deal of "snow" on the screen. This display interference occurs when the program writes directly into the display buffer. You won't see this interference with the monochrome adapter or with the color/graphics adapter in the 40-column mode. We'll see why this is, and how to get around it, when we discuss the hardware of the IBM Personal Computer.

There are other uses for multiple SEGMENT statements in a program. If a program requires a data area greater than 64K, it must manage the access to that data. Quite commonly, you'll handle the data area with some memory management scheme. In such a situation, you would manage all of the data area (with the exception of a few fixed areas) through indirect references.

As an example, let's look at the way the command interpreter for DOS loads programs. DOS loads a transient program at the paragraph boundary following the resident portion of DOS. The length of the resident portion can vary depending on the number of diskette drives in the system. Also, the use of DOS interrupt INT 27H, which causes a program to exit but remain resident, effectively increases the length of DOS. However, the DOS program loader must address the Program Segment Prefix (PSP) of the program it is loading. The easiest way to define this data structure is with a separate SEGMENT statement.

Figure 6.13 shows a SEGMENT declaration that might be used in two different places. If we could see the source code for the DOS loader, we might find such a definition there. For a program using an .EXE structure, we might have such a segment structure to allow access to the variables in the PSP. In Figure 5.6, the DOS example, a .COM file structure was used. This allowed us to reference the various locations in the PSP with an offset relative to the PSP. DOS loaded the program code into the same segment that contained the PSP, making it a pretty simple task.

For the .EXE file, the PSP is in a different segment than the code. Since DOS points the DS and ES registers at the PSP when control goes to the .EXE program, it makes sense to handle the PSP as a separate segment. The fragment of

```
The IBM Personal Computer MACRO Assembler 01-01-83              PAGE    1-1
Figure 6.13 Program Segment Prefix

 1                                                 PAGE     ,132
 2                                                 TITLE    Figure 6.13 Program Segment Prefix
 3        0000                             PROGRAM_SEGMENT_PREFIX   SEGMENT
 4
 5        0000      02 [                   INT_20             DB       2 DUP(?)
 6                        ??
 7                          ]
 8
 9        0002    ????                     MEMORY_SIZE        DW       ?
10        0004      05 [                   LONG_CALL          DB       5 DUP(?)
11                        ??
12                          ]
13
14        0009    ????????                 TERMINATE_ADDR    DD       ?
15        000D    ????????                 CTRL_BREAK        DD       ?
16        005C                                       ORG      05CH
17        005C      10 [                   FCB1               DB       16 DUP(?)
18                        ??
19                          ]
20
21        006C                                       ORG      06CH
22        006C      10 [                   FCB2               DB       16 DUP(?)
23                        ??
24                          ]
25
26        0080                                       ORG      080H
27        0080      80 [                   DTA                DB       128 DUP(?)
28                        ??
29                          ]
30
31
32        0100                             PROGRAM_SEGMENT_PREFIX   ENDS
33
34        0000                             CODE     SEGMENT
35                                                  ASSUME   CS:CODE,DS:PROGRAM_SEGMENT_PREFIX
36
37        0000    A1 0002 R                          MOV      AX,MEMORY_SIZE
38
39        0003                             CODE     ENDS
40                                                  END
```

Figure 6.13   Program Segment Prefix

code in the CODE segment of Figure 6.13 indicates how you might access the data in the PSP.

Notice that the PSP segment in Figure 6.13 does not actually contain any values for the data variables. For example, we know that the first two bytes of the PSP contain the code for INT 20H. However, we have chosen to show that there is a two-byte data field at that location, without any reference to the data contained there. We have to do this so that the linker and loader do not attempt to store any data in memory as a result of this segment declaration. We are actually using this segment as a data declaration tool. The segment statement defines a data structure that we call the Program Segment Prefix. It is not a fixed area, but is located by one of the segment registers. In our example in Figure 6.13, it is located by the DS register.

We can use the same method to identify any type of data structure that might be randomly located in the memory area of the 8088. The data structure might be a control block for the operating system. It might be a single line of text for a text editor. Or it might even be the parameter block for a particular subroutine. Each instance of the data structure resides in its own segment. That is, a program references each element of the data structure with the segment register pointing to the beginning (or near the beginning) of the element. The program doesn't access two different elements using the same value of the segment register. It always sets the segment value for each element.

At this point, we should talk a little about memory allocation strategies for the 8088. The IBM Personal Computer with the 8088 processor can address up to 1 megabyte of storage, but a single segment can handle only 64K bytes. Even with the four segment registers, there is no way that a program can get to all of the memory without some segmentation strategies.

If the data can all fit within 64K bytes, there is no need to do anything exciting. Just put all of the data in the same segment. If we assume that a program requires a data area exceeding 64K bytes, we must solve the problem of storage management. There are two strategies that you can employ. In both cases we'll assume that the data can be broken up into smaller units (such as single variables, lines of text, control blocks, or data arrays), each of which is smaller than 64K bytes.

You should use this first allocation method when conserving memory space is your overriding concern. In this method, you locate data objects at the first free location in memory. This requires that the program managing the data areas use a four-byte pointer to each data variable. Two bytes are for the offset, and two more for the segment value. When the program wants to access the data, it recovers the address of the data from the address storage area with an LDS or LES instruction. If you require even greater space savings you can actually contain the pointer in a three-byte field. Two bytes have the segment address of the data. The single remaining byte in the offset of the object in that segment. The starting offset should always be a value between 0 and 15, since the segment value can be a multiple of 16.

While this method is most space efficient in the allocation of data, there are a couple of drawbacks. The maximum size of a data object is slightly less than 64K bytes. In the worst case for this allocation strategy, the absolute address of the data object ends in 0FH, which requires a starting offset of 0FH. Since the maximum offset in any segment is 0FFFFH, the maximum length of the variable is 64K − 15, or 65,521 bytes. A second drawback for this method is the storage required to save the pointers to the data objects. If there are a large number of objects, the sum of all the four-byte (or three-byte) data pointers consumes a great deal of storage.

An example of this method of storage allocation is the File Control Block (FCB). In the previous DOS example we allocated the FCB at an arbitrary location in the program. There was no alignment of the data structure. Then, when we called DOS to perform a file operation, the program needed a four-byte pointer. The DS:DX register pair identified the FCB for DOS.

The second method of data allocation places all data objects on a paragraph boundary. This immediately simplifies the pointer that identifies the data object. The pointer is only two bytes. This two-byte value locates the segment in which the data reside. Since the allocation is always on a paragraph boundary, the starting offset for the data is always zero. This method, however, is wasteful of data space. Each time you allocate a new object in storage, it is possible to waste 15 bytes of storage. This occurs if the last byte of the preceding object is right on the paragraph boundary. The next paragraph boundary is 15 bytes away, and the 15 bytes in between are wasted. Also, the minimum size for an object is 16 bytes. If any data area is smaller than that, the remaining bytes are useless anyway.

As we have discussed, the DOS loader uses the second method of allocating storage when it loads programs. DOS loads the program at the next paragraph boundary. Since DOS assumes that a small number of large objects reside in memory, this method is not particularly wasteful of storage. If, however, your application requires many small objects, paragraph alignment may be too expensive.

The second method of allocation, using paragraph alignment, lets you define the data area using SEGMENT data structures. If you wish to use the first method, you need a different method of defining the data structure. The next section discusses just such a data declaration tool.

STRUCTURES

A data structure is an arrangement of the data that is meaningful to the programmer. As a rule of thumb, we usually define data structures when more than one program or programmer is using the same set of data. By defining the data structure, both parties have a clear image of the data. When program A passes data to program B, the defined data structure ensures that each program looks for the data in the same location.

We already have a good example of a data structure. The File Control Block (FCB) is a data structure. Programs use the FCB to communicate file information to DOS. The FCB holds important data about the open file—values such as the current record number, file size, and so forth. The FCB also contains data that are used only by DOS—the reserved field. All of the data required by DOS and the application program are in the FCB. This data structure communicates the file parameters between DOS and the application program.

We now need a way of defining data structures so that a program can use them conveniently. For the IBM Macro Assembler, there is an assembler operator called STRUC, which lets you define a data structure. From the programmer's viewpoint, it seems as if the data structure is another segment. The data definition assembles just as normal data statements do, and the structure is terminated with an ENDS statement, just like a segment. However, the structure does not actually create the data. The STRUC command identifies the structure of the data for the assembler. In a later portion of the assembly, the program uses the name of the structure to create the data area.

When viewed in that perspective, the STRUC statement is more like a MACRO. A program defines the structure in one section and invokes the structure at a later time. When you invoke the structure the data are actually created. Figure 6.14 will help us to understand the operation of the STRUC statement.

```
The IBM Personal Computer MACRO Assembler 01-01-83          PAGE    1-1
Figure 6.14   Structures

 1                                              PAGE    ,132
 2                                              TITLE   Figure 6.14  Structures
 3
 4                                      FCB     STRUC
 5      0000  00                        DRIVE           DB      0               ; Drive Number
 6      0001  20 20 20 20 20 20 20      FILE_NAME       DB      '          '    ; File name
 7            20 20
 8      0009  20 20 20                  FILE_EXT        DB      '   '           ; Extension
 9      000C  0000                      CURRENT_BLOCK   DW      0               ; Current block number
10      000E  0080                      RECORD_SIZE     DW      80H             ; Logical record size
11      0010  00 00 00 00               FILE_SIZE       DD      0               ; Size of the file, in bytes
12      0014  0000                      DATE            DW      0               ; Date the file was created
13      0016      0A [                  RESERVED        DB      10 DUP(?)       ; Reserved, can't be overriden
14                    ??
15                       ]
16
17      0020  00                        SEQ_NUMBER      DB      0               ; Record in block for sequential
18      0021  00 00 00 00               RANDOM_NUMBER   DD      0               ; Record in file for random
19      0025                            FCB     ENDS
20
21      0000                            STACK   SEGMENT STACK
22      0000      40 [                          DW      64 DUP(?)
23                    ????
24                       ]
25
26      0080                            STACK   ENDS
27
28      0000                            CODE    SEGMENT
29                                              ASSUME  CS:CODE
30
31      0000  01                        INPUT   FCB     <1,'FIG6-14','INP'>
32      0001  46 49 47 36 2D 31
33            34 20
34      0009  49 4E 50
35      000C  0000
36      000E  0080
37      0010  00 00 00 00
38      0014  0000
39      0016      0A [
40                    ??
41                       ]
42      0020  00
43      0021  00 00 00 00
44
45
46      0025  02                        OUTPUT  FCB     <2,'EXAMPLE','TST'>
47      0026  45 58 41 4D 50 4C
48            45 20
49      002E  54 53 54
50      0031  0000
51      0033  0080
52      0035  00 00 00 00
53      0039  0000
54      003B      0A [
55                    ??
56                       ]
57      0045  00
58      0046  00 00 00 00
59
60
61      004A                            STRUCTURES      PROC    FAR
62      004A  1E                                PUSH    DS              ; Set return address
63      004B  B8 0000                           MOV     AX,0
64      004E  50                                PUSH    AX
65      004F  0E                                PUSH    CS              ; Set DS into CODE segment
66      0050  1F                                POP     DS
67                                              ASSUME  DS:CODE
68      0051  8D 16 0000 R                      LEA     DX,INPUT        ; Open the input file
69      0055  B4 0F                             MOV     AH,0FH
70      0057  CD 21                             INT     21H
71
72      0059  8D 16 0025 R                      LEA     DX,OUTPUT       ; Create the output file
73      005D  B4 16                             MOV     AH,16H
74      005F  CD 21                             INT     21H
75
76      0061  8D 1E 0000 R                      LEA     BX,INPUT
77      0065  C7 47 0E 0010                     MOV     [BX].RECORD_SIZE,16   ; Set record size for input file
78      006A  C6 47 20 01                       MOV     [BX].SEQ_NUMBER,1     ; Skip first record
79
80      006E  C7 06 0033 R 0010                 MOV     OUTPUT.RECORD_SIZE,16 ; Set record size for output
81
82      0074  8D 16 0000 R                      LEA     DX,INPUT        ; Read second record in file
83      0078  B4 14                             MOV     AH,14H
84      007A  CD 21                             INT     21H
85
86      007C  8D 16 0025 R                      LEA     DX,OUTPUT       ; Write that record to ouput
87      0080  B4 15                             MOV     AH,15H
88      0082  CD 21                             INT     21H
89
```

Figure 6.14   Structures

```
90      0084  B4 10                          MOV     AH,10H                    ; Close the output file
91      0086  CD 21                          INT     21H
92
93      0088  CB                             RET
94      0089                   STRUCTURES    ENDP
95      0089                   CODE    ENDS
96                                           END     STRUCTURES
```

The IBM Personal Computer MACRO Assembler 01-01-83   PAGE   Symbols-1
Figure 6.14 Structures

Structures and records:

	Width	# fields		
N a m e	Shift	Width	Mask	Initial
FCB.	0025	000A		
DRIVE.	0000			
FILE_NAME.	0001			
FILE_EXT	0009			
CURRENT_BLOCK.	000C			
RECORD_SIZE.	000E			
FILE_SIZE.	0010			
DATE	0014			
RESERVED	0016			
SEQ_NUMBER	0020			
RANDOM_NUMBER.	0021			

Figure 6.14 *Continued*

Figure 6.14 contains a very simple program that uses DOS files. This program opens a DOS file on drive A:, reads the second record of that file, and writes that record to a DOS file on drive B:. It's unlikely that you would ever write such a program to do anything important, but it gives us a chance to use the data structure for the FCB.

The first portion of the program in Figure 6.14 defines the data structure FCB. The assembler operator STRUC marks the beginning of the structure definition. The label FCB names this particular structure. The example defines each of the fields of the FCB in the structure. Notice that the assembler generates the assembler code for the structure in the left-hand columns. However, when the assembled object code is linked, there is no data area in the program. The assembler has included an assembled version of the data structure only for your reference.

Just as if it were a macro, the name FCB has become a new assembler operator. The first statement in the CODE segment is an invocation of the FCB data structure. The example gives this data structure the name INPUT. This FCB identifies the input data set. Notice that there are operands together with the FCB statement. These operands replace, or override, the values that were included in the original definition of the data structure.

When we compare the object code for the definition of the FCB structure with the object code for the INPUT structure we see that they differ in the first three fields of the structure. The definition contains a 0 in the DRIVE field, while INPUT has a 1. The first operand in the angle brackets of the INPUT definition is a 1. This replacement value overrides the original defined value of 0. Similarly, the example overrides the second and third fields, which name the file. The closing angle bracket in the INPUT definition ends the replacement values for the fields of the structure. The remainder of the INPUT structure is identical to the FCB definition.

A program can change any of the fields in the FCB structure if the original definition of the field contains only a single entry. For this example, the program can modify every field in FCB with the exception of the RESERVED field. We defined this field as 10 separate entries, and it can't be changed. Similarly, if a field is defined as

    DB   10,20

you can't override it. You can only change fields with a single entry in the STRUC invocation. The assembler treats a character string, composed of multiple characters, as a single entry. In this example, the field FILE_NAME has multiple characters, but is a single entry that you can override.

The operands in the angle brackets replace the defined operands on a positional basis, just as they do in a macro. If you don't want to modify a defined value, but wish to change the following field, you must include a null parameter in the list of values. For example, to modify the FILE_NAME and the CURRENT_BLOCK, while leaving the default value for the DRIVE and FILE_EXT, you would invoke the FCB structure with this statement:

    EXAMPLE   FCB   <,NEWNAME,,12>

The first parameter field is null, so the assembler uses the default. NEWNAME replaces the blank string in the next field. The default blank string is used for FILE_EXT, and finally 12 replaces 0 as the value in CURRENT_BLOCK.

The next source line of the Figure 6.14 program defines the FCB for the output file, naming it OUTPUT. Here again the example modifies the first three fields of the data definition by including the new values in the operand field of the FCB statement.

The value of using a data structure shows in the actual instructions for the program. The program may reference INPUT and OUTPUT as any other labels in the program. You can see this in the section of code that opens the INPUT file, with the

    LEA   DX,INPUT

statement used to establish the address of the input FCB.

We can use each of the fields of the data structure in the program. The value of this symbol is the offset of that field in the data structure. For example, the program sets the BX register with the address of the INPUT FCB. We then access the RECORD_SIZE and SEQ_NUMBER fields using a base register addressing mode. Since BX already points to the FCB, we must specify the offset from that base. The address mode

    [BX].RECORD_SIZE

tells the assembler to generate an instruction that adds the offset in the data structure of RECORD_SIZE to the base value in the BX register. When you examine the machine language for the instructions, you can see that the offset for

RECORD_SIZE (0EH) and SEQ_NUMBER (20H) appear in the instructions. The "." symbol identifies the field names as offsets in a data structure.

Besides based and indexed addressing modes, you can use the data structure for direct addressing. The next portion of the program modifies the RECORD _SIZE field of the OUTPUT FCB directly. The program names this field as OUTPUT.RECORD_SIZE. The symbol OUTPUT identifies the particular data structure. RECORD_SIZE names the field in that data structure.

Before we leave this example, let's look at what the assembler knows about the data structure. The figure includes a portion of the symbol table. The assembler sets aside a section of the symbol table for structures and records. The assembler shows you the information it has about the structure. This section has the title "Structures and records." For the FCB structure in the example, the first line shows that the structure is 25H bytes in length and contains 0AH fields. The assembler also shows each of the fields indented under the structure name. The symbol table shows the offset of each field. For structures, the assembler uses the two columns labeled "width" and "# fields." The second row of column labels is used with records. In the next section we'll discuss data structures known to the assembler as records.

This example program in Figure 6.14 doesn't do anything useful. It also doesn't contain any error handling. However, it does illustrate the use of the STRUC statement. This data definition tool is particularly useful for often-used data structures. The use of the field names for offset values is very useful when you are modifying the data structures during program development. If you change the data structure, the assembler automatically changes the offset values when the program is reassembled. Also, using data structures helps make an assembly program more readable and understandable.

RECORDS

The structures of the preceding section are intended for multiple-byte structures. There are times when you need to identify data objects bit by bit. For this, the Macro Assembler provides a data definition mechanism named RECORD.

RECORD is similar to STRUC and MACRO in its operation. The RECORD statement defines the data structure. The name given to the RECORD becomes another operator for the assembler. You can use that record name to define specific occurrences of the data. RECORD differs from STRUC in that it defines objects at the bit level. The RECORD statement gives names to each of the fields, together with the width of each field in bits. You can use the RECORD statement to generate bit fields up to a total of 16 bits.

Here again, we'll work with an example. In Figure 6.15 there is another do-nothing program, this one concerned with finding the date of a file. The definition of the File Control Block contains a 16-bit field containing the date when DOS

```
The IBM Personal Computer MACRO Assembler 01-01-83          PAGE    1-1
Figure 6.15  Records

 1                                       PAGE    ,132
 2                                       TITLE   Figure 6.15  Records
 3
 4                              DATE_WORD        RECORD  YEAR:7,MONTH:4,DAY:5
 5
 6      0000                    STACK   SEGMENT STACK
 7      0000      40 [                  DW      64 DUP(?)
 8                      ????
 9                           ]
10
11      0080                    STACK   ENDS
12
13      0000                    CODE    SEGMENT
14                                      ASSUME  CS:CODE
15
16      0000                    FCB     LABEL   BYTE
17      0000   01               DRIVE           DB      1            ; Drive Number
18      0001   46 49 47 36 2D 31 FILE_NAME      DB      'FIG6-15 '   ; File name
19             35 20
20      0009   41 53 4D         FILE_EXT        DB      'ASM'        ; Extension
21      000C   0000             CURRENT_BLOCK   DW      0            ; Current block number
22      000E   0080             RECORD_SIZE     DW      80H          ; Logical record size
23      0010   00 00 00 00      FILE_SIZE       DD      0            ; Size of the file, in bytes
24      0014   00 00            DATE            DATE_WORD   <>       ; Date the file was created
25      0016      0A [          RESERVED        DB      10 DUP(?)    ; Reserved, can't be overriden
26                      ??
27                           ]
28
29      0020   00               SEQ_NUMBER      DB      0            ; Record in block for sequential
30      0021   00 00 00 00      RANDOM_NUMBER   DD      0            ; Record in file for random
31
32      0025                    RECORDS         PROC    FAR
33      0025   1E                       PUSH    DS                   ; Set return address
34      0026   B8 0000                  MOV     AX,0
35      0029   50                       PUSH    AX
36      002A   0E                       PUSH    CS                   ; Set DS into CODE segment
37      002B   1F                       POP     DS
38                                      ASSUME  DS:CODE
39      002C   8D 16 0000 R             LEA     DX,FCB               ; Open the file
40      0030   B4 0F                    MOV     AH,0FH
41      0032   CD 21                    INT     21H
42
43      0034   A1 0014 R               MOV     AX,DATE
44      0037   25 FE00                 AND     AX,MASK YEAR          ; Isolate the year
45      003A   B1 09                   MOV     CL,YEAR               ; Right justify the value
46      003C   D3 E8                   SHR     AX,CL
47      003E   8A F8                   MOV     BH,AL                 ; Store year in BH
48
49      0040   A1 0014 R               MOV     AX,DATE
50      0043   25 01E0                 AND     AX,MASK MONTH
51      0046   B1 05                   MOV     CL,MONTH
52      0048   D3 E8                   SHR     AX,CL
53      004A   8A D8                   MOV     BL,AL                 ; Store month in BL
54
55      004C   A1 0014 R               MOV     AX,DATE
56      004F   25 001F                 AND     AX,MASK DAY           ; Store day in AL
57
58      0052   CB                      RET
59      0053                   RECORDS          ENDP
60      0053                   CODE    ENDS
61                             END     RECORDS

The IBM Personal Computer MACRO Assembler 01-01-83          PAGE    Symbols-1
Figure 6.15  Records
```

Structures and records:

Name	Width Shift	# fields Width	Mask	Initial
DATE_WORD.	0010	0003		
YEAR	0009	0007	FE00	0000
MONTH.	0005	0004	01E0	0000
DAY.	0000	0005	001F	0000

Figure 6.15   Records

created or last updated the file. When DOS opens a file, DOS fills this field in the FCB from the date information stored in the diskette directory. The date field contains the year, month, and day encoded in the 16 bits. The RECORD statement of Figure 6.15 shows the layout of this word.

In Figure 6.15, the example gives the name DATE_WORD to the RECORD. The operand field of RECORD shows that there are three fields in

DATE_WORD. The first 7 bits are the YEAR, the next 4 bits are the MONTH, with the last 5 bits containing the DAY. Just as with a MACRO, this source instruction merely defines the particular record type called DATE_WORD. The RECORD statement does not create the data in storage until you use the RECORD name as an assembly operator.

The example generates DATE using the DATE_WORD definition in the FCB. The label DATE identifies this data area, and DATE_WORD generates the 16 bit data area. As we'll see later, there are methods of defining the default and override values for the field values in a record. In this example, we haven't done anything to modify the normal value of zero for each of the fields.

Besides showing you the structure of the RECORD statement, the program in Figure 6.15 shows you some of the operations that the RECORD statement makes simple. The first portion of the program opens the file named in the FCB. The remainder of the program takes the date information from the FCB and moves the individual fields into the registers of the 8088.

The program first isolates the year value from the data in the FCB. After it moves the DATE word into AX, it sets the month and day values in the word to zero with an AND instruction. Notice here that the immediate operand is MASK YEAR. Since YEAR is a field within a record, the MASK operator returns a value that isolates the YEAR within the word. In this case, MASK YEAR returns a value 0FE00H. As you can see, the first 7 bits are one, with the remainder zero. This mask value corresponds to the bits that form the YEAR value in the word. ANDing this value with the rest of the record leaves only the YEAR field.

In the next instructions, the program moves the YEAR field to the rightmost portion of the word. The field name YEAR has a value equal to the shift count necessary to move the field to the rightmost end of the word. In this case, the value is nine. Shifting right by nine leaves the year as a number in AL. (Remember that DOS encodes the year as a number from 0 to 119. These values correspond to the years 1980 to 2099.)

In the next series of instructions, the example extracts the MONTH field from the record. Here again, the program uses the MASK and shift values from the DATE_WORD record. Similarly, it removes the DAY field from the record.

This example doesn't do any useful work, since the values placed in the registers are lost when the routine returns to DOS. However, you can run the program in DEBUG, and set a breakpoint at the return instruction. Debug displays the BH, BL, and AL registers so you can see the date. A more usable program would take the date values and convert them to ASCII for display. Or you could rewrite this routine as a subroutine, providing date information for another program.

There are several other features of the RECORD operation that we should discuss. Figure 6.15 contains a portion of the symbol table from the assembly. This table shows the information that the assembler has about each of the fields in the record. In this symbol table listing, we'll use the second row of column headers, "Shift Width Mask Initial." As the symbol table shows, the

DATE_WORD record is 16 bits wide with three fields. Each of the fields has four attributes. The shift value is the number of bits in the record to the right of the field. This value tells the assembler how far to shift the field to right-justify it. The mask value isolates the field. A "1" entry in the mask field indicates that that position is part of the field.

The width of the field is available in the assembler for any field of a RECORD. You can determine the width of a field at assembly time with the operator WIDTH. For example,

    MOV AL, WIDTH YEAR

stores the value seven in the AL register in this example.

The initial column of the symbol table tells you what value the assembler fills in when it creates the RECORD. You may specify records with initial values other than zero. You may also override these values at the time the data area is generated. To define initial values, you follow each field designation in the RECORD statement by an equal sign and the value. The DATE_WORD record, with initial values of January 1, 1983, would be

    DATE_WORD   RECORD   YEAR:7=3,MONTH:4=1,DAY:5=1

You can override these values in the same way that you did for structures. When you create the record, the angle brackets contain the specific values for this generation. If you want the date to be January 5, 1984, you could generate a record like this:

    DATE   DATE_WORD   <4,,5>

Just as with macros and structures, the arguments are position dependent. Since the month value is left null, the assembler uses the initial value specified in the RECORD statement.

Notice that the program in Figure 6.15 defined the FCB structure, but did not use the STRUC of the preceding section. We couldn't use STRUC because each of the fields in a structure must be one of the DEFINE data operators. We can't use a RECORD name as one of the fields in the structure. The way we did it in Figure 6.15 is one method of working around the problem.

We can solve this problem in another fashion. Even though the assembler does not generate a data area until the record name is used as an operator, the assembler records the field definitions when the RECORD is defined. This allows a program to define the DATE_WORD record, without using it to specify the DATE field in the structure. This is the same as defining a macro but never invoking it. The remainder of the program is the same. The various field names in the DATE_WORD record have meaning, and can be used as shift counts and MASK values.

The same is true for STRUC. The definition of the structure defines the offsets to the assembler, even if you never use the structure name to define a data area. You can use this to locate the default FCB at location 05CH of the Program

```
 1                                              PAGE    ,132
 2                                              TITLE   Figure 6.16   Structure and Record
 3
 4                              DATE_WORD        RECORD  YEAR:7,MONTH:4,DAY:5
 5
 6                              FCB     STRUC
 7       0000  00               DRIVE            DB      0                  ; Drive Number
 8       0001  20 20 20 20 20 20  FILE_NAME      DB      '          '       ; File name
 9             20 20
10       0009  20 20 20         FILE_EXT         DB      '   '              ; Extension
11       000C  0000             CURRENT_BLOCK    DW      0                  ; Current block number
12       000E  0080             RECORD_SIZE      DW      80H                ; Logical record size
13       0010  00 00 00 00      FILE_SIZE        DD      0                  ; Size of the file, in bytes
14       0014  0000             DATE             DW      0                  ; Date the file was created
15       0016     0A [          RESERVED         DB      10 DUP(?)          ; Reserved, can't be overriden
16                  ??
17                     ]
18
19       0020  00               SEQ_NUMBER       DB      0                  ; Record in block for sequential
20       0021  00 00 00 00      RANDOM_NUMBER    DD      0                  ; Record in file for random
21       0025             FCB     ENDS
22
23       0000             STACK   SEGMENT STACK
24       0000     40 [                    DW      64 DUP(?)
25                  ????
26                     ]
27
28       0080             STACK   ENDS
29
30       0000             CODE    SEGMENT
31                                ASSUME  CS:CODE
32
33
34       0000             RECORDS          PROC    FAR
35       0000  1E                          PUSH    DS                       ; Set return address
36       0001  B8 0000                     MOV     AX,0
37       0004  50                          PUSH    AX
38                                ASSUME  DS:CODE                           ; DS really points to PSP
39       0005  BA 005C                     MOV     DX,05CH                  ; Location of FCB in PSP
40       0008  B4 0F                       MOV     AH,0FH                   ; Open the file
41       000A  CD 21                       INT     21H
42
43       000C  BB 005C                     MOV     BX,05CH                  ; Location of FCB
44       000F  8B 47 14                    MOV     AX,[BX].DATE
45       0012  25 FE00                     AND     AX,MASK YEAR             ; Isolate the year
46       0015  B1 09                       MOV     CL,YEAR                  ; Right justify the value
47       0017  D3 E8                       SHR     AX,CL
48       0019  8A F0                       MOV     DH,AL                    ; Store year in BH
49
50       001B  8B 47 14                    MOV     AX,[BX].DATE
51       001E  25 01E0                     AND     AX,MASK MONTH
52       0021  B1 05                       MOV     CL,MONTH
53       0023  D3 E8                       SHR     AX,CL
54       0025  8A D0                       MOV     DL,AL                    ; Store month in BL
55
56       0027  8B 47 14                    MOV     AX,[BX].DATE
57       002A  25 001F                     AND     AX,MASK DAY              ; Store day in AL
58
59       002D  CB                          RET
60       002E             RECORDS          ENDP
61       002E             CODE    ENDS
62                                END     RECORDS
```

Figure 6.16   Structure and Record

Segment Prefix. This FCB always exists, so there is no need to use the structure
to generate the data area. The program in Figure 6.16 is nearly identical to Figure
6.15, except for several details. The program defines an FCB with the STRUC
statement, rather than a collection of DEFINE statements. Notice that the
example invokes neither the DATE_WORD record nor the FCB structure in the
assembly. They serve merely to define the data area offsets.

A final word about the use of records and structures. We use these
mechanisms because they let us write a program without specific knowledge of
the data structure. With a STRUC definition, we can reference every field as an
offset into the structure. The programmer doesn't have to know the actual offset
that the field has. The same is true for a bit record. If the program uses the MASK

and shift count operators, it must specify the bit locations in the field only in the RECORD statement.

The value of programming with these tools becomes apparent when you work on a large project that has lots of programmers or lots of programs. Invariably, you will modify the data structures as the programs are developed. If you write your program using these data structure models, it is simple to change the models and the associated programs. You can modify the data structure and then reassemble all the programs using that structure. The programs themselves don't have to be changed. Even better, you can keep the data structure as a separate file, and INCLUDE it into every assembly, so there will be only one version of the data structure. Using these tools simplifies the process of developing a large program as it goes through evolutionary changes.

CHAPTER

7

The 8087
Numeric
Data Procesor

The designers of the Intel 8088 have provided a special feature for the micro-processor, one that is unique to the 8086/8088 family. The design of the processor allows a system to have 'a coprocessor. A coprocessor is a device which extends the capabilities of the central processor in some fashion. The 8087 numeric data processor (NDP) is a coprocessor for the 8088 central processor that adds numeric instructions and floating-point registers. These additional arithmetic capabilities become an extension of the 8088, and significantly increase the processing power when a program does floating-point or high-precision numeric operations.

IBM designed the Personal Computer so that a coprocessor could be installed. There is an empty 40-pin socket next to the 8088 on the system board. IBM designed this socket to accept any architecturally compatible coprocessor for the 8088. The 8087 NDP fits, in architectural definition, and in the socket. To add this numeric processing capability, you need only plug the 8087 into the empty socket. You should set a switch on the system board to indicate the existence of the coprocessor. This switch is necessary only to ensure that the processor receives the 8087 exception condition interrupts. The actual operation of the 8087 does not depend on any external switches.

8087 OPERATION

The 8087 coprocessor handles floating-point instructions by monitoring the instructions executed by the 8088. The NDP "watches" the 8088 execute instructions. When the 8087 sees an instruction that it should execute, it steps in and begins working on the instruction. The 8087 executes its numeric instructions in parallel with the 8088. That is, while the 8087 is executing the arithmetic instruction, the 8088 can continue to execute its instructions. In this fashion, true coprocessing can occur. The 8088 can be executing an instruction while the 8087 is handling a different instruction. This can be particularly valuable when the 8087 instruction takes a long time to execute, as some floating-point operations can.

Since the two processors can execute simultaneously, there must be some synchronization between them. The WAIT instruction of the 8088 does this job. The 8087 is wired to the 8088 so that when the NDP is busy (executing a floating-point instruction) the test input of the 8088 is inactive. The WAIT instruction stops 8088 instruction processing until the test input becomes active, signaling the completion of the 8087 instruction. In this way, the 8088 can make sure that the 8087 has finished an operation before attempting to give it another instruction to execute. It can also prevent the 8088 from accessing any data stored by the 8087 before the instruction has completed.

The processor and coprocessor communicate only through the external control lines of the processors such as the test input. The 8088 cannot read the internal registers of the 8087, and vice versa. All data that pass between them must be placed in memory, which both processors can access. But since the addressing registers are in the 8088, it should be difficult for the 8087 to address memory efficiently, using the same address modes as the 8088. To allow the 8087 to address memory using the addressing modes of the 8088, the two processors cooperate on the execution of a floating-point instruction.

The 8088 instruction set contains an Escape (ESC) instruction, which does not execute in the 8088. In a system without an 8087 processor, the ESC is identical to a NOP—except that it takes longer to execute. However, the ESC instructions do have addressing information built in. Specifically, they have a mod-r/m byte for address computation as part of the instruction. Even though the ESC acts as a NOP, the 8088 does the effective address calculation. The 8088 does a memory read with the resulting address, although the 8088 does nothing with the data. (If the mod-r/m byte specifies an 8088 register rather than a memory operand, no memory read is done.)

The 8087, in the meantime, has been watching the sequence of instructions executed by the 8088. When the 8088 executes an ESC, the 8087 recognizes it as an instruction for the 8087 to execute. The 8087 waits for the 8088 to do the dummy memory read. When that address is on the system bus, the 8087 captures it. The 8087 now knows where the data are in memory, without doing the address calculations. The 8088 does the address calculation, the 8087 does the rest of the instruction. The 8087 can now "steal" some memory cycles to read or write the data it requires, while the 8088 continues execution.

The 8087 adds arithmetic capability to the system, but doesn't replace any of the 8088 instructions. The ADD, SUB, MUL, and DIV instructions discussed in Chapter 4 are still executed by the 8088. The NDP contains additional, and more powerful, instructions for arithmetic processing. From a programming point of view, a system with an 8087 installed should be viewed as a complete processor, with a larger instruction set than the simple 8088. There is little value remembering which processor executes which instruction. Only when the 8088 will be immediately accessing an 8087 result, and the synchronizing WAIT instruction is required, does the distinction in processors become necessary.

There is a problem in writing programs that use the 8087 instruction set when you use the IBM Macro Assembler. The Macro Assembler does not include the mnemonic codes for the 8087 instructions. To use the 8087, you must form the 8087 instructions using the WAIT and ESC operation codes. The best way to do this is with a set of macros, which allow you to write the 8087 instructions. Chapter 6 developed some of the macros necessary for the 8087. If you intend to program the 8087, you should expand those examples into the full set of 8087 instruction macros.

8087 DATA TYPES

The 8087 has an expanded set of data types to support its increased arithmetic function. While the 8088 can operate directly only on byte or word operands, the 8087 has seven numerical data types. Six of these data types are unique to the 8087. Figure 7.1 shows the seven data types that the 8087 supports. Four of the formats are for integers and three are for real, or floating-point, numbers. One of the integer data formats is for an extended BCD number rather than a binary integer.

Figure 7.2 shows the way the 8087 stores those numbers in memory. As with the 8088 data formats, all data are stored with the least significant portion of the operand at the lowest address. The sign bit always appears in the byte of the highest memory address. We'll discuss the meanings of the various fields as we cover the data types.

The 8087 can access three kinds of integers: word, which is 16 bits and identical to the word operand of the 8088; short integer, a 32-bit value; and long integer, a 64-bit value. These are two's-complement numbers.

A program specifies a word integer with the DW operator. This integer can be in the range $-32,768$ to $32,767$. We have already used this integer format in 8088 instruction set. This is the only data format shared by the 8088 and the 8087.

The short integer requires a data operator for a 32-bit data field. The Define Doubleword (DD) operator does this, specifying integers in the range -2^{32} to $2^{32} - 1$. Remember that the DD operator can also specify a SEGMENT:OFFSET address pair. The assembler determines which form to generate based on the operand. If the operand is an address, it creates the SEGMENT:OFFSET. If the operand is a value, it assembles the appropriate integer.

The long integer of 64 bits needs the Define Quadword (DQ) operator. This directive tells the assembler to create a data area with four words (eight bytes). This type of integer operand can represent values in the range -2^{64} to $2^{64} - 1$.

This assembler operator, just like the DB, DW, and DD operators, can define a constant data value, an undefined area using "?" and a multiplicity of eight-byte fields using the DUP command.

The remaining integer data type is the packed decimal representation. This data type represents an integer as a packed BCD value. The data occupy 10 bytes. One byte is reserved for the sign and the remaining nine bytes specify 18 decimal digits. This packed decimal storage representation is identical to that of the 8088 decimal operands, except that it handles 18 digits at a time. The 8088 packed decimal adjust instructions allow only two decimal digits at a time. The 8088 packed BCD values also require the programmer to define the method of handling

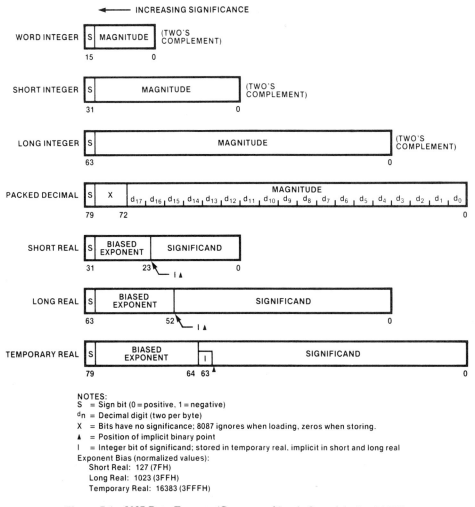

Figure 7.1 8087 Data Formats (Courtesy of Intel; Copyright Intel 1980)

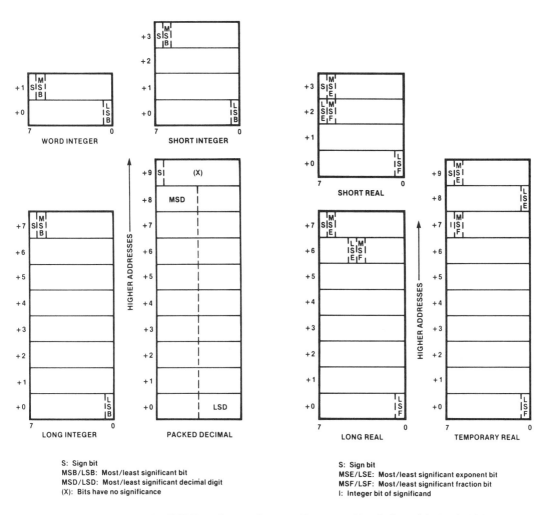

S: Sign bit
MSB/LSB: Most/least significant bit
MSD/LSD: Most/least significant decimal digit
(X): Bits have no significance

S: Sign bit
MSE/LSE: Most/least significant exponent bit
MSF/LSF: Most/least significant fraction bit
I: Integer bit of significand

Figure 7.2 8087 Data Storage Layouts (Courtesy of Intel; Copyright Intel 1980)

the sign of the number, if negative numbers are used. The 8087 packed BCD has a sign bit in the highest-order byte. The packed BCD value is stored in sign-magnitude representation, with the most significant bit of the 10-byte field indicating the sign (0 = positive, 1 = negative).

The assembler uses the Define Tenbyte (DT) operator for the packed BCD field. This operator sets aside a 10-byte data area. To assemble a packed BCD value in this area, the program must use hexadecimal notation. If an integer value is in the field, the assembler converts it into two's-complement representation, not the packed BCD. Fortunately, it's easy to convert a decimal number into the required hexadecimal notation for packed BCD. Just write the number as you would in decimal, and then follow it with the "H" to indicate hexadecimal. It's

```
The IBM Personal Computer MACRO Assembler 01-01-83              PAGE   1-1
Figure 7.3 8087 Integer Data Formats

 1                                              PAGE    ,132
 2                                              TITLE   Figure 7.3 8087 Integer Data Formats
 3
 4      0000                             CODE    SEGMENT
 5
 6      0000  04D2                       WORD            DW      1234
 7      0002  FB2E                                       DW      -1234
 8
 9      0004  40 E2 01 00                SHORT_INTEGER   DD      123456
10      0008  C0 1D FE FF                                DD      -123456
11
12      000C  D2 02 96 49 00 00          LONG_INTEGER    DQ      1234567890
13            00 00
14      0014  2E FD 69 B6 FF FF                          DQ      -1234567890
15            FF FF
16      001C  ???????????????????                        DQ      ?
17
18      0024  78 56 34 12 90 78          PACKED_BCD      DT          123456789012345678H
19            56 34 12 00
20      002E  78 56 34 12 90 78                          DT      80123456789012345678H    ; Negative of previous
21            56 34 12 80
22      0038     02 [                                     DT      2 DUP(?)
23                     ?????????
24                     ??????????
25                  ?
26                     ]
27
28
29      004C                             CODE    ENDS
30                                               END
```

Figure 7.3   8087 Integer Data Formats

slightly more difficult to enter a negative value. If you precede the decimal number with a ''−'' sign, the assembler converts it to the two's-complement value, even with the ''H.'' So to indicate a negative packed BCD value, you must count the decimal digits and make the number 20 digits long. The first two digits must be 80, to get the negative indicator into the sign bit. Thus, to enter −1234 in packed BCD, the assembler expression is

DT   80000000000000001234H

Figure 7.3 is an assembly listing that shows the assembler-generated values for the four integer types.

FLOATING-POINT DATA REPRESENTATION

There are three data formats for representing real numbers with the 8087. Two of the floating-point representations conform to the proposed Institute of Electrical and Electronic Engineers (IEEE) standard for such numbers. The short real format uses 32 bits; the long real format requires 64 bits. The third format specifies the number as an 80-bit field. This format does not conform to the IEEE standard. The 8087 uses this ''temporary real'' format internally to give very high precision to intermediate results.

The remainder of this section is for those who have no experience with floating-point numbers as represented in a computer. You can skip this section if you have an understanding of the general scheme of representing floating-point numbers, both on paper and within a computer. The next section will deal with the specific method used in the 8087.

Integer schemes are the best way to represent many numbers. Integers are simple to understand and use, and map well to binary representation. However, integers do not work well for very large values. A very large integer usually ends with a long string of zeros. For example, the sun is about 93,000,000 miles from earth. Integer methods also cannot show a number that contains a fraction. A computer can't store the number $\frac{1}{2}$ in an integer representation. And fractions that are less than 1, such as $\frac{1}{3}$ and $\frac{1}{5}$, are also impossible to represent using integer methods.

Scientists and mathematicians long ago developed a way of representing these problem numbers in a consistent fashion. The first step is to introduce a decimal point. This symbol, a ".", indicates the separation between the integer portion and the fractional portion of the number. With an integer, the number position that represents units, or ones, is always located at the extreme right edge of the number. When a decimal point is used, the numbers to the right of the decimal point represent values less than 1.

With integers, each position in the number corresponds to a power of 10. Thus, 1234 is

$$1234 = 1000 + 200 + 30 + 4 = 1 \times 10^3 + 2 \times 10^2 + 3 \times 10^1 + 4 \times 10^0$$

The decimal point now defines the break between the position corresponding to 10^0 and the fractional part. In the fraction, number positions are once again powers of 10, but now they are negative powers of 10. The number 1.234 is

$$1.234 = 1 + 0.2 + 0.03 + 0.004 = 1 \times 10^0 + 2 \times 10^{-1} + 3 \times 10^{-2} + 4 \times 10^{-3}$$

The decimal point allows fractions to be written. The number $1\frac{1}{2}$ is now 1.5, while $\frac{1}{4} = 0.25$ and $\frac{1}{5} = 0.2$.

Since each position in a decimal number varies from its neighbor by a factor of 10, multiplying a number by 10 is equivalent to moving the decimal point one position to the right. Similarly, dividing by 10 moves the decimal point one position to the left. We can use this knowledge to shift the decimal point to an appropriate position. We move the decimal point, and at the same time, adjust the number by some factor of 10. This is known as "floating-point" representation, since the decimal point "floats" in the number. The decimal point no longer marks the absolute point between units and fractions. We can choose the decimal point position for convenience, and then multiply the number by the correct power of 10 to produce the true value.

For example, the sun is about 93,000,000 miles from earth. This form is awkward to handle because of all the zeros. Instead, we can write it in floating-point notation, 9.3×10^7. That is 93,000,000 is equivalent to 9.3 times 10 to the seventh power. In fact,

$$93,000,000 = 9.3 \times 10^7 = 93 \times 10^6 = 930 \times 10^5$$

and so on. We can move the decimal point anywhere in the number by changing the power of 10.

The decimal floating-point number has two components. There is the significant part of the number, called the mantissa or significand. In the example above, the value 9.3 is the mantissa. In practice, the mantissa is normally kept in the range $1 \le$ mantissa < 10. Thus, a mantissa might be 1.3, 7.6, or 9.97. The other component of a floating-point number is the exponent. This is the power to which 10 must be raised before multiplying it times the mantissa. Thus, 9.3×10^7 has a mantissa of 9.3 and an exponent of 7. Once the base of the number system has been determined, in this case 10, the mantissa and exponent are the only two values that must be defined to reconstruct the original number.

Floating-point representation allows us to write very large numbers (e.g., 1.234×10^{85}), or very small numbers (e.g., 1.234×10^{-85}), in a compact fashion. To write out these numbers without an exponent of 10 would require a long string of zeros.

Binary floating-point representation is very similar to decimal floating point. The base of the number system is 2 rather than 10. The mantissa is a value between $1 \le$ mantissa < 2, and the exponent is a power of 2. Thus, the number 1.101×10^{100} in binary notation means that the mantissa 1.101B is multiplied by 2^4, or 16. The value of the mantissa is determined by the same positional relationship as decimal fractions are, except that the number base is now 2. For locations to the right of the binary point, the positions represent negative powers of 2. The table in Figure 7.4 shows the value of the first five positions.

We can now calculate the decimal value of the example number.

$$1.101B = 1 + \tfrac{1}{2} + \tfrac{1}{8} = 1\tfrac{5}{8} = 1.625$$

$$10^{100}B = 2^4 = 16$$

$$1.101 \times 10^{100}B = 1\tfrac{5}{8} \times 16 = 26$$

Alternatively, we could calculate the value just as we do for decimal numbers. The exponent value tells how many positions to shift the binary point. In this case, since the exponent value is 4, we'll shift the binary point four places to the right. So

$$1.101 \times 10^{100}B = 11010B = 26$$

Both methods are valid and produce identical results. In the first, we evaluated the fraction and then multiplied it by the exponent. In the second method, we did the exponent multiplication before evaluating the mantissa.

How then are these numbers represented in a computer? The area set aside

Binary Value	Decimal Value
0.1	1/2
0.01	1/4
0.001	1/8
0.0001	1/16
0.00001	1/32

Figure 7.4 Negative Powers of 2

for the storage of a floating-point number is divided into two fields. One field contains the sign and value of the mantissa. The other field contains the sign and value of the exponent.

The size of the mantissa field determines the precision or accuracy of the number. The more bits that the computer allots to the mantissa field, the higher the precision. For example, the decimal fraction 1.234 is more precise than the fraction 1.2. The two extra digits of the fraction allow a more precise rendition of the value.

In order to maintain the maximum precision, computers almost always store the mantissa as a normalized number. This means that the mantissa is a number between 1 and 2 ($1 \leq$ mantissa < 2). Two considerations make this a necessity. First, any leading zeros of a number do not contribute to the precision of a number. (This is not true of trailing zeros. We consider the number 1.000 to be more precise than the number 1.0.) If we allow leading zeros in the floating-point mantissa, the precision of the number is reduced. Second, the storage of a floating-point mantissa assumes that the binary point is in a fixed position. In fact, the mantissa's binary point is assumed to follow the first binary digit. Thus, normalizing the mantissa forces the first bit to be a one, leaving the mantissa value in the range between 1 and 2. The computer adjusts the exponent portion of the number to the appropriate value to support the normalization.

There are exceptions to the normalization of the mantissa. The most obvious exception is when the value is zero. In that case, the entire mantissa is zero. The second exception is not as readily apparent, and occurs when the number is approaching the lower bound of its range. Let's see what that means.

Just as the size of a number's mantissa determines its precision, the size of the exponent field determines the range of a number. The exponent field contains a power of 2. The more bits in this field, the larger (or smaller) the number can be.

If three binary digits are available for the exponent field (expressed as a two's-complement number), the largest number is $1.111 \ldots \times 10^{011B}$. The mantissa is a number slightly smaller than 2, while the exponent is 2^3, or 8. Thus, the maximum number is slightly less than 16. The smallest nonzero positive number is $1.000 \ldots \times 10^{100B}$, or 1×2^{-4}, or $\frac{1}{16}$. Since floating-point representations use a sign-magnitude representation for the mantissa, the range of negative numbers is similar. With a 3-bit exponent, the range of positive numbers is from $\frac{1}{16}$ to 16. Negative numbers go from -16 to $-\frac{1}{16}$.

If 4 bits are used for the exponent field, the largest number is $1.111 \ldots \times 10^{0111B} < 2 \times 2^7 = 256$. The smallest nonzero positive number is $1.000 \ldots \times 10^{1000B} = 1 \times 2^{-8} = \frac{1}{256}$. So 4 exponent bits give a range from $\frac{1}{256}$ to 256. You can see that the greater the number of exponent bits, the greater the range that the number can represent.

It's important to note that even though the range might increase with an increase in the number of exponent bits, the precision does not. In the examples above, we'll assume that there are 4 bits of mantissa available. If we pick a particular number that falls within the range of both examples, it will have the same precision regardless of the exponent range. For example, the number 1.010 × 10^{001B} = $2\frac{1}{2}$. Extending the number of exponent bits does not increase the precision of the number. For any particular number within the range of the system, the mantissa size is the sole limitation on precision.

Exponent values are not stored as two's-complement numbers. For computational ease, computers store the exponent as a biased number. This means that the actual exponent value has a bias value added to it before it is stored. The bias value is chosen to allow exponents to be compared using simple unsigned integer comparison. This is particularly useful when comparing two floating-point numbers. The exponent and mantissa are stored as a single data entity, with the exponent preceding the mantissa. With a biased exponent, a program can compare the numbers bitwise, from high-order to low-order bit positions. The first unequal comparison identifies the order of the numbers. No other portions of the numbers must be checked. The bias value is determined by the size of the exponent field. Let's take an example from the 8087 formats.

The short real format in the 8087 uses 32 bits, of which 8 are for the exponent. Thus, the exponent can be in the range −128 to 127. However, the 8087 reserves the value of −128 for a special, indefinite, number, so the exponent range is −127 to 127. The exponent is not a two's-complement number. The 8087 adds the bias value of 127 to the exponent before it is stored in the real format. The table in Figure 7.5 shows some of the possible exponent values, and the resulting stored value.

Exponent Value	Biased Value
−127	000H
−1	07EH
0	07FH
1	080H
127	0FEH

Figure 7.5 Biased Exponents

As the table in Figure 7.5 shows, the bias adjusts the exponent field so that the smallest exponent corresponds to the smallest real number. Similarly, the largest exponent value belongs to the largest number. If two floating-point numbers differ in their exponent values, a simple comparison of the exponent fields orders the two numbers. Since this comparison also carries into the mantissa field, a program can easily order two floating-point numbers. This simplicity is due to the biasing of the exponent.

8087 REAL DATA FORMATS

There are three floating-point data formats supported by the 8087. These formats appear in Figures 7.1 and 7.2. Figure 7.1 shows the logical layout of the numbers, while Figure 7.2 indicates the location of the components when the value is stored in memory.

The short and long real data formats correspond to the proposed IEEE standard for floating-point representation. The short real number requires 32 bits or four bytes of storage. This format is often called a single-precision floating-point number. The mantissa contains 23 bits, which is about equal to six or seven decimal digits of precision. That is, a seven-digit decimal number is about as precise as a 23-bit binary number. The 8-bit exponent has a bias value of 127 or 07FH. The exponent has a range of 2^{-127} to 2^{127}, which is about equivalent to 10^{-38} to 10^{38}. The remaining bit of the number determines the sign of the entire number. Notice that there are two sign bits within a floating-point number. One is for the sign of the exponent, and is contained within the exponent field (and is modified by the bias value). The other sign indicates whether the number itself is positive or negative.

The long real format requires 64 bits, or eight bytes of storage. This double-precision floating-point number has a mantissa of 52 bits, which is about 15 to 16 decimal digits of precision. The 11-bit exponent has a range of 2^{-1023} to 2^{1023} and a bias value of 1023 or 03FFH. In decimal values, the range is about 10^{-307} to 10^{307}.

The 8087 always stores the long and short real numbers as normalized numbers. Once again, this means that the first bit of the mantissa is a one. Since this bit is always a one, there is no reason to include it. It is always assumed to be there. The picture of Figure 7.2 shows this. Below the data layout for long and short real numbers there is a 1 preceding the binary point. The bit is not in memory, but we all know that it's really there.

We should note that the six data formats for the 8087 that we have discussed so far—four integer and two real—exist only outside the 8087. That is, the 8087 places data into these formats only when it stores them into memory. The 8087 can also read data in these formats. The 8087 holds all of the data inside it in the seventh format—temporary real. This means that the program you write using the 8087 has the benefit of the extended range and precision of the temporary real format whenever the numbers are processed with the 8087. The external data formats are for your convenience in representing or storing the data.

The temporary real floating-point representation is the most precise and widest ranging representation. This representation requires 80 bits, or 10 bytes. The mantissa is 64 bits long. This gives a precision equivalent to about 19 decimal digits. The mantissa is generally normalized, but under certain conditions it may be denormalized. For this reason, the temporary real format does not assume that the highest bit of the mantissa is a 1. The picture in Figure 7.2 shows the normalized leading 1 very plainly as part of the mantissa, and not assumed. The 15-bit exponent field is biased with a value of 16383 or 03FFFH. This exponent gives a range of $2^{-16,383}$ to $2^{16,383}$ or about 10^{-4932} to 10^{4932}.

Because the 8087 may denormalize the mantissa of the temporary real, the lower bound of the range is extended even further. As the number is denormalized, leading zeros occur in the fraction. This allows the total number to be even smaller than the exponent range allows. As an example, let's look at the simple form we used earlier, with a 3-bit exponent and a 4-bit mantissa. The smallest positive number this can represent is

$$1.000 \times 10^{000\text{B}} = 1 \times 2^{-3} = \tfrac{1}{8}$$

This example assumes that the exponent is biased with a value of 3. If we now denormalize the mantissa, we can represent an even smaller number, such as

$$0.100 \times 10^{000\text{B}} = \tfrac{1}{2} \times 2^{-3} = \tfrac{1}{16}$$

The smallest positive number that a denormalized value can represent is

$$0.001 \times 10^{000\text{B}} = \tfrac{1}{8} \times 2^{-3} = \tfrac{1}{64}$$

Denormalizing the mantissa extends the lower bound of the range.

This extra range didn't come free. As we introduced leading zeros, we reduced the precision of the mantissa. The temporary real format of the 8087 allows precision to be sacrificed to extend the range of the number when it's required. This feature comes into play primarily in the intermediate steps of long calculations. Sometimes an application subtracts two numbers that are nearly equal before it does another operation. The result of the subtraction is a number much smaller than either of the original numbers. That difference may be very significant. By allowing the range to extend in these special cases, the computation can continue. The only other alternative would be to set the result of the subtraction to 0. In this method, all significance is lost.

REAL NUMBER DATA DEFINITION

The assembler sets aside data areas for the real numbers with four-, eight-, and ten-byte fields. For a short real, this is the DD operator. For long reals, it is the DQ command. And for temporary real, it is the DT operator.

Unfortunately, the IBM Macro Assembler doesn't support the floating-point representation of the 8087. If you specify a real number as the operand in a DD or DQ field, there will be a indecipherable collection of ones and zeros created for the data. That floating-point format corresponds to the data format used internally by the Basic interpreter, and is not the IEEE format used by the 8087. So an 8087 program must use a different method of creating real numbers.

There are two methods that you can use for real number data fields. The first method is the human assembly approach. You figure out the real number using paper and pencil, and place it into the correct format. This operation entails reading the format very carefully, converting the decimal (usually) number into the correct binary form, separating exponent and mantissa, applying the bias to the exponent, and finally converting it all into binary or hexadecimal constants. This is a feasible method, but one that requires a fair amount of skill and a great deal of time on the part of the programmer.

The second method of creating real numbers is an indirect approach that requires a greater amount of execution time, but much less programmer time. You write the real number as the product or quotient of two or more integers. The assembler can handle the integers directly using the DW, DD, or DQ commands. Following the initialization of the 8087, the program can build the desired real numbers by performing the required multiplications or divisions. For example, the program needs the real number 1.234×10^5 as a memory constant in the program. The programmer can do this one easily as an integer, using this assembly statement:

```
DD      123400
```

Notice that the number is too large for a DW representation, but easily fits in the constraints of the 32-bit integer.

Suppose, however, that the number is 1.234×10^{-5}, a very small fraction. In this case, the program needs two integers. One integer corresponds to the mantissa value, the other to the exponent. The program can use these definitions

```
DW      1234
DD      100000000
```

to create the number in the program. The program divides the fraction, 1234, by the exponent, 10^8, to produce the number.

A problem with this approach is very large or small numbers. These numbers require exponents much larger than any integer we would like to write. For that purpose, we'll do an example later which shows the real format for every third power of 10. We'll defer that program until we have covered the instructions for it. With these real representations for powers of 10, it will be simple to assemble real numbers with values of 10^{36} or 10^{-24}. The program can break up the value into the integer portion and a power of 10. Multiplication or division produces the correct value. The 8087 also offers other methods of performing these scaling operations, but the methods using integers and powers of 10 have the greatest simplicity, particularly for people using the 8087 for the first time.

8087 PROGRAMMING MODEL

Although the 8087 is a separate processor, you should view it as an extension of the 8088 processor, adding capabilities to the 8088 processor. The capabilities include additional data types, additional instructions, and additional registers. Figure 7.6 shows the programming model of the 8087. These registers are taken together with the registers of the 8088 to form the register set of the entire programming system.

Register Stack

The 8087 has four special-purpose registers and an eight register stack to hold the numeric operands. The register stack is the primary method of operating with the 8087, so we'll look at it first.

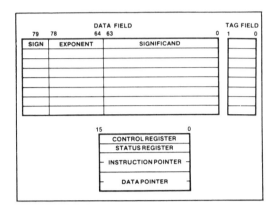

Figure 7.6 8087 Register Model
(Courtesy of Intel; Copyright
Intel 1980)

The NDP register stack has eight positions, each of which is 80 bits wide. The 8087 stores all entries in temporary real format, no matter how they were represented in the processor memory. The 8087 converts integers and real numbers to the internal format. As we noted before, this representation allows very high precision and great range. For integer operations, the 8087 obtains exact results up to 2^{64}. The floating-point internal format should be of little concern to anyone doing integer arithmetic with the 8087.

The registers of the 8087 operate as a push-down stack, just as the stack of the 8088. However, there are a limited number of positions available, just eight. The 8087 has another register inside the processor that is not easily available to the programmer. This register contains "tag" words for each position on the stack. This register allows the 8087 to keep track of which stack positions are in use and which are free for further use. Any attempt to push an item onto the stack into a position that is already occupied results in an invalid operation exception condition. In just a moment, we'll discuss the exception conditions and how a program can handle the stack overflow problem.

A program may move data into the 8087 stack with a load instruction. All the load instructions push data onto the top of the stack. If the number in main storage is not in temporary real format, the 8087 converts it into the 80-bit representation as part of the load operation. Similarly, the store instructions take a value from the 8087 stack and place it into main memory. If data conversion is required, the 8087 does it as part of the store. A store to memory doesn't automatically pop the 8087 stack. Some forms of the store instruction leave the top of stack intact, for further operations.

Once a program pushes data onto the 8087 stack, it may use the value with any of the numeric instructions. The 8087 numeric instructions allow register-to-register arithmetic as well as memory-to-register arithmetic. Just as with the 8088, for any two operand arithmetic operation, one of the operands must come from the registers. For the 8087, one of the operands must always be the top element of the stack. The other operand may come from memory, or it may come from the register stack. The register stack of the 8087 must always be the destination of any arithmetic operation. The NDP cannot store the result directly into memory with the same instruction that does that arithmetic. A separate store instruction (or store and pop) is required to move the operand back into memory. Some arithmetic instructions also pop the top element from the stack and discard it, without storing it to memory.

Control Word

The 8087 contains two 16-bit control registers. One register is for control input, the other for status output. The control register allows the programmer to specify the execution mode of the 8087. We'll only mention some of the possibilities in this text. The use of all of the control variations is beyond the scope of this book. Figure 7.7 shows the layout of the control register.

The control word allows one of the two different types of infinity to be selected. The default method of closing the number system is projective closure. With projective closure, the 8087 treats both positive and negative infinity as a single unsigned infinity. The other method is affine closure, which has both a

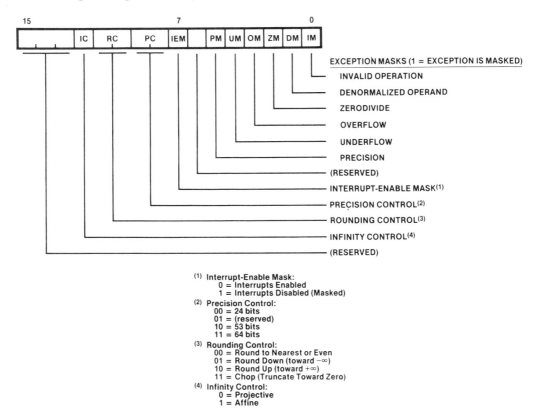

Figure 7.7 8087 Control Word Format (Courtesy of Intel; Copyright Intel 1980)

positive and a negative infinity. Although it may seem that projective closure loses information, projective closure doesn't generate misleading results. A program should use affine closure only when it needs the additional information and is prepared to deal with the possibly misleading results.

The 8087 allows you to pick one of four ways to round numbers. Rounding occurs when the result requires more precision than the number system allows. The method of rounding determines which number is selected as the result. Rounding methods include selecting the next greater number in the system, the next smaller, always rounding toward zero, or always rounding toward the even number. The 8087 also allows a program to decrease the 64-bit precision of the temporary real format. This fulfills a requirements of the proposed IEEE format. This action does not improve execution times and should not be used only to make the 8087 instructions compatible with some previously existing processing.

The 8087 can detect a variety of error conditions, known as exceptions. The 8087 may also generate interrupts to signal these exception conditions. The control word contains a set of bits that let the programmer determine which exception conditions will result in an interrupt and which will be handled in other fashions. These bits are known as interrupt masks, since they can be used to mask, or prevent, the occurrence of an interrupt.

It isn't necessary to allow each of these exceptions to generate an interrupt. The 8087 has an extensive range of exception handling built into it. For each of the possible exceptions, the 8087 has a default method of dealing with the problem. For example, dividing by zero causes an exception interrupt if it is enabled (unmasked). However, if the programmer has not enabled that exception interrupt, the 8087 uses a value of infinity as the result of the division by zero. This value is propagated through the remaining calculations, producing a result that will immediately indicate that an error of some form occurred during the processing.

However, for your particular floating-point program, it might be necessary to handle an exception condition immediately. You may wish to substitute your own routines to handle the exceptions. The IBM Personal Computer connects the 8087 exception interrupt to the Non Maskable Interrupt (NMI). This is the same interrupt that signals parity checks. If a program uses the 8087 interrupt mechanism, it must modify the NMI vector to point to an 8087 interrupt handler. This interrupt handler must respond to any parity checks that occur. Chapter 10 will show a method of replacing an interrupt handler with one of your own choosing.

As an example of exception condition, consider the stack overflow mentioned above. If a program pushes a ninth stack entry, the 8087 responds with an exception interrupt. If this interrupt is not enabled, the 8087 marks the operation as an invalid operation and makes the result a special value, known as NAN (Not A Number). However, if you plan to do complex arithmetic that requires more than eight stack positions, the exception interrupt can be used to your advantage. When the stack overflow occurs, the exception interrupt handler can remove some of the lower entries from the stack, using the store instructions. The program can free these stack positions for further use. There is also a corresponding stack underflow exception interrupt. That interrupt occurs when an empty stack position is used. The exception routine can handle this stack underflow. It can restore the stack to its previous values from the save area.

We'll see later that the 8087 contains state information that makes it possible to handle these exception conditions in an interrupt handler. The 8087 provides complete information about the instruction that caused the exception.

Status Word

The status word of the 8087 tells the current state of the coprocessor. Figure 7.8 shows the bit layout for the status word. The status word contains bits to indicate each of the exception conditions, so that the exception interrupt handler can determine the reason for the problem. The status word also has a bit indicating whether it is busy or not. This is the same bit that is communicated externally to allow processor synchronization with the 8088. The status word also contains the pointer to the current top of stack within the 8087 register set.

Probably the most often used section of the 8087 status word is the condition code register. The status word contains 4 bits that can be set by 8087 operations. Two of these condition code bits correspond directly to the carry and zero flags of the 8088. In fact, they are aligned at the same bit positions within the high byte of the 8087 status word. You can take advantage of this alignment by storing the

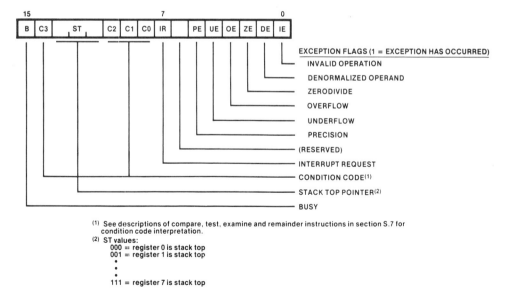

Figure 7.8   8087 Status Word Format (Courtesy of Intel; Copyright Intel 1980)

status word into memory. You move the high byte of the status word into the AH register. The SAHF instruction then sets the carry and zero flags according to the results of the 8087 compare operation. Since all numbers in the 8087 are signed real numbers, the two flags are sufficient to determine the ordering of any two numbers. Later we will work with examples that use the status word for number comparison. The remaining 2 bits of the condition code register are used with a special 8087 instruction to test for all of the special condition numbers that the 8087 supports. Since many of these numbers require special processing, the condition code register provides a mechanism for sorting them out.

8087 INSTRUCTION SET

The program should view the 8087 instructions as an extension of the 8088 instructions. The 8087 adds instructions to the total set. Memory addressing is done identically to the 8088. As we saw earlier, this is because the 8088 actually generates the memory addresses, while the 8087 processes the numeric operations.

The 8087 has a set of eight floating-point registers, arranged as a stack. The 8087 locates the top of stack with a 3-bit pointer, contained in the status word. When you read the status word, you can see which of the eight registers is currently the top of the stack. As we'll see, a program seldom requires this information.

All addressing of the 8087 register stack is relative to the current top of the stack. The Stack Top is abbreviated ST(0) or ST in the assembler mnemonics. The element of the stack just below the stack top is ST(1). The second element is ST(2), and so on, to the last element in the stack, ST(7). For ease in using macros, we'll drop the parentheses in the stack elements, using instead ST0, ST1, ST2, and so on.

Let's see how a program can access the stack elements. The instruction

    FADD   ST0,ST3

adds the stack top to the fourth element in the stack and places the result in the stack top. Figure 7.9(a) shows the actions of this instruction. The reference to the ST and ST3 registers is strictly related to the stack pointer. Part (a) added the values represented by A and D, with the result A + D replacing A as the stack top. In Figure 7.9(b), a program has pushed another element, E, onto the stack prior to the execution of the same instruction. This instruction still adds the top of the stack to the fourth element in the stack. In part (b) this adds E and C, with the result E + C replacing E. The act of pushing the element E onto the stack did not affect the positioning of the operands within the 8087, but it did affect their positioning relative to the stack top. ST3 is always the fourth element in the stack, irrespective of where the stack pointer is located.

We can divide the 8087 instructions into three broad categories. The first

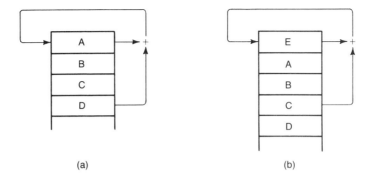

Figure 7.9 Action of FADD ST0,ST3

category is data transfer—the loads and stores of data to and from the 8087. The second area is processor control—the instructions that handle the housekeeping chores of the 8087. The third group of instructions provides the power of the 8087, the number-processing instructions. We'll look at each of the groups in some detail. This text will not provide an exhaustive coverage of the 8087 instructions. We'll use examples to convey a fair amount of the instruction meaning in context. It is beyond the scope of this book to cover all of the uses of the numeric power of the 8087.

Data Transfer Instructions

The data transfer group for the 8087 has just three basic instructions. The load instruction takes data and pushes them onto the 8087 register stack. Normally, these data come from system memory, but the load instruction may also take a value from the stack and replicate it on the stack top. The store instruction moves data from the top of stack and places them into system memory. The exchange instruction swaps two numbers in the 8087 register stack.

Figure 7.10 shows the assembly of the data transfer instructions. The assembly included a set of 8087 macros at the beginning of the program, using

```
IF1
INCLUDE 87MAC.LIB
ENDIF
```

This sequence of instructions includes the 8087 macros during the first pass of the assembler, when the macro expansions must take place. The assembler doesn't read the macro file during the second pass, since it is no longer needed. The ENDIF is the only instruction that shows in the assembly listing.

The first data transfer instruction we'll consider is the load instruction. All of the 8087 instructions begin with an "F." So, to load the 8087, the instruction is FLD for Floating LoaD. Unlike the 8088 instruction set, where the MOV operation code handled all forms of data, there are different load mnemonics for

```
The IBM Personal Computer MACRO Assembler 01-01-83          PAGE   1-1
Figure 7.10 8087 Data Transfer Instructions


  1                                                  PAGE   ,132
  2                                                  TITLE  Figure 7.10 8087 Data Transfer Instructions
  3                                          ENDIF
  4
  5      0000                                 CODE   SEGMENT
  6                                                  ASSUME  CS:CODE, DS:CODE
  7
  8      0000                                 word_integer     label    word
  9      0000                                 short_integer    label    dword
 10      0000                                 long_integer     label    qword
 11      0000                                 bcd_integer      label    tbyte
 12      0000                                 short_real       label    dword
 13      0000                                 long_real        label    qword
 14      0000                                 temporary_real   label    tbyte
 15
 16                                                  FILD   WORD_INTEGER
 17      0000  9B                          +         DB     09BH
 18      0001  DF 06 0000 R                +         ESC    38H,WORD_INTEGER
 19                                                  FILD   SHORT_INTEGER
 20      0005  9B                          +         DB     09BH
 21      0006  DB 06 0000 R                +         ESC    18H,SHORT_INTEGER
 22                                                  FILD   LONG_INTEGER
 23      000A  9B                          +         DB     09BH
 24      000B  DF 2E 0000 R                +         ESC    03DH,LONG_INTEGER
 25                                                  FBLD   BCD_INTEGER
 26      000F  9B                          +         DB     09BH
 27      0010  DF 26 0000 R                +         ESC    03CH,BCD_INTEGER
 28                                                  FLD    SHORT_REAL
 29      0014  9B                          +         DB     09BH
 30      0015  D9 06 0000 R                +         ESC    8,SHORT_REAL
 31                                                  FLD    LONG_REAL
 32      0019  9B                          +         DB     09BH
 33      001A  DD 06 0000 R                +         ESC    40,LONG_REAL
 34                                                  FLD    TEMPORARY_REAL
 35      001E  9B                          +         DB     09BH
 36      001F  DB 2E 0000 R                +         ESC    01DH,TEMPORARY_REAL
 37
 38                                                  FLD    ST2
 39      0023  9B D9 C2                    +         DB     09BH,0D9H,0C0H+ST2
 40
 41                                                  FIST   WORD_INTEGER
 42      0026  9B                          +         DB     09BH
 43      0027  DF 16 0000 R                +         ESC    03AH,WORD_INTEGER
 44                                                  FIST   SHORT_INTEGER
 45      002B  9B                          +         DB     09BH
 46      002C  DB 16 0000 R                +         ESC    01AH,SHORT_INTEGER
 47                                                  FST    SHORT_REAL
 48      0030  9B                          +         DB     09BH
 49      0031  D9 16 0000 R                +         ESC    10,SHORT_REAL
 50                                                  FST    LONG_REAL
 51      0035  9B                          +         DB     09BH
 52      0036  DD 16 0000 R                +         ESC    02AH,LONG_REAL
 53
 54                                                  FST    ST2
 55      003A  9B DD D2                    +         DB     09BH,0DDH,0D0H+ST2
 56
 57                                                  FISTP  WORD_INTEGER
 58      003D  9B                          +         DB     09BH
 59      003E  DF 1E 0000 R                +         ESC    03BH,WORD_INTEGER
 60                                                  FISTP  SHORT_INTEGER
 61      0042  9B                          +         DB     09BH
 62      0043  DB 1E 0000 R                +         ESC    01BH,SHORT_INTEGER
 63                                                  FISTP  LONG_INTEGER
 64      0047  9B                          +         DB     09BH
 65      0048  DF 3E 0000 R                +         ESC    03FH,LONG_INTEGER
 66                                                  FBSTP  BCD_INTEGER
 67      004C  9B                          +         DB     09BH
 68      004D  DF 36 0000 R                +         ESC    03EH,BCD_INTEGER
 69                                                  FSTP   SHORT_REAL
 70      0051  9B                          +         DB     09BH
 71      0052  D9 1E 0000 R                +         ESC    0BH,SHORT_REAL
 72                                                  FSTP   LONG_REAL
 73      0056  9B                          +         DB     09BH
 74      0057  DD 1E 0000 R                +         ESC    02BH,LONG_REAL
 75                                                  FSTP   TEMPORARY_REAL
 76      005B  9B                          +         DB     09BH
 77      005C  DB 3E 0000 R                +         ESC    01FH,TEMPORARY_REAL
 78
 79                                                  FSTP   ST2
 80      0060  9B DD DA                    +         DB     09BH,0DDH,0D8H+ST2
 81
 82                                                  FXCH   ST2
 83      0063  9B D9 CA                    +         DB     09BH,0D9H,0C8H+ST2
 84
 85                                                  FLDZ
```

Figure 7.10   8087 Data Transfer Instructions

```
86    0066  9B D9 EE        +      DB    09BH,0D9H,0EEH
87                                 FLD1
88    0069  9B D9 E8        +      DB    09BH,0D9H,0E8H
89                                 FLDPI
90    006C  9B D9 EB        +      DB    09BH,0D9H,0EBH
91                                 FLDL2T
92    006F  9B D9 E9        +      DB    09BH,0D9H,0E9H
93                                 FLDL2E
94    0072  9B D9 EA        +      DB    09BH,0D9H,0EAH
95                                 FLDLG2
96    0075  9B D9 EC        +      DB    09BH,0D9H,0ECH
97                                 FLDLN2
98    0078  9B D9 ED        +      DB    09BH,0D9H,0EDH
99
100   007B                 CODE   ENDS
101                                END
```

Figure 7.10 *Continued*

different data types. This is because the assembler can distinguish between four-byte and eight-byte operands, but can't tell if an operand is a real number or an integer.

The assembler uses FILD whenever the operand is an integer. Thus, FILD loads a word (16 bits), a short integer (32 bits), or a long integer (64 bits). To load the packed decimal value (80 bits), we use the operation code FBLD. The "B" indicates BCD values. Finally, FLD loads real numbers. The assembler (and the 8087 macro constructions) determine which type of integer or real number you wish to load.

The assembler uses the naming convention of "F" followed by an "I" for integer, "B" for BCD numbers, or no extra character for real numbers for all of the 8087 instructions that reference memory. We'll see that the store instructions use the same convention, as do the arithmetic operations that specify a memory operand.

As you can see in Figure 7.10, there is a load instruction for each of the seven data types that the 8087 supports. The load instruction specifies the data field in memory. The 8087 converts the data from their external representation into the temporary real format. The converted number is pushed onto the stack, increasing the size of the stack by one. If you attempt to push a value onto a stack with eight values already on it, the 8087 signals an exception condition—stack overflow. Unless the program handles the exception with its own routine, the built-in exception handler marks the loaded value as "indefinite." That means that further operations using that number generate indefinite results. If you make a mistake, the 8087 will make sure that it doesn't go unnoticed.

The remaining form of the load instruction takes one of the elements in the stack and pushes it onto the top of the stack. For example, the code

        FLD   ST0

duplicates the top of the stack. The top two elements have the same value.

        FLD   ST3

pushes a copy of the fourth element in the stack onto the stack. Notice that the value that was ST3 is now ST4.

Let's take a look at the machine language actually generated by these instructions. Since this text generates the 8087 instructions with macros, it makes it easy to see where the different values come from. First, every instruction begins with a byte of 09BH. This is the WAIT instruction. As you recall, the 8087 must be synchronized with the 8088 execution. If the 8088 attempted to execute another 8087 instruction before the 8087 had finished the previous one, the 8087 would produce erroneous results. Virtually all of the 8087 macros have the WAIT instruction to provide synchronization. (Those instructions without synchronization are all control instructions that normally don't require the last result. You can identify these instructions easily, since they begin with "FN," where the "N" indicates no synchronization.)

You can also see from the macro expansion that the 8087 instructions are forms of the ESC instructions. To specify a memory address, the ESC instruction contains two operands. The first identifies which ESC instruction it is, the second names the memory location. The ESC instruction may be either two, three, or four bytes long, depending on the size of the displacement field created by the mod-r/m byte. When combined with the WAIT instruction, the maximum size of an 8087 instruction is five bytes.

The store instruction comes in two flavors. The first variation of the instruction takes the top of stack and stores it in the named memory location. The 8087 does the conversion of the data from temporary real form to the desired external form as part of the operation. These are the FST and FIST operation codes. (Notice that the instruction naming convention continues here.) You may also store the stack top register into another location within the stack with this instruction.

You should notice that the FST instruction does not allow you to store all possible external data types. Only the "big four" data types are allowed—word and short integer, short and long real. This instruction doesn't support all of the external data types because the 8087 designers felt that it wasn't necessary. They felt that way because of the next instruction.

The second variation of the store instruction also manipulates the stack pointer besides storing the data. The FSTP (and FISTP and FBSTP) instructions perform the same operation of storing data from the 8087 into memory. However, the instruction also pops the value from the top of the stack. This set of instructions does support all of the external data types. The 8087 designers had to economize on instructions somewhere, so only the FLD and FSTP instructions support all of the external data types. All other instructions that reference memory can access only the "big four" data types. They felt that those four would be the most prevalent, and the use of the other formats could be reserved only for FLD and FSTP.

The exchange instruction (FXCH) is next in the data transfer group. FXCH exchanges the stack top with another register in the stack. Notice that this instruction can only use another element of the stack as an operand. You can't exchange the stack top with a memory location in a single instruction. It takes

Instruction	Constant
FLDZ	0
FLD1	1
FLDPI	PI
FLDL2T	LOG2(10)
FLDL2E	LOG2(e)
FLDLG2	LOG10(2)
FLDLN2	LOGe(2)

Figure 7.11   8087 Constants

several instructions, and a temporary storage area somewhere. Unlike the 8088, the 8087 can can only do a memory read or a memory write, but not both, in a single instruction.

The remaining instructions in the data transfer group handle numeric constants. These instructions load a predefined constant into the stack top. These values cover the range of constants that programs need in numeric processing. These values were chosen to facilitate the processing of the transcendental and trigonometric functions. We'll use some of these constants in our example programs. The table in Figure 7.11 shows the value loaded into ST0 for each instruction. The instruction mnemonic has been chosen in each case to indicate the constant value.

Control Instructions

The control instructions of the 8087 don't do any arithmetic. However, they are necessary to control the operation of the 8087. Figure 7.12 shows the assembly of the 8087 control instructions.

Many of the control instructions can execute without waiting for the completion of the previous 8087 operation. Figure 7.12 has assembled these instructions in the form that includes the WAIT operation. The operation code in the comment field shows the instruction without the WAIT. The assembler

```
The IBM Personal Computer MACRO Assembler 01-01-83            PAGE    1-1
Figure 7.12   8087 Control Instructions

 1                                          PAGE    ,132
 2                                          TITLE   Figure 7.12  8087 Control Instructions
 3                                  ENDIF
 4      0000                        CODE    SEGMENT
 5                                          ASSUME  CS:CODE
 6
 7      0000                        status_word     label   word
 8      0000                        control_word    label   word
 9      0000                        environment     label   byte    ; 14 byte area
10      0000                        state           label   byte    ; 94 byte area
11
12                                          FINIT                   ; FNINIT
13      0000  9B DB E3        +             DB      09BH,0DBH,0E3H
14                                          FENI                    ; FNENI
15      0003  9B DB E0        +             DB      09BH,0DBH,0E0H
16                                          FDISI                   ; FNDISI
17      0006  9B DB E1        +             DB      09BH,0DBH,0E1H
18                                          FLDCW   control_word
19      0009  9B              +             DB      09BH
```

Figure 7.12   8087 Control Instructions

```
20      000A    2E: D9 2E 0000 R      +       ESC    0DH,control_word
21                                            FSTCW    control_word      ; FNSTCW
22      000F    9B                   +       DB     09BH
23      0010    2E: D9 3E 0000 R      +       ESC    0FH,control_word
24                                            FCLEX                      ; FNCLEX
25      0015    9B DB E2             +       DB     09BH,0DBH,0E2H
26                                            FSTENV   environment       ; FNSTENV
27      0018    9B                   +       DB     09BH
28      0019    2E: D9 36 0000 R      +       ESC    0EH,environment
29                                            FLDENV   environment
30      001E    9B                   +       DB     09BH
31      001F    2E: D9 26 0000 R      +       ESC    0CH,environment
32                                            FSAVE    state             ; FNSAVE
33      0024    9B                   +       DB     09BH
34      0025    2E: DD 36 0000 R      +       ESC    02EH,state
35                                            FRSTOR   state
36      002A    9B                   +       DB     09BH
37      002B    2E: DD 26 0000 R      +       ESC    02CH,state
38                                            FINCSTP
39      0030    9B D9 F7             +       DB     09BH,0D9H,0F7H
40                                            FDECSTP
41      0033    9B D9 F6             +       DB     09BH,0D9H,0F6H
42                                            FFREE    ST2
43      0036    9B DD C2             +       DB     09BH,0DDH,0C0H+ST2
44                                            FNOP
45      0039    D9 D0                +       DB     0D9H,0D0H
46                                            FWAIT
47      003B    9B                   +       DB     09BH
48      003C              .                 CODE    ENDS
49                                            END
```

Figure 7.12   *Continued*

indicates "no-wait" operation codes by a "FN" as the first two characters of the mnemonic.

Figure 7.13 summarizes the actions of the 8087 control instructions.

The FENI, FDISI, and FCLEX instructions all deal with the exception conditions of the 8087. The control register contains an interrupt mask that selects which exceptions may cause an interrupt. The FENI and FDISI instructions control an overall interrupt mask register for the 8087. These instructions are similar to STI and CLI on the 8088, except that they control only the interrupts

Instruction	Action
FINIT	Initialize the 8087. Software reset
FENI	Enable the exception interrupts
FDISI	Disable the exception interrupts
FLDCW	Load the 8087 control register from memory
FSTCW	Store the 8087 control register into memory
FSTSW	Store the 8087 status register into memory
FCLEX	Clear the exception indicators
FSTENV	Store the 8087 environment into memory
FLDENV	Load the 8087 environment from memory
FSAVE	Save the 8087 state into memory
FRSTOR	Load the 8087 state from memory
FINCSTP	Increment the stack pointer
FDECSTP	Decrement the stack pointer
FFREE	Free the stack register
FNOP	Do nothing
FWAIT	Identical to WAIT

Figure 7.13   Control Actions (Courtesy of Intel; Copyright Intel 1980)

from the 8087. The FCLEX instruction clears the exception bits of the status register. The 8087 remembers all exception conditions, so that if a sequence of instructions generates more than one type of error, they are all reported in the status register. The FCLEX instruction is the only way to clear these flags.

We covered the control and status words as part of the 8088 programming model. The control instructions FLDCW, FSTCW, and FSTSW load and store these registers.

The environment of the 8087 contains all of the registers of the 8087, except for the data stack. The environment contains 14 bytes of data. Figure 7.14 shows the layout of the environment when the 8087 stores it in memory. Storing the environment is a convenient way to act on exception conditions from the 8087. The environment contains all of the data about the exception. One 20-bit address locates the last 8087 instruction executed. The other address points at the last data location accessed. The last 8087 instruction is also in the environment.

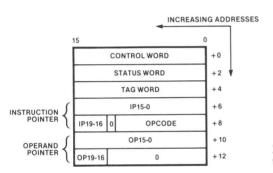

Figure 7.14 8087 Environment (Courtesy of Intel; Copyright Intel 1980)

The state of the 8087 is the environment plus the data registers. Since there are eight registers of 10 bytes in the 8087, the state contains 94 data bytes. Figure 7.15 shows the layout of the 8087 state when it is stored in memory. The state layout is identical to the environment, with the register stack added at the end. A program can store the 8087 state when it performs a task switch, or if an interrupt handler requires the use of the 8087. It can restore the state when the previously executing task once again regains control.

The two instructions that manipulate the stack pointer do just that. They move only the stack pointer. Any data in the registers remain there; that is, the tag word is not modified. Incrementing the stack pointer is not equivalent to popping the stack, because the tag value for that location still indicates that data are present in the register. Attempting to load a number on top of that will result in a stack overflow exception. The FFREE command frees a stack location, setting the tag value for that location to indicate that there are no valid data there. But FFREE doesn't change the stack pointer. If you just want to throw away the top value on the stack, we'll see an arithmetic instruction later that does the job in most cases.

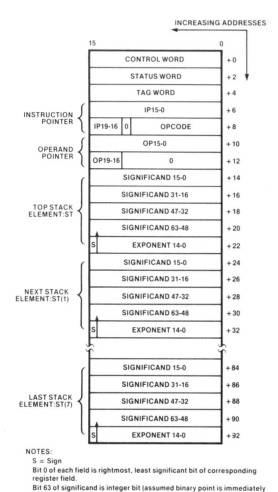

NOTES:
S = Sign
Bit 0 of each field is rightmost, least significant bit of corresponding register field.
Bit 63 of significand is integer bit (assumed binary point is immediately to the right).

Figure 7.15   8087 State (Courtesy of Intel; Copyright Intel 1980)

Arithmetic Instructions

The arithmetic instructions are the real heart of the 8087. The 8087 excels in fast, high-precision execution of numeric operations. The 8087 has instructions not only for the basic four functions of add, subtract, multiply, and divide, but also for the transcendental and trigonometric functions necessary to do the full range of numeric processing.

Figure 7.16 shows some of the assembled instructions for the basic four functions. The example shows only the FADD instruction in all possible configurations. Before looking at the actual instructions, we'll examine the processing possibilities. Figure 7.17 shows the different variations.

As Figure 7.17(a) shows, there are five different methods of executing an arithmetic instruction. The data used for every arithmetic operation can be identified in the five cases of part (a). In case 1, the instruction specifies only the operation code. The stack top and ST1 participate in the operation, with the result replacing the stack top. Notice that Figure 7.17(a) contains an example for each

```
The IBM Personal Computer MACRO Assembler 01-01-83          PAGE    1-1
Figure 7.16  Arithmetic Instructions of 8087

 1                                                PAGE    ,132
 2                                                TITLE   Figure 7.16  Arithmetic Instructions of 8087
 3                                        ENDIF
 4    0000                        CODE    SEGMENT
 5                                        ASSUME  CS:CODE,DS:CODE
 6    0000                        word_integer    label   word
 7    0000                        short_integer   label   dword
 8    0000                        short_real      label   dword
 9    0000                        long_real       label   qword
10
11                                        FADD
12    0000  9B D8 C1          +                   DB      09BH,0D8H,0C1H
13                                        FADD    ST2
14    0003  9B D8 C2          +                           DB      09BH,0D8H,0C0H+ST2
15                                        FADD    ST0,ST2
16    0006  9B D8 C2          +                           DB      09BH,0D8H,0C0H+ST2
17                                        FADD    ST2,ST0
18    0009  9B DC C2          +                           DB      09BH,0DCH,0C0H+ST2
19                                        FIADD   word_integer
20    000C  9B               +                           DB      09BH
21    000D  DE 06 0000 R     +                           ESC     030H,word_integer
22                                        FIADD   short_integer
23    0011  9B               +                           DB      09BH
24    0012  DA 06 0000 R     +                           ESC     010H,short_integer
25                                        FADD    short_real
26    0016  9B               +                                   DB      09BH
27    0017  D8 06 0000 R     +                                   ESC     0,short_real
28                                        FADD    long_real
29    001B  9B               +                                   DB      09BH
30    001C  DC 06 0000 R     +                                   ESC     32,long_real
31                                        FADDP   ST2,ST0
32    0020  9B DE C2         +            DB      09BH,0DEH,0C0H+ST2
33
34                                        FSUB    ST2
35    0023  9B D8 E2         +                           DB      09BH,0D8H,0E0H+ST2
36                                        FISUB   word_integer
37    0026  9B               +                           DB      09BH
38    0027  DE 26 0000 R     +                           ESC     034H,word_integer
39                                        FSUBP   ST2,ST0
40    002B  9B DE E2         +            DB      09BH,0DEH,0E0H+ST2
41
42                                        FSUBR   ST2,ST0
43    002E  9B DC EA         +            DB      09BH,0DCH,0E8H+ST2
44                                        FISUBR  short_integer
45    0031  9B               +                           DB      09BH
46    0032  DA 2E 0000 R     +                           ESC     015H,short_integer
47                                        FSUBRP  ST2,ST0
48    0036  9B DE EA         +            DB      09BH,0DEH,0E8H+ST2
49
50                                        FMUL    short_real
51    0039  9B               +                                   DB      09BH
52    003A  D8 0E 0000 R     +                                   ESC     1,short_real
53                                        FIMUL   word_integer
54    003E  9B               +                           DB      09BH
55    003F  DE 0E 0000 R     +                           ESC     031H,word_integer
56                                        FMULP   ST2,ST0
57    0043  9B DE CA         +            DB      09BH,0DEH,0C8H+ST2
58
59                                        FDIV    ST0,ST2
60    0046  9B D8 F2         +                           DB      09BH,0D8H,0F0H+ST2
61                                        FIDIV   short_integer
62    0049  9B               +                           DB      09BH
63    004A  DA 36 0000 R     +                           ESC     016H,short_integer
64                                        FDIVP   ST2,ST0
65    004E  9B DE F2         +            DB      09BH,0DEH,0F0H+ST2
66
67                                        FDIVR   ST2
68    0051  9B D8 FA         +                           DB      09BH,0D8H,0F8H+ST2
69                                        FIDIVR  word_integer
70    0054  9B               +                           DB      09BH
71    0055  DE 3E 0000 R     +                           ESC     037H,word_integer
72                                        FDIVRP  ST2,ST0
73    0059  9B DE FA         +            DB      09BH,0DEH,0F8H+ST2
74
75    005C                    CODE        ENDS
76                                        END
Open conditionals: 13
```

Figure 7.16 Arithmetic Instructions of 8087

Instruction Form		FADD Example		Action
1. Fop		FADD		ST0←ST0+ST1
2. Fop	STi	FADD	ST2	ST0←ST0+STi
Fop	ST0,STi	FADD	ST0,ST2	ST0←ST0+STi
Fop	STi,ST0	FADD	ST2,ST0	ST2←ST0+ST2
3. FopP	STi,ST0	FADDP	ST2,ST0	ST2←ST0+ST2, Pop stack
4. Fop	real_mem	FADD	REAL	ST0←ST0+REAL
5. FIop	integer_mem	FIADD	INTEGER	ST0←ST0+INTEGER

(a)

Operation	Action
ADD	destination ← destination + source
SUB	destination ← destination − source
SUBR	destination ← source − destination
MUL	destination ← destination × source
DIV	destination ← destination / source
DIVR	destination ← source / destination

(b)

Figure 7.17 Arithmetic Operations. (a) Data Combinations; (b) Arithmetic Functions for the 8087 NDP (Courtesy of Intel; Copyright Intel 1980)

case, using the addition operation. The figure also shows a schematic of the operation.

Case 2 shows an operation performed with two registers on the 8087 stack. The stack top must be one of the registers. If the stack top is the destination, it may be omitted, with only the source register identified. If any register other than the stack top is the destination, both destination and source must be specified.

Case 3 performs a stack operation. This form does the function on two stack operands, and then discards the stack top. Since the stack top is popped following the operation, the stack top cannot be the destination of this instruction. If the destination is ST1, this becomes the classical stack operation. The classical stack operation removes the top two elements from the stack, combines them in the desired function, and pushes the result back onto the stack. Of course, any of the registers may be specified for destination in this operation.

The two remaining cases deal with memory operands. In case 4, the memory operand is a short or long real. In case 5, the operand is a word or short integer. Just as with load and store, the "I" is indicates the memory operand is an integer.

Referring back to Figure 7.16, the assembly listing, you can see that there are only four memory operands defined for FADD. There are two integers—word and short, and two reals—short and long. The arithmetic instructions cannot operate directly on BCD, long integer, and temporary real forms. The program must load those values into a register before doing arithmetic on them.

Figure 7.17(b) shows the six arithmetic operations available. Notice that the 8087 extends the standard four functions by providing reverse operations for both subtraction and division. Since addition and multiplication are commutative, they don't require reverse operations. The ordering of the operands for subtraction and division is critical. Sometimes the value currently in the source is not the value that you want to subtract from the destination. In that case, the reverse function does the job.

Comparison Instructions

Just like the 8088 instruction set, the 8087 has instructions that compare two numbers. The 8087 discards the result of the comparison, but sets the status flags according to the result. The program must store the status word in memory before it can interrogate the status flags. The simplest way is to move the status flags to AH, and then to the 8088 flags for easy conditional testing.

Figure 7.18 shows the assembly listing of the comparison instructions for the 8087. Since the stack top always participates in the comparison, the program must identify only the register or memory operand. Following the comparison, the status word contains an indication of the ordering of the two numbers. The table in Figure 7.19 shows the relationship. Only two of the status bits are necessary to reflect the comparison. Refer to Figure 7.8 for the location of C3 and C0 within the status word.

The source program in Figure 7.20 shows a sample code fragment that compares the stack top to a word in memory. The code branches based on the result of the comparison. Notice that one of the four cases indicates that the two

```
The IBM Personal Computer MACRO Assembler 01-01-83          PAGE    1-1
Figure 7.18  Comparison Instructions of 8087

 1                                         PAGE    ,132
 2                                         TITLE   Figure 7.18  Comparison Instructions of 8087
 3                                   ENDIF
 4      0000                         CODE    SEGMENT
 5                                           ASSUME  CS:CODE,DS:CODE
 6      0000                         word_integer    label   word
 7      0000                         short_integer   label   dword
 8      0000                         short_real      label   dword
 9      0000                         long_real       label   qword
10
11                                           FCOM
12      0000  9B D8 D1        +               DB      09BH,0D8H,0D1H
13                                           FCOM    ST2
14      0003  9B D8 D2        +               DB      09BH,0D8H,0D0H+ST2
15                                           FICOM   word_integer
16      0006  9B             +               DB      09BH
17      0007  DE 16 0000 R   +               ESC     032H,word_integer
18                                           FCOM    short_real
19      000B  9B             +               DB      09BH
20      000C  D8 16 0000 R   +               ESC     2,short_real
21
22                                           FCOMP
23      0010  9B D8 D9        +               DB      09BH,0D8H,0D9H
24                                           FICOMP  short_integer
25      0013  9B             +               DB      09BH
26      0014  DA 1E 0000 R   +               ESC     013H,short_integer
27                                           FCOMP   long_real
28      0018  9B             +               DB      09BH
29      0019  DC 1E 0000 R   +               ESC     35,long_real
30
31                                           FCOMPP
32      001D  9B DE D9        +               DB      09BH,0DEH,0D9H
33
34                                           FTST
35      0020  9B D9 E4        +               DB      09BH,0D9H,0E4H
36                                           FXAM
37      0023  9B D9 E5        +               DB      09BH,0D9H,0E5H
38
39      0026                         CODE    ENDS
40                                           END
Open conditionals: 2
```

Figure 7.18 Comparison Instructions of 8087

C3	C0	Order
0	0	ST > source
0	1	ST < source
1	0	ST = source
1	1	ST and source cannot be compared

Figure 7.19   Comparison Ordering (Courtesy of Intel; Copyright Intel 1980)

numbers could not be compared. This occurs if one of the numbers is a NAN (Not A Number) or one of the forms of infinity. Notice that the 8087 places the C3 and C0 status flags in just the right places. They line up directly with the zero (C3) and carry (C0) flags of the 8087 flag register. As the code fragment shows, if the program moves the high byte of the 8087 status word into the 8088 flag register, it can do the conditional branching with direct testing of the flags through the conditional jumps. The individual bits of the status word do not have to be masked and tested.

By the way, this chapter will list the 8087 example programs in source form rather than the assembled listing. We'll do this since the macro expansions tend to clutter up the listing, making it difficult to follow the logic of the program. Whenever there is something significant to be seen from the actual assembly of a program, we'll include the assembly listing rather than the source.

Returning to the assembly listing of Figure 7.18, there are other variations of the FCOM instruction. Of course, there is the integer version, FICOM. The FCOMP and FICOMP instructions are identical to FICOM, except that the 8087 pops the stack top following the instruction. This allows you to compare two numbers using the 8087 without worrying about clearing the first operand from the stack following the comparison.

The FCOMPP instruction has no user-specified operands. It always com-

```
          PAGE    ,132
          TITLE   Figure 7.20  Comparison branching
IF1
INCLUDE 87MAC.LIB
ENDIF
          CODE    SEGMENT
          ASSUME  CS:CODE, DS:CODE

WORD_INTEGER   LABEL   WORD
STATUS_WORD    DW      ?

;----- This code compares the stack top to word_integer

          FICOM   WORD_INTEGER   ; Compare word to ST
          FSTSW   STATUS_WORD    ; Store the status word
          FWAIT                  ; Wait for store complete
          MOV     AH,BYTE PTR STATUS_WORD+1     ; Get into AH
          SAHF                   ; Move to flags [C0=CF, C3=ZF]
          JB      CONTINUE       ; Test C0 flag, jump if zero
          JNE     ST_GREATER     ; Test C3 flag
ST_EQUAL:                        ; Here if C3=1, C0=0
;          . . .
ST_GREATER:                      ; Here if C3=0, C0=0
;          . . .
CONTINUE:
          JNE     ST_LESS        ; Test C3 flag
UNORDERED:                       ; Here if C3=1, C0=1
;          . . .
ST_LESS:                         ; Here if C3=0, C0=1
;          . . .

CODE      ENDS
          END
```

Figure 7.20   Comparison Branching

pares the top two elements of the stack. Following the comparison, it pops both operands from the stack.

The compare and pop instructions offer a convenient way to clear values from the stack. Since the 8087 has no instruction to pop an operand from the stack conveniently, you can use the compare and pop instructions instead. Of course, these instructions also modify the status register. They can't be used when the status bits are important. In most cases these instructions present a quick way to pop either one or two operands from the stack. Since the 8087 gives an invalid operation error if the stack overflows, you must remove any operands from the stack when you finish your computation.

There are two special comparison instructions. The first, FTST, is a comparison of the stack top to zero. This instruction allows you to determine the sign of the stack top quickly. The table of 7.19 once again shows the status of the comparison. You need to substitute the value zero for ''source'' wherever it appears in the table.

The FXAM instruction is, strictly speaking, not a comparison instruction. Although it operates on the stack top, it does not compare the stack top to any other value. Rather, the FXAM instruction sets the four status register flags (C3 through C0) to indicate what kind of number is in the stack top. Since the 8087 can handle many forms of numbers other than the normalized floating-point number, the FXAM instruction tells you what is currently in the stack top. Figure 7.21 shows the setting of the status bits for each of the possible numbers.

If your arithmetic processing is not doing anything fancy or pressing the limits of the 8087 data representation, you won't see some of these FXAM states. You should expect to see positive or negative normal or zero. Finding the stack top empty should be limited to an error condition. A subroutine might do this test to check a parameter passed on the stack top.

The remaining number values are responses of the 8087 to an error condition. Whenever the 8087 detects an error condition, it attempts to execute an exception interrupt, with the appropriate bit set in the status word. However, if the exception is masked through the control word, the 8087 takes action on its own. It decides which action is appropriate for the particular error and presses on with the peculiar number in the register. A NAN (Not a Number) occurs when an

C3	C2	C1	C0	Meaning	C3	C2	C1	C0	Meaning
0	0	0	0	+ Unnormal	1	0	0	0	+ 0
0	0	0	1	+ NAN	1	0	0	1	Empty
0	0	1	0	− Unnormal	1	0	1	0	− 0
0	0	1	1	−NAN	1	0	1	1	Empty
0	1	0	0	+ Normal	1	1	0	0	+ Denormal
0	1	0	1	+ Infinity	1	1	0	1	Empty
0	1	1	0	− Normal	1	1	1	0	− Denormal
0	1	1	1	− Infinity	1	1	1	1	Empty

Figure 7.21 FXAM Condition Code Interpretation (Courtesy of Intel; Copyright Intel 1980)

operation is not defined, such as the square root of a negative number. Infinity occurs when the result of an operation is too big for the floating-point representation.

The denormalized and unnormalized numbers occur at the other end of the floating-point representation. When a number becomes so small that the exponent field can no longer contain it, the number is denormalized. Instead of setting the value to zero, the 8087 sets the exponent to the smallest possible value and unnormalizes the fractional part. This means that precision is lost from the value, since there are leading zeros in the fraction. However, the denormalized result is still more precise than the alternate, zero. This is an instance of a condition where the 8087 continues on and gives you the best possible response to a bad condition. The flagging of the value as a denormal number alerts you to the condition. The bit in the exception register is also set, and remains set until FCLEX clears the exception bits. With these two flags, a program can detect the occurrence of an error condition and regard the results with suspicion.

Functions and Transcendentals

The remaining group of 8087 instructions do high-powered mathematics. These instructions allow the 8087 to perform the more complicated arithmetic functions that require logarithmic, exponential, or trigonometric functions. Figure 7.22 is a list of these instructions. When you look at this set of instructions, you won't see the same operations that you find on a pocket calculator. The 8087 designers could not provide all of the desired functions within the chip, which is already quite

```
The IBM Personal Computer MACRO Assembler 01-01-83          PAGE     1-1
Figure 7.22  Stack Top Arithmetic Instructions

 1                                                PAGE     ,132
 2                                                TITLE    Figure 7.22  Stack Top Arithmetic Instructions
 3                                        ENDIF
 4      0000                              CODE    SEGMENT
 5                                                ASSUME   CS:CODE,DS:CODE
 6
 7                                                FSQRT
 8      0000  9B D9 FA            +                DB       09BH,0D9H,0FAH
 9                                                FSCALE
10      0003  9B D9 FD            +                DB       09BH,0D9H,0FDH
11                                                FPREM
12      0006  9B D9 F8            +                DB       09BH,0D9H,0F8H
13                                                FRNDINT
14      0009  9B D9 FC            +                DB       09BH,0D9H,0FCH
15                                                FXTRACT
16      000C  9B D9 F4            +                DB       09BH,0D9H,0F4H
17                                                FABS
18      000F  9B D9 E1            +                DB       09BH,0D9H,0E1H
19                                                FCHS
20      0012  9B D9 E0            +                DB       09BH,0D9H,0E0H
21                                                FPTAN
22      0015  9B D9 F2            +                DB       09BH,0D9H,0F2H
23                                                FPATAN
24      0018  9B D9 F3            +                DB       09BH,0D9H,0F3H
25                                                F2XM1
26      001B  9B D9 F0            +                DB       09BH,0D9H,0F0H
27                                                FYL2X
28      001E  9B D9 F1            +                DB       09BH,0D9H,0F1H
29                                                FYL2XP1
30      0021  9B D9 F9            +                DB       09BH,0D9H,0F9H
31
32      0024                              CODE    ENDS
33                                                END
```

Figure 7.22   Stack Top Arithmetic Instructions

complex. So, instead, they have provided a set of lower-level functions, from which a program can do the calculator functions. For example, there are no trigonometric functions, such as sine and cosine. Instead, there is a partial tangent function. This instruction returns a ratio which is equal to the tangent of the angle. From this ratio, a program can determine the sine, cosine, tangent, or any other trigonometric value. Going the other direction is the partial arctangent operation, which takes a ratio of values and returns the angle for that tangent. These partial functions allow you to construct the arcsine, arccosine, and others without having them as explicit instructions.

Below is a listing of the instructions within this group, together with a short explanation of the operation of each. None of these instructions contain programmer defined operands. In general, they all operate on the stack top, and possibly, on ST1 also.

SQRT   (Square Root)
                  ST ← Square Root (ST)
FSQRT   ST must be nonnegative.
FSCALE   (Scale)
                  ST ← ST * 2^{ST1}

This instruction is necessary for exponentiation. The only other exponentiation function has a limited range for the exponent value. This instruction raises the number by integer values of 2. Later we'll do an example of raising 10 to a power.

FPREM   (Partial Remainder)
                  ST ← ST partial mod(ST1)

FPREM does not do the complete modulo operation. It reduces the stack top by a maximum of 2^{64} in a single instruction. The instruction does an exact remaindering and requires a significant amount of time to reduce a very large number by a very small base. By setting a maximum reduction for each execution of the instruction, the programmer can allow interrupts during the execution of a total remainder operation. FPREM sets the condition code flag C2 to "1" if the function is incomplete. FPREM sets the other status flags of C3, C1, and C0 with the low 3 bits of the quotient when it completes the remaindering. When FPREM is used in conjunction with the trigonometric primitives to limit the angle range, it is necessary to determine the octant of the original angle. We'll do a trigonometric example later also, to illustrate this instruction.

FRNDINT   (Round to Integer)
                  ST ← Integer (ST)

This instruction rounds the current stack top to an integer. The current rounding control set in the control word determines the direction of rounding.

FXTRACT   (Extract)
                  ST ← Fraction of ST
                  ST1 ← Exponent of ST

This instruction breaks up the current stack top into its component parts. The current stack top is the argument to the function. The exponent value of the argument replaces the stack top value. The fractional part of the argument is pushed onto the stack, becoming the new stack top. This instruction is complementary to the FSCALE instruction. Starting with a value on the stack top, executing FXTRACT and FSCALE in succession leaves the same value on the top. However, FSCALE does not remove the exponent value from the stack, so there will now be one additional value on the stack.

> FABS   (Absolute Value)
> ST ← Absolute value of ST

This instruction sets the sign of the stack top to "0" (indicating a positive number) for the absolute value.

> FCHS   (Change Sign)
> ST ← −ST

This instruction changes the sign of the stack top.

The following functions handle the transcendental operations of trigonometry, logarithms, and exponentiation.

> FPTAN   (Partial Tangent)
> ST ← X
> ST1 ← Y, where Y/X = TAN(Angle)

This function is the gateway to all of the trigonometric functions, such as sine, cosine, and tangent. The input on the stack top is an angle in radians, which must be in the range $0 < \text{Angle} < \text{PI}/4$. FPREM can reduce the angle to the correct range. The output is a ratio, Y/X, which is the tangent of the angle. Y replaces the angle on the stack top, and then X is pushed on. The other trig functions can be calculated using these values. For example, cosine is $\text{COS(Angle)} = \text{X/SQR(X**2 + Y**2)}$

> FPATAN   (Partial Arctangent)
> ST ← Arctan(Y/X) = Arctan(ST1/ST)

This function is complementary to the preceding operation, FPTAN. FPATAN calculates the angle corresponding to the ratio of values in ST1 and ST0. It pops the X value from the stack, and the angle result overwrites the Y value as the new stack top. The input values must obey the inequality

> $0 < Y < X < \text{Infinity}$

> F2XM1   (2 to the X Minus 1)
> ST ← $(2^{ST}) - 1$

This function does exponentiation. It raises 2 to the power indicated in the stack top. However, the input value must be in the range $0 \le \text{ST} \le 0.5$. To calculate an exponent value greater than 0.5, this instruction must be used in combination with the FSCALE function. With the FLD constant functions, a program may raise values other than 2 to a power, using these formulas:

$$10^X = 2^{X \cdot Log_2 10}$$
$$e^X = 2^{X \cdot Log_2 e}$$
$$Y^X = 2^{X \cdot Log_2 Y}$$

We'll do an example showing how to raise 10 to an arbitrary value.

FYL2X   (Y Times Log base 2 of X)
                 $ST \leftarrow Y \cdot Log_2 X = ST1 \cdot Log_2 ST$

This function does the logarithm operation. It takes the logarithm to the base 2 of the stack top value and then multiplies it by ST1. The FYL2X pops the X value and the result replaces the Y value. The parameters must observe the following inequalities:

$0 < X <$ Infinity and $-$Infinity $< Y <$ Infinity

This function optimizes the calculation of a logarithm to a base other than 2. The formula

$Log_n 2 \times Log_2 X$

gives the logarithm of a value to the base n. You can calculate $Log_n 2$ as $l/(Log_2 n)$.

FYL2XP1   (Y Times Log base 2 of X Plus 1)
                 $ST < - Y \cdot Log_2(X + 1) = ST1 \cdot Log_2(ST + 1)$

This function is identical to FYL2X except for the addition of 1 to X. This function has stricter bounds on X, and is for calculation of logarithms where X is very close to 1. This function gives improved accuracy, provided that

$$0 < ABS(X) < 1 - \frac{\sqrt{2}}{2}$$

EXAMPLES

This section of the chapter should teach you how to use the 8087 by example rather than by explanation. This section includes examples for most of the common operations using the 8087. All of the examples are simple. That is, they don't try to handle all possible error conditions or detect any of the peculiar numbers that the 8087 can manipulate. The 8087 is quite capable of doing those things, but those are more advanced operations. These examples show you how to use the 8087, assuming that you have no prior knowledge. Once you have mastered the simple techniques, you can add the touches to these examples that will make them into truly general-purpose routines.

Powers of 10

The source program in Figure 7.23 is the first example. This program prints out the short real representation for the powers of 10 from 10^3 to 10^{39}. As we discussed in the data representation section, the IBM Macro Assembler has no provisions for directly entering real numbers. Having this table of values makes it easy for you to enter powers of 10 as constants. By referring to this table, you can determine the correct hexadecimal value to include in your program.

This program generates only every third power of 10, and it uses short real representation. If you are dealing with much larger numbers, or you require more precision, you should do this example using long real numbers, and should generate every power of 10. We will leave that as an exercise for the student.

The primary purpose of this example is as an introduction to the 8087 and its operation. The program is a stand-alone program, intended to be executed as an .EXE file. Before we get into the program itself, notice that the program includes a STACK segment, required for an .EXE file. The data areas appear first in the CODE segment, and the program begins with the label CALCULATE_POWER. Looking ahead to the END statement, you can see that CALCULATE_POWER is the first instruction executed, since it is listed on the END statement.

The first part of the program does the initialization. The program pushes the return address for an .EXE file onto the stack before setting the DS register into the CODE segment. The 8087 is initialized with the FINIT instruction, which is identical to the hardware reset. It leaves the 8087 set with all of the default-exception-handling conditions, which is fine for all the examples in this book. The FINIT also clears the 8087 register stack, leaving all eight positions available for our use. A program should use FINIT only when the program is starting out. FINIT should not be part of an 8087 subroutine, for example.

The next instructions load the value 1000 into ST1 and the value 1 into ST0. All subsequent operations with the 8087 use these two registers on the stack. ST0 holds the current power of ten, while ST1 has 10^3. We'll use the value in ST1 to bump the value in ST0 after each loop of the program. The integer variable POWER tracks the power of 10 currently in ST0.

In POWER_LOOP, ST0 is multiplied by ST1 (which has 1000 in it) to bump ST0 by 10^3. The FST instruction stores the result into a memory area. The remainder of POWER_LOOP prints out the results of the operation. The subroutine TRANSLATE converts a byte hexadecimal value into a two-character ASCII string, so that the program can print it. The current POWER of 10, and the hexadecimal string stored by the 8087 are both converted into ASCII. The DOS function prints the string on the display. The POWER_LOOP continues until the last printed value is greater than 10^{38}. We chose this value because 10^{38} is the maximum value that the short real form can represent. If we had chosen to print out the long real forms of the number, this maximum number would be 10^{308}. The final part of Figure 7.23 shows the output of this program as it looks on the display.

```
                PAGE    ,132
                TITLE   Figure 7.23 Powers of Ten
        1F1
        INCLUDE 87MAC.LIB
        ENDIF
        STACK   SEGMENT STACK
                DW      64 DUP(?)
        STACK   ENDS
        CODE    SEGMENT
                ASSUME  CS:CODE
        POWER_OF_TEN    DD      ?               ; Data area for 10**x, short real
        OUTPUT_POWER    DB      2 DUP(' ')      ; Buffer for power value
                        DB      'H      '
        OUTPUT_STRING   DB      8 DUP(' ')      ; Hexadecimal string output
                        DB      'H',13,10,'$'   ; String ending
        POWER           DB      0               ; Current power of ten
        THOUSAND        DW      1000            ; Constant
        CONTROL_87      DW      03BFH
        CALCULATE_POWER PROC    FAR
                        PUSH    DS                      ;Set return address
                        MOV     AX,0
                        PUSH    AX
                        PUSH    CS
                        POP     DS
                        ASSUME  DS:CODE         ; Addressing to data area
                        FINIT                   ; Initialize the 8087
                        FILD    THOUSAND        ; Load 10**3
                        FLD1                    ; Load starting value
        POWER_LOOP:
                        FMUL    ST1             ; Multiply st0 * st1
                        FST     POWER_OF_TEN    ; Store into ram
                        ADD     POWER,3         ; Update power of ten
                        MOV     AL,POWER        ; Get power
                        MOV     BX,OFFSET OUTPUT_POWER
                        CALL    TRANSLATE
                        MOV     CX,4
                        MOV     BX,OFFSET OUTPUT_STRING
                        MOV     SI,OFFSET POWER_OF_TEN+3
                        STD                     ; Backwards
        VALUE_OUTPUT:
                        LODSB                   ; Get byte of power
                        CALL    TRANSLATE       ; Write to output string
                        LOOP    VALUE_OUTPUT    ; Do it for all bytes of string

                        MOV     DX,OFFSET OUTPUT_POWER
                        MOV     AH,9
                        INT     21H
                        CMP     POWER,38
                        JB      POWER_LOOP
                        FCOMPP                  ; Pop two items from stack
                        RET
        CALCULATE_POWER ENDP

        TRANSLATE       PROC    NEAR
                        PUSH    AX              ; Save input value
                        PUSH    CX
                        MOV     CL,4            ; Move high nybble to
                        SHR     AL,CL           ;  low nybble
                        POP     CX
                        CALL    XLAT_OUTPUT     ; Output low nybble
                        POP     AX              ; Parameter back
                        CALL    XLAT_OUTPUT     ; Output high nybble
                        RET
        TRANSLATE       ENDP

        ASCII_TABLE     DB      '0123456789ABCDEF'
        XLAT_OUTPUT     PROC    NEAR
                        AND     AL,0FH          ; Isolate low nybble
                        PUSH    BX
                        MOV     BX,OFFSET ASCII_TABLE  ; Translate table
                        XLAT    ASCII_TABLE     ; Convert to ASCII
                        POP     BX
                        MOV     [BX],AL         ; Store in output string
                        INC     BX              ; Point to next in string
                        RET
        XLAT_OUTPUT     ENDP
        CODE    ENDS
                END     CALCULATE_POWER

                Figure 7.23(a)

        A>PRINT10
        03H     447A0000H
        06H     49742400H
        09H     4E6E6B28H
        0CH     5368D4A5H
        0FH     58635FA9H
        12H     5D5E0B6BH
        15H     6258D727H
        18H     6753C21CH
        1BH     6C4ECB8FH
        1EH     7149F2CAH
        21H     76453719H
        24H     7B4097CEH
        27H     7F800000H

            Figure 7.23(b)
```

Figure 7.23 (a) Powers of 10; (b) Display from Powers-of-10 Routine.

You should look at the TRANSLATE section of the program, even though it doesn't use any 8087 instructions. This code is an example of preparing values for output. In particular, the XLAT instruction converts the hexadecimal nybble value (0 to 0FH) into the correct ASCII character ("0" to "F") for printing. You can't just add a value to the nybble value, since the characters "A" through "F" don't immediately follow the characters "0" through "9" in the ASCII set. The translate instruction makes it all work very nicely. We'll use a method similar to this when we convert a floating-point number into a printed decimal number later.

Ten to the X

The second example of 8087 operations takes us much deeper into the 8087 execution. This program is a subroutine. In fact, we'll use this subroutine in a later program. The program assumes that the input parameter is a value X in the stack top. On the return from the subroutine, the value in the stack top is 10 raised to the value X. The source listing for this subroutine is given in Figure 7.24.

There is no 8087 instruction to raise 10 to an arbitrary number, but we can

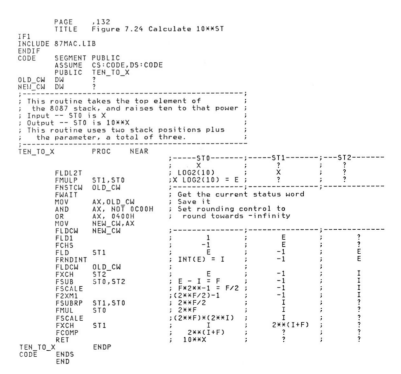

```
                PAGE    ,132
                TITLE   Figure 7.24 Calculate 10**ST
        IF1
        INCLUDE 87MAC.LIB
        ENDIF
        CODE    SEGMENT PUBLIC
                ASSUME  CS:CODE,DS:CODE
                PUBLIC  TEN_TO_X
        OLD_CW  DW      ?
        NEW_CW  DW      ?
        ;---------------------------------------------------;
        ; This routine takes the top element of             ;
        ;   the 8087 stack, and raises ten to that power    ;
        ; Input -- ST0 is X                                 ;
        ; Output -- ST0 is 10**X                            ;
        ; This routine uses two stack positions plus        ;
        ;   the parameter, a total of three.                ;
        ;---------------------------------------------------;
        TEN_TO_X        PROC    NEAR
                                        ;-----ST0-------;-----ST1-------;---ST2-------
                                        ;     X         ;      ?        ;    ?
                FLDL2T                  ; LOG2(10)      ;      X        ;    ?
                FMULP   ST1,ST0         ;X LOG2(10) = E ;      ?        ;    ?
                FNSTCW  OLD_CW          ;--------------;---------------;--------------
                FWAIT                   ; Get the current status word
                MOV     AX,OLD_CW       ; Save it
                AND     AX, NOT 0C00H   ; Set rounding control to
                OR      AX, 0400H       ;   round towards -infinity
                MOV     NEW_CW,AX
                FLDCW   NEW_CW          ;--------------;---------------;--------------
                FLD1                    ;      1        ;      E        ;    ?
                FCHS                    ;     -1        ;      E        ;    ?
                FLD     ST1             ;      E        ;     -1        ;    E
                FRNDINT                 ; INT(E) = I    ;     -1        ;    E
                FLDCW   OLD_CW          ;              ;               ;
                FXCH    ST2             ;      E        ;     -1        ;    I
                FSUB    ST0,ST2         ; E - I = F     ;     -1        ;    I
                FSCALE                  ; F*2**-1 = F/2 ;     -1        ;    I
                F2XM1                   ;(2**F/2)-1     ;     -1        ;    I
                FSUBRP  ST1,ST0         ; 2**F/2        ;      I        ;    ?
                FMUL    ST0             ; 2**F          ;      I        ;    ?
                FSCALE                  ;(2**F)*(2**I)  ;      I        ;    ?
                FXCH    ST1             ;      I        ; 2**(I+F)      ;    ?
                FCOMP                   ;   2**(I+F)    ;      ?        ;    ?
                RET                     ;   10**X       ;      ?        ;    ?
        TEN_TO_X        ENDP
        CODE    ENDS
                END
```

Figure 7.24   Calculate 10**ST

raise 2 to some value. Therefore, we have to use the formula

$$10^{**}X = 2^{**}(X^*Log2(10))$$

The first two 8087 instructions form this new exponent for 2. The program loads the constant value Log2(10), and then multiplies it by the input value X, giving the desired exponent of 2, called E. Notice that the example uses the comment field of the program to indicate the stack locations of the 8087. The ''?'' symbol indicates that the value of that stack element is unknown. This subroutine uses a total of three stack locations, so there are three columns in the comment field.

Now that we have the required exponent of 2, there is no 8087 instruction that does the job in a single step. The instruction F2XM1 raises 2 to the X power, but only for X less than or equal to one-half. This means that we have to separate the exponent E into the integer portion and the fractional portion. The FSCALE instruction can raise 2 to the integer value, and F2XM1 will handle the fractional part.

Before the program separates E, it does some housekeeping. The next sequence of 8087 instructions reads the control word and sets the rounding control to round down. This guarantees that when we take the integer value of the exponent, the value will be rounded down, toward Minus Infinity. This ensures that the fractional part of the exponent will be a positive number, also required for F2XM1.

Notice the use of the FWAIT instruction following the FNSTCW instruction. We don't need to wait for the multiply to finish before storing the control word, since the multiply doesn't change the value in the control word. However, before we read the control word from main memory and modify it, we have to be sure that the 8087 has placed it there. Thus, we must FWAIT until it gets there.

Once the rounding control has been set, the FRNDINT instruction rounds the exponent E to an integer value. Since we also saved the original value of E on the stack, we can subtract the integer part from E to give the fractional part of the exponent. Thus, we now have E = I + F, and we can calculate

$$2^{**}E = 2^{**}I * 2^{**}F$$

One more item before we can do that, however. The fraction F might be a value greater than one-half, and therefore can't be an argument to F2XM1. We'll use the value of −1 previously placed on the stack to divide the F value by 2, giving F/2. We used FSCALE to do that, since FSCALE multiplies ST0 by 2 raised to the value of ST1. Since ST1 is a −1, the net effect is multiplying ST0 by one-half. We are now sure that ST0 is less than one-half.

The F2XM1 instruction now raises 2 to the F/2 power, and the minus one on the stack can take care of the minus one produced as a result of the F2XM1 instruction. Notice that a reverse subtraction, with pop, gets rid of the value −1 on the stack. The 2**(F/2) is multiplied by itself to give 2**F in ST0. Since the integer portion of the exponent has now migrated to ST1, the FSCALE instruction takes 2**I and multiplies it times the 2**F already in ST0, and produces the desired result. The FCOMP instruction removes the value of I from the stack before executing the return from the subroutine.

Floating-Point Display

The next subroutine that we'll do converts the value in the stack top into a printable character string. In fact, we'll write the routine so that it removes the value from the stack top and sends the value to the display. We'll use this routine in the next two examples, to display the results of those programs. The subroutine source listing appears in Figure 7.25.

This routine does a very simpleminded determination of the correct ASCII string to be displayed. If the input parameter is a NAN or infinity or some other peculiar number of the 8087, the result is incorrectly displayed. The first portion of this routine would be a good place to use the FXAM instruction, which determines the type of number in the stack top register. We'll omit that operation from this example, and assume that the input to this routine is always well behaved.

This routine also does a very meager job of formatting the output. The output always consists of a sign (either blank or "−") and a one-digit integer portion. Following the decimal point are eight decimal locations. The "E" is followed by the sign of the exponent and three digit positions for the power of 10. The result of this routine is not as nice as you might wish it to be, but it will certainly allow us to view the output of our programs in a human-readable form. To make a nicer conversion of the number would require a lot more instructions, and very few of them would enhance our understanding of the 8087.

The conversion program works something like this. It first determines the order of magnitude of the number. For example, the number 1234 has an order of magnitude of 3. This means that it is between 10^3 and 10^4. Having found the correct order of magnitude, the program saves that value (it is the exponent of the result) and divides the input number by 10 raised to that value. This converts the input value into a number between 1 and 10. The routine then multiplies the

```
        PAGE    ,132
        TITLE   Figure 7.25 Floating point to ASCII Conversion
IF1
INCLUDE 87MAC.LIB
ENDIF

CODE    SEGMENT PUBLIC
        ASSUME  CS:CODE,DS:CODE,ES:CODE
        EXTRN   TEN_TO_X:NEAR
OLD_CW          DW      ?
NEW_CW          DW      ?
EXPONENT        DW      ?
BCD_RESULT      DT      ?
BCD_EXPONENT    DT      ?
TEN8            DD      100000000
PRINT_STRING    DB      '        .         E       ',10,13,'$'
        PUBLIC  FLOAT_ASCII
;-----------------------------------------------------;
; This routine takes the top element of the           ;
;  8087 stack and displays the floating point         ;
;  value.                                             ;
; Input -- ST0 of the 8087                            ;
; Output -- Value is displayed, stack is popped       ;
;-----------------------------------------------------;
```

Figure 7.25   Floating Point-to-ASCII Conversion

```
FLOAT_ASCII     PROC    NEAR
                                ;------ST0------;------ST1------;------ST2----
                                ;       X       ;               ;
        FLD     ST0             ;       X       ;       X       ;     ?
        FABS                    ;      |X|      ;       X       ;     ?
        FLD1                    ;       1       ;       X       ;     X
        FXCH    ST1             ;       X       ;       1       ;     X
        FYL2X                   ;     LOG2(X)   ;       X       ;     ?
        FLDL2T                  ;     LOG2(10)  ;     LOG2(X)   ;     X
        FDIVRP  ST1,ST0         ;E=LOGX/LOG10   ;       X       ;     ?
        FNSTCW  OLD_CW          ;               ;               ;
        FWAIT                   ;               ;               ;
        MOV     AX,OLD_CW       ;               ;               ;
        AND     AX, NOT 0C00H   ;               ;               ;
        OR      AX, 0400H       ;               ;               ;
        MOV     NEW_CW,AX       ;               ;               ;
        FLDCW   NEW_CW          ;               ;               ;
        FRNDINT                 ; I= INT(E)     ;       X       ;     ?
        FLDCW   OLD_CW          ;               ;               ;
        FIST    EXPONENT        ;       I       ;       X       ;     ?
        FCHS                    ;      -I       ;       X       ;     ?
        CALL    TEN_TO_X        ; 10 **(-I)     ;       X       ;     ?
        FMULP   ST1,ST0         ; X/10**I       ;       ?       ;     ?
        FIMUL   TEN8            ; ADJUSTED FRAC ;       ?       ;     ?
        FBSTP   BCD_RESULT      ;       ?       ;       ?       ;     ?
        FILD    EXPONENT        ;       I       ;       ?       ;     ?
        FBSTP   BCD_EXPONENT    ;       ?       ;       ?       ;     ?
;----- Display the values stored as BCD strings

        CLD
        MOV     DI,OFFSET PRINT_STRING
        MOV     AL,BYTE PTR BCD_RESULT+9     ; Point at output string
        CALL    PRINT_SIGN                  ; Print the sign
        MOV     AL,BYTE PTR BCD_RESULT+4
        CALL    PRINT_NYBBLE                ; Print the leading digit
        MOV     AL,'.'                      ; The decimal point
        STOSB
        MOV     BX,OFFSET BCD_RESULT+3
        MOV     CX,4                        ; Loop through the 8
DO_BYTE:                                    ;  digits following
        CALL    PRINT_BYTE                  ;  the decimal point
        LOOP    DO_BYTE
        MOV     AL,'E'                      ; Exponent indicator
        STOSB
        MOV     AL,BYTE PTR BCD_EXPONENT+9
        CALL    PRINT_SIGN                  ; Print exponent sign
        MOV     AL,BYTE PTR BCD_EXPONENT+1
        CALL    PRINT_NYBBLE                ; Print first digit
        MOV     BX,OFFSET BCD_EXPONENT
        CALL    PRINT_BYTE                  ; Last two digits of exp
        MOV     DX,OFFSET PRINT_STRING
        MOV     AH,9
        INT     21H                         ; Use DOS to print the string
        RET
FLOAT_ASCII     ENDP

;----- This routine prints a ' ' or '-'

PRINT_SIGN      PROC    NEAR
        CMP     AL,0                        ; Test for minus sign
        MOV     AL,' '                      ; Positive
        JZ      POSITIVE
        MOV     AL,'-'                      ; Mark as negative
POSITIVE:
        STOSB                               ; Put sign in the print string
        RET
PRINT_SIGN      ENDP

;------ This routine prints the two decimal
;------ digits pointed to by [BX]

PRINT_BYTE      PROC    NEAR
        MOV     AL,[BX]                     ; Get BCD byte
        PUSH    CX
        MOV     CL,4
        SHR     AL,CL                       ; Shift high nybble to low portion
        POP     CX
        CALL    PRINT_NYBBLE                ; Print high nybble
        MOV     AL,[BX]                     ; Get original value back
        CALL    PRINT_NYBBLE                ; Print low nybble
        DEC     BX                          ; Move to next byte in string
        RET
PRINT_BYTE      ENDP

;------ Print as decimal the AL value

PRINT_NYBBLE    PROC    NEAR
        AND     AL,0FH                      ; Isolate low nybble
        ADD     AL,'0'                      ; Convert to ASCII value
        STOSB                               ; Store in print string
        RET
PRINT_NYBBLE    ENDP
CODE    ENDS
        END
```

Figure 7.25 *Continued*

number by 10^8. Storing this number as a BCD value gives nine BCD digits. The highest-order digit is the integer portion; the eight low-order digits are the decimal positions.

The first portion of the program determines the correct order of magnitude for the input parameter. We determine the base 10 logarithm of a number with the formula

Log10(X) = Log2(X)/Log2(10)

We round the order of magnitude toward Minus Infinity by once again setting the rounding control. The previous example, which calculates 10^X, gets the correct value to multiply the input value. This reduces the input to the range 1 to 10. We use the constant value TENB (which has the integer 10^8 in it) to get the value into the correct range. Finally, the FBSTP instruction twice converts the numbers into BCD representation. The first time we use it to get the nine digits of the fractional part of the number, the second time to get the three digits of the exponent.

The remaining portion of the subroutine does the character manipulation necessary to convert the BCD representations into character strings. The routine determines and displays the sign of the number and the exponent. It unpacks the BCD bytes and converts them into ASCII characters. The PRINT_BYTE routine does the unpacking, while the PRINT-NYBBLE routine does the conversion to ASCII. Notice that this case does not require the XLAT instruction, since the numbers are in the range 0 through 9. (However, if the input number is one of the undefined numbers, the character string will have some strange characters in it.)

This program correctly prints out any of the numbers in the range of the long reals. Any number which exceeds that representation (for example, 10^{1234}) has its exponent field truncated to only three digits. Of course, you can modify the program to handle four digits in the exponent field if you so desire. There is, however, one number that is handled correctly by the program, but that you may wish to change. If the entry parameter is 0, the result is printed as 0.00000000E-932. This is because of the bias in the exponent field of the 8087. The 8087 represents the number 0 with the smallest possible exponent (-4932) as well as with a mantissa of 0. When this program converts the number to ASCII, it prints the mantissa and exponent correctly (except that it has truncated the exponent to three digits). However, you probably would like to handle the exponent differently. You can change the program by inserting a test for zero (perhaps using the FTST instruction) at the beginning of the program, and treating it as a special case. Once again, it is left as an exercise for the student.

Quadratic Equation

We'll now do two examples that will use the floating-point display routine. The first example is the solution to the quadratic equation. Given the formula

0 = A*X**2 + B*X + C

we will solve for the roots of the equation. We know from high school that the solution is

$$X = (-B + - SQR(B^{**}2 - 4^*A^*C))/2^*A$$

The program to solve this equation is straightforward and shown in Figure 7.26. The program assumes that the three parameters A, B, and C, are stored as integer variables in the program. Of course, if you use this program for more than an example, you need to provide some method of entering the different factors into the program.

This example does not handle complex arithmetic. There is a test for a negative discriminant (B**2−4*A*C). If this value is negative, the program terminates with an error message. There is no reason why you can't include

```
                PAGE    ,132
                TITLE   Figure 7.26 Quadratic Equation roots
        IF1
        INCLUDE 87MAC.LIB
        ENDIF
        STACK   SEGMENT STACK
                DW      64 DUP(?)
        STACK   ENDS

        CODE    SEGMENT PUBLIC
                ASSUME  CS:CODE,DS:CODE,ES:CODE
                EXTRN   FLOAT_ASCII:NEAR
        A       DW      1
        B       DW      -5
        C       DW      6
        STATUS  DW      ?
        FOUR    DW      4
        TWO     DW      2
        ERROR_MSG       DB      'Roots are imaginary',10,13,'$'

        QUADRATIC       PROC    FAR
                PUSH    DS              ; Return address for .EXE
                SUB     AX,AX
                PUSH    AX
                MOV     AX,CS
                MOV     DS,AX
                MOV     ES,AX

                FINIT                   ;------ST0------;-----ST1-------
                FILD    B               ;       B       ;
                FMUL    ST0             ;      B**2     ;
                FILD    A               ;       A       ;      B**2
                FIMUL   FOUR            ;      4*A      ;      B**2
                FIMUL   C               ;     4*A*C     ;      B**2
                FSUBRP  ST1,ST0         ;  D=B**2-4AC   ;       ?
                FTST                    ;
                FSTSW   STATUS
                FWAIT
                MOV     AH,BYTE PTR STATUS+1
                SAHF
                JB      IMAGINARY
                FSQRT                   ; SQR(D)        ;
                FLD     ST0             ; SQR(D)        ;    SQR(D)
                FCHS                    ; -SQR(D)       ;    SQR(D)
                FIADD   B               ; B-SQR(D)      ;    SQR(D)
                FCHS                    ; -B+SQR(D)     ;    SQR(D)
                FXCH    ST1             ;   SQR(D)      ; -B+SQR(D)
                FIADD   B               ; B+SQR(D)      ; -B+SQR(D)
                FCHS                    ;N1= -B-SQR(D)  ;N2= -B+SQR(D)
                FIDIV   A               ;   N1/A        ;      N2
                FIDIV   TWO             ; ROOT1 =N1/2A  ;      N2
                CALL    FLOAT_ASCII     ;      N2       ;
                FIDIV   A               ;     N2/A      ;
                FIDIV   TWO             ; ROOT2 = N2/2A ;
                CALL    FLOAT_ASCII     ;      ?        ;
                RET
        IMAGINARY:
                MOV     DX,OFFSET ERROR_MSG
                MOV     AH,9
                INT     21H             ; Display error message
                RET
        QUADRATIC       ENDP
        CODE    ENDS
                END     QUADRATIC
```

Figure 7.26   Quadratic Equation Roots

complex arithmetic in the program. However, we have chosen not to in this example. You should remember, however, that the 8087 does not automatically handle complex or imaginary arithmetic. You must write the program to manage both the real and imaginary parts of the complex numbers separately.

The FTST instruction tests for a negative discriminant. This instruction is just like a compare, with the source value of zero built in. Notice that the program stores the status word into memory and then loads it into the flag register of the 8088. This allows the quick test (JB for Jump Below) to determine if the discriminant is less than zero. The remainder of the program does the work of calculating the two roots of the equation. The program does take advantage of the fact that the parameters are available in memory. This technique minimizes the amount of 8087 stack required. However, if you modify this program to work as a subroutine for some other program, you probably want to pass the parameters to the program on the 8087 stack. This approach would necessitate a modification in the way the routine handles some values.

SIN of an Angle

The final example we'll do using the 8087 is the SIN of an angle. The 8087 does not have an instruction to do the SIN function. The best the 8087 can offer is FPTAN, the partial tangent instruction. We'll use that instruction, together with the FPREM (partial remainder) instruction, to do the SIN operation.

The program to do SIN is shown in Figure 7.27. This program calculates and prints the SIN of angles from 1/2 through 6 for every half radian. This program produces an output very similar to the BASIC program.

```
10   FOR X = .5 TO 6.0 STEP .5
20   PRINT SIN(X)
30   NEXT X
```

We'll use the floating-point print routine of Figure 7.25 for the output.

```
            PAGE    ,132
            TITLE   Figure 7.27 Sine computation
      IF1
      INCLUDE 87MAC.LIB
      ENDIF
      STACK     SEGMENT STACK
                DW      64 DUP(?)
      STACK     ENDS
      CODE      SEGMENT PUBLIC
                ASSUME  CS:CODE,DS:CODE,ES:CODE
                EXTRN   FLOAT_ASCII:NEAR
      NUM_ANGLE     DW      1
      DEN_ANGLE     DW      2
      STATUS   DW     ?
      FOUR     DW     4
      C3       EQU    40H
      C2       EQU    04H
      C1       EQU    02H
      C0       EQU    01H
      ERROR_MSG     DB      'Angle is too large',10,13,'$'
      SIN      PROC   FAR
      PUSH     DS
      SUB      AX,AX
      PUSH     AX
      MOV      AX,CS
```

Figure 7.27   Sine Computation. (a) SIN routine; (b) Display from SIN routine.

```
            MOV     DS,AX
            MOV     ES,AX
DO_AGAIN:
            FINIT                       ;------STO------;-----ST1-------
            FILD    NUM_ANGLE           ;
            FIDIV   DEN_ANGLE           ;  X= ANGLE     ;
            FLDPI                       ;    PI         ;      X
            FIDIV   FOUR                ;   PI/4        ;      X
            FXCH                        ;    X          ;     PI/4
            FPREM                       ;    R          ;     PI/4
            FSTSW   STATUS
            FWAIT
            MOV     AH,BYTE PTR STATUS+1
            TEST    AH,C2
            JNZ     BIG_ANGLE
            TEST    AH,C1               ; Determine if PI/4 subtract needed
            JZ      DO_R                ; If zero, then no subtract
            FSUBRP  ST1,ST0             ; A=PI/4-R      ;      ?
            JMP     SHORT DO_FPTAN
DO_R:
            FXCH                        ;   PI/4        ;      R
            FCOMP                       ;    R          ;      ?
DO_FPTAN:
            FPTAN                       ;   OPP         ; ADJ where OPP/ADJ=TAN(A)

;------ Determine if sin or cos required

            TEST    AH,C3 OR C1         ; Look at both
            JPE     DO_SINE
            FXCH                        ;   ADJ         ;     OPP
DO_SINE:                                ;    D          ;      N

;------ Calculate N/SQR(N**2 + D**2)

            FMUL    ST0                 ;  D**2         ;      N
            FXCH    ST1                 ;    N          ;    D**2
            FLD     ST0                 ;    N          ;      N         ;      D**2
            FMUL    ST0                 ;  N**2         ;      N         ;      N         ;    D**2
            FADD    ST2                 ; N**2+D**2     ;      N         ;      N         ;    D**2
            FSQRT                       ;SQR(N2+D2)     ;      N         ;      N         ;    D**2
            FDIVRP  ST1                 ;  SIN(X)       ;    D**2        ;
            FXCH    ST1                 ;   D**2        ;    SIN(X)      ;
            FCOMP                       ;  SIN(X)
            TEST    AH,C0
            JZ      SIGN_OK
            FCHS
SIGN_OK:
            CALL    FLOAT_ASCII
            INC     NUM_ANGLE
            CMP     NUM_ANGLE,13
            JA      RETURN_INST
            JMP     DO_AGAIN
RETURN_INST:
            RET
BIG_ANGLE:
            MOV     DX,OFFSET ERROR_MSG
            MOV     AH,9
            INT     21H
            RET
SIN         ENDP
CODE        ENDS
            END     SIN
```

Figure 7.27(a) SIN routine

```
A>SIN
 4.79425539E-001
 8.41470985E-001
 9.97494987E-001
 9.09297427E-001
 5.98472144E-001
 1.41120008E-001
-3.50783228E-001
-7.56802495E-001
-9.77530118E-001
-9.58924275E-001
-7.05540326E-001
-2.79415498E-001
 2.15119988E-001
```

Figure 7.27(b) Display from SIN routine

Figure 7.27 *Continued*

The first portion of the program initializes it for an .EXE file. The 8087 loads the two integer values and divides them to form the angle input for the routine to process. Here is an example of using two integer values to form a floating-point value (in this case, 1/2) that can't be done directly with the assembler.

As you recall from trigonometry, SIN is a repeating function. That is, the function produces the same results for input values that differ by exactly 2*PI. Therefore, the first task of the SIN program is to change the input angle to the corresponding value within the range

$$0 \le X < 2\text{*PI}$$

The FPTAN instruction requires that the angle be in the range

$$0 \le X < \text{PI/4}$$

This means that even though the angle is less than 2*PI, we have to reduce it even further to satisfy the constraints of FPTAN. Fortunately, if the input angle is reduced to a value less than PI/4, we can still determine the correct value for any of the trigonometric functions. To do so, however, we must know where in the range 0 to 2*PI the original angle was.

The FPREM instruction does this for us. Not only does the instruction produce the remainder, but it also gives us the three low bits of the quotient determined during the remaindering process. It stores these bits in the status word. This means that although we have reduced the angle to a value in one-eighth of the original range, we can still determine the octant in which the angle falls. Knowing this, we can apply some trigonometry and determine the appropriate formula for the SIN calculation. The table in Figure 7.28 shows the relationship between the original octant, and the method for calculating the SIN of the angle. The table assumes that the value R is the remainder of the input angle after it is reduced to less than PI/4. The octant values are expressed as the values that appear in C3-C1-C0 following the FPREM instruction.

With this table, we can determine the correct formula to apply at each step within the program. After setting up the radian-angle value, the program loads the constant PI and divides it by 4 to do the FPREM operation. The status value is captured at this point. If the remaindering process doesn't complete in this single step it means that the input angle was greater than 2^{64}. Since this value is so much larger than the appropriate range for trigonometric values, we discard these values

Octant					
C0	C3	C1	Range		SIN(X) =:
0	0	0	0	PI/4	SIN(R)
0	0	1	PI/4	PI/2	COS(PI/4-R)
0	1	0	PI/2	3*PI/4	COS(R)
0	1	1	3*PI/4	PI	SIN(PI/4-R)
1	0	0	PI	5*PI/4	− SIN(R)
1	0	1	5*PI/4	3*PI/2	− COS(PI/4-R)
1	1	0	3*PI/2	7*PI/4	− COS(R)
1	1	1	7*PI/4	2*PI	− SIN(PI/4-R)

(R is the remainder, 0<R<PI/4)

Figure 7.28   SIN(X) in the Eight Octants

as being too large for reasonable processing. This won't happen with the values we have chosen for this example, but we have included it here for illustration.

The routine checks in C1 in the status register to decide if it should use the remainder R, or if it should subtract R from PI/4. Since PI/4 is still in one of the registers, this step is simple. If the subtraction is not required, the FCOMP instruction pops the unneeded value of PI/4 from the stack.

The FPTAN instruction does the partial tangent. The result is indicated as OPP/ADJ (for opposite divided by adjacent), which is equal to the tangent of the angle R or PI/4-R depending on which was selected. With these two values, we can now determine the SIN or COS of the angle. For example, we can calculate the SIN, given OPP/ADJ, with the formula

SIN(X) = OPP/SQR(OPP**2 + ADJ**2), where TAN(X) = OPP/ADJ

To calculate the COS, we change the numerator value to ADJ. We decide whether the SIN or COS is correct by looking at the saved octant designators, and testing the values in C3 and C1. The TEST instruction isolates those values, and the JPE instruction jumps if they are both 0 or they are both 1. In that case, we calculate the SIN. If they are different, we calculate the COS, which is set up by exchanging OPP and ADJ on the register stack.

The next sequence of 8087 instructions calculates the SIN (or COS) value from the partial tangent value. The only step yet to handle is the determination of the final sign of the result. For SIN, the result is negative if it was in the fourth through the seventh octants. Testing C0 determines the correct sign for the result. The FLOAT_ASCII routine of Figure 7.25 displays the value as a floating-point number. The loop control goes back for more if it hasn't gone through all of the octants yet. The latter part of Figure 7.27 shows the output of this program.

DEBUGGING WITH THE 8087

Before we leave the discussion of the 8087, we should talk a little about debugging 8087 programs. The problem that we face with this processor is that the DEBUG utility in DOS does not support the 8087. This means that when DEBUG encounters a breakpoint, the register display does not include the contents of the 8087 registers. This makes it very difficult to follow the execution of a program that is modifying the 8087 registers.

This book offers a method that can be used to debug 8087 programs, using the DOS DEBUG program. This method may not be the best for everyone, but it worked for the example programs in this chapter.

The major obstacle is the inability of the DEBUG program to display the contents of the 8087 register stack. Short of rewriting the DEBUG program, this method gives you the essential information needed to debug an 8087 program. This debug method requires that you write your program as a stand-alone routine, either as an .EXE or a .COM file. Even if you're writing a subroutine, debug it as a main routine first. One of the first instructions in the program is a FINIT instruction, which resets the 8087 to its state at power on. You must do this so that you can rerun the program over and over, always starting from the beginning. The method suggested here for debugging doesn't allow you to stop, examine the 8087 registers, and continue from that point. Instead, this method relies on the ability to start over from the beginning after every breakpoint.

You should also include all of the parameters for the routine as memory locations in the program. The program should load these values into the appropriate registers following the FINIT instruction. You can use this method even when dealing with a program that accepts parameters passed on the register stack. The first debugging of the program proceeds using parameters contained in memory locations. After the arithmetic logic of the program has been debugged, you can modify the program to accept parameters from the register stack.

The goal of these modifications is to allow the program to execute without outside intervention. This means that you can start the program from the first location, and execute it to any instruction. Restarting the program from the first instruction executes the program in exactly the same manner. You need this capability since the proposed register display method destroys the contents of the 8087 stack. Once the stack has been modified, you can't resume the program from where you left off. You must restart from the beginning and stop the program at another location. These suggestions allow you to set up the program to do that. The last two example programs, quadratic equations and sine function, are both set up in this manner. The parameters are in memory locations and they begin with the FINIT instruction.

The next step for successful debugging requires placing a special section of code at a known location in your program. The examples chose 200H, since none of the examples is more than 500 bytes long. This code fragment is only for the purposes of debugging your program, and you'll remove it before delivering the final version. This code fragment is shown in Figure 7.29. As you can see, it is very short, consisting of only three instructions and two data areas. The first data value is a constant, in this example 10^6, or 1,000,000. The choice of the particular value is left to you. If your program will be dealing with numbers much smaller than 10^{-6} or larger than 10^{12}, a different constant value might be appropriate.

The theory of this code fragment is that it will convert the stack top into a number that you can look at. The code multiplies the current stack top by a number with lots of zeros. This has the effect of shifting the decimal point to the right. For this example, if the stack top contains 1/2, the multiplication converts it to 500,000.

Now that the number has been changed into a large integer rather than a fractional value, the FBSTP instruction stores it as packed BCD. The storage area for this value is also in this special code fragment. The INT 3 instruction returns control to the DEBUG routine. You can now use the Display command of DEBUG to look at the 10 bytes of data stored by the FBSTP instruction. Of course, you must read the display value backward, since that's the way the 8087

TEN6	DD	1000000	
	ORG	200H	
BCD_TEMP		DT	?
	ORG	210H	
	FIMUL	TEN6	
	FBSTP	BCD_TEMP	
	INT	3	

Figure 7.29 Debug Routine for NDP

stores BCD numbers. You must take into account the modification of the decimal point that the multiplication did.

The debugging of an 8087 program goes something like this. After you have decided that your program doesn't work correctly, you pick a breakpoint from your program listing. Using the Unassemble command doesn't tell you much, because all of the 8087 instructions are unassembled as ESC instructions. So, using a program listing is essential.

You now execute the program from the beginning to the breakpoint. This is why you designed the program to be rerun from the beginning without any further setup. Each time you set a new breakpoint, you must execute from the beginning of the program.

When routine executes the breakpoint, control returns to DEBUG. You can now execute the special code fragment you've included in the your program. The INT 3 of that special code gives control back to DEBUG, so you can look at the BCD data area and see what value was on the stack top when the original breakpoint was executed. Since you used the FBSTP instruction, it popped the stack top as it stored the value in memory. You can rerun the debug code fragment again, to display the second value on the stack, ST1. You can repeat as many times as you wish. When this method displays a BCD value with 0FFH as both the highest-order and sign byte, you know that you have popped an empty value from the stack. You can now set a new breakpoint in your program, and once again execute the program from the beginning. In this fashion you can step your way through the entire program until you find the problem area. Once you find the problem, you can either modify it in place ("patch" the problem), or exit back to DOS to edit and reassemble the program. When the program finally runs correctly and you don't need to DEBUG any longer, you can remove the debugging code fragment from the program. You may also wish to modify the program at that time to handle parameters as stack registers rather than as storage variables.

CHAPTER

8

The IBM
Personal Computer

This chapter explains the hardware of the IBM Personal Computer. Since this book is devoted to assembly language programming for the IBM Personal Computer, it is appropriate to discuss the underlying hardware. This chapter is not for engineers and technicians. Rather the chapter is primarily for those who write assembly language programs that execute on the IBM Personal Computer.

As we have discussed before, assembly language programming is not always the appropriate programming language. Being able to program directly at the machine level allows the programmer to exercise a great deal of control over the machine. But for a large programming project, the overwhelming detail required in assembly language makes it difficult to retain concentration on the actual goal. So it's best to use assembly language only when it's needed.

One of the reasons that you use assembly language is that you want to take advantage of direct control of the hardware. To do that job correctly, you need to know what the hardware is and what it does. That's the reason for this chapter. The information in this chapter is directed to the programmer and not the engineer. We'll discuss the various pieces of hardware and how you can program them.

The information in this chapter is a supplement to the descriptions in the Personal Computer Technical Reference Manual. You should also refer to the Technical Reference Manual for some specifics of the programming aspects of the hardware. You can also gain some additional information from the specification sheets for the different hardware devices. This chapter does not repeat those data. Where appropriate, the text reproduces some of the hardware data to illustrate a particular programming activity. Of course, we will do examples illustrating the operation of the hardware.

We will defer until the next chapter a discussion of the Basic Input/Output System (BIOS) that is in the read-only memory (ROM) of the computer. The BIOS routines provide the device-level control for the I/O devices of the IBM Personal Computer. This chapter explains what the hardware can do. The next chapter details what is done with the hardware, and the final chapter will help you with some ways to do things with the hardware that weren't done in the ROM BIOS.

SYSTEM HARDWARE

We'll cover the significant portions of the IBM Personal Computer I/O in sections. This section deals with the standard components of the hardware—those available on the main processor board in the system unit. Other sections deal with the individual I/O adapter cards that you may optionally install in the system.

The central processor for the IBM Personal Computer is the Intel 8088. This, of course, is the processor that we discussed at length in the first sections of the book. Hopefully, there is little more that we need to say about the processor. Next to the 8088 on the system board is an empty socket that accepts an Intel 8087 Numeric Data Processor. The NDP was featured in Chapter 7 and should now be familiar to you.

The remainder of the components on the system board provide the function that turns the microprocessor into a computer. The system board contains up to 64K bytes of read/write memory, and 40K bytes of read-only memory (ROM). This ROM contains the Basic interpreter, as well as the ROM BIOS that we'll discuss in the next chapter.

There are lots of components on the system board that are crucial to the operation of the IBM Personal Computer. We'll look at those components that are programmable and useful. On the system board, these components are the 8255 Programmable Peripheral Interface, the 8253 Timer/Counter, the 8259 Interrupt Controller, and the 8237 Direct Memory Access Controller. The rest of the parts have hardware functions that can't be modified by programming. However, we won't study these parts on a component-by-component basis. To do that, you should refer to the Intel Component Data Catalog, or some other reference material. Instead, we'll look at the I/O functions that are implemented on the system board of the IBM Personal Computer. As we control those devices, we'll be using the components mentioned above.

SPEAKER

The IBM Personal Computer has a small speaker in the cabinet. A program can control the tones generated by this speaker. To do this, you must control some of the output bits of the 8255 and the tone generator in the 8253.

Figure 8.1 is a program that controls the speaker using two different methods. The first method, indicated by the label DIRECT on the program listing, directly controls the speaker. Bit 1 of output port 61H is connected directly to the speaker. Each time a program changes the value of this bit, the speaker cone moves, either in or out. By rapidly changing the value of this bit, a program generates a tone. The first part of Figure 8.1 does just this, changing the value of bit 1, and producing a very high pitched tone. The rate at which the program changes bit 1 determines the frequency of the tone.

To assume direct control of the speaker, you must first manipulate the output

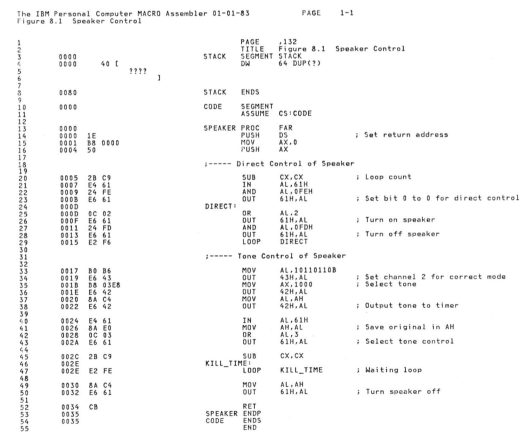

```
The IBM Personal Computer MACRO Assembler 01-01-83        PAGE    1-1
Figure 8.1  Speaker Control

1                                              PAGE    ,132
2                                              TITLE   Figure 8.1  Speaker Control
3          0000                       STACK   SEGMENT STACK
4          0000       40 [                     DW      64 DUP(?)
5                             ????
6                         ]
7
8          0080                       STACK   ENDS
9
10         0000                       CODE    SEGMENT
11                                             ASSUME  CS:CODE
12
13         0000                       SPEAKER PROC    FAR
14         0000    1E                         PUSH    DS              ; Set return address
15         0001    B8 0000                    MOV     AX,0
16         0004    50                         PUSH    AX
17
18                                   ;----- Direct Control of Speaker
19
20         0005    2B C9                      SUB     CX,CX           ; Loop count
21         0007    E4 61                      IN      AL,61H
22         0009    24 FE                      AND     AL,0FEH
23         000B    E6 61                      OUT     61H,AL          ; Set bit 0 to 0 for direct control
24         000D                       DIRECT:
25         000D    0C 02                      OR      AL,2
26         000F    E6 61                      OUT     61H,AL          ; Turn on speaker
27         0011    24 FD                      AND     AL,0FDH
28         0013    E6 61                      OUT     61H,AL          ; Turn off speaker
29         0015    E2 F6                      LOOP    DIRECT
30
31                                   ;----- Tone Control of Speaker
32
33         0017    B0 B6                      MOV     AL,10110110B
34         0019    E6 43                      OUT     43H,AL          ; Set channel 2 for correct mode
35         001B    B8 03E8                    MOV     AX,1000         ; Select tone
36         001E    E6 42                      OUT     42H,AL
37         0020    8A C4                      MOV     AL,AH
38         0022    E6 42                      OUT     42H,AL          ; Output tone to timer
39
40         0024    E4 61                      IN      AL,61H
41         0026    8A E0                      MOV     AH,AL           ; Save original in AH
42         0028    0C 03                      OR      AL,3
43         002A    E6 61                      OUT     61H,AL          ; Select tone control
44
45         002C    2B C9                      SUB     CX,CX
46         002E                       KILL_TIME:
47         002E    E2 FE                      LOOP    KILL_TIME       ; Waiting loop
48
49         0030    8A C4                      MOV     AL,AH
50         0032    E6 61                      OUT     61H,AL          ; Turn speaker off
51
52         0034    CB                         RET
53         0035                       SPEAKER ENDP
54         0035                       CODE    ENDS
55                                             END
```

Figure 8.1   Speaker Control

port of the 8255 on the system board. The 8255 Programmable Peripheral Interface (PPI) contains a total of three input or output ports. The IBM Personal Computer initializes the 8255 to provide two input ports—ports 60H and 62H—and one output port—61H. Port 60H primarily reads keyboard values. You may also use port 60H to read the switch values on the system board. However, the switches are normally read only once, during the power-on initialization of the system. The ROM BIOS stores the results in memory for use thereafter. So, for our purposes, port 60H strictly handles the keyboard input. An input port does an important job. The port serves as a buffer between the processor and the I/O device. The port presents the data to the processor only when the processor requests it—during an IN instruction. At other times, the input port holds the data and doesn't allow them to affect the operation of the processor.

Port 62H, the other input port on the 8255, handles a variety of other inputs. Four of the input bits correspond directly to switch inputs, indicating the amount of memory attached in the system I/O channel. The other 4 input bits have individual meanings. Two indicate system errors of some form. The Non Maskable Interrupt (NMI) routine uses these error bits to determine the cause of a system failure. Bit 5 of port 62H is a feedback mechanism from one of the timer/counter channels. This bit indicates the current output of channel two of the 8253. Bit 4 of port 62H has the current state of the cassette input. The IBM Personal Computer has a cassette connection at the back, next to the keyboard connector. When you read data from the cassette, you use this input bit to determine the current cassette data value.

Port 61H is the output port of the 8255 in the IBM machine. An output port captures (or "latches") the data values output by the program. If the hardware doesn't latch the values, they go away within a microsecond or so. This data latch holds the values until they are once again modified by the program. Thus, when we output a value to change the speaker, that value remains set until it is again modified by the program.

Figure 8.2 shows the bit values for port 61H. These data are from the Technical Reference Manual.

For our discussion of the speaker control, only bits 0 and 1 come into play. Of the others, only bit 3—cassette motor control—and bit 7—keyboard clear— have

Bit	Meaning
0	Timer 2 gate (speaker control)
1	Speaker direct control
2	Multiplex port 62H
3	Cassette motor control
4	Enable parity check on system board memory
5	Enable parity check on I/O channel memory
6	Keyboard clock control
7	Keyboard clear/multiplex port 60H

Figure 8.2 Port 61H Bit Meanings

any meaning for our programs. The remaining bits are intended only for initialization and diagnostic purposes. To understand them fully requires a detailed examination of the system wiring diagrams.

Going back now to the discussion of speaker control, we can see that bits 0 and 1 are used for direct control. As Figure 8.1 shows, setting bit 0 to a "0" initiates the direct control of the speaker. This disables the tone-generating mechanism of the 8253. We'll use that method in the second half of the program.

Notice how the program resets bit 0. The OUT instruction sets all 8 bits of port 61H. There is no mechanism to change only bit 0 and leave all of the others untouched. Since the program wants to modify only bit 0, it must read in the current value of the port. Fortunately, the 8255 allows a program to read the output ports directly. The code sequence

```
IN        AL,61H
AND       AL,0FEH
OUT       61H,AL
```

reads the current value of the output port. The AND instruction turns off the lowest-order bit, and the OUT sends that value as the control byte. If the program had output a value of 0 directly to the port, the speaker would work correctly, but the keyboard wouldn't. In dealing with any bit-significant output port you must ensure that the program doesn't interfere with any of the other bits, unless you intend to modify them.

The remainder of the first program in Figure 8.1 alternates the value of bit 1 of the output port. The original value of port 61H is already in AL, so the program doesn't have to read it during each pass of the loop. It uses the CX register to go through the loop 64K times. When you execute this program, you may have trouble hearing the first tone produced by the program. In that case, try inserting some additional (NOP) instructions in the DIRECT loop. This has the effect of lowering the tone.

The second portion of Figure 8.1 deals with the 8253 Timer/Counter to produce an output tone. Before we go further, we'll discuss the operation of the 8253 to see how it is used in the system. The Intel 8253 provides three 16-bit counters that may be used for timing or counting in the system. A program loads a 16-bit value into one of the counters. The counter is decremented by one for each input from the clock. The clock input to each of the three channels is 1.19 MHz. This means that the counter decrements once very 840 nanoseconds. Each of the three channels has an output. The output control line changes whenever the counter reaches zero. Control instructions to the 8253 determine the method it uses to count.

The outputs of these time/counter channels are connected to different devices on the system board. Channel 0 connects to the 8259 interrupt controller. The system uses it to provide a time-of-day interrupt. Channel 1 is connected the 8237 DMA controller, and you shouldn't use that channel of the 8253. Changing the value in that counter could very likely destroy your program, together with all of the other data in system memory. Channel 2 is connected to the speaker for tone output.

We'll come back to channel 0 of the 8253 later. Channel 2 provides a tone output to the speaker. To set up the timer channel, a program sends the value 0B6H to port 43H, the control port of the 8253. This sets channel 2 of the timer/counter to act as a frequency divider. The timer divides the input frequency—in this case, 1.19 MHz—by whatever 16-bit value the program loads into the channel 2 register. The channel 2 register is located at port address 42H (channel 0 is port 40H and since you should never modify channel 1, we'll leave it to you to determine that port address). The example program loads the value 1000 into the channel register. This means that you will hear an output frequency of 1190 Hz. Actually, you'll hear a fundamental frequency of 1190 Hz, plus overtones caused by the square-wave output of the timer.

Notice that 1000 is a 16-bit number, while port 42H is an 8-bit port. The mode command that we gave to port 43H told the 8253 to expect the 16-bit value as two 8-bit values. The low-order byte goes first, followed by the high-order byte. This two-step process loads the correct value into the channel register.

The program must now set the control port at 61H to allow the tone to pass on to the speaker. The program sets bits 0 and 1 of the control port to 1. Notice that the code saves the original value of the control port, and restores it at the end. This turns the speaker off following the tone. If this method is not sufficient—for example, the program sounds the tone during a time when it isn't sure that the speaker is already off—you may force the speaker off by setting bit 1 of port 61H to 0.

These two methods of controlling the speaker are the most straightforward. However, you can try combinations of these methods if you're looking for interesting effects. After establishing a tone output using the 8253, you can modulate the output using bit 1 or bit 0 or both of port 61H. Also, you can change the channel counter value while the speaker is on. You could modify the program of Figure 8.1 to output the value in the CX register during each loop of the program. This causes the speaker pitch to rise from a very low to a very high pitch. With these three control values to work with, you can create a variety of interesting effects.

KEYBOARD

The next I/O device we'll look at is the keyboard. The keyboard is free standing, connected to the system unit with a four conductor cable. Although there is a microprocessor inside the keyboard unit, there is no convenient way to write programs for it. So we'll leave the programming of the keyboard to the engineers at IBM. However, we can deal with the information that the keyboard sends.

The keyboard circuitry on the system board is connected to the interrupt system. Whenever the circuitry receives a keystroke, it signals an interrupt to the system. This interrupt transfers control to the keyboard interrupt handler. This routine takes the keyboard data and saves them for later use. The keyboard interrupt handler also handles the special cases, such as System Reset (CTL-ALT-DEL) and a program break (CTL-BREAK). However, we won't discuss how this is done until the next chapter, since the ROM BIOS handles this. But we will look at how you can control the hardware for the keyboard.

When the keyboard signals an interrupt the signal goes through the 8259 Interrupt Controller before going on to the 8088 processor. The 8259 handles nearly all facets of the interrupt system for the IBM Personal Computer.

The 8259 can handle up to eight interrupting devices. The IBM Personal Computer connects the system timer, keyboard, asynchronous communications adapter, fixed disk, diskette, and printer to interrupt lines. The remaining interrupt levels are available for use by other I/O devices installed in the system I/O channel. The hardware design assigns each of these interrupting devices to a particular interrupt input on the 8259. The interrupt input that a device connects to is called the interrupt level for that device. As we'll see in a monent, the 8259 prioritizes interrupts according to level. Figure 8.3 shows the interrupt level for each of the IBM devices.

You may enable or disable each of the interrupting devices individually. Just as the 8088 has an interrupt flag that allows or disallows interrupts using the STI and CLI instructions, so does the 8259. Only for the 8259 are there eight interrupt flags, one for each possible interrupting device. The Interrupt Mask Register (IMR) contains these bits and is located at port address 21H. Bit 7 corresponds to interrupt 7, bit 6 to interrupt 6, and so on. When you set the bit to 1, the device can't interrupt. If you clear the bit to 0, the interrupt controller passes the device interrupt on to the 8088. Of course, even if the IMR allows a particular interrupt, the 8088 interrupt flag must also be enabled before an interrupt can occur.

The interrupt controller assigns a priority to each of the interrupting devices, depending on the interrupt level of the device. The hardware connection determines the interrupt level and can't be changed by programming. Interrupt 0 is the highest priority, interrupt 7 is the lowest. If any two devices attempt to interrupt at the same time, the high-priority device gets the interrupt. The lower-priority device is held off until the system has taken care of the higher-priority device. The internal control circuitry of the 8259 handles this prioritization, but your program

Level	Device
0	Timer channel 0
1	Keyboard
2	—
3	Asynchronous communications
4	Alternate asynchronous communications
5	Fixed disk
6	Diskette
7	Printer

Figure 8.3 Interrupt Levels for the 8259

must participate in the interrupt control. The program must tell the 8259 when it has finished with the currently interrupting device. This command, called an End Of Interrupt (EOI) instruction, tells the 8259 that it has finished with the higher-priority device and that a lower-priority device may now interrupt the system.

The 8259 also prevents a lower-priority device from interrupting the processor if the system is currently handling a higher-priority interrupt. The 8259 remembers the currently active interrupt, and assumes that the processor is handling that interrupt until it receives the EOI command. The 8259 manages this by maintaining two registers internally. The first identifies those devices currently requesting interrupts, and is called the Interrupt Request Register (IRR). Another register tracks the currently executing interrupts and is known as the In Service Register (ISR). If you forget to issue that EOI command, only higher-priority devices can interrupt the processor. If you don't issue an EOI command after a timer interrupt, the system comes to a halt. Since the timer has the highest priority, failing to end that interrupt prevents any other interrupts from occurring.

The 8259 also vectors the interrupts. This means that the controller makes the processor go to the correct interrupt handler. When the controller acknowledges an interrupt, it forces the 8088 to begin execution at a location pointed to one of the 256 interrupt vectors in the first 1K bytes of memory. The IBM Personal Computer maps the eight interrupt levels of the 8259 to the interrupt vectors 8 through 0FH. Thus, when the keyboard (interrupt level 1) interrupts, the program begins execution at the CS:IP location identified by the doubleword at interrupt vector 9, or locations 24H through 27H.

Let's see how this all goes together in the IBM Personal Computer. First, the power-on self-test (POST) initializes the 8259 with the appropriate control and vectoring information. During this time, the POST unmasks the timer, keyboard, and diskette interrupts in the 8259 interrupt mask register. At the completion of POST the interrupt system is enabled with an STI instruction. The system is now ready to accept interrupts.

Now you depress a key on the keyboard. The keyboard sends the character to the system board, which stores it in a register and signals interrupt level 1. Now the 8259 takes over. It sets bit 1 of the IRR to indicate a request. If neither bit 0 nor bit 1 of the ISR is set, indicating a higher-priority interrupt in service, the controller activates the interrupt line to the 8088. When the 8088 is ready to accept the interrupt, the processor executes an interrupt acknowledge cycle. The 8088 pushes the current flag register, CS and IP registers onto the stack. The 8259 responds to the cycle with the interrupt number, in this case, interrupt 9. The controller sets bit 1 of the ISR, indicating that interrupt 1 is in service. Meanwhile, the 8088 fetches the CS:IP value from locations 24H and 27H and begins execution at that location.

The processer now executes the keyboard interrupt handler routine. Figure 8.4 shows a skeleton interrupt handler for the keyboard. Notice that the first operation of the interrupt handler is to save the AX register on the stack. The program does this because it modifies the AX register. If the interrupt handler

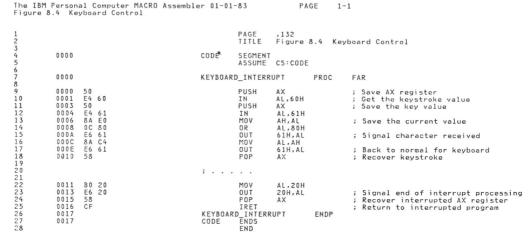

```
The IBM Personal Computer MACRO Assembler 01-01-83          PAGE    1-1
Figure 8.4  Keyboard Control

1                                         PAGE    ,132
2                                         TITLE   Figure 8.4  Keyboard Control
3
4      0000                       CODE    SEGMENT
5                                         ASSUME  CS:CODE
6
7      0000                       KEYBOARD_INTERRUPT       PROC    FAR
8
9      0000   50                          PUSH    AX          ; Save AX register
10     0001   E4 60                       IN      AL,60H      ; Get the keystroke value
11     0003   50                          PUSH    AX          ; Save the key value
12     0004   E4 61                       IN      AL,61H
13     0006   8A E0                       MOV     AH,AL       ; Save the current value
14     0008   0C 80                       OR      AL,80H
15     000A   E6 61                       OUT     61H,AL      ; Signal character received
16     000C   8A C4                       MOV     AL,AH
17     000E   E6 61                       OUT     61H,AL      ; Back to normal for keyboard
18     0010   58                          POP     AX          ; Recover keystroke
19
20                               ; . . . . .
21
22     0011   B0 20                       MOV     AL,20H
23     0013   E6 20                       OUT     20H,AL      ; Signal end of interrupt processing
24     0015   58                          POP     AX          ; Recover interrupted AX register
25     0016   CF                          IRET                ; Return to interrupted program
26     0017                       KEYBOARD_INTERRUPT       ENDP
27     0017                       CODE    ENDS
28                                         END
```

Figure 8.4 Keyboard Control

doesn't restore this register to its original value before it returns to the interrupted program, execution errors will occur. It's tough enough to write correct programs without another program randomly changing the register contents during the execution of a program. If the interrupt handler requires more registers, it must also save and restore them.

The interrupt handler reads the key value, called a scan code, from port 60H. The program must "clear" the interrupt, by telling the I/O device to remove the interrupt request. The program clears the keyboard interrupt by toggling bit 7 of port 61H. This not only removes the interrupt request, but also tells the keyboard that it can send another character to the 8088. The interrupt routine can now process the key stroke.

When the interrupt service is complete, the interrupt handler sends an EOI command to the 8259. This resets bit 1 of the ISR, so that any lower-priority interrupts waiting for service may now interrupt. The EOI command consists of sending the value 20H to port 20H. The interrupt service routine restores the AX register and the IRET instruction restores the IP, CS, and flag registers to their values prior to the interrupt.

This same sequence of events occurs for any interrupt handled by the 8088 that comes through the 8259. The only difference is the particular interrupt that occurs. This changes the bits set in the IRR and ISR, and the interrupt vector number given to the 8088. The interrupt handler routine must still preserve the state of the processor at the time of the interrupt. The program must issue the EOI command following the interrupt service routine, or whenever the interrupt handler has determined that the program can accept a lower-priority interrupt. Also, a note of caution. Your interrupt handler should not issue two EOI commands. If the currently executing interrupt handler had interrupted another lower-priority interrupt handler, the second EOI takes the place of the command from that lower-priority routine. This might lead to unacceptable actions, so you should avoid this.

Now that we've handled the keyboard interrupt and set all the bits and commands correctly, what have we got? The keyboard sends "scan codes" to the 8088. These values represent the key locations on the keyboard and have nothing to do with the value printed on the key top. For example, the ESC key returns scan code 1, the "1" key returns scan code 2, and so on. The DEL key returns scan code 83. Each key has its own unique scan code. The data in port 60H can't be interpreted as an ASCII character. You must translate the scan code value into the correct character value.

The keyboard sends more than just these 83 scan codes. The first 83 scan codes, from 1 to 83, are known as the "make" codes. The keyboard sends the make scan code when the key is depressed. When the key is released, the keyboard sends a second scan code, the "break" code. The keyboard forms the break code by adding 128 to the "make" scan code. Thus, the break codes are in the range 129 through 211. Break codes are easily indentified since bit 7 is on.

Since the keyboard sends a different code for each key depression and release, a program can track every key on the keyboard. You know when the key is depressed since the keyboard sends a make code. The key remains down until you receive the break code, indicating that the key was released. For most keys this isn't important information. However, for the shift keys this is vital information. For example, you form capital letters only when the shift key is held down. Since this information is available for every key on the IBM keyboard, it's no problem to deal with the shift keys. If you wish to modify the keyboard encoding to make your own keyboard layout, any key can be treated as a shift key.

Finally, every key on the IBM keyboard is typamatic. If you hold down a key for more than 1/2 second, the keyboard starts sending make scan codes at the rate of 10 a second. For normal keys this is great, especially the cursor control keys. You just hold them down and the cursor moves to the desired location. However, if you have a key that produces some action only when it is first depressed (and absolutely cannot be a typamatic or "machine-gun" key), you must once again track the ups and downs of the key. Only the first make code following the key depression produces the action. You must ignore the other make codes.

TIME OF DAY

Timer channel 0 of the 8253 has a special purpose on the IBM Personal Computer. The output of this timer channel is connected to interrupt level 0 of the 8259. This means that whenever the output of channel 0 goes to the active level, an interrupt occurs (assuming that everything else is set correctly). The power-on self-test initializes channel 0 of the timer by loading it with the value 0. This gives the largest (not the smallest) count that a program can store in the counter. With the input frequency of 1.19 MHz, the counter counts back to 0 in slightly under 55 milliseconds. The initialization routine sets the timer so that it runs continuously. This means that interrupt 0 occurs 18.2 times a second.

As we'll see in the next chapter, ROM BIOS uses this constant timer interrupt to keep track of the current time. Every time an interrupt occurs, BIOS advances the time of day clock by one tick. With the appropriate calculations, you can convert the number of timer ticks into hours, minutes, and seconds.

Why was the value 18.2 chosen? Why wasn't the counter set to provide an interrupt 20 times a second, or some other "nice" number? The next example should show you why.

The system timer can provide a timing function other than time of day. Time of day is great for determining time intervals measured in seconds or minutes. But in some I/O control situations, you need to measure time intervals of 1 or 2 milliseconds. Normally, programs do these timing intervals with a timing loop. For a timing loop, the program looks something like this:

```
        MOV     CX,LOOP_VALUE
HERE:LOOP       HERE
```

You select the constant LOOP_VALUE so that the loop executes just the right number of times. If you need to delay for a certain amount of time, this method is very good. For the example above, an initial LOOP_VALUE of OFFFFH will take about 250 milliseconds to execute.

However, suppose that you wish to monitor an external event and determine how long it took for that event to occur. You can use a variation of the timing loop, something like this:

```
        MOV         CX,0
HERE:
; --- Test for event occurring
        IN          AL,DX
        TEST        AL,MASK_BIT
        LOOPNE      HERE
DONE:
; -- CX has the number of loop iterations
```

In this method you count the number of times through the loop to figure out how long it took. This method assumes that the event occurs before CX reaches 0 for the second time. However, if the resolution you need is measured in microseconds, this method may not work well. The loop may require 10 to 20 microseconds for each iteration. The system timer provides a better solution. Since the timer changes value every 840 nanoseconds, you can determine the length of an event to within a microsecond.

Figure 8.5 has an example program that calculates the time of an event using the system timer. This example uses the timer channel 2 output as the event to

```
 1                                          PAGE    ,132
 2                                          TITLE   Figure 8.5  System Timer
 3     0000                         STACK   SEGMENT STACK
 4     0000   40 [                          DW      64 DUP(?)
 5              ????
 6                   ]
 7
 8     0080                         STACK   ENDS
 9     0000                         CODE    SEGMENT
10                                          ASSUME  CS:CODE
11     0000                         TIMER   PROC    FAR
12     0000   1E                            PUSH    DS              ; Set return address
13     0001   B8 0000                       MOV     AX,0
14     0004   50                            PUSH    AX
15
16     0005   B0 B6                         MOV     AL,10110110B    ; Set timer 2
17     0007   E6 43                         OUT     43H,AL
18     0009   B8 0500                       MOV     AX,500H
19     000C   E6 42                         OUT     42H,AL          ; Timer 2 divisor will be 500H
20     000E   8A C4                         MOV     AL,AH
21     0010   E6 42                         OUT     42H,AL
22
23     0012   E8 001D R                     CALL    LOW_TO_HIGH     ; Get time of first low to high
24     0015   8B D8                         MOV     BX,AX           ; Save that value in BX
25     0017   E8 001D R                     CALL    LOW_TO_HIGH     ; Get time of second low to high
26     001A   2B D8                         SUB     BX,AX           ; Subtract to get cycle time
27     001C   CB                            RET
28     001D                         TIMER   ENDP
29                                  ;------------------------------------
30                                  ; This subroutine waits for the
31                                  ;   first low-to-high transition
32                                  ;   of the timer channel 2 output.
33                                  ;   The timer 0 count at that time
34                                  ;   is returned in AX.
35                                  ;------------------------------------
36     001D                         LOW_TO_HIGH  PROC   NEAR
37     001D   E4 62                          IN      AL,62H          ; Test the timer channel 2 bit
38     001F   A8 20                          TEST    AL,20H
39     0021   75 FA                          JNZ     LOW_TO_HIGH     ; Loop until it is low
40     0023                         WAIT_HIGH:
41     0023   E4 62                          IN      AL,62H          ; Test the bit again
42     0025   A8 20                          TEST    AL,20H
43     0027   74 FA                          JZ      WAIT_HIGH       ; Loop until it goes high
44
45     0029   B0 00                          MOV     AL,0            ; Send command to timer control register
46     002B   E6 43                          OUT     43H,AL          ;  that "freezes" the count in timer 0
47     002D   90                             NOP
48     002E   90                             NOP                     ; Delay necessary for 8253
49     002F   E4 40                          IN      AL,40H
50     0031   8A E0                          MOV     AH,AL           ; Read the low byte of the count
51     0033   90                             NOP
52     0034   E4 40                          IN      AL,40H          ; Read the high byte of the count
53     0036   86 E0                          XCHG    AH,AL           ; Move into correct positions
54     0038   C3                             RET                     ; Return current count in AX
55     0039                         LOW_TO_HIGH  ENDP
56     0039                         CODE    ENDS
57                                          END
```

Figure 8.5   System Timer

measure. The first part of the program initializes timer channel 2 to a known value. We chose the value 500H arbitrarily. Notice that this section of the code is identical to the way of generating tones using timer channel 2.

The program calls a subroutine, LOW_TO_HIGH, which returns the current timer value when a transition from a low value to a high value is seen on the output of timer channel 2. The program looks for the transition. If it looked for a high value only, it wouldn't know whether the signal had just gone high or whether the signal was just about ready to go low. The subroutine sends a zero value to the timer control register (port 43H) to "freeze" the current value of timer 0. This allows it to read the current value while the timer keeps on counting. If a program couldn't stop the timer temporarily, it couldn't read the 16-bit timer value without error.

Notice that the subroutine of Figure 8.5 includes some NOP instructions. The program has these instructions strictly for timing purposes. If we read the specifications for the 8253 very carefully, we'll notice that there is a minimum time of 1 microsecond between INs and OUTs to the chip. The NOP instructions take up just enough time to ensure that we don't violate the timing requirements for the chip.

After the return from the subroutine, the program saves in the BX register the value of the timer at the first low-to-high transition. The program once again calls the subroutine, to detect the next low-to-high transition of timer channel 2. It subtracts the two values to determine the cycle time of channel 2.

Earlier we mentioned that setting the timer 0 register with the count value of 0 was really a good idea. This program shows it, since the program subtracts the two timer values without regard to which is larger or smaller. Since timer 0 is running asynchronously to the execution of this program, there is no guarantee that the first number read is larger than the second number read. For example, suppose that the first low-to-high transition occurs when timer 0 has a value of 100H. After 500H counts, the value in timer 0 is 0FC00H. The timer 0 counter automatically "rolls over" from 0 to 0FFFFH. So the second value read is larger numerically than the first value read. But since the timer register, after counting down to 0, begins again at 0FFFFH, we can always subtract the two numbers. Sometimes there is a carry, other times there is no carry. But the difference between the two numbers is always equal to the number of counts that have occurred.

To convince you that this is true, consider the case where the counter was initialized to 8000H. If the first transition occurs at a count of 6000H, the second would be at 5B00H, and the difference would be 500H. However, if the first transition occurs at a count of 100H, the second would occur at a count of 7C00H. The difference here would be 8500H. To handle this situation successfully, the program would have to test for a timer rollover during the timing period.

If you run this program, you'll find out that the value in the BX register is about 0A00H. This isn't the 500H you would expect to find. This is because the timer is operating in a mode where it decrements the count by two for every clock input. To understand the operation of the 8253, we need to consult the programming guide for it.

Figure 8.6 summarizes the control word for the 8253. You output this control value to port 43H to set up one of the channels for a particular operation. We have already seen several values output to port 43H. We sent a zero to the port to freeze the counter, and a 0B6H to set up the tone generation. Let's see where those values come from.

The 2 highest-order bits of the control word select the timer channel. The next 2 bits select the operation to perform. When we output the 0, it selected timer 0 and latched the data in the counter. The next 3 bits select the mode of operation for the selected timer. These bits aren't needed when the counter is latched, but are required when the timer is initialized. The final bit determines whether the counter runs as a 16-bit binary counter or as a four-digit BCD counter.

Control Word Format

D_7	D_6	D_5	D_4	D_3	D_2	D_1	D_0
SC1	SC0	RL1	RL0	M2	M1	M0	BCD

Definition of Control

SC — Select Counter:

SC1	SC0	
0	0	Select Counter 0
0	1	Select Counter 1
1	0	Select Counter 2
1	1	Illegal

RL — Read/Load:

RL1	RL0	
0	0	Counter Latching operation (see READ/WRITE Procedure Section)
1	0	Read/Load most significant byte only.
0	1	Read/Load least significant byte only.
1	1	Read/Load least significant byte first, then most significant byte.

M — MODE:

M2	M1	M0	
0	0	0	Mode 0
0	0	1	Mode 1
X	1	0	Mode 2
X	1	1	Mode 3
1	0	0	Mode 4
1	0	1	Mode 5

BCD:

0	Binary Counter 16-bits
1	Binary Coded Decimal (BCD) Counter (4 Decades)

Figure 8.6 Timer/Counter Programming (Courtesy of Intel; Copyright Intel 1981)

The control value of 0B6H we used for tone generation can be determined this way:

0B6H = 10110110B = 10 11 011 0

This control word selects timer 2. The timer counter handles a 16-bit value, with the low byte of the value loaded into the counter first. The final bit indicates that binary counting will be done. Also, we can see that mode 3 was selected.

The 8253 can operate in six different modes. For our uses, only two of the modes are convenient in the IBM system configuration. Mode 3 is the default method of running all three channels of the timer. This mode is the square-wave generator. The output from the timer is at a low level half of the time, and at a high level half of the time. The counter handles this by counting by two rather than one as it counts down from the selected value. During the first count down, the output is low. Then, during the second count, the output is high. Since the timer is counting by twos, the output is high exactly half of the time, and low half of the time. Since timer 0 normally runs in mode 3, the example in Figure 8.5 ended up with a count value of 0A00H, rather than the 500H expected. Each timer count decrements the counter by two.

Because the counter counts by twos, the counter rolls over every 27 microseconds. If you want to time an event longer than 27 microseconds, you'll need to use a different timing mode.

The other timer mode that has application for the IBM Personal Computer is Mode 0. This mode is known as Interrupt on Terminal Count. In this mode, the timer does not run constantly. After you select the mode, the timer doesn't begin to count (by ones) until the full value has been loaded into the timer register. The counter then counts down at the clock rate until the count reaches 0. At that time, the timer output goes high. Since the timer 0 output is connected to interrupt 0 of the 8259, a system interrupt occurs.

The interrupt on terminal count mode is useful if you want to signal a program with an interrupt at some time in the future. Because the counter is limited to 16 bits, the maximum time interval is 55 milliseconds. If this time period is too short, you'll need a different method.

If you want to measure a time period in seconds, you should leave the timer in its normal mode of operation. The ROM BIOS provides a method of gaining control every 55 milliseconds. At each of those timer ticks you can decide if the desired amount of time has expired.

If the time period you want to delay for is somewhere between 55 milliseconds and 5 seconds, you might want to use a different method than the ROM BIOS. Say you wanted to delay for 150 milliseconds. Using the interrupt on terminal count mode, you set the timer to interrupt after 50 milliseconds (this requires a count value of about 59500). You program the interrupt handler to reset the timer for another 50 milliseconds the first two times that it gains control. On the third timer interrupt, the 150 milliseconds have elapsed, and you can take the desired control action.

Whenever you are dealing with the timer, you must take some care. As we mentioned above, timer 1 provides an important hardware function. If you modify the value in timer 1, your program will probably die right on the spot. Using timer 2 is reasonably safe. Timer 2 is connected only to the speaker and the cassette output. Of course, this means that you shouldn't use timer 2 for timing values at the same time you try to play music on the speaker. Finally, the ROM BIOS uses the services of timer 0 for several system functions. As we will see in the discussion of ROM BIOS, the time-of-day interrupt controls not only the current time, but also handles the diskette motor timing. Before you reuse timer 0 for any new functions, you must understand the functions that you might be changing.

SYSTEM FEATURES

This section of the chapter describes the programming aspects of some of the system features. Not all systems have all of the features that we'll describe. We'll discuss the features that you can find on many systems. The discussion includes the two display adapters, the diskette adapter, the printer adapter, the asynchronous communications adapter, and the game control adapter.

DISPLAY ADAPTERS

You can purchase the IBM Personal Computer with either of two different display adapters. One adapter is the Monochrome Display and Printer Adapter (we'll call it the monochrome adapter or sometimes the black-and-white card). This display adapter is best suited for business applications. The black-and-white card drives the IBM Monochrome Display. The monochrome adapter operates in only one mode, and can display only monochrome text on the screen. This adapter also contains the hardware circuitry necessary to drive the printer. This combination card makes it particularly attractive for business applications.

The other display adapter is the Color/Graphics Monitor Adapter (we'll call it the color card). The color card is used with displays that operate at normal TV frequencies. The adapter also produces color displays, rather than the single color of the monochrome adapter. There are several modes of operation, including modes in which you can individually control the dots on the screen.

Monochrome Display and Printer Adapter

We'll talk about the monochrome display first. It's the simplest of the two adapters. We'll postpone a discussion of the printer adapter portion of the card until we talk about the printer adapter. The circuitry for the printer adapter on the monochrome card is identical to the stand-alone printer adapter, so the programming aspects are also identical.

The black-and-white card operates in a single mode. The display adapter produces 25 rows of characters with 80 characters per row, known as an 80 × 25 display. You place characters on the screen by storing the ASCII value of the character into the display buffer. The display buffer is a special section of memory, located at 0B0000H in the address space. This memory is part of the adapter card, and is not part of the system memory. Once you store the ASCII code for the character in the display buffer, the character appears on the screen in the corresponding location. The conversion of the character from its ASCII representation to the dots on the screen is all handled by the hardware.

Each character on the display also has an attribute. Character attributes determine the way that the adapter displays the character on the screen. Figure 8.7 shows the character attributes and the values for them. You need to know this value, because you must store that value into the display buffer also. Every character position in the display buffer occupies two bytes. The even-numbered byte of the pair contains the character-code value. The odd byte contains the attribute value. By referring to Figure 8.7, you can determine the attribute value to store for a character. Normally, you want to display a white (actually green) character on a black background. The attribute value for this is 07H. To create reverse video, you change the attribute value to 70H. The attribute value 00H makes a character invisible. Even though you store an ASCII code value in the character byte, the attribute value keeps the character from displaying.

The display buffer for the black-and-white card contains 4K bytes. This is sufficient to provide a character and attribute byte for each of the 2000 character positions on the screen. The first character in the display buffer appears at the upper left corner of the screen. The next two bytes display as the next character to the right, and so on. The first character in the second row is at bytes 160 and 161. You can determine the address of any character position on the screen. First, we define the character position at the upper left corner of the screen to be row 0 and column 0. The bottom right corner is row 24 and column 79. The formula for an arbitrary row and column is then

address = 2 × (row × 80 + column) + 0B0000H

The multiplication by two adjusts for two bytes per character position. The addition of 0B0000H reflects the starting address of the display buffer. Normally, your program sets the DS or ES register to 0B000H, and the remainder of the program deals with offsets into the display buffer.

As an example program for the monochrome display, Figure 8.8 contains a program that moves the contents of the screen one character position to the right. It discards the rightmost column while placing a blank column along the left. If you want to try this program but only have a color card in your system, the program works if you change the DISPLAY segment to 0B800H. The two display

Value	Attribute
00H	Nothing is displayed
01H	Underlined character
07H	White character, black background
0FH	Intense white character, black background
70H	Black character, white background
80H	When added to any of the above, the character will blink

Figure 8.7 Character Attributes for Monochrome Adapter

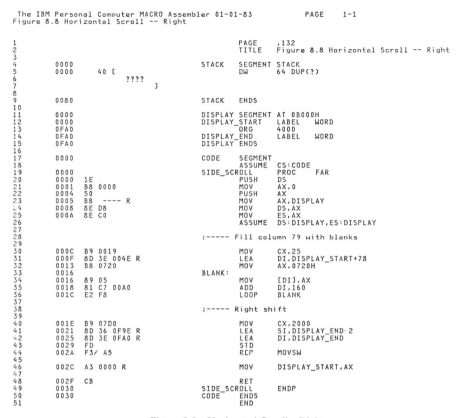

The IBM Personal Computer MACRO Assembler 01-01-83   PAGE   1-1
Figure 8.8 Horizontal Scroll -- Right

Figure 8.8   Horizontal Scroll—Right

adapters are very similar in text operation, and differ only in memory and I/O addresses.

The program of Figure 8.8 does the horizontal scroll using a very simple method. The right-hand column is turned into blanks by writing 25 blanks into memory every 160 bytes. Then the program shifts the entire display buffer one byte higher in memory. Since the display buffer continues directly from one row to the next, the character that was at column 79 of row 0 becomes column 0 of row 1 after the move. Finally, the program replaces the first character in the buffer with a blank.

The monochrome adapter also has some I/O ports that you can use in programming the display. However, we'll pass over the use of these ports very quickly. The construction of the monochrome adapter uses these I/O ports primarily as a convenience for the hardware design. Also, the I/O programming appearance of the black-and-white card is very similar to the color card. Since the color card has a lot more opportunity to use the I/O ports, we'll talk more about them in that section.

The monochrome adapter generates the horizontal and vertical timing signals necessary for a display with the Motorola 6845 CRT (Cathode Ray Tube) Controller. This device has two I/O addresses, at I/O ports 3B4H and 3B5H. The adapter also has a control port at 3B8H and a status port at 3BAH. Once the adapter has been initialized, there is little reason to modify the values in these ports. There may be other modes of operation possible with the monochrome card, but we'll concentrate our efforts on the color card. Complete details of the monochrome adapter I/O ports can be found in the Technical Reference Manual.

Color/Graphics Monitor Adapter

The Color/Graphics Monitor Adapter is the other display adapter available for the IBM Personal Computer. IBM designed the color card to attach to TV-like devices. Where the black-and-white adapter works only with the IBM Monochrome display, you can attach the color card to any color or black-and-white monitor that uses standard TV frequency signals. Or you may separately purchase an RF modulator that allows you to connect the color card output to your home TV. The color card can be connected to a variety of monitors since it operates at TV frequencies.

The color card has many different modes of operation. IBM programming supports some of these modes. Other modes are left for you to handle. The color card has a great deal more flexibility than the monochrome adapter.

There are two text modes available on the color/graphics adapter. One text mode creates a screen that has 25 rows of 80 characters, identical to the monochrome adapter. A second text mode reduces the number of characters per line to 40. This lower resolution mode is necessary if you want to use the color card with a low-resolution monitor or with your home TV. You may find an 80-character display unreadable on some displays. To use the full capabilities of the color card, you must use a high-quality monitor. A high-resolution monitor allows you to display the full 80-character lines without distortion.

The color card also has two graphics modes. In these modes, you can control each individual dot on the screen. In the text modes, each character position is independent. In graphics modes, each dot is independent. The medium-resolution graphics mode provides 200 rows with 320 dots per row. Each of these dots can have one of four possible colors. This means that you control each dot with 2 bits for the four colors. The high-resolution graphics mode has 200 lines with 640 dots per line. In this mode, only two colors are allowed, black and white.

Text Mode

The two text modes of the color/graphics adapter provide a simple method of displaying characters on the screen. In the text modes, the color card is similar to the monochrome adapter. The color card lets you specify the colors for each character. Just like the monochrome card, each character position for the color

Bit number   7 6 5 4 3 2 1 0

| B | BACK | I | FORE |

Figure 8.9 Attribute Byte for
Color/Graphics

card has an attribute byte. This attribute byte determines the foreground and background colors for each character position.

Figure 8.9 shows the layout for the color text attribute byte. The three bytes labeled BACK determine the background color, one of eight colors. The 3 bits labeled FORE specify the foreground color. The I bit also affects the foreground color. Setting the bit intensifies the foreground color. This lets you select one of 16 colors for the foreground. The attribute byte controls a single character, so you may pick any combination of foreground and background colors for each character position. The highest-order bit, labeled B, usually causes the foreground character to blink. Setting the blink bit to "1" alternates the character between the foreground and background color, at a rate of about four times a second. Since a character displayed in the background color becomes invisible, the effect is character blinking. You can change the blink bit to become the fourth background color bit, allowing 16 foreground and 16 background colors. There's a bit in the color select register that does this. Another thing to notice is that setting the foreground and background colors to an identical value means that you can't see the character. The character is there, but it's just like trying to see a polar bear in a snowstorm—everything's the same color. Figure 8.10 shows the 16 colors possible in the text mode.

If you compare the color/graphics attribute byte to the monochrome attribute in Figure 8.7, you'll see that they are similar. Of course, you can't specify colors with the monochrome adapter, but everything else matches up. Since the underline attribute isn't supported by the color card, you set the monochrome

I	R	G	B	Color
0	0	0	0	Black
0	0	0	1	Blue
0	0	1	0	Green
0	0	1	1	Cyan
0	1	0	0	Red
0	1	0	1	Magenta
0	1	1	0	Brown
0	1	1	1	Light gray
1	0	0	0	Dark gray
1	0	0	1	Light blue
1	0	1	0	Light green
1	0	1	1	Light cyan
1	1	0	0	Light red
1	1	0	1	Light magenta
1	1	1	0	Yellow
1	1	1	1	White

Figure 8.10 Colors (Courtesy of IBM, Copyright IBM 1981)

attribute to blue foreground on black background to underline the monochrome character.

This alignment of the attribute bytes is an attempt to make the two display adapters as identical as possible. Each character is at the even value in the display buffer, the attribute byte at the odd location. The memory for the color display is on the display adapter, but at a different memory address. The monochrome display is at memory address 0B0000H, while the color display buffer is at 0B8000H. To see just how similar the displays are, if you modify the monochrome display program in Figure 8.8 by changing the AT value of the segment to 0B800H, the program runs correctly on the color card. Thus, with minimum modifications, the same program executes using either display adapter.

The color/graphics card also uses the 6845 CRT Controller to control the adapter. The two I/O ports of the controller are at I/O addresses 3D4H and 3D5H. The 6845 controller really has 18 internal registers. The two I/O ports access all of the registers with an indirect addressing scheme. To address a 6845 register, you first load the register index into port 03D4H. You then read or write port 3D5H to access the register.

Let's do an example to see just how this works. Figure 8.11 lists the 18 registers of the 6845. For this example, we'll use registers R10 and R11. These registers determine the starting and ending scan line for the cursor. On the color card, each character is made up of eight scan lines, numbered 0 to 7. You can place the cursor anywhere in these eight scan lines. Register R10 tells the 6845 which scan line starts the cursor, while register R11 specifies the last scan line for the cursor. The ROM BIOS initializes the cursor on lines 6 and 7. This is done by setting R10 to 6 and R11 to 7.

The program in Figure 8.12(a) modifies the cursor on the color/graphics card. It moves the cursor so that it appears as the top five scan lines rather than the bottom two. First it sets the CRT index register (3D4H) to 10, and then writes the data register (3D4H) with the start line, 0. Setting the index register to 11, it writes the ending scan line, 4. The cursor now appears as a blinking block in the top part of a character position, rather than as a blinking underline. Cursor modification techniques similar to this are used by several editing programs on the Personal Computer, including the BASIC interpreter. When you enter insert mode during editing, the cursor becomes fatter. The BASIC interpreter does that by changing the 6845 parameters.

Referring back to Figure 8.11, you can see that there are many other registers in the 6845. Most of them control the horizontal and vertical timing signals required for the TV raster signal. You can modify these values to do things to the display. In fact, the DOS MODE command, which can shift the display on the screen, modifies R2, the horizontal sync position.

If you try experimenting with these registers, you should write short programs to do the changes. If you try to change the registers using DEBUG, it probably won't work. Registers R14 and R15 control the cursor position. If

Register #	Register File	Program Unit	Read	Write
R0	Horizontal Total	Char.	No	Yes
R1	Horizontal Displayed	Char.	No	Yes
R2	H. Sync Position	Char.	No	Yes
R3	H. Sync Width	Char.	No	Yes
R4	Vertical Total	Char. Row	No	Yes
R5	V. Total Adjust	Scan Line	No	Yes
R6	Vertical Displayed	Char. Row	No	Yes
R7	V. Sync Position	Char. Row	No	Yes
R8	Interlace Mode	–	No	Yes
R9	Max Scan Line Address	Scan Line	No	Yes
R10	Cursor Start	Scan Line	No	Yes
R11	Cursor End	Scan Line	No	Yes
R12	Start Address (H)	–	No	Yes
R13	Start Address (L)	–	No	Yes
R14	Cursor (H)	–	Yes	Yes
R15	Cursor (L)	–	Yes	Yes
R16	Light Pen (H)	–	Yes	No
R17	Light Pen (L)	–	Yes	No

Figure 8.11 6845 Registers (Courtesy of Motorola, Inc.)

DEBUG moves the cursor between your output to the index register and your output to the data register, the change won't occur. That's because DEBUG has changed the index register of the 6845, so it's no longer pointing at the internal register you want to modify.

Another interesting 6845 register pair is the Start Address pair, R12 and R13. The color/graphics display adapter has 16K bytes of memory, compared to the 4K bytes on the monochrome card. The color card uses the extra storage for the graphics modes. But it's there for your use in the text modes. The 80 × 25 text mode requires 4K bytes, so there's room for four different pages of text in the buffer. You can scroll the data on the screen by moving the data from one location to another, as we did in Figure 8.8. But for vertical scrolling, you can just change the start address of the 6845. Normally, the start address is 0. If you change it to 80 (the number of characters on a line), the display begins with the characters of the second line. This has the immediate effect of scrolling all of the data on the screen up one line.

In actuality, you haven't scrolled the data. Rather you have moved the viewport into the display memory. You can think of the 80 × 25 display as being a window with which you can look into the 8192 character display buffer.

The problem with using the start address to scroll data occurs when you run into the 16K-byte boundary. The display will "wraparound" at this point. The top lines of the display come from the end of the buffer, while the bottom lines are taken from the beginning of the display buffer. You can certainly handle this problem, but it takes some thought and experimentation.

The IBM Personal Computer MACRO Assembler 01-01-83   PAGE   1-1
Figure 8.12 Color/Graphics Control Programs

```
1                                                PAGE    ,132
2                                                TITLE   Figure 8.12 Color/Graphics Control Programs
3
4       0000                                     STACK   SEGMENT STACK
5       0000        40 [                                 DW      64 DUP(?)
6                          ????
7                                ]
8
9       0080                                     STACK   ENDS
10
11      0000                                     DISPLAY_BUFFER   SEGMENT AT 0B800H
12      0000                                     DISPLAY_START    LABEL   WORD
13      0000                                     DISPLAY_BUFFER   ENDS
14
15      = 03D4                                    CRT_INDEX        EQU     03D4H
16      = 03D5                                    CRT_DATA         EQU     03D5H
17      = 03DA                                    CRT_STATUS       EQU     03DAH
18      = 000A                                    CURSOR_START     EQU     10           ; Cursor registers
19      = 000B                                    CURSOR_END       EQU     11           ;   within the 6845
20
21      0000                                     CODE    SEGMENT
22                                                       ASSUME  CS:CODE
23      0000                                     COLOR_GRAPHICS  PROC    FAR
24      0000   1E                                        PUSH    DS                    ; Set return address
25      0001   2B C0                                     SUB     AX,AX
26      0003   50                                        PUSH    AX
27
28                                               ;----- Figure 8.12(a) Modify cursor value
29
30      0004   BA 03D4                                   MOV     DX,CRT_INDEX
31      0007   B0 0A                                     MOV     AL,CURSOR_START       ; Point 6845 index register
32      0009   EE                                        OUT     DX,AL                 ;   at the cursor start register
33      000A   42                                        INC     DX
34      000B   B0 00                                     MOV     AL,0
35      000D   EE                                        OUT     DX,AL                 ; Set cursor start scan line
36
37      000E   4A                                        DEC     DX
38      000F   B0 0B                                     MOV     AL,CURSOR_END
39      0011   EE                                        OUT     DX,AL                 ; Point at cursor end register
40      0012   42                                        INC     DX
41      0013   B0 04                                     MOV     AL,4
42      0015   EE                                        OUT     DX,AL                 ; Set cursor end scan line
43
44                                               ;----- Figure 8.12(b) Use of status register
45
46      0016   B8 J002                                   MOV     AX,2
47      0019   CD 10                                     INT     10H                   ; Select 80x25 text mode
48      001B   B8  ---- R                                MOV     AX,DISPLAY_BUFFER
49      001E   8E C0                                     MOV     ES,AX                 ; Address video buffer
50      0020   B8 0720                                   MOV     AX,0720H              ; Start with " " character
51      0023                                    NEXT_CHAR:
52      0023   BF 0000                                   MOV     DI,0
53      0026   B9 0050                                   MOV     CX,80
54      0029   F3/ AB                                    REP     STOSW                 ; Write a line of 80 characters
55      002B   FE C0                                     INC     AL                    ; Next character
56      002D   75 F4                                     JNZ     NEXT_CHAR
57
58      002F   BB 0720                                   MOV     BX,0720H
59      0032                                    NEXT_CHAR_1:
60      0032   B9 0050                                   MOV     CX,80
61      0035   BF 0000                                   MOV     DI,0
62      0038   BA 03DA                                   MOV     DX,CRT_STATUS         ; Status port for color card
63      003B                                    WAIT_NO_RETRACE:
64      003B   EC                                        IN      AL,DX
65      003C   A8 01                                     TEST    AL,1
66      003E   75 FB                                     JNZ     WAIT_NO_RETRACE       ; Test retrace bit
67      0040   FA                                        CLI                           ; Wait until it is displaying
68      0041                                    WAIT_RETRACE:                          ; Can't allow interrupts
69      0041   EC                                        IN      AL,DX
70      0042   A8 01                                     TEST    AL,1
71      0044   74 FB                                     JZ      WAIT_RETRACE          ; Wait for non-display
72      0046   8B C3                                     MOV     AX,BX                 ; Get character
73      0048   AB                                        STOSW                         ; Store in buffer
74      0049   FB                                        STI                           ; Interrupts back on
75      004A   E2 EF                                     LOOP    WAIT_NO_RETRACE
76      004C   FE C3                                     INC     BL
77      004E   75 E2                                     JNZ     NEXT_CHAR_1
78
79                                               ;----- Figure 8.12(c) Draw a diagonal line in APA mode
80
81      0050   B8 0004                                   MOV     AX,4
82      0053   CD 10                                     INT     10H                   ; Select 320x200 APA mode
83
84      0055   06                                        PUSH    ES
85      0056   1F                                        POP     DS
```

Figure 8.12   Color/Graphics Control Programs

```
86    0057  B3 32                      MOV       BL,50              ; Number of row groups
87    0059  B1 02                      MOV       CL,2               ; Shift count
88    005B  BF 0000                    MOV       DI,0
89    005E                   DOT_LOOP:
90    005E  B0 C0                      MOV       AL,0C0H            ; First dot in byte
91    0060  88 05                      MOV       [DI],AL
92    0062  81 C7 2000                 ADD       DI,2000H           ; Move to odd row
93    0066  D2 E8                      SHR       AL,CL              ; Shift to next pel in byte
94    0068  88 05                      MOV       [DI],AL
95    006A  81 EF 1FB0                 SUB       DI,2000H-80        ; Move to even row
96    006E  D2 E8                      SHR       AL,CL
97    0070  88 05                      MOV       [DI],AL
98    0072  81 C7 2000                 ADD       DI,2000H           ; Move to odd row
99    0076  D2 E8                      SHR       AL,CL
100   0078  88 05                      MOV       [DI],AL
101   007A  81 EF 1FAF                 SUB       DI,2000H-81        ; Move to even row, one byte over
102   007E  FE CB                      DEC       BL
103   0080  75 DC                      JNZ       DOT_LOOP
104
105                            ;----- Restore system to 80x25 text and return
106
107   0082  B8 0002                    MOV       AX,2
108   0085  CD 10                      INT       10H
109   0087  CB                         RET
110   0088              COLOR_GRAPHICS  ENDP
111   0088              CODE            ENDS
112   0088                              END
```

Figure 8.12 *Continued*

The color/graphics adapter has three other I/O registers. The mode register is at I/O address 03D8H. This register sets the hardware controls for the different modes of displaying data. For example, you can set bit 5 of this register to "0" and allow 16 background colors in the text modes. Setting bit 5 to "1" selects the blinking function. The complete layout of this register, and all others, are given in the Technical Reference Manual.

The color select register is at I/O address 3D9H. This register sets the border color for the text modes. Since the actual text doesn't fill the full screen, you can surround the text with a selected color. The color select register can also pick different color palettes for the graphics modes, as we'll discuss in the next section. The low 4 bits of this register selects one of the 16 colors in Figure 8.10 for the border color.

Finally, the status register at I/O address 3DAH provides feedback information from the color card to a program. A program reads this register to determine the current state of the light pen, if one is attached to the system. More important, the status register tells when it's safe to read and write the data in the display buffer.

Without going into the technical details, reading and writing data in the color card's display buffer can cause "snow" on the screen if you do it at the wrong time. This happens only in the high-resolution text mode, 80 × 25. You'll recall that we did an example earlier, Figure 6.12, which constantly wrote a value into the buffer. If you used the color card for that example, there was a lot of interference on the screen. We can use the status register to avoid that problem.

There are times when it is safe to handle data in the display buffer. Bit 0 of the status register is "1" during those times. You have to wait for bit 0 to be "1," and then read or write the data. Figure 8.12(b) shows a program to write a character on the display. The first lines of the example write data into the buffer without using the status register. The program writes the 80 characters on the first line of the display 224 times. This is equivalent to filling the screen about nine times. When you run the program, you'll see a brief flash of interference as the data are written.

The second portion of part (b) repeats the action, this time checking for the status bit. Notice that the program tests the status bit in two ways. First, it waits until the status bit is a "0." Then, as soon as it becomes "1," the program writes the data. It is done this way because there is only a short interval during which the data can be written. If the program tested only for a "1," it might just catch the status bit before it went back to "0." The processor can't write the data out fast enough in that case to avoid interference. So the program loop makes sure that it sees the status bit the first time that it goes to "1."

Using the status bit, you won't see any interference on the screen. You will notice that the program takes much longer to execute. The extra time, spent waiting for the status bit, makes the program take longer. If you want to write a lot of data into the screen—for example, the horizontal scrolling example of Figure 8.8—you'll want another method. The easiest way is to turn off the display in the mode register. There is a bit (bit 3) in the mode register (3D8H) that controls the video display. When you set that bit to "0," the screen goes blank. To move a lot of data into the color display buffer, you can turn off the display and move the data without testing the status bit. Since the display is off, the interference won't appear on the screen. When the block move is complete, turn the display on. You'll see a brief blink as the display is turned off and then back on. IBM used this method to handle vertical scrolling with the color display.

Graphics Mode

The color/graphics adapter has two display modes which control the individual dots on the screen. These modes are called All Points Addressable (APA), since they can address and change individual points. Actually, the color card allows you to set up more than two APA display modes, but we'll look at those two that are suppported by the programming system. With the information in the Technical Reference Manual, you can try the others.

The medium-resolution graphics mode has 320 dots in 200 lines. Each of these dots can be one of four colors. This means that each dot requires 2 bits to represent the four colors. There are four dots, or pixels (for picture element, also called a pel), in each byte of the graphics storage. If you multiply the horizontal and vertical dimensions, and divide by 4 for the number of dots per byte, you'll see that the medium-resolution mode requires 16,000 bytes. That's why the color card has 16K bytes of storage.

Figure 8.13 shows the layout of the pixels within each byte. The pair of bits at bit location 7 and 6 become the first dot displayed. Bits 1 and 0 represent the last dot displayed from this byte. The first 80 bytes of the graphics storage contain the 320 dots of row 0, the first row on the screen.

However, byte 80 does not contain the first four dots of row 1. For hardware

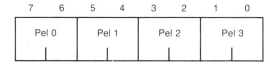

Figure 8.13 Bit Layout for 320 × 200 Graphics

reasons, the even and odd rows are maintained at separate ends of the graphic storage. All the odd rows are offset 2000H bytes from the corresponding even row. So row 1 is in bytes 2000H through 204FH. Row 2, an even row, is found at bytes 50H through 9FH. Row 3 is at 2050H through 209FH, and so on.

Figure 8.12(c) contains a program that shows the layout of the graphics storage. This program draws a diagonal line on the 320 × 200 display. The line goes from (0,0), the upper left corner, to (199,199), at the bottom and slightly to the right of center. The first part of the program places the display into the medium-resolution APA mode, using the ROM BIOS. The next chapter covers how this is done.

The program uses the DI register to point to the correct byte in the display buffer. The program displays a total of 200 dots. Register BL is set to 50, since the inner loop writes four dots for each loop. The program initializes CL to 2, for a shift-count value. The loop sets AL to 0C0H, which sets the two highest bits for color 3. The other three pixels in the byte are 0, the background color. After the loop stores that dot, it shifts AL right 2 bits, so it's now dealing with the second pel in the byte. Adding 2000H to DI moves the pointer to the odd field. The third dot of the inner loop is found by once again shifting AL and then subtracting (2000H-80) from DI. This moves DI back into the even field for row 2, and moves it down to the second set of 80 bytes. Finally, after the loop stores the fourth byte, it resets DI once again to the even field, but also increments it to point to the next byte in the row. This example chose to handle four bytes within the loop, since there are four pixels per byte.

Color in 320 × 200 APA Mode

Now let's cover the colors that you can get in the medium-resolution graphics mode. Two bits per pixel lets you specify one of four colors for each dot. Color 0 (00B) is the background color. You can choose any of the 16 colors shown in Figure 8.10 for the background color. You store this 4-bit value in the color select register (3D9H). IBM has predefined the remaining three colors. You can't arbitrarily choose the colors 1, 2, and 3. IBM has defined two different color palettes. Figure 8.14 shows the two different palettes. You choose the palette by setting bit 5 of the color select register.

As Figure 8.14 shows, if you set bit 5 to "0," you have the colors green, red, and yellow to go along with the selected background color. Setting bit 5 to "1" gives cyan, magenta, and white. You can also modify the palette values with another bit in the color select register. Setting bit 4 to "1" intensifies the colors in

Color Value	Palette 0 Color	Palette 1 Color
1 (01B)	Green	Cyan
2 (10B)	Red	Magenta
3 (11B)	Yellow	White
	Bit 5 = 0	Bit 5 = 1

Figure 8.14 Color Palettes for 320 × 200 Graphics

the palette. The ROM BIOS initialization routines normally set the color select register to 30H. This sets the background color to 0 (black) and selects palette 1 intensified.

High Resolution Graphics

The other APA mode gives you 640 dots across the screen, with 200 rows. In this mode there is only a single bit per pixel. If that bit is "0," black is displayed. If that bit is "1," the color is displayed. You select the color with the color select register. Normally, this register is 1111B (white), producing a black-and-white display. You may choose any other color.

The pixel mapping is nearly identical to the medium-resolution graphics mode. The exception is that there are eight dots per byte. The most significant bit (bit 7) is displayed first, bit 0 is displayed last. Here again, there are 80 bytes per row. Just like medium resolution, the even rows are at the beginning of the display buffer. The odd rows begin at location 2000H.

PARALLEL PRINTER ADAPTER

You need the parallel printer adapter to operate the IBM Printer or any other printer that attaches through a parallel interface. This adapter is built into the Monochrome and Parallel Printer Adapter. Or if you have a Color/Graphics Monitor Adapter, you also need a separate Parallel Printer Adapter. The two adapters are identical for the printer interface, except for the I/O address. The monochrome card places the printer ports at 3BCH through 3BEH. The separate printer card goes at 378H through 37AH.

The printer adapter has two output ports and one input port. It is quite similar to the 8255 part used for the keyboard interface. In fact, the original design of the printer card used an 8255. However, IBM determined that it would be better to build the adapters using discrete parts.

The 8-bit data output port at 3BCH or 378H communicates the data to the printer. The adapter sends the ASCII character value placed in this port to the printer. The second output port has 5 output bits. This port is at address 3BEH or 37AH. This port contains control signals for the printer. These lines control the initialization and operation of the printer. In particular, bit 0 transmits the data to the printer. Storing the data in the data output port doesn't send the ASCII character to the printer. You must set the strobe bit (bit 0 of 3BEH or 37AH) to "1" and then back to "0" before the printer receives the character. Figure 8.15 shows you a short program that transmits a character string to the printer. The subroutine named PRINT actually transmits the character to the printer.

Notice that the PRINT subroutine reads a value from the input port (3BCH or 379H). This input port returns status information from the printer to the program. In this example, the program checks to ensure that the printer is ready to accept the next character. Bit 7 of the status input port indicates the busy state of the printer. If this bit is "1," the printer can accept another character for printing. Otherwise, the program must wait. The remaining 4 input bits in this port reflect error conditions that might occur at the printer, such as Out of Paper. Our example doesn't check for these conditions. The Technical Reference Manual

```
The IBM Personal Computer MACRO Assembler 01-01-83           PAGE    1-1
Figure 8.15 Printer Output

1                                       PAGE    ,132
2                                       TITLE   Figure 8.15 Printer Output
3
4      0000                      STACK   SEGMENT STACK
5      0000      40 [            DW      64 DUP(?)
6                     ????
7                         ]
8
9      0080                      STACK   ENDS
10
11     = 0378                    BASE    EQU     378H
12
13     0000                      CODE    SEGMENT
14                                       ASSUME  CS:CODE
15
16     0000  46 69 67 75 72 65   MSG     DB      'Figure 8.15',13,10,'$'
17           20 38 2E 31 35 0D
18           0A 24
19
20     000E                      MAIN    PROC    FAR
21     000E  1E                          PUSH    DS              ; Set return address
22     000F  2B C0                       SUB     AX,AX
23     0011  50                          PUSH    AX
24
25     0012  2E: 8D 1E 0000 R            LEA     BX,MSG
26     0017                      PRINT_LOOP:
27     0017  2E: 8A 07                   MOV     AL,CS:[BX]      ; Get character string byte
28     001A  3C 24                       CMP     AL,'$'          ; Is this the end of the string
29     001C  74 06                       JE      MAIN_RETURN
30     001E  E8 0025 R                   CALL    PRINT           ; Print the character
31     0021  43                          INC     BX
32     0022  EB F3                       JMP     PRINT_LOOP      ; Do the next character
33     0024                      MAIN_RETURN:
34     0024  CB                          RET
35     0025                      MAIN    ENDP
36
37                              ;----- This routine prints the character in AL
38
39     0025                      PRINT   PROC    NEAR
40     0025  BA 0378                     MOV     DX,BASE         ; Data output port
41     0028  EE                          OUT     DX,AL           ; Put the character in the output port
42     0029  42                          INC     DX              ; Status port address
43     002A                      WAIT_BUSY:
44     002A  EC                          IN      AL,DX           ; Get the status
45     002B  A8 80                       TEST    AL,80H          ; Test the busy bit
46     002D  74 FB                       JZ      WAIT_BUSY       ; Loop if it's still busy
47     002F  42                          INC     DX              ; Point to control port
48     0030  B0 0D                       MOV     AL,0DH          ; Control value for strobe high
49     0032  EE                          OUT     DX,AL
50     0033  B0 0C                       MOV     AL,0CH          ; Control value for strobe low
51     0035  EE                          OUT     DX,AL
52     0036  C3                          RET
53     0037                      PRINT   ENDP
54     0037                      CODE    ENDS
55                                       END     MAIN
```

Figure 8.15 Printer Output

describes the bit layouts for the input and output I/O ports on the printer adapter card.

One of the control bits in port 3BEH or 37AH controls the printer interrupt line. Before the printer can send its interrupt signal back to the 8259 on the system board, this bit must be set to "1." However, the printer adapter uses the wrong signal for the interrupt. The chosen signal doesn't cause a reliable interrupt. Therefore, you shouldn't try to write a program that uses the interrupt capability of the printer adapter (unless you want to physically modify your printer card). We'll do an example that gets around this problem by using the system timer.

ASYNCHRONOUS COMMUNICATIONS ADAPTER

The Asynchronous Communications Adapter gives a serial communication capability to the IBM Personal Computer. This adapter gives you the capability to communicate with other computers, data base services, and other information vendors. We won't discuss how asynchronous communications work in general, but we will talk about the methods of programming this particular adapter for the IBM Personal Computer.

The communication integrated circuit does all the work in sending and receiving characters over the asynchronous line. You can program the 8250 Asynchronous Communication Element (ACE) to handle a wide variety of line disciplines. Character size, baud rate, stop characters, and parity bits are all under program control when you initialize the ACE. The adapter also lets you test and control the normal modem (modulator–demodulator) control signals.

You transmit characters using the ACE by writing the character value into the transmit register. The chip handles everything else, according to the values you have initialized the chip with. To receive a character, you merely read it from the receive buffer. There is a status register—called the line status register—that indicates when the transmit buffer is empty and can accept another character. Another bit in the status register tells you when the ACE has received a character from another system.

The Technical Reference Manual shows you the other registers that are part of the 8250 ACE. These registers provide the means to control the modem and determine its state. You can allow various conditions that occur in the ACE to cause an interrupt. This lets your program respond quickly to any change in external conditions.

The program in Figure 8.16 shows you the basic mechanisms necessary to initialize the ACE, send a character and then receive a character. The base I/O address for the adapter card is 3F8H, so the ACE registers vary from 3F8H to 3FEH. You can also modify the IBM Asynchronous Communications Adapter to respond to I/O addresses 2F8H through 2FEH. With this modification, you can install a second adapter in the IBM Personal Computer and communicate with two different external devices. In fact, it's possible to attach a printer to the system using serial communication rather than the parallel attachment. In that situation, you'll need two adapters. One card talks to the serial printer, the other handles external communications.

One of the I/O ports of the ACE does several jobs. The transmit and receive buffers are both at I/O address 3F8H. When you write to that location, it's the transmit buffer, but when you read it, you get the last character received by the ACE. This I/O port also does a third job. The divisor value that determines the baud rate for the adapter is stored in that I/O port. The ACE divides the input clock frequency by the value placed in the divisor latch, allowing you to select any baud rate from 50 to 9600. A bit in a control register determines the use of port 3F8H.

The first section of the example program initializes the 8250 ACE. The first

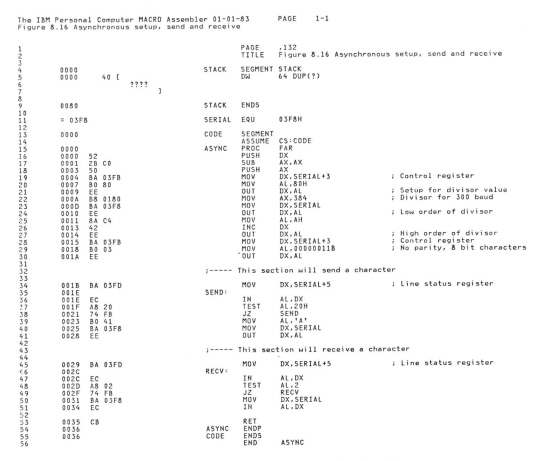

```
The IBM Personal Computer MACRO Assembler 01-01-83      PAGE    1-1
Figure 8.16 Asynchronous setup, send and receive

 1                                      PAGE    ,132
 2                                      TITLE   Figure 8.16 Asynchronous setup, send and receive
 3
 4      0000                    STACK   SEGMENT STACK
 5      0000        40 [                DW      64 DUP(?)
 6                       ????
 7                           ]
 8
 9      0080                    STACK   ENDS
10
11      = 03F8                  SERIAL  EQU     03F8H
12
13      0000                    CODE    SEGMENT
14                                      ASSUME  CS:CODE
15      0000                    ASYNC   PROC    FAR
16      0000    52                      PUSH    DX
17      0001    2B C0                   SUB     AX,AX
18      0003    50                      PUSH    AX
19      0004    BA 03FB                 MOV     DX,SERIAL+3     ; Control register
20      0007    B0 80                   MOV     AL,80H
21      0009    EE                      OUT     DX,AL           ; Setup for divisor value
22      000A    B8 0180                 MOV     AX,384          ; Divisor for 300 baud
23      000D    BA 03F8                 MOV     DX,SERIAL
24      0010    EE                      OUT     DX,AL           ; Low order of divisor
25      0011    8A C4                   MOV     AL,AH
26      0013    42                      INC     DX
27      0014    EE                      OUT     DX,AL           ; High order of divisor
28      0015    BA 03FB                 MOV     DX,SERIAL+3     ; Control register
29      0018    B0 03                   MOV     AL,00000011B    ; No parity, 8 bit characters
30      001A    EE                      OUT     DX,AL

                                ;----- This section will send a character

34      001B    BA 03FD                 MOV     DX,SERIAL+5     ; Line status register
35      001E                    SEND:
36      001E    EC                      IN      AL,DX
37      001F    A8 20                   TEST    AL,20H
38      0021    74 FB                   JZ      SEND
39      0023    B0 41                   MOV     AL,'A'
40      0025    BA 03F8                 MOV     DX,SERIAL
41      0028    EE                      OUT     DX,AL

                                ;----- This section will receive a character

45      0029    BA 03FD                 MOV     DX,SERIAL+5     ; Line status register
46      002C                    RECV:
47      002C    EC                      IN      AL,DX
48      002D    A8 02                   TEST    AL,2
49      002F    74 FB                   JZ      RECV
50      0031    BA 03F8                 MOV     DX,SERIAL
51      0034    EC                      IN      AL,DX
52
53      0035    CB                      RET
54      0036                    ASYNC   ENDP
55      0036                    CODE    ENDS
56      0036                            END     ASYNC
```

Figure 8.16 Asynchronous Setup, Send, and Receive

```
The IBM Personal Computer MACRO Assembler 01-01-83              PAGE    1-1
Figure 8.17  Asynchronous Interrupts

1                                     PAGE    ,132
2                                     TITLE   Figure 8.17  Asynchronous Interrupts
3      0000                    ABS0    SEGMENT AT 0
4      002C                            ORG     0BH*4
5      002C           ASYNC_INTERRUPT LABEL   WORD
6      002C                    ABS0    ENDS
7      0000                    STACK   SEGMENT STACK
8      0000    40 [                    DW      64 DUP(?)
9                      ????
10                          ]
11
12     0080                    STACK   ENDS
13
14     0000                    CODE    SEGMENT
15                                     ASSUME  CS:CODE
16     0000  0049 R            BUFFER_POINTER  DW      BUFFER
17
18     0002                    SET_INTERRUPT   PROC    FAR
19     0002  2B C0                     SUB     AX,AX
20     0004  8E D8                     MOV     DS,AX
21                                     ASSUME  DS:ABS0         ; Addressing to interrupt vectors
22
23                             ;----- Set up the interrupts on the 8250
24
25     0006  C7 06 002C R 0024 R       MOV     ASYNC_INTERRUPT,OFFSET INT_HANDLER
26     000C  8C 0E 002E R              MOV     ASYNC_INTERRUPT+2,CS   ; Set the 8259 interrupt vector
27
28     0010  BA 03F9                   MOV     DX,03F9H        ; Interrupt Enable Register
29     0013  B0 04                     MOV     AL,04H          ; Receive line status interrupt
30     0015  EE                        OUT     DX,AL           ; Set the register
31
32     0016  E4 21                     IN      AL,21H          ; 8259 Interrupt mask register
33     0018  24 F7                     AND     AL,0F7H         ; 0 at bit 3
34     001A  E6 21                     OUT     21H,AL          ; Interrupt unmasked
35
36     001C  BA 03FC                   MOV     DX,3FCH         ; Modem control register
37     001F  B0 08                     MOV     AL,08H          ; OUT2 bit
38     0021  EE                        OUT     DX,AL           ; Interrupts enabled at async card
39
40     0022  EB FE             HERE:   JMP     HERE            ; Program done, wait for interrupt
41     0024                    SET_INTERRUPT   ENDP
42
43                             ;----- Interrupt handler for receive characters
44
45     0024                    INT_HANDLER     PROC    FAR
46     0024  50                        PUSH    AX
47     0025  53                        PUSH    BX              ; Save interrupted register
48     0026  52                        PUSH    DX
49     0027  BA 03FD                   MOV     DX,3FDH         ; Line status register
50     002A  EC                        IN      AL,DX
51     002B  A8 01                     TEST    AL,01H          ; Make sure a char was received
52     002D  74 12                     JZ      INT_RETURN      ; Something wrong, return
53     002F  BA 03F8                   MOV     DX,3F8H         ; Receive data register
54     0032  EC                        IN      AL,DX           ; Get input char
55     0033  2E: 8B 1E 0000 R          MOV     BX,BUFFER_POINTER
56     0038  2E: 88 07                 MOV     CS:[BX],AL      ; Store the input in buffer
57     003B  43                        INC     BX
58     003C  2E: 89 1E 0000 R          MOV     BUFFER_POINTER,BX
59     0041                    INT_RETURN:
60     0041  5A                        POP     DX
61     0042  5B                        POP     BX              ; Restore registers
62     0043  B0 20                     MOV     AL,20H          ; EOI command
63     0045  E6 20                     OUT     20H,AL
64     0047  58                        POP     AX
65     0048  CF                        IRET                    ; Return from interrupt
66     0049                    INT_HANDLER     ENDP
67     0049    80 [            BUFFER  DB      128 DUP(0)
68                 00
69                          ]
70
71     00C9                    CODE    ENDS
72                                     END     SET_INTERRUPT
```

Figure 8.17 Asynchronous Interrupts

action of the program establishes the baud rate for the adapter. A divisor value of 384 gives the desired 300-baud rate. Notice that the program sets port 3FBH, the control register, bit 7 to "1" before setting the divisor value. The final output to port 3FBH establishes the line characteristics. This example chose to handle 8-bit characters with no parity.

The remaining two sections of the example send a character and receive a character. The line status register at port 3FDH has a status bit for the transmit buffer and another for the receive buffer. You can't send a character until the transmit buffer is empty. And you certainly can't read a character before the adapter has received it.

The Asynchronous Communications Adapter also supports interrupts. The OUT2 signal in the modem control register connects the interrupt signal from the ACE to the system. The interrupt enable register in the ACE selects which of the possible state changes will set an external interrupt condition. The asynchronous adapter generates interrupts on level 3 of the 8259 interrupt controller chip.

Let's see how you would go about setting up the interrupt on the asynchronous card to receive characters. Figure 8.17 shows the sequence of events that are required to enable the interrupt system. For the hardware interrupt, the program sets the interrupt vector corresponding to interrupt level 3 of the 8259 (interrupt 0BH at location 58H) to the address of the interrupt service routine. It clears the interrupt mask register at the bit location corresponding to the interrupt from the communications card. At the 8250 ACE the program sets the interrupt enable register to allow receive line status interrupts. Finally, the program turns on the OUT2 line to send the interrupts to the system. After all of this work, there is no problem handling the characters as they are received by the system. This example sticks them into a buffer where another program can look at them at leisure.

GAME CONTROL ADAPTER

The Game Control Adapter connects joysticks or paddles to the system. These are analog devices—that is, they don't work in ones and zeros. A joystick or paddle input is a resistance value, not a binary value that the computer can read directly. The game control adapter converts the resistive value into something that a computer can deal with.

The game control adapter doesn't convert the resistance value directly into a binary value. Rather, the adapter converts the resistance into a time delay. The larger the resistance, the longer the time delay. The computer can measure this time delay. A program can convert the time delay into a number that corresponds to the position of the joystick. Our problem is to write the program that converts the time delay into a number.

The game control adapter handles up to four resistive inputs. The time delay mechanism for each of these inputs is connected to a separate bit in I/O port 201H. When you output any value to port 201H, the 4 low-order bits of the port go to "0." The bits return to a "1" state after a variable amount of time. The resistance value connected to the adapter determines the time delay. The program in Figure 8.18 is an example of determining the resistance value of two of the four input ports. This scheme uses a simple method. Instead of determining the time delay of all four inputs at the same time, they are handled sequentially. The amount of time

```
The IBM Personal Computer MACRO Assembler 01-01-83          PAGE    1-1
Figure 8.18  Game Control Adapter

1                                         PAGE     ,132
2                                         TITLE    Figure 8.18  Game Control Adapter
3
4      = 0201                             GAME_PORT      EQU     201H
5
6      0000                               STACK    SEGMENT STACK
7      0000        40 [                            DW      64 DUP(?)
8                          ????
9                               ]
10
11     0080                               STACK    ENDS
12
13     0000                               CODE     SEGMENT
14                                                  ASSUME  CS:CODE
15     0000                               GAME_CONTROL   PROC     FAR
16     0000   1E                                   PUSH    DS               ; Set up return address
17     0001   2B C0                                SUB     AX,AX
18     0003   50                                   PUSH    AX
19     0004   BA 0201                              MOV     DX,GAME_PORT
20     0007   B8 B000                              MOV     AX,0B000H        ; Display buffer segment
21     000A   8E D8                                MOV     DS,AX
22
23     000C   B5 21                                MOV     CH,21H           ; Character to write in buffer
24     000E   B1 00                                MOV     CL,0             ; Switch settings
25     0010                               WRITE_LOOP:
26     0010   B4 01                                MOV     AH,1             ; Get X position
27     0012   E8 0042 R                            CALL    POSITION
28     0015   8B D8                                MOV     BX,AX            ; Save X position
29     0017   D1 EB                                SHR     BX,1
30     0019   D1 EB                                SHR     BX,1             ; Divide by 4
31     001B   B4 02                                MOV     AH,2             ; Get Y position
32     001D   E8 0042 R                            CALL    POSITION
33     0020   D0 E8                                SHR     AL,1
34     0022   D0 E8                                SHR     AL,1
35     0024   D0 E8                                SHR     AL,1
36     0026   D0 E8                                SHR     AL,1             ; Divide by 16
37     0028   B4 A0                                MOV     AH,160
38     002A   F6 E4                                MUL     AH               ; Convert to buffer offset
39     002C   03 D8                                ADD     BX,AX
40     002E   88 2F                                MOV     [BX],CH          ; Store a character there
41     0030   EC                                   IN      AL,DX
42     0031   24 10                                AND     AL,10H
43     0033   3A C1                                CMP     AL,CL
44     0035   74 D9                                JE      WRITE_LOOP
45     0037   8A C8                                MOV     CL,AL
46     0039   80 F9 10                             CMP     CL,10H
47     003C   75 D2                                JNE     WRITE_LOOP
48     003E   FE C5                                INC     CH               ; Next character
49     0040   EB CE                                JMP     WRITE_LOOP
50
51     0042                               GAME_CONTROL   ENDP
52
53                                        ;----- AH has mask bit
54
55     0042                               POSITION       PROC     NEAR
56     0042   51                                   PUSH    CX
57     0043   2B C9                                SUB     CX,CX            ; Set loop control value
58     0045   EE                                   OUT     DX,AL            ; Start the timing
59     0046                               POS_LOOP:
60     0046   EC                                   IN      AL,DX
61     0047   84 C4                                TEST    AL,AH
62     0049   E0 FB                                LOOPNE  POS_LOOP         ; Loop while the bit is still on
63     004B   B8 0000                              MOV     AX,0             ; Determine count value
64     004E   2B C1                                SUB     AX,CX            ; Range is 0 - 255
65     0050   59                                   POP     CX
66     0051   C3                                   RET
67     0052                               POSITION       ENDP
68     0052                               CODE     ENDS
69                                                 END     GAME_CONTROL
```

Figure 8.18 Game Control Adapter

that an individual delay takes is short. Therefore, handling the two in sequence rather than all at once works out all right.

The latter part of the Figure 8.18 program takes the X-Y position determined from the joystick inputs and writes a character at that position on the display. The game control adapter also allows four switch inputs, which can be read as the high-order of port 201H. The example program interrogates one of those switch bits to move from one character value to the next for display on the screen.

DISKETTE DRIVE ADAPTER

The Diskette Drive Adapter is the interface between the processor and the diskette drives. The circuitry on this adapter handles all of the functions necessary to save and recover data on a diskette. The adapter does all of the physical formatting of the data required for diskette usage.

The central part in the IBM Diskette Drive Adapter is the NEC μPD765 Floppy Disk Controller (FDC). This part is also available as the Intel 8272. The FDC controls the flow of data to and from the diskette. The FDC has two I/O control ports, one for data and one for status. The data port is at I/O address 3F4H, the status port at 3F5H. The data port is bidirectional. That is, at different times you may read or write data to that I/O port. The status register is read-only, and it may be read at any time. The status register tells you how the data port should be handled at any time.

There are 2 bits in the status port that you use during diskette operations. Bit 6 is Data Input/Output (DIO). This bit tells what the controller expects you to do with the data register. If DIO is "1," the FDC expects you to read the data register. If DIO is "0," the FDC is waiting for you to write something into the data register. Bit 7 of the status port is the Request For Master (RQM) bit. This is similar to the "busy" bit of the printer. When RQM is "1," the FDC is ready for you to either read or write the data register. If you don't pay attention to RQM, you'll get the FDC confused, and then nothing will work.

The data register is not really a single register. Like the 6845 CRT Controller, the data port is actually a group of registers. Unlike the 6845, there is no index register for the data register. The data that you send to the controller must be in the correct order. Similarly, when you read data from the data port, information comes in a specific order.

The Technical Reference Manual contains a chart showing the output and input combinations for all of the diskette operations. Let's look at a simple command to the FDC, Sense Drive Status. You perform this operation if you want to learn something about the current state of the diskette drive. Figure 8.19 shows the data for the Sense Drive Status command. Figure 8.20 is a program that performs the Sense Drive Status operation.

Every action by the diskette controller has three phases: command, execution, and result. For the command phase, the FDC expects data, and the DIO bit reflects this. When the FDC sets RQM to indicate it is ready to accept data, the program may send a command to the controller. For Sense Drive Status, it outputs two command bytes to the FDC. The first byte, 04H, is the operation code

Command...04H	
Command modifier................................00H	**Figure 8.19** Sense Drive Status
Returned status.....................................ST3	Command

```
The IBM Personal Computer MACRO Assembler 01-01-83          PAGE    1-1
Figure 8.20 Sense Drive Status


 1                                              PAGE    ,132
 2                                              TITLE   Figure 8.20 Sense Drive Status
 3
 4       0000                            STACK   SEGMENT STACK
 5       0000      40 [                          DW      64 DUP(?)
 6                          ????
 7                                 ]
 8
 9       0080                            STACK   ENDS
10
11                                       FDC_STATUS      RECORD  RQM:1,DIO:1,OTHER:6
12
13       0000                            CODE    SEGMENT
14                                               ASSUME  CS:CODE
15       0000                            SENSE   PROC    FAR
16       0000      1E                            PUSH    DS              ; Set return address
17       0001      2B C0                         SUB     AX,AX
18       0003      50                            PUSH    AX
19
20       0004      BA 03F4                       MOV     DX,03F4H        ; Status port for FDC
21       0007      B4 04                         MOV     AH,04H          ; Sense drive status command
22       0009      E8 001E R                     CALL    OUTPUT          ; Send to controller
23       000C      B4 00                         MOV     AH,0            ; Second byte of command
24       000E      E8 001E R                     CALL    OUTPUT
25
26                                       ;----- Read the status from the FDC
27
28       0011                            IN_DIO:
29       0011      EC                            IN      AL,DX           ; Wait until DIO indicates
30       0012      A8 40                         TEST    AL,MASK DIO     ;  input from FDC
31       0014      74 FB                         JZ      IN_DIO
32       0016                            IN_RQM:
33       0016      EC                            IN      AL,DX           ; Wait until RQM indicates
34       0017      A8 80                         TEST    AL,MASK RQM     ;  FDC is ready
35       0019      74 FB                         JZ      IN_RQM
36
37       001B      42                            INC     DX              ; Point to data port
38       001C      EC                            IN      AL,DX           ; Read in the sense status
39       001D      CB                            RET                     ; End of example
40       001E                            SENSE   ENDP
41
42                                       ;----- Routine to send byte to FDC
43
44       001E                            OUTPUT  PROC    NEAR
45       001E      EC                            IN      AL,DX           ; Wait until DIO says FDC ready
46       001F      A8 40                         TEST    AL,MASK DIO     ;  for output to it
47       0021      75 FB                         JNZ     OUTPUT
48       0023                            OUT_RQM:
49       0023      EC                            IN      AL,DX           ; Wait until RQM says FDC ready
50       0024      A8 80                         TEST    AL,MASK RQM
51       0026      74 FB                         JZ      OUT_RQM
52
53       0028      42                            INC     DX              ; Point at data port
54       0029      8A C4                         MOV     AL,AH           ; Get data value
55       002B      EE                            OUT     DX,AL           ; Send the value
56       002C      4A                            DEC     DX              ; Back to status port
57       002D      C3                            RET
58       002E                            OUTPUT  ENDP
59       002E                            CODE    ENDS
60                                               END     SENSE
```

Figure 8.20   Sense Drive Status

for this status operation. The second byte tells the FDC which diskette drive to test. During the command phase, DIO always indicates that the FDC is waiting for data, and the program uses RQM to determine when it is safe to output the byte.

The controller now enters the execution phase. During this phase, the controller executes the command. In this example, it senses the status of the drive. During this time RQM tells the program to leave the data port alone. After the execution is completed, DIO switches to a "1," telling the program to read the data register. When RQM allows, the program can read in the single byte of status from this operation. Once it has read all of the status information, the DIO returns to "0," awaiting the input of the next command.

As you can see from the table in the Technical Reference Manual, the Sense Drive Status command is one of the simplest. The Read Data command requires nine bytes of data during the command phase. When the operation is complete, the program must read seven status bytes from the controller. Execution doesn't begin until the sixth command byte is sent, and you can't begin another command until all seven status bytes have been read.

At I/O address 3F2H, there is a digital output register for the diskette controller. This output port performs some auxiliary diskette control operations. The primary use of this port is to control the diskette motors. For the 5 1/4-inch diskette drives used in the IBM Personal Computer, the diskette motor does not run continuously. The program must turn the motor on before it reads or writes on the diskette, and turn it off after the operation. If you leave the motor on all the time, you'll wear out the diskette. When the motor is on, the red light on the front of the diskette drive is on.

The adapter also uses the digital output register for several other functions. Two of the bits select the drive. The register also provides a way to reset the FDC, since there are error conditions which send the controller into an unknown state. In those instances, the only resource is to reset the controller and try again.

DIRECT MEMORY ACCESS

The diskette adapter card is an IBM feature card that uses the Direct Memory Access (DMA) capability of the system. Direct memory access allows the I/O device to transfer data directly to or from memory. The processor does not have to supply the data. The printer, for example, requires the processor to transmit every character to be printed. For diskette data transfer, the processor would be hard-pressed to provide the data quickly enough. A program to transfer diskette data would be very similar to the code in Figure 8.15, where characters were sent to the printer. That is, the program would loop, reading the RQM bit to test for another byte of data. However, if the processor does not respond fast enough for the diskette, the data are lost.

For DMA data transfers, the processor only has to initialize the operation. The Intel 8237 DMA controller on the system board handles the rest. For a diskette read, the program initializes the DMA to handle the data transfer. The program then sends the command to the diskette controller to execute the read. During the execution phase, the program does not have to move the data, the DMA controller does the job. When the operation is complete, the program executes the result phase as before.

Let's see how you set up the DMA for a diskette read operation. Figure 8.21 shows the code required to do the job. The DMA has four channels. The diskette is connected to channel 2 of the DMA. Channels 1 and 3 are available on the system I/O channel for other I/O devices, while channel 0 is reserved for a very important hardware function—keeping the memory refreshed. If you interfere with the operation of DMA channel 0, all of the system memory will probably change.

Each channel of the DMA has two registers: an address register and a count register. The address register locates the memory region where the data are transferred. For our example read operation, the value in the address register marks the beginning of the data buffer. As the diskette controller reads each byte from the diskette, the DMA controller places that byte into memory at the location identified by the address register. The DMA controller then increments the address register so that it's pointing to the next location in the data buffer.

In Figure 8.21, BUFFER is the name of the data region. The program determines the absolute address of the BUFFER in the system. This program does that by adding the offset of BUFFER to the shifted value of the CS register, which contains the segment value for BUFFER. The program places the low 16 bits of the address in the DMA address register for channel 2. The high 4 bits of

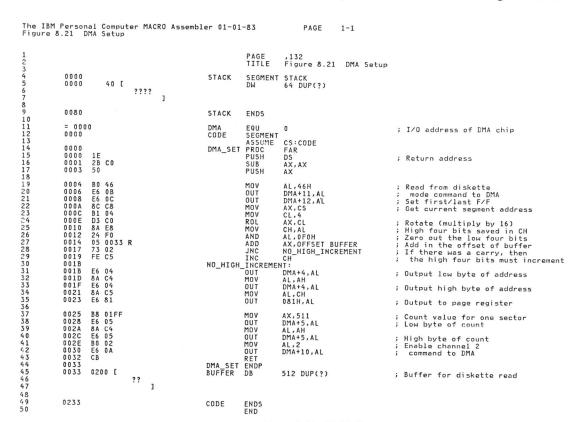

```
The IBM Personal Computer MACRO Assembler 01-01-83          PAGE    1-1
Figure 8.21  DMA Setup


1                                      PAGE     ,132
2                                      TITLE    Figure 8.21   DMA Setup
3
4       0000                   STACK   SEGMENT STACK
5       0000     40 [                  DW       64 DUP(?)
6                      ????
7                            ]
8
9       0080                   STACK   ENDS
10
11      = 0000                 DMA     EQU      0                        ; I/O address of DMA chip
12      0000                   CODE    SEGMENT
13                                     ASSUME  CS:CODE
14      0000                   DMA_SET PROC     FAR
15      0000    1E                     PUSH     DS                       ; Return address
16      0001    2B C0                  SUB      AX,AX
17      0003    50                     PUSH     AX
18
19      0004    B0 46                  MOV      AL,46H                   ; Read from diskette
20      0006    E6 0B                  OUT      DMA+11,AL                ;   mode command to DMA
21      0008    E6 0C                  OUT      DMA+12,AL                ; Set first/last F/F
22      000A    8C C8                  MOV      AX,CS                    ; Get current segment address
23      000C    B1 04                  MOV      CL,4
24      000E    D3 C0                  ROL      AX,CL                    ; Rotate (multiply by 16)
25      0010    8A E8                  MOV      CH,AL                    ; High four bits saved in CH
26      0012    24 F0                  AND      AL,0F0H                  ; Zero out the low four bits
27      0014    05 0033 R              ADD      AX,OFFSET BUFFER         ; Add in the offset of buffer
28      0017    73 02                  JNC      NO_HIGH_INCREMENT        ; If there was a carry, then
29      0019    FE C5                  INC      CH                       ;   the high four bits must increment
30      001B                   NO_HIGH_INCREMENT:
31      001B    E6 04                  OUT      DMA+4,AL                 ; Output low byte of address
32      001D    8A C4                  MOV      AL,AH
33      001F    E6 04                  OUT      DMA+4,AL                 ; Output high byte of address
34      0021    8A C5                  MOV      AL,CH
35      0023    E6 81                  OUT      081H,AL                  ; Output to page register
36
37      0025    B8 01FF                MOV      AX,511                   ; Count value for one sector
38      0028    E6 05                  OUT      DMA+5,AL                 ; Low byte of count
39      002A    8A C4                  MOV      AL,AH
40      002C    E6 05                  OUT      DMA+5,AL                 ; High byte of count
41      002E    B0 02                  MOV      AL,2                     ; Enable channel 2
42      0030    E6 0A                  OUT      DMA+10,AL                ;   command to DMA
43      0032    CB                     RET
44      0033                   DMA_SET ENDP
45      0033    0200 [         BUFFER  DB       512 DUP(?)               ; Buffer for diskette read
46                      ??
47                            ]
48
49      0233                   CODE    ENDS
50                                     END
```

Figure 8.21   DMA Setup

the address are placed in a special "page" register. The 8237 DMA controller can really handle only 16-bit addresses. The IBM Personal Computer has added this page register so that your program can read the data into any location in memory. There are three page registers, one each for channels 1, 2, and 3. The page register is only 4 bits, so the high 4 bits of AL don't matter when outputing the page value.

The program also sends the number of bytes to the DMA controller. The diskette controller uses this value, stored in the channel 2 count register, to terminate the data read operation. The DMA sends a special control signal, called Terminal Count, to the device when it stores the last byte of data in memory. The final operation to the DMA device enables channel 2 for operation. The program can now enter the command phase with the diskette controller.

The Diskette Drive Adapter brings together many of the components in the system. The diskette adapter uses both DMA and an interrupt to handle the operation of the diskette. The diskette controller itself is a complicated, "intelligent" control device that requires a "program" before it will execute. In the next chapter, we'll bring all of this together when we discuss the ROM BIOS control of the diskette drive.

CHAPTER

9

The ROM
BIOS

In the preceding chapter, we studied the hardware of the IBM Personal Computer. IBM provides a standard control program for many of those hardware components. These control programs are in the system ROM and are called the ROM BIOS (Basic Input/Output System). This chapter explains the functions that are available as part of the ROM BIOS. You should use this chapter together with Chapter 3 and Appendix A of the Technical Reference Manual. Chapter 3 describes the ROM BIOS, particularly some of its special functions. Appendix A contains the complete assembly language listing of the ROM BIOS for the IBM Personal Computer.

We'll study the ROM BIOS routines for two reasons. They provide an example of assembly language programming techniques, especially for controlling system hardware. But more important, these ROM BIOS routines play an important role in the development of assembly language programs for the IBM Personal Computer. We have used some of the ROM BIOS functions in previous examples. Since IBM has given us these functions, there's no reason to duplicate them. It's a good idea to use them whenever possible.

The second reason for using the ROM BIOS routines is program portability. IBM provides the ROM BIOS routines to enforce a level of system interface on the assembly language programmer. At the time IBM developed the Personal Computer, the system designers knew that no matter how good a job they did the first time, there would always be a better way to do it. In fact, as time goes on, the evolution of technology provides a better way to do the job.

As new hardware is developed for the Personal Computer, there will be new programming interfaces for the hardware. If you write your programs using the hardware specifications, you'll have to modify those programs every time you change the system hardware. Now that isn't a big deal for individual programmers, but it can be if you're writing a program that many people will use. Or if you intend to sell your program, you would like it to have a long shelf life. That is, you don't want to ship new programs to the dealers every time someone offers new system hardware.

The ROM BIOS interface is an attempt to solve this problem. IBM has defined an interface to the different components of the system. Manufacturers will endeavor to maintain that BIOS interface for all new hardware. This means that even if the hardware changes, the BIOS interface should remain the same. Your program will not require modification.

Of course, as the hardware develops more function, you must modify your program to take advantage of that new function. For that purpose, IBM will probably provide additional BIOS interfaces. However, your old programs, which ran perfectly on the old machines, will continue to run on the new machines. Of course, they won't use the new function. If your program served a useful purpose before, it is likely that it still has value and will continue to be used.

Let's look at a possible ROM BIOS example. Suppose that IBM decided to modify the diskette controller card. They might do this for several reasons. They might want to reduce the manufacturing cost of the card, or they might want to include some additional function on the controller. In either case, the programming interface to the hardware, such as we examined in the preceding chapter, would be different. However, the ROM BIOS that IBM supplies with that new controller will probably have a similar interface. That means that the calling sequence and parameter passing methods for the interface will remain identical. If you write a program that uses the diskette, and use the ROM BIOS interface for all your diskette access, the program will run correctly. If, however, you write your program to manipulate the diskette controller directly, that program will probably not work with the new controller card.

The ROM BIOS consists of several separate functions. The first is the power-on self-test (POST). This routine executes whenever the power is turned on, or whenever you enter a System Reset (depress Control–Alternate–Delete simultaneously). The POST routine tests the system hardware and initializes some of the devices for operation.

The ROM BIOS also contains device drivers. These routines control the actions of the hardware devices. IBM provides device routines for all of the commonly used hardware. However, IBM has not provided for all the devices. Similarly, not every desirable function is available. There simply is not enough ROM space to provide for every function that you might desire.

Finally, the ROM BIOS contains a set of system services. These routines don't directly control any system devices, but they do provide valuable data about the operation of the system.

This chapter discusses the different components of the ROM BIOS. We'll start with the POST, since it's first in the listing and in the power on sequence. System services are all related to the system board, so they'll come next. Finally, we'll see how IBM has provided operations for the different I/O features of the system.

NOTES ON THE ROM BIOS LISTING

The ROM BIOS listing is given in Appendix A of the Technical Reference Manual. This listing describes the contents of the 8K-byte ROM module located at 0FE000H in the 8088 address space. This ROM is one of five modules placed on the system board by IBM. The other four ROM modules contain the BASIC interpreter. Just like DOS, the source code for the BASIC routines is proprietary information and is not printed in the Technical Reference Manual. However, IBM has published the ROM BIOS routines so that everyone can learn how to use the interfaces of the BIOS routines.

The assembly listing given in Appendix A of the Technical Reference Manual is an assembly of the entire contents of the ROM. The assembly was not done with the IBM Macro Assembler. That's because the Macro Assembler didn't exist at the time IBM developed the ROM BIOS. The Intel Macro Assembler was used for the BIOS development and produced the listing you see. The Intel assembler is similar to the IBM assembler in usage and syntax. As you can see, the Intel Assembler does not print the address fields in the same fashion, and some of the assembler pseudo-operations are different. It should be easy for you to deal with those minor differences.

The ROM BIOS listing describes six different segments. Only three of these are really of interest to us. The ABS0 segment, located at address 0, contains the interrupt vectors that the ROM BIOS and POST deal with. This segment does not contain any initialized data definitions. The segment merely locates the vectors. Since this area is RAM, the ROM BIOS must initialize it after the power is turned on. The DATA segment, located at paragraph 40H or absolute location 400H, defines all of the data areas used by the ROM BIOS. Similarly, this segment defines the variable locations but not their initial values. Finally, the CODE segment begins at paragraph 0F000H. The first 56K bytes of this segment have nothing in them. The first byte in the CODE segment appears at absolute address 0FE000H or offset 0E000H in the segment. These data, from 0FE000H to 0FFFFFH, represent the 8K bytes in the BIOS ROM module. This code, together with the BASIC ROM modules, are the only instructions available when the machine begins execution.

One additional note. IBM did not develop the ROM BIOS as one large source module. Each function was developed as a separate module, and the modules were linked together to form the ROM BIOS. You may be able to see some of the linkages in the code. For publication, IBM combined the code modules into a single source module and assembled them all at once. This single assembly allows the publication to list the absolute addresses of each of the ROM BIOS functions.

POWER-ON SELF-TEST

The IBM Personal Computer performs the ROM power-on self-test following every reset of the system, including the time when power is first turned on. This test has two purposes: it performs a quick test of the basic elements of the system; and it initializes the major hardware components for use.

As a system test, the POST forms the first part of a three-pronged diagnostic package for the IBM Personal Computer. The POST executes every time the system is turned on. This quick test validates the system operation and spots a problem before it affects a running program. The second level of diagnostic comes with every machine in the Guide to Operations. This diskette (or cassette) contains a customer diagnostic that tests every part of the machine. The customer diagnostic determines which part of the machine the customer should return for service if a fault is found. Finally, IBM offers an Advanced Diagnostic tool. This feature, available as an extra cost option, determines which of the replaceable units has failed. This diagnostic tool is designed for use by service personnel in their work on the machines. There is, of course, no reason why you can't purchase the Advanced Diagnostic for your own use.

The beginning of POST may be difficult for you to find. That's because the beginning of POST is at the very end of the program listing. When the 8088 processor is reset (as it is when power is first turned on), it begins execution at location 0FFFF:0000H. This location is just 16 bytes away from the end of the 8088 address space. There is just enough room there for a jump instruction to the real POST routine. As you can see, the FAR JMP instruction there transfers control to the label START, which is the real beginning of the POST. IBM uses the remaining bytes at the end of the ROM to hold a date value. This date tells when IBM released the ROM for production.

The beginning of POST also tells you why IBM locates the ROM for the Personal Computer at the high end of memory. That's where the processor begins execution following a reset. The system ROM, which contains the initialization program for the machine, must have some control information at 0FFFF:0000H. So it makes sense to put all of the ROM at that end of memory. Also, it makes sense to leave the interrupt vectors in low memory as RAM locations. Our ability to modify those vector values greatly enhances the versatility of the ROM BIOS.

The POST contains generally uninteresting code. Many of the instruction sequences don't make any sense. If you examine the first sequence of instructions, you'll see that they don't do anything—unless there's a problem with the processor. Unless you are interested in writing a diagnostic program, there's little reason for examining the programming techniques of the POST.

We can note some of the actions that POST takes to show you the extent of error testing. POST tests all of the ROM on the system board by performing a checksum. This test adds together all of the bytes in the ROM module. As it does the addition, it discards any carry from the 8-bit result. If the final result is zero, the ROM passes the test. Of course, IBM made sure that each ROM adds up to zero before it's placed in manufacturing. If the ROM is bad, this test detects an error.

The POST also tests all of the read/write memory of the system. The switches on the system board tell the POST how much memory is in the system. Each bit of the memory is tested to see if it can be set to one and reset to zero. On completion

Hardware Interrupts

Interrupt Number		ROM BIOS Usage
2	02H	Parity error in memory
5	05H	Print screen
8	08H	Time of day
9	09H	Keyboard
14	0EH	Diskette

BIOS Device Drivers

Interrupt Number		ROM BIOS Usage
16	10H	Video
17	11H	Equipment check
18	12H	Memory size
19	13H	Diskette
20	14H	Asynchronous
21	15H	Cassette
22	16H	Keyboard
23	17H	Printer
24	18H	Cassette BASIC entry point
25	19H	Bootstrap routine entry point
26	1AH	Time of day

User-Supplied Routines

Interrupt Number		ROM BIOS Usage
27	1BH	Keyboard break
28	1CH	Timer tick

BIOS Parameter Blocks

Interrupt Number		ROM BIOS Usage
29	1DH	Video parameters
30	1EH	Diskette parameters
31	1FH	Video graphics characters

Figure 9.1 Interrupt Vectors Used by ROM BIOS

of the test, POST writes zeros to all memory locations. This means that if you write a program that runs immediately following POST, all of memory will be set to zero. However, it's bad programming practice to rely on some other program to initialize your data areas. It's better to do it yourself and be sure.

The final thing we'll note about the POST is that it initializes the software interrupt vectors for the ROM BIOS. A program accesses the ROM BIOS routines through the software interrupt vectors. The routines themselves are in the ROM module, the same one that contains the POST. Before POST passes control to the operating system, it makes sure that each of the BIOS entry points is stored in the correct interrupt vector. The BIOS uses most of the interrupt vectors from interrupt 2 through interrupt 01FH. The Technical Reference Manual contains an Interrupt Vector Listing which shows the interrupt number and the initial value of that vector. Figure 9.1 contains part of that table, which we'll use in our discussion of the ROM BIOS.

ROM BIOS INTERRUPTS

As the table in Figure 9.1 shows, ROM BIOS uses the interrupt vectors of the 8088. These vectors serve several different purposes. The first block of vectors deal directly with the hardware interrupts. The routines for these vectors gain control when a hardware interrupt occurs. For example, the keyboard interrupt uses the interrupt vector 9, located at 9*4 or 24H. The ROM BIOS does not use all of the interrupts possible with the 8259 interrupt controller. Some of the interrupts are reserved for IBM devices, while others can be used for your own purposes. And, of course, even though IBM has reserved a particular interrupt vector, you can use it for something different if it works in your system. However, if you want to market a program, you must remember that everyone's system will not be the same as yours.

DEVICE DRIVERS

The device driver routines are the heart of the ROM BIOS. These routines give the assembly language programmer a method of controlling the hardware devices of the IBM Personal Computer. Any program can control the devices with the correct sequence of instructions. However, for many programs you won't want to do anything special with the hardware devices. In those cases you just want to use the devices in a standard fashion. For example, very few programs do anything with the diskette other than read and write. We wrote our own routine to read the diskette drive status in Chapter 8. If we want to read a particular sector on the diskette, we can use the ROM BIOS and not have to recreate that code ourselves. The assembly language programmer should view the ROM BIOS routines as a tool. These routines minimize the work the programmer must do.

A program uses the function of ROM BIOS by issuing a software interrupt for the desired action. A program passes parameters to and from the BIOS function with the 8088 registers. For example, these instructions determine the current mode of the display

```
MOV     AH,15
INT     10H
```

The INT 10H instruction invokes the Video BIOS routine. The Video routine can do lots of different jobs. Setting AH to 15 tells the routine that we want to know the current video state. The BIOS routine returns the state information in the AL register.

Each of the BIOS device drivers has its own parameters for input and output. In general, the AH register identifies the particular function for that BIOS routine. The BIOS routine uses the other registers for any other parameters required for input or output. The ROM BIOS listing contains the input and output specifications for each routine. At the beginning of each BIOS routine, there is a prologue that identifies the input and output parameters. Each function is briefly described, together with other important notes. We'll refer to those listings for the individual routines. Before we do that, however, let's look at the other interrupt vectors.

User Routines

There are some system functions that require immediate program intervention. The two interrupts for user routines provide that mechanism. The first vector, at interrupt 1BH, is the keyboard break. The system user types a Control-Break keystroke to interrupt the current program. Normally, this returns control to the current system, such as DOS or BASIC. If we write a program that honors the keyboard break operation, we have to check the keyboard constantly (using the BIOS routine) to see if the user has typed a break character. Or we can use the break interrupt. The ROM BIOS keyboard routine issues the software interrupt 1BH whenever the CTL-Break keystroke occurs. Normally, this interrupt points to a dummy return—an IRET instruction—so that nothing happens. If we want our program to know about the CTL-Break immediately, we set the 1BH interrupt to point to a special routine in the program. That routine knows immediately when the user wants to exit the program, and can set the appropriate conditions.

Similarly, we may write a program that requires periodic interruption. For example, a game program constantly needs to know the position of the game paddles. The ROM BIOS calls interrupt 1CH every time the timer ticks. As we saw before, this occurs about 18.2 times a second, or once every 55 milliseconds. We can write a routine that checks the game paddles every eighteenth time BIOS calls this routine, allowing the program to update the game paddle position about once a second. This method gives us a periodic entry into a particular routine within the program.

Parameter Blocks

The parameter blocks of the ROM BIOS give flexibility to the hardware programs in the ROM. The parameter block interrupt vectors point to tables that are used by the ROM BIOS routines. The diskette parameter block contains the values which the BIOS routine uses to control the diskette drive. Since different diskette drives have different characteristics, the ROM BIOS has a table for the drives that IBM supplies. If you choose to use a different diskette drive, you can modify the parameter table, and use that drive successfully.

Similarly, there is a parameter table for the video initialization parameters. If your display device requires some slightly different timings, you can modify this table. For example, many television sets cannot display the full width of the 40 character display. One of the parameters in the video table controls the left–right positioning of the data on the display. The DOS MODE command, which can shift the characters on the screen, modifies the parameter table specifically for that purpose.

The last parameter block that uses a BIOS interrupt vector is actually a table of character shapes. The ROM BIOS has the ability to display characters on the screen even when the color/graphics display is in a graphics mode. The BIOS does this by constructing the characters out of the appropriate dot configurations. You can see a table in the ROM for the first 128 characters, located at offset 0FA6EH in the CODE segment. The interrupt vector 01FH points at the table used for the second 128 characters. There was no room in the ROM for this table, so it's up to the user to supply it. This lets you substitute your own set of characters for the ones that IBM chose for the upper 128. Just design your own dot patterns, point the 01FH interrupt vector at that table, and use the graphics mode BIOS to write characters. This capability can be a very useful extension to your graphics programming. It allows you to design and use your own character set.

For all of the parameter blocks, you need only to modify the interupt vector to change the parameters. You construct your table of parameters anywhere in your program. Then modify the interrupt vector to point to that table. When you use ROM BIOS and the BIOS requires a parameter, it goes to your table rather than the default table built into the ROM. These parameter tables make BIOS very flexible. Although the instructions are in a ROM module, you can alter the effects of ROM BIOS without substituting a new ROM or replacing any of the BIOS routines.

ROM BIOS DATA AREA

The DATA segment located at paragraph 40H contains the variables used by the ROM BIOS. We won't go through a list of every variable now, and what each does. Each of these is covered in the appropriate device routine.

IBM will not change any of these data locations without good reason. Some of the ROM BIOS routines do nothing more than return these data values. It may be more advantageous for a program to read the variables directly. We'll do an example in the next chapter that requires us to modify one of the variables maintained by the ROM BIOS. Changing that value gives us an additional method using the system.

Since IBM will probably not be changing any of the variable locations, it's reasonably safe to use the data locations directly. There is a possible concern. Some of the variables may not make sense as people develop new versions of the hardware. For example, if IBM were to develop a system that didn't have any memory (an extremely unlikely possibility), there would be no use for the variable locations that hold the current memory size. In that instance, IBM might find another use for that variable location. But if the function exists in a form that resembles the current form, the variable will probably be used in the same way.

DEVICE DRIVER ROUTINES

We'll now discuss the device driver routines, one by one. Instead of taking them in numerical order, let's look at them in the order of complexity. The simplest ones are the system services, so let's start there.

SYSTEM SERVICE

Two of the ROM BIOS routines perform system services in a rather simple fashion. These two entry points are for memory size determination and equipment check.

Memory size determination has no input parameters. The BIOS routine returns in the AX register the amount of memory in the system. The AX register returns the amount of memory available in thousands of bytes. If the system has 64K bytes, the AX register returns with the value 64. Any application program that uses all of system memory should read this memory size value to determine the end of memory. An application program could determine the amount of memory by writing and then reading back memory locations until it found the location where the value read was not identical to the value written. However, as an example in the next chapter will show, it's advantageous to force all applications to use the memory size routine to determine the end of memory. It's certainly more efficient, since each program doesn't need to write the memory size routine. By changing the value of the upper limit of memory, it's possible to reserve a section of high memory. After a program changes the total memory size value, a properly written application program will not disturb it.

The equipment check routine has no input parameters. The routine returns a 16-bit value in the AX register that indicates the devices attached to the particular system. The prolog for the equipment check routine tells you just what each bit means. This BIOS function is an easy way to determine if a particular feature is present or not.

The final system service routine handles the time of day. This routine has two functions: read the time or set the time. Time is measured as timer ticks since midnight, or whenever the machine was turned on. The BIOS routine does not convert the count value into hours, minutes, and seconds. The BIOS listing does show the appropriate values to use for the conversion. To determine the time in hours, divide the 24-bit timer value by 65,543, the number of ticks per hour. To determine the minute, divide the remainder from the previous division by 1092, the number of ticks per minute, and so on.

If you're not too critical of the converted time value, there is an easy way to do it. Since 24 hours of ticks won't fit within a single word, the timer value is a three-byte integer. The highest-order byte is within 1% of being the time in hours. The low-order word can be divided by 1092 to determine the number of minutes. Dividing the remainder by 18 gives the number of seconds.

The time-of-day function requires a hardware interrupt, the timer tick interrupt. This interrupt is level 0 on the 8259 interrupt controller, and is vectored through software interrupt 8 of the 8088. This routine gains control once every 55 milliseconds. The primary job of this routine is to increment the timer tick value for the time of day routine. If a program turns off the interrupts for a significant period of time, it's probable that the time of day is no longer correct.

The timer tick interrupt also does a diskette function. The diskette motors are not on all the time. BIOS turns on the motors only for the duration of the diskette access. However, the ROM BIOS does not turn the motor off immediately following the operation. There is a delay from the time the motor is turned on until the motor is going fast enough that data can be read from the diskette. If a program uses the diskette again almost immediately, it's better to leave the motor on rather than turning it off and then back on. The timer routine takes care of this. The diskette routine sets a variable called MOTOR_COUNT when the diskette operation is completed. The timer tick interrupt decrements the count value. When MOTOR_COUNT reaches 0, the timer tick interrupt turns the diskette motor off. The diskette routine tests the motor value when it's about ready to write on the diskette. If the motor is already on, there is no need to delay the operation. If the motor isn't on yet, there is a delay until the diskette is rotating at the correct speed. Normally, the diskette motor continues to run for two seconds after the access completes. This is one of the values in the diskette parameter block, and you can change it to a different value. The selection of this value trades off performance against the wear and tear on the diskette media.

All three of the service BIOS routines transmit memory location values to the calling routine. You can avoid using the BIOS routines by reading the memory locations directly. However, in most cases it's easier to call the BIOS routine than it is to establish addressing to the BIOS DATA segment. From a "purity" viewpoint, it's better to use the BIOS routine.

PRINTER AND ASYNCHRONOUS COMMUNICATIONS

The ROM BIOS routines for printer and asynchronous communications are very similar. The major difference is the ability to read characters from the asynchronous adapter card. Both routines have a function to initialize the adapter, one to send a character and one to read the current status of the adapter. Figure 9.2 summarizes the functions available with these BIOS routines.

As you can tell from the table, the two BIOS routines are not matched. The AH value to do a particular job is different for the two routines. But that's the way it is, and we're going to have to live with it.

These BIOS routines support more than one adapter card. The BIOS data area at 40:0H has an eight-word data area. BIOS reserves this area for the base address of printer and asynchronous adapters. The four words at offset 0, labeled RS232_BASE, are a place to put the base address for up to four asynchronous communication adapter cards. At offset 8, labeled PRINT_BASE, is a corresponding area for printer adapters. The POST initializes this data area depending on the devices that it finds in the system. For the printer, POST looks for the black-and-white card first, then the printer adapter at I/O address 378H and finally a printer adapter at address 278H. If POST finds a printer adapter at any of those addresses, it places that base address value into the data area. The POST does a similar job for the asynchronous adapters, looking first for the card at I/O address 3F8H and then for the card at address 2F8H.

The BIOS routines are written independent of the I/O address of the particular adapter card. The DX register is an input parameter, specifying which of the available cards BIOS is to use. For example, if you have a monochrome card, with the printer port at I/O address 3BCH as part of that card, that base address appears first in the PRINT_BASE table. If you call the print BIOS routine with DX set to 0, BIOS directs all I/O operations to that adapter. If you also have the stand-alone printer adapter, located at I/O address 378H, setting DX to 1 communicates with it. As you look at the printer and asynchronous BIOS code, you can see that it uses the input value of DX to pick the appropriate value from the base address table in the BIOS DATA segment. After BIOS determines that value, it does all I/O operations using some modification of that base address value. The routines contain a number of increment and decrement instructions for the DX register. This allows the BIOS routine to address the different registers of the I/O adapter without using absolute values. All I/O references are relative to the original value determined from the base address table.

The print initialization function requires no user input parameters. The

ID (AH Value)	Print Function	Async Function
0	Print character	Initialize adapter
1	Initialize	Transmit a character
2	Read status	Receive a character
3	—	Read the status

Figure 9.2   Print and Asynchronous Functions

initialization program resets the printer and sets up the printer adapter control port for further action. The RS232 initialization, on the other hand, requires the programmer to supply information about the line parameters. Details for the initialization value, passed to the routine in the AL register, are shown in the prolog for the asynchronous routine.

The other BIOS functions for print and asynchronous communications allow you to write (and read, for the asynchronous) values to the device. The important thing to notice about these BIOS routines is that the I/O operation is done synchronously. This means that when a program transfers control to the BIOS routine to do the function, control does not return until the job is done. When printing a character, the print routine remains in control until it transmits the character to the printer. If the printer is busy, the BIOS routine loops, waiting for the printer to finish its current activity. When transmitting a character through the asynchronous communication BIOS, the routine waits until the hardware allows another character transmission. Similarly, the receive routine for the asynchronous communications waits until the adapter receives a character. If the external device never sends a character, the program that called BIOS to read the character never regains control.

For this reason, both routines have a status function. This allows a program to decide if the BIOS routine can perform an operation at the current time. The print status function tells if the printer is currently busy. The asynchronous status routine indicates whether a character can be transmitted and whether a character can be read. A program can use these status routines to determine if the operation can proceed immediately. You may decide to do something else in your program until the I/O operation can proceed. If you're testing for some external event, such as a character received by the adapter, the status routine doesn't tie up the program until the character is sent. Testing to see if the character has arrived allows you to continue on with other things until it does.

Another important thing to notice about the BIOS routines is their error handling. With the BIOS routines, it is very difficult to "hang" the system. Except for the case where you are waiting for a character from an external asynchronous communication device, the BIOS routines always return to the caller, even if the external hardware fails. BIOS uses a count in every loop that's waiting for the hardware to perform some action. For example, when the print routine is waiting for the printer to finish its current activity, the BL and CX registers hold a count value. If the count value in these registers goes to zero before the printer becomes not busy, the BIOS routine returns with a time-out error. This means that turning off the printer while you're trying to print doesn't cause the system to hang. The BIOS routine eventually returns with an error, indicating the failure of the printer.

The PRINT routine has a minor problem because of the time-out values. When a Form Feed character (0CH) is sent to the printer, the printer ejects the paper to the top of the page. If there are more than 51 lines in the current page, it takes longer for the printer to move the paper than the time-out value allows. It's possible to get an error indication even when the printer is working correctly. This value was modified in the second version of the ROM BIOS to correct the problem. If your system has the original version, you may have to retry an operation to the printer that results in a time-out error. Retrying the error once ensures that it wasn't a BIOS error.

KEYBOARD

The keyboard BIOS routines offer an example of several different programming techniques. Primarily, the keyboard BIOS has a large interrupt handler that does the conversion from keyboard scan codes to ASCII codes. The interrupt handler handles the normal shift keys and the toggle shift keys. The keyboard routine also buffers up to the last 15 keystrokes in a circular buffer, allowing you to type faster than the program can accept keystrokes.

Keyboard Data

The keyboard BIOS data area begins at offset 17H in the DATA segment. The two flag variables, KB_FLAG and KB_FLAG_1, are bit significant, and track the current setting of the shift keys. The equates following the definition of these variables shows the various bit assignments. For example, bit 3 of KB_FLAG follows the ALTernate shift key. If it's depressed, the bit is "1." If the ALT key is not depressed, the bit is "0." The bits of KB_FLAG define the current state of all the keyboard shift keys, both normal and toggle. The toggle shift keys use the bits of KB_FLAG_1. These keys change the state of the keyboard each time they are pressed. For example, the CAPS LOCK key toggles from capitals to normal, or vice versa, each time the key is pressed.

BIOS uses the bits in flag 1 to keep track of whether the CAPS LOCK key (and the other toggle shifts) is currently depressed. BIOS must do this because all of the keys on the keyboard are typamatic. If BIOS toggled the CAPS_STATE each time a "make" scan code arrived for the CAPS LOCK key, the typamatic action of the key would make it impossible for the keyboard operator to figure out which state the keyboard was in. The BIOS toggles the CAPS_STATE bit when the first make scan code arrives. BIOS ignores any other make scan codes until it receives the break code for the CAPS LOCK key, which indicates that the key was released.

BIOS uses the ALT_INPUT variable for the special character entry in alternate shift. When the alternate shift key is depressed, you can enter a decimal value with the numeric keypad. The keyboard routine returns the ASCII character corresponding to that decimal value when you release the ALT shift key. This technique allows an operator to enter any of the character codes for the IBM Personal Computer, even those that aren't available on the keyboard. For example, depress ALT, type "1," "1," "1" on the numeric keypad, and then release ALT. The character "o" appears. This character has decimal value 111 in the ASCII code set.

The ALT_INPUT variable holds the current ASCII value typed in during ALT shift. When a number is typed at the numeric keypad, and the keyboard state indicates ALT shift, BIOS multiplies the current value of ALT_INPUT by 10, and adds the new value to it. When the ALT shift key is released, the value of ALT_INPUT becomes a character output. ALT_INPUT is normally set to zero, and BIOS does not treat zero as a valid ALT keypad input. This allows the operator to depress and release the ALT shift key for use with other keys (as in the BASIC supershift keys, where ALT-A produces the character string AUTO), without entering the ASCII code of 0 when the ALT key is released.

The remaining keyboard variables form the keyboard buffer. As characters are typed at the keyboard, an interrupt occurs. The BIOS routine KB_INT accepts the keyboard interrupt, reads the scan code from port 60H, and determines the ASCII value of the keystroke. BIOS stores this value in the keyboard buffer, KB_BUFFER. This buffer has a total of 16 words—each keystroke is stored as a word value. The first byte is the ASCII value of the keystroke, the second byte is the scan code, or extended scan code of the keystroke. Using the extended scan code allows keystrokes with non-ASCII values to be given to the application.

There are two pointers for the buffer. The BUFFER_HEAD variable contains the offset in the DATA segment of the first keystroke in the buffer, the one typed longest ago. The BUFFER_TAIL points at the most recently entered keystroke. If the pointers have the same value, the buffer is empty.

When the BIOS interrupt handler gets a valid keystroke, it places the keystroke into the buffer. If the buffer is not full, the keyboard interrupt handler places the character at the location pointed to by the BUFFER_TAIL variable. It increments BUFFER_TAIL by two to point to the next location in the buffer. If incrementing the tail pointer takes it past the end of the buffer, the pointer is moved to the beginning of the buffer. This means that the keyboard buffer "wraps around." After the sixteenth keystroke, the next character goes at the first position in the buffer. This arrangement is also known as a circular buffer, since the positions in the buffer are treated as if they were arranged in a circle rather than as linear positions.

The BIOS keyboard routine at INT 16H has three functions. One operation removes a character from the buffer. The BUFFER_HEAD pointer locates the first character in the buffer. If the buffer is not empty (indicated by head = tail), BIOS removes the word at BUFFER_HEAD and increments the head pointer by two. Here again, if the pointer exceeds BUFFER_END, it is moved back to the beginning of the buffer. The subroutine K4 in the keyboard BIOS performs the pointer increment and wrap around when necessary.

Another keyboard function returns the current status of the keyboard buffer. This tells the calling program if there is a character in the buffer or not. A program can use this information to avoid waiting for a keystroke if there is another operation to perform in the meantime. You might use such a status call in a program to determine when to exit a loop. On each pass through the loop you can test to see if a character has been entered at the keyboard. If not, the loop continues. If a character has been entered, the loop exits. If the looping program used the BIOS function that reads the keyboard instead, the loop would never execute.

Figure 9.3 shows an assembly routine that adds one to a four-byte integer each time through the loop. When the operator presses the space key, the routine exits. This routine uses two of the keyboard BIOS functions. When AH is set to 1, BIOS returns the status of the keyboard buffer. If the zero flag is set, there is no character available. If a character is available, the routine must also read that character. Otherwise, that character remains in the buffer until the next program (or the same program, later in execution) asks for a character. This example takes the character from the buffer using the BIOS function with AH set to zero. BIOS returns the charcter in AL, and the routine compares the character value with a space. This example shows how you can test for certain character every pass through a loop.

Inside the Keyboard BIOS

We aren't going to do a line-by-line analysis of the keyboard BIOS. There are, however, several sections of the code that are interesting. Some of these we mentioned earlier, such as the K4 routine to increment the buffer pointer.

The KB_INT routine uses several tables of keystroke values. If you go through the code you'll see these tables used in several ways. The tables that have

```
The IBM Personal Computer MACRO Assembler 01-01-83          PAGE     1-1
Figure 9.3   Keyboard Status

1                                          PAGE    ,132
2                                          TITLE   Figure 9.3   Keyboard Status
3       0000                       STACK   SEGMENT STACK
4       0000    40 [                       DW      64 DUP(?)
5                       ????
6                               ]
7
8       0080                       STACK   ENDS
9       0000                       CODE    SEGMENT
10                                          ASSUME  CS:CODE
11      0000  0000               LITTLE  DW      0
12      0002  0000               BIG     DW      0
13      0004                     COUNT   PROC    FAR
14      0004  1E                         PUSH    DS
15      0005  2B C0                      SUB     AX,AX           ; Set return address
16      0007  50                         PUSH    AX
17      0008                     ADD_ONE:
18      0008  2E: FF 06 0000 R            INC     LITTLE
19      000D  75 05                       JNZ     STILL_LOW
20      000F  2E: FF 06 0002 R            INC     BIG
21      0014                     STILL_LOW:
22      0014  B4 01                       MOV     AH,1            ; Keyboard status routine
23      0016  CD 16                       INT     16H
24      0018  74 EE                       JZ      ADD_ONE         ; No character available
25      001A  B4 00                       MOV     AH,0
26      001C  CD 16                       INT     16H             ; Read the character
27      001E  3C 20                       CMP     AL,' '          ; Is it a space
28      0020  75 E6                       JNZ     ADD_ONE
29      0022  CB                          RET                     ; All done
30      0023                     COUNT   ENDP
31      0023                     CODE    ENDS
32                                          END     COUNT
```

Figure 9.3   Keyboard Status

scan code values are used for pattern matching. BIOS compares the scan code from the keyboard against the values in the table. The REPNE SCASB instruction, such as used just after label K16, lets BIOS look through the table for a match with one of the shift keys. When BIOS finds a match in the scan code table, it uses the offset in the table to get the bit mask value used in the KB_FLAG variable. Since all the shift keys are represented as bits in the flag variables, a single routine, together with the tables, can control all of the shift keys.

BIOS uses other tables to convert the scan codes into ASCII codes. Once it determines the current shift state, BIOS points the BX register to the correct ASCII table. The routine converts the keyboard scan code to the correct origin value for that particular table (by subtracting the starting value in the table). The XLAT instruction gives the correct ASCII code for that scan code. This method is used at label K63, where BIOS generates the pseudo-scan codes for the numeric keypad in the CONTROL shift state.

The subroutine ERROR_BEEP is an example of speaker control that we explored in the preceding chapter. BIOS sounds this alarm whenever the operator enters a character and the keyboard buffer is full. Since this beep occurs when the system is handling the keyboard interrupt, it would be unwise to change the value of the timer channel driving the speaker. For that reason, the keyboard BIOS uses the direct control of the speaker. If any tone is being generated, that tone is cut off and the buffer overflow beep occurs. If you listen carefully to the overflow beep, you'll notice that it "warbles" slightly. The timer interrupt, occurring 18 times a second, interrupts the timing loop and consequently modifies the output tone. As suggested in the preceding chapter, you can explore the consequences of using several timing loops on the output of the speaker. Here's an inadvertent example.

CASSETTE

The cassette BIOS is an example of controlling a serial device with timing loops. However, because of the timing differences in the instructions, cassette BIOS uses the 8253 timer/counter for all critical timing sections. We'll look at two of the timing routines here, READ_HALF_BIT and WRITE_BIT.

The Technical Reference Manual contains a complete description of the encoding method for data stored on the cassette tape. The WRITE_BIT routine writes out one data bit cell to the tape. The output from channel 2 of the timer/counter connects directly to the cassette output port. So writing a data bit consists of setting the correct frequency in the channel 2 counter and waiting for one complete cycle. The WRITE_BIT routine does this, except in the reverse order. When WRITE_BIT gets control, the previous bit is still in the process of writing. The two wait loops in WRITE_BIT wait for each half-cycle of the previous bit to complete. When the bit is finished, BIOS places the new frequency value in channel 2 of the timer. The WRITE_BIT routine returns to the calling routine while the new frequency starts going to the tape. The cassette routine is fast enough (or the bit rate to the cassette is slow enough—it depends on your viewpoint) that the WRITE_BIT routine is called again before the timer completes the first half-cycle of the bit.

The READ_HALF_BIT routine does the opposite job. This routine waits until the cassette input bit (bit 4 of port 62H) changes state. Each change of that bit corresponds to half of a bit cell. Cassette BIOS subtracts the current timer value from the timer value at the previous bit change. This value represents the amount of time it took the cassette input to go from one state to the other. Adding the two half-bit transitions produces the total length of the cycle for this bit. Since the cycle times are different for ones and zeros, the READ_BYTE routine can determine the value of the current bit. It puts together 8 of these bits to form a single byte.

The READ_HALF_BIT routine illustrates the use of timer channel 0 for timing purposes. BIOS freezes the timer count and then reads it into the AX register. Using a count value of 0 in the timer 0 counter allows it to subtract any two timer values without regard to which is larger or smaller. The correct difference appears in either case.

The cassette BIOS routine has four functions available. Two of these are block I/O operations—read a block or write a block. For tape efficiency, data are stored on the cassette in blocks of 256 bytes each. BIOS checks these blocks for errors using a cyclic redundancy check (CRC). The CRC error checking detects nearly all errors that can occur with the tape. This allows the IBM Personal Computer to use the cassette as a storage medium with a fair degree of confidence that the data are correct when they are read back in. BIOS also places the data in blocks because of the inefficiencies of the tape mechanism when writing any size block of data. The routine must delay for a period of time to ensure that the cassette motor is on and running at the correct speed. The routine must also write synchronization patterns on the tape to ensure that the processor can get back in synch with the data when they are read. Finally, BIOS writes the CRC word and a trailer following the block. All of this overhead goes along with any block of data, whether it's one byte or 10,000 bytes. IBM chose a block size of 256 as a compromise between block overhead and tape usage.

The other two cassette BIOS functions are simple bit controls. These routines turn the cassette motor on or off. If you are thinking of developing a simple attachment for the IBM Personal Computer, the cassette port offers an attractive method to attach it. Through the cassette connector at the back of the system unit you can connect to a serial input and a serial output line. There is also a relay control that lets you control a low-voltage, low-current motor. There is one thing to beware of. The cassette output bit connects directly to the cassette input bit when the motor relay is not turned on. This connection allows the IBM diagnostic routines to test the cassette input and output circuits without writing and reading data on the cassette itself. In order to use the serial input and output separately, you must turn the motor on—even if there isn't one.

DISKETTE

The diskette BIOS routine provides block-level I/O operations for the diskette adapter. The BIOS interface allows the calling program to specify a track and sector address for a diskette read or write operation. The BIOS code controls the adapter and drive for the operation, and moves the data to or from the user-specified buffer. Following the operation, BIOS summarizes the results of the operation and presents them as part of the output parameters of diskette BIOS. The calling program doesn't have to handle the different functions of the diskette controller and worry about the timings.

Diskette Data Areas

The diskette BIOS data area begins at offset 3EH in the BIOS DATA segment. The first four bytes of the data area preserve status information about the diskette drives from operation to operation. The seven-byte buffer named NEC_STATUS holds the status information returned by the NEC diskette controller following a diskette read or write. As you can see from the diskette control code, this buffer area allows the BIOS to decode any error conditions into a simplified set of error codes. BIOS places these error codes in the DISKETTE_STATUS byte, and also returns that code to the calling program in the AH register following the diskette operation. The equates following DISKETTE_STATUS summarize the error codes that a calling program can see.

The NEC diskette controller knows the position of the read/write head in each of the four diskette drives that it can handle. However, the controller must be in synchronization with those drives before it can accurately track the current position of the heads. So, when power is first turned on, or following a reset of the diskette controller, the NEC controller doesn't know where the drive heads are located. The SEEK_STATUS byte uses the 4 low-order bits, one for each drive, to determine whether the controller knows the current location of the head for that drive. The diskette BIOS resets that byte to zeros when it does a reset to the controller. For every diskette operation, BIOS tests the seek byte before the operation. If the bit corresponding to the drive being used in this operation is zero, BIOS sends a recalibrate command to the drive before the seek command. The recalibration step drives the read/write head to track 0, and the controller and the drive are now in agreement for the head location. All further seek operations with the drive can proceed without a recalibration action.

The recalibrate operation also performs a valuable error correction function in normal operation. The recommended action following any type of diskette error is to reset the controller. This ensures that the error-causing condition is cleared in the controller. This also forces the SEEK_STATUS byte to zero. So before the application program retries the operation (a failing operation should be retried at least three times, since most diskette errors are soft errors—they don't repeat)

BIOS recalibrates the drive. This automatically handles the diskette error caused by a failed seek operation, such as the drive not stepping to the correct track. Recalibrating and reseeking to that track clears the error normally.

The MOTOR_STATUS and MOTOR_COUNT bytes control the running of the diskette motors. The diskette adapter has a control register that lets you select which diskette motor is running at any time. That control register is write only, so the MOTOR_STATUS byte is a memory image of that data. Before a write operation you must let the diskette motor come up to the correct speed, by waiting for some period of time, about half a second. If the motor is already running, there is no need to wait. Reading the particular bit in this status value allows BIOS to determine whether the wait is required.

Similarly, it is advantageous to let the motor keep running following the operation. This is a bet that the diskette will be accessed again in a short time. The diskette wear is traded against the gain in access time for the next diskette operation. But since BIOS doesn't want to let the diskette run forever, the value in MOTOR_COUNT is the count-down value. Each timer tick decrements this count value. When the value reaches zero, all of the diskette motors are turned off. Using the default timing parameter, this allows the diskette motor to run for about 2 seconds following the operation.

As you look through the diskette BIOS code, you'll also see that the MOTOR_COUNT value is set to 255 in one of the first steps. This ensures that the timer tick doesn't turn the diskette motor off in the middle of a diskette operation. The final value, representing two seconds, is stored in the count byte as the BIOS code returns to the calling routine.

Figure 9.4 summarizes the diskette BIOS commands. The reset command initializes the controller with the drive parameters such as step rate and DMA mode. The reset command also does a hardware reset to the controller. IBM recommends this action following any diskette error. It's necessary because some of the errors (particularly the time-out error that happens if there's no diskette in the drive) really confuse the controller. After those errors, the only way you can get the controller back in operation is to reset it.

Read and Write Commands

The read and write commands use the 8088 registers as the input parameters to specify the track, sector, head, and diskette drive where the operation will take place. The calling program locates a buffer with the ES:BX register pair, and the

AH	Function
0	Reset the diskette adapter
1	Read status of last operation
2	Read from diskette to memory
3	Write from memory to diskette
4	Verify the diskette
5	Format a diskette track

Figure 9.4 Diskette BIOS Functions

diskette BIOS sets up the DMA operation to use that buffer. The subroutine DMA_SETUP performs the address calculation. This routine calculates the total number of bytes to transfer based on the input parameter giving the number of sectors, and the table parameter that tells the sector size. The routine sends the count value and the calculated address to the DMA controller. Notice that the routine determines if the buffer crosses a 64K-address boundary. Since the 4-bit page register doesn't increment if the DMA address register goes past 0FFFFH, the data transfer will be incorrect if the buffer crosses a boundary. This routine sets an error condition that won't let the diskette operation continue if it would be in error.

Verify Command

The verify operation is identical to the read operation, except that the data are thrown away rather than stored in memory. There is a special command for the DMA called verify, in which the DMA controller responds to the requests from the diskette controller and provides the correct bus cycles. But the DMA controller doesn't do the other half of the DMA cycle that writes the data into memory. You can use the verify command to ensure that data were written correctly on the diskette. DOS uses the verify operation as part of the FORMAT command. Verify tests for any bad spots on the diskette. When verify identifies these bad areas, DOS can set them aside in the diskette directory. This allows the system to use an imperfect diskette, rather than discarding it.

The verify command, although it can determine if there is an error in the data on the diskette, doesn't guarantee that the data were written to the diskette. Suppose that there is a problem with the diskette write circuitry. The error is such that it doesn't cause an error during the write operation, but no data get written on the diskette. If you verify the data area, the verify command reads the previous data (that you were expecting to modify) with no error, and you'll think that everything went OK. If your data absolutely, positively must be on the diskette, you should read the data back into a different buffer after writing, and then compare the two buffers. This guarantees that the data were written correctly.

Format Command

The format command initializes a brand new diskette. When you format the diskette, you are writing the sector identification markers onto the diskette. The controller uses these ID fields during read and write operations to locate the sector(s). During a read operation, for example, the BIOS sends four bytes of sector identification to the diskette controller. These four bytes normally correspond to the track number, head number, sector number, and sector length, known as Cylinder-Head-Record-Number (CHRN). The controller uses the CHRN value as a match against the values written on the diskette in the sector identification fields during the format operation.

This means that the controller doesn't care what values are actually in the CHRN field on the diskette. Sectors don't have to be numbered one through eight on each track. As long as the controller finds a sector matching the CHRN values it was given, it reads that sector. The controller places the CHRN values on the diskette during the format operation. You have the opportunity to write any values you choose as CHRN values. The data buffer for the format command contains the CHRN bytes for every sector that it writes on the diskette. Normally, this means that the data buffer contains values something like

DB	10,0,1,2,10,0,2,2
DB	10,0,3,2,10,0,4,2

. . .

for track 10 on side 0 of the diskette. This is the data field that the DOS FORMAT command uses, for example. Figure 9.5 is a program that formats a single-sided diskette with the normal values. You shouldn't substitute this program for the

```
The IBM Personal Computer MACRO Assembler 01-01-83          PAGE    1-1
Figure 9.5  Diskette Format


 1                                           PAGE    ,132
 2                                           TITLE   Figure 9.5  Diskette Format
 3       0000                         STACK   SEGMENT STACK
 4       0000      40 [                       DW      64 DUP(?)
 5                       ????
 6                              ]
 7
 8       0080                         STACK   ENDS
 9
10       0000                         CODE    SEGMENT
11                                            ASSUME  CS:CODE,ES:CODE
12       0000   00 00 01 02 00 00     ID_BUFFER DB    0,0,1,2,0,0,2,2
13              02 02
14       0008   00 00 03 02 00 00               DB    0,0,3,2,0,0,4,2
15              04 02
16       0010   00 00 05 02 00 00               DB    0,0,5,2,0,0,6,2
17              06 02
18       0018   00 00 07 02 00 00               DB    0,0,7,2,0,0,8,2
19              08 02
20
21       0020                         FORMAT  PROC    FAR
22       0020   1E                            PUSH    DS
23       0021   2B C0                         SUB     AX,AX
24       0023   50                            PUSH    AX              ; Set return address
25       0024   2E: 8D 1E 0000 R              LEA     BX,ID_BUFFER    ; Set buffer address
26       0029   0E                            PUSH    CS              ;  in ES:BX
27       002A   07                            POP     ES
28       002B   B9 0001                       MOV     CX,1            ; Track 0, sector 1
29       002E   BA 0000                       MOV     DX,0            ; Drive 0, head 0
30       0031                         TRACK_LOOP:
31       0031   2E: 8D 3E 0000 R              LEA     DI,ID_BUFFER    ; Need to reset C value in ID_BUFFER
32       0036   B0 08                         MOV     AL,8
33       0038                         ID_SETUP:
34       0038   26: 88 2D                     MOV     ES:[DI],CH      ; Set value for this cylinder
35       003B   83 C7 04                      ADD     DI,4            ; Go to next value in table
36       003E   FE C8                         DEC     AL
37       0040   75 F6                         JNZ     ID_SETUP        ; Loop through ID_BUFFER
38       0042   B8 0501                       MOV     AX,501H         ; Format command
39       0045   CD 13                         INT     13H
40       0047   FE C5                         INC     CH              ; Move to next cylinder   *
41       0049   80 FD 28                      CMP     CH,40           ; Are we done yet?
42       004C   75 E3                         JNE     TRACK_LOOP      ; Move on to next track
43       004E   CB                            RET                     ; Return to DOS
44       004F                         FORMAT  ENDP
45       004F                         CODE    ENDS
46                                            END     FORMAT
```

Figure 9.5 Diskette Format

DOS FORMAT program, since DOS also verifies the diskette and writes the directory and File Allocation Table on the diskette. Another problem you might notice is that the example starts immediately formatting the diskette in drive A:. You'd better be ready for that if you run this program. But this example does show the method of using diskette BIOS.

You can use the format command to your advantage if you want to copy protect a diskette. Copy protection means that the diskette has been encoded in a fashion that makes it difficult to copy. Since the DOS DISKCOPY utility assumes that the diskette sector IDs were written in the normal fashion, the DISKCOPY routine doesn't copy any diskette with a strange sector value. By writing a diskette with a sector ID different from the norm, you can copy protect the diskette.

As an example, let's copy-protect a diskette by writing a strange sector value on track 10. The example above shows the normal sector values. Instead, if the data buffer contains

```
DB      10,0,10,2,10,0,2,2
DB      10,0,3,2,10,0,4,2
. . .
```

track 10 won't have a sector 1. Instead, it has a sector 10, which you don't normally find on a DOS diskette. This DISKCOPY program will not copy track 10 correctly. If our program tests (with the verify command) for a track 10 sector 10 on the diskette, a successful result means that the diskette is the original, not an attempted copy.

This copy protection scheme is not foolproof. A knowledgeable user (and even some copy programs) can figure out this protection scheme and circumvent it. You also don't have a free hand in modifying the sector IDs. The BIOS code uses the track value to determine the seek address, so the cylinder value must match the cylinder of the sector. The value in the head byte determines an electronic switch setting that selects the correct head, so that value must be correct. The length field comes from the parameter table and isn't a register input parameter, so it's harder to change. Also, both BIOS and the controller use that value to determine the length of the sector, so you can't change it without some thought. This leaves only the sector value. Before you begin to change them, remember that if you still intend for this diskette to be a DOS diskette, DOS will try to use the sector that you've replaced with your strange one unless you modify the diskette tables to reserve that sector. If you want to do multiple sector reads (which BIOS allows), the sectors must be numbered consecutively, but not necessarily starting at one.

In summary, the format command gives you some measure of diskette copy protection. No truly foolproof method has yet been found. A good selection of encryption techniques may help you keep the honest people honest.

VIDEO

The video BIOS controls the operation of the two display adapters available for the IBM Personal Computer. We've saved this one for last because it's the biggest and most complicated of the BIOS routines.

Video Data Areas

The section of the ROM BIOS DATA area entitled VIDEO DISPLAY DATA AREA, starting at offset 49H, contains the variables used by the Video BIOS routines. All of these data locations hold values that are currently in effect with the display adapter. Many of these values are kept in write-only registers on the display adapters. BIOS needs to know the current settings of these variables, such as CRT_MODE_SET and CRT_PALLETTE, when it must modify the registers. Unlike the output data port on the system planar board (port 61H), BIOS can't read these registers before modifying and rewriting them. This means that BIOS must maintain a memory image of the register.

All of the data variables have descriptive comments that should make sense if you work your way through the BIOS code as well as the data area. The CURSOR_POSN array deserves some comment. Since the Color/Graphics adapter can support more than one display page when used in the text mode, there is a storage location for the cursor on each of the display pages. The 6845 CRT Controller handles only the currently displayed cursor. When the BIOS switches from page to page, it remembers the cursor location for each page. Since the color card can have a maximum of eight pages in the 40-column text mode, there are eight locations to store the current cursor position in each of the display pages.

Video BIOS Functions

The routine for the display BIOS contains a large number of functions. Figure 9.6 shows the functions that the BIOS can do.

Because the Video BIOS has so many functions, this BIOS routine uses a jump table to get to the different functions. The table named M1 contains the offset of each entry point in the display BIOS. The first part of the VIDEO_IO routine takes the AH value and converts it into a jump address in the BIOS ROM. The first part of the code does some other things, including examining the EQUIP _FLAG.

IBM wrote the Video BIOS so that it can deal with either display adapter— either the Color/Graphics adapter or the Monochrome adapter. But BIOS also assumes that only one or the other is active at any one time. This means that you can't use the BIOS to write a character on the color display and then immediately use the BIOS to write a character on the monochrome display. BIOS can deal with only one display adapter at a time.

Each time a program calls the Video BIOS, it determines which display

AH	Function
0	Initialize the display adapter
1	Set the cursor size and shape
2	Set the cursor position
3	Read the cursor position
4	Read the light pen position
5	Select active page
6	Scroll up
7	Scroll down
8	Read character
9	Write character and attribute
10	Write character only
11	Select color pallette
12	Write dot
13	Read dot
14	Write teletype

Figure 9.6   Functions of Video BIOS

adapter is in the system. It does this by examining the bits of EQUIP_FLAG—specifically looking at the bits for the current display. If bits 5 and 4 are both "1," the monochrome adapter is in the system. Any other bit setting indicates the color card is in the system. IBM wrote the code this way since they assumed that a system would have only a single display adapter. You must set the planar board switches to indicate the display adapter to be used when the machine is first powered on.

The equipment flag information determines which buffer address BIOS uses. BIOS sets the ES register to 0B000H for the monochrome card, 0B800H for the color card. This allows the remaining BIOS display routines to operate without knowing which adapter is in the system. All references to the display buffer are made relative to the ES register.

You might think that since the EQUIP_FLAG indicates the current display adapter, you could switch from one to the other merely by changing the bits in the flag word. Unfortunately, this isn't so. The I/O address of the 6845 differs for the two adapters, and BIOS stores the base address of the current display adapter in the BIOS data area. BIOS sets the ADDR_6845 variable only when initializing the adapter (the AH = 0 command). Therefore, switching from one display to another also requires a change of this variable.

Even though the CURSOR_POSN variable has eight positions, it can't handle the change from one adapter to another. You must reset the cursor position in the BIOS data area each time you switch to the other display adapter. If you don't, the cursor display on the screen won't match the cursor position in the data area. When a character is written to the screen, it will probably appear in the wrong location.

IBM has published methods of changing from one display to another, either from an assembly language program or from BASIC. These published methods require that you modify the EQUIP_FLAG to indicate the display adapter you wish to use, and then issue a Video interrupt (INT 10H) with AH set to 0. This function initializes the display adapter and ensures that all of the BIOS variables are set correctly. BIOS can now work only with the display adapter just specified. Any data displayed on the other adapter remains visible. Similarly, the display buffer for that adapter continues to display any modifications to the text or graphics images stored in it. So you can modify the contents of the display buffer directly through your program (rather than using BIOS) to update the information on the screen that you just switched from.

Let's go through a simple example. You have an IBM Personal Computer that has both the Color/Graphics adapter and the Monochrome Adapter, and each adapter has a display connected to it. When you first turn the computer on, the system uses the monochrome display. You must set the planar board switches this way, because the Monochrome Display can be damaged if it isn't initialized shortly after powering up. The Guide to Operations recommends that you set the planar board switches to indicate that the monochrome adapter is in the system.

You may now use the Video BIOS with the monochrome display. To change to the color adapter, you can run the program in Figure 9.7. This routine turns on the color adapter in 80-column text mode. The characters displayed on the monochrome display remain there. You may now use the Video BIOS to work with the color/graphics display. However, if you wish to change the contents of the Monochrome Display, you can do so by writing new characters or attributes in the display buffer located at segment 0B000H. Doing this doesn't change the cursor position, but does modify the contents of the display. In this example, if you want to modify the text on both the color and monochrome displays simultaneously, you must write your own routine to handle the monochrome display. Or, you can figure out just what values must be modified in the Video

```
The IBM Personal Computer MACRO Assembler 01-01-83            PAGE    1-1
Figure 9.7  Switch to Color Card

1                                          PAGE    ,132
2                                          TITLE   Figure 9.7  Switch to Color Card
3        0000                      STACK   SEGMENT STACK
4        0000    40 [              DW      64 DUP(?)
5                        ????
6                             ]
7
8        0080                      STACK   ENDS
9        0000                      ABS0    SEGMENT AT 0
10       0410                              ORG     410H
11       0410              EQUIP_FLAG       LABEL   BYTE    ; Only will modify low byte of flag
12       0410                      ABS0    ENDS
13       0000                      CODE    SEGMENT
14                                         ASSUME  CS:CODE,DS:ABS0
15       0000                      COLOR   PROC    FAR
16       0000  1E                          PUSH    DS
17       0001  2B C0                       SUB     AX,AX           ; Return address
18       0003  50                          PUSH    AX
19       0004  8E D8                       MOV     DS,AX           ; Set up ABS0 segment
20       0006  80 26 0410 R CF             AND     EQUIP_FLAG,11001111B   ; Zero out display field
21       000B  80 0E 0410 R 20             OR      EQUIP_FLAG,00100000B   ; Indicate 80 column color card
22       0010  B8 0003                     MOV     AX,3            ; Mode set for 80 column color
23       0013  CD 10                       INT     10H             ; Reset the card
24       0015  CB                          RET                     ; All done
25       0016                      COLOR   ENDP
26       0016                      CODE    ENDS
27                                         END
```

Figure 9.7   Switch to Color Card

BIOS data area that lets BIOS switch back and forth without reinitializing the adapter each time.

Mode Setting

When a program issues an INT 10H with AH set to 0, it invokes the mode-set function of the Video BIOS. If the EQUIP_FLAG says that there is a monochrome card in the system, it doesn't matter what mode value has been set in AL. In that case, BIOS sets the monochrome adapter to mode 7, which is the 80 × 25 text mode supported by the black-and-white card.

For the color/graphics card, the value in AL determines to which of the two text modes and two graphics modes BIOS sets the display adapter. You can see that there are black-and-white modes to go along with the color modes for text modes and the 320 × 200 graphics. These black-and-white modes don't really turn off the color. Those modes turn off the color burst signal that a color TV uses to determine the color of each dot. If you're using a direct drive monitor, the colors will still be there. If you are using a color (or black-and-white) monitor, setting black-and-white modes with the color card turns off the colors and produces a slightly sharper image on the screen. If you're doing an application that doesn't need color, you'll probably produce a better display image by selecting one of the black-and-white modes rather than the corresponding color mode.

When the mode set routine executes, it sets up the adapter and the BIOS data areas to handle the requested operating mode. The mode set routine fills the display buffer with blanks, and positions the cursor in the upper left-hand corner of the screen. You should use the BIOS to do mode sets until you become very familiar with the display hardware. Although there's nothing wrong with changing the values on your own, it's very difficult to debug a program that modifies the display. If you do something wrong, the display becomes inoperative, and there's no way to figure out what went wrong.

The BIOS routines for AH from 1 to 5 serve as a way to manipulate the registers of the 6845. As you recall from the system hardware, the 6845 has a number of registers that control the cursor shape and position, and other screen timings. These routines of the Video BIOS let you modify the screen display without knowing the base address of the 6845. These routines exist primarily as service routines provided by the BIOS.

Scrolling

The scroll routines move all of the text information on the screen either up or down, depending on the routine. The scroll routines provide some measure of windowing—that is, BIOS doesn't scroll the entire contents of the screen. The input parameters to the scroll routine define a rectangle on the screen. This specifies the upper left and lower right corners of the scroll area. BIOS scrolls only the text in this window. The remainder of the screen is left untouched.

We can see the use of scroll windows by examining DOS and BASIC when they use the BIOS to scroll the screen. If we assume an 80-character display, DOS sets the upper left corner of the scroll window as (0,0) and the lower right corner as (24,79). This scrolls the entire screen. However, BASIC uses the twenty-fifth line as a status display area, and uses only the top 24 lines for program display. When BASIC calls BIOS to scroll the screen, it likewise sets the upper left to (0,0), but sets the lower right to (23,79). Since the last line is out of the scroll window, it doesn't move during the scroll operation. The next chapter contains an example of a scroll window called from a BASIC program.

Video BIOS does the scroll operations by moving the characters and attributes in the display buffer. The BIOS scroll routine does not change the start address for the display buffer. That method of scrolling would be much faster, but would not allow the application program to determine where the individual characters go on the screen. The BIOS scrolling technique is adequate for the normal operation of the screen. Notice also that the routine scrolls by more than one line if so desired. Normally, a program moves the screen contents by only a single line. However, the BIOS scroll function allows the calling program to move the screen by multiple lines. In fact, if the scroll amount is set to zero, BIOS blanks the window. This is a quick way of clearing the screen, or some portion of the screen.

When a program is operating in the 80-column mode of the color graphics adapter, it can't read or write the text at any time it wishes. Unless the program picks specific times to modify the buffer, the display shows interference. Since the scroll routine reads and writes large quantities of data, it must be sensitive to the interference problem. If you examine the code for the scroll operation, you can see that BIOS handles the 80 × 25 color card mode (CRT_MODE set to either 2 or 3) as a special case. For scroll operations, the BIOS routine waits until vertical retrace occurs. This means that the adapter hardware has written the entire contents of the buffer to the display, and the adapter is about to start again at the top of the screen. (The adapter hardware goes through this process of refreshing the screen 60 times every second.) At vertical retrace, BIOS turns off the display and does the scroll. When the scroll routine has moved all the characters, it turns the display back on. This causes a quick "blink" of the display. If you look closely at the display during a scroll, you can see that the top six lines of the display are somewhat dimmer than the rest. This occurs because it takes the scroll operation slightly longer than one refresh interval to scroll the screen. So the top six lines are turned off for a total of two refresh intervals, while the remainder of the screen is off for only one refresh interval. The alternative of allowing interference on the screen is so unsightly that this method is preferable. You may want to write your own programs to test the different methods.

There is another section of the scroll routine that comes into play when the screen is in the graphics mode. Although this is a valuable feature of the ROM

BIOS, we won't discuss it now. We'll defer the discussion of this feature until we've discussed reading and writing characters on the screen.

Character Read and Write

The Video BIOS routines for AH between 8 and 10 handle characters on the display. These three routines all work with the current cursor location. To write a character to a specific position on the screen, the program must first set the cursor position using the Video BIOS with AH equal 2. The BIOS does not automatically advance the cursor after it writes the character. If the program wants to write more than one character, it must advance the cursor to the next character position before writing. The same is true for reading characters from the display. Since all character operations are at the current cursor position, the program using Video BIOS doesn't have to determine where the character belongs in the display buffer. The read and write character routines determine just where the character is located in the buffer. The calling program only has to know the row and column position of the character.

There are two forms of the character write routine. One routine requires the program to specify both the character and the attribute (e.g., blinking, highlight, colors, etc.) to be displayed at the current cursor position. The other character write routine writes only the character and does not modify the attribute at that location. These different forms of the write routine exist to allow the calling program to accept the current attribute at the character location, without having to know just what it is. The character read function returns both the character and the attribute at the cursor location. There's no need for two separate functions here. The information is available if you wish to use it.

Because of the interference problem with the color/graphics card, the character read and write routines have the horizontal retrace test in them. This test is required to ensure that "snow" doesn't appear on the screen during the processor operation. BIOS does this test every time that it writes characters to the screen, no matter what the display mode is. BIOS even does this test when the monochrome adapter is in use. The maximum waiting time for the horizontal retrace signal is about 63 microseconds, or 63 millionths of a second. This wait is minimal in the process of displaying a character on the screen. IBM didn't have the additional ROM space necessary to put in the instructions to test for the special cases. So the BIOS always tests for the noninterference signal before reading or writing.

Text in Graphics Modes

One of the significant features of the IBM ROM BIOS is the ability to display text on the screen even though the color/graphics adapter is in one of the graphics modes. The BIOS does this with the character shape table at offset 0FA6EH. This table has the character shapes for the first 128 characters. If a user so desires, the program can point interrupt vector 01FH at a character shape table for the second 128 characters.

As the BIOS listing indicates, when the color card is in a graphics mode, the character write routine branches to a special section called GRAPHICS_WRITE. This code takes the character shape from the ROM table or the user-supplied table and places dots in the appropriate positions of the APA display. There are several interesting things in this routine. In the medium-resolution graphics mode, BIOS expands the 8-bit-wide character shape to 16 bits wide. This is because there are two bits per pixel in the 320×200 graphics mode. The subroutine S21 (EXPAND_BYTE) takes the row of the character shape in AL and expands it into a full word value in AX for the return.

The character write routine must also handle the even and odd field addressing of the color/graphics card. In the GRAPHICS_WRITE routine BIOS writes the different rows of the character shape into bytes located 2000H apart. This is most apparent in the high-resolution character write routine. In this mode, BIOS can store the character shape directly into the display buffer. But instead of a REP MOVSB instruction to move the eight bytes, there is a loop at label S4 that handles the even and odd fields. First BIOS writes the even field using an STOSB instruction. Then BIOS writes the odd field with a MOV instruction using an address of [DI + 2000H − 1].

Another feature of the character write routines is the ability to write characters to the screen using the exclusive-or function. This method is invaluable for writing characters on a graphics display that you'll want to remove later. When BIOS writes a character on the display with the XOR bit on, BIOS takes the exclusive-or of the current contents of the display buffer with the character shape. Normally, this displays the character in a readable fashion, but the actual appearance of the character depends on the background into which it is written. However, when BIOS writes the character back into the same location, once again using the XOR function, the character disappears, and the screen returns to its original display. This method is preferable to writing the character, and then erasing it by writing blanks. Writing blanks does not restore the display to its value before the characters were written. You can use this write and erase later feature quite effectively in instances where you want to display temporarily some text on the display.

The character read routine also works when the color card is in an APA mode. The BIOS code extracts the character shape from the display buffer, and then compares that shape to the shapes in the character tables. When it finds a match, it reports the character read at that location as the one that it matched. This routine works only on an exact match, so if another portion of the graphics figure has invaded the character box for that character, the BIOS read routine won't figure it out. But even so, this routine gives the programmer the capability of treating the APA modes identically with the text modes. As long as the program works at the BIOS level, it can handle text independently of the display mode.

You recall that the scroll routines also had special code sections to handle the graphics mode cases. If you review that section of BIOS, you can see that BIOS determines the scroll windows within the graphics display, and scrolls the characters in a fashion that looks identical to the text mode scroll. Scrolling in the graphics modes is somewhat slower than scrolling in text mode, primarily because the routine must move all 16,000 bytes of the display buffer, rather than 2000 or 4000 bytes necessary in the text modes. This multiplies the scroll time by 4 to 8, and it is noticeably slower.

The ability of BIOS to handle characters while the display is in a graphics mode gives you a great deal of flexibility. It is no problem to draw a graph or picture and then use the characters to label portions of the picture. Similarly, you can devote a portion of the screen to a graphics picture, and another window for the text. You can write normal text into this window using the BIOS character routines. You can scroll the text in that window with the BIOS routines. In other applications, you can write characters to the screen without caring about the current mode of the display. BIOS determines which mode the display is in, and writes the characters correctly.

Graphics

The Video BIOS has several functions to help you with graphics on the IBM Personal Computer. By setting AH to 11, a program can make the color selection for the graphics mode. This routine is structured so that it resembles a true palette rather than the prearranged palettes of the color/graphics card. If the 320×200 APA mode had a true palette, there would be a mapping from the four colors possible for each pixel to the four colors that the program wanted to use. The background color in the medium-resolution mode does that now. You can choose any color to be color 0, the background color. The interface for this routine was designed to allow a true palette color definition if IBM ever modifies the hardware to allow it.

To achieve that goal, you identify the pixel value in the BH register. The BL register identifies the color that the adapter displays for that pixel value. For example, when BH is 0, BL contains the color value for the background color. This BIOS routine only handles BH equal to 0 or 1, since you can choose only the background color, and one of two prearranged palettes. The BIOS prologue identifies the values for each of the palettes. Notice that you can also specify the border color for the text modes using this BIOS function.

The other two graphics routines allow you to either read or write a specific pixel on the graphics screen. For simple operations, this BIOS function allows you to specify row and column locations without determining the mapping into the display buffer. However, for drawing large pictures, or doing any other kind of graphics operation, these functions are very time consuming. The program must call the BIOS routine once for every dot on the screen. For the high-resolution mode, 640×200, the program would have to call the BIOS 128,000 times to set each dot correctly. Even though the BIOS routine executes fairly rapidly, it must calculate the display address each time from the row and column information. This action requires a multiply and several additions, and consequently takes some time. Generally, a program writes a graphics figure using a starting dot location and offsets from that dot position. This means that the program calculates the first dot position using the buffer mapping algorithm, and positions the remaining dots using some additive modification of the current buffer address.

Write Teletype

The write teletype function of the Video BIOS is for programs that want to use the display in the simplest possible manner. This function treats the display just like a teletype. This BIOS routine handles the cursor positioning and character writing. After BIOS writes the character at the current cursor position, it moves the cursor to the next position. If the cursor moves off the end of the line, BIOS scrolls the display up by one line, and places the cursor at the first position of the bottom line.

Besides being a handy method of writing characters to the screen, the write teletype BIOS routine serves as a good example of using the Video BIOS for character handling. This routine writes characters, positions the cursor, and scrolls the screen when necessary. The routine also responds to several control characters. Backspace moves the cursor back one location, carriage return moves the cursor to the beginning of the line, and line feed moves the cursor to the next line, scrolling the screen if necessary. Finally, the BELL character (ASCII code 7) generates a tone using the speaker. The DOS uses this BIOS function to handle most of its display functions.

CHAPTER

10

Assembly Language Extensions and Subroutines

This chapter explains the method of using assembly language programs in the context of a larger program. The previous examples have been stand-alone assembly programs. No other programming language lets you control the hardware the way assembly language does. However, assembly language may not be the correct choice in many cases. Many times the best choice is a high-level language combined with an assembly language subroutine.

This chapter explores two areas where assembly language programs are used. In the first case, we'll write assembly language programs that extend the ROM BIOS. These routines add new function to the existing hardware. You must load these routines permanently into memory before using them. Then your application invokes these new functions as an extension of the normal BIOS function. We'll do two examples, using two different methods of loading the programs into memory.

The second area is assembly language subroutines for a high-level language. The machine language program does a job that would be difficult or impossible to do from the high-level language. We'll do several examples to illustrate the different techniques that a program can use. The examples deal primarily with additional hardware function, but you can use the concepts for any machine language program.

BIOS EXTENSIONS

For some device driver functions, we want to load the program so that it becomes a permanent extension of the system. Certainly, the ROM BIOS is a good example of this type of program. By placing the device drivers in ROM, IBM made them a permanent part of the system. These routines are available to all the applications that run on the IBM Personal Computer, since the BIOS is always there.

Most of us, however, don't have the luxury of putting our programs in ROM. It just doesn't make sense to spend thousands of dollars to manufacture a single ROM module unless you are planning to market the program widely. There is, however, an alternative that costs much less. There are some types of ROM modules that you can program yourself if you have the right equipment. Several companies sell PROM (Programmable ROM) programmers that let you put your program into a ROM module. The special hardware to program the PROMs costs hundreds of dollars, and the individual PROMs will be $10 to $50.

For some programs, you may need to have this level of code permanence. In fact, the IBM Personal Computer has an empty socket for a ROM module. You may plug a standard 8K-byte ROM or PROM into that socket. This makes your program a permanent part of the machine. We won't discuss any further how to do ROMs or PROMs. Those operations require specialized hardware and are different for every user.

Instead, we'll look at ways you can load a program into the read/write memory in such a way that it becomes a permanent part of the system. Your program stays loaded until the machine is turned off. The advantage here is that your function is not permanently built into the machine. You can modify it without taking the machine apart. If you find a problem in the program, you can modify it without redoing all the ROM steps.

DOS EXIT AND STAY RESIDENT

The first way to write and load a permanent function in a DOS system is the Exit and Stay Resident function of DOS. This function is INT 27H.

The normal DOS exit is INT 20H. Or the program can jump to location 0 of the Program Segment Prefix, as we have done with our EXE programs. This action returns control to DOS. DOS recovers the storage that it had allocated to the program. The next program you load following an INT 20H loads into the same region used by the previous application.

The INT 27H exit to DOS is different. Control returns to DOS just as in INT 20H, but some portion of the program storage is not returned to DOS for later use. The DX register points to just beyond the last location you want to reserve. The DOS reserves this section of storage as part of the DOS. This means that your program becomes another part of DOS. There is no way to remove this program from memory short of rebooting DOS and starting all over.

When you exit to DOS with an INT 27H, the CS register must be the address of the Program Segment Prefix. The most convenient way to do that is to write all programs that use INT 27H as .COM programs. It's very difficult to write an .EXE program that leaves the CS and DX registers set correctly on exit. Since we discussed the creation of a .COM program in Chapter 5, we'll assume that all of our exit but stay resident programs are invoked as .COM programs.

The example we'll use for DOS INT 27H is pretty complicated. Not only does this example show the use of INT 27H, but it also shows the methods of replacing the current ROM BIOS with another version. In this example we'll even play some tricks with the timer to speed up processing.

Figure 10.1 contains the example. This program provides a print buffer. Normally, each time a program prints a character, it calls INT 17H, the ROM BIOS printer driver. This ROM BIOS function sends the character to the printer after checking for errors and waiting for the printer to be ready. Normally, this provides adequate performance. But suppose that you are writing several programs. You want to list the programs on the printer. When you do so, you can't use the system while the printer is in operation. You must wait until the printing is complete before you go on to edit or assemble another section of the program.

```
The IBM Personal Computer MACRO Assembler 01-01-83          PAGE    1-1
Figure 10.1 Print Buffer


1                                      PAGE    ,132
2                                      TITLE   Figure 10.1 Print Buffer
3       0000                  ABS0     SEGMENT AT 0
4       0020                           ORG     4*8H
5       0020  ????????        TIMER_INT DD     ?           ; Hardware interrupt for timer
6       005C                           ORG     4*17H
7       005C  ????????        PRINT_INT DD     ?           ; BIOS Print interrupt
8       0408                           ORG     408H
9       0408  ????            PRINTER_BASE DW  ?           ; Base address for printer adapter
10      040A                  ABS0     ENDS
11      0000                  CODE     SEGMENT
12      0100                           ORG     100H        ; .COM file
13                                     ASSUME  CS:CODE,DS:CODE,ES:CODE
14      0100  EB 09 90                 JMP     START
15
16      0103  ????????        PRINT_VECTOR DD  ?           ; Store original INT 17H
17      0107  ????????        TIMER_VECTOR DD  ?           ; Store original INT 9
18
19      010B                  START:
20      010B  2B C0                    SUB     AX,AX                 ; Establish addressing
21      010D  8E C0                    MOV     ES,AX
22                                     ASSUME  ES:ABS0
23      010F  26: A1 005C R            MOV     AX,WORD PTR PRINT_INT  ; Get original vectors
24      0113  26: 8B 1E 005E R         MOV     BX,WORD PTR PRINT_INT+2
25      0118  26: 8B 0E 0020 R         MOV     CX,WORD PTR TIMER_INT
26      011D  26: 8B 16 0022 R         MOV     DX,WORD PTR TIMER_INT+2
27      0122  A3 0103 R                MOV     WORD PTR PRINT_VECTOR,AX      ; Save in this segment
28      0125  89 1E 0105 R             MOV     WORD PTR PRINT_VECTOR+2,BX
29      0129  89 0E 0107 R             MOV     WORD PTR TIMER_VECTOR,CX
30      012D  89 16 0109 R             MOV     WORD PTR TIMER_VECTOR+2,DX
31
32                            ;----- No interrupts while setting new values
33
34      0131  FA                       CLI
35      0132  26: C7 06 005C R 0162 R  MOV     WORD PTR PRINT_INT,OFFSET PRINT_HANDLER
36      0139  26: 8C 0E 005E R         MOV     WORD PTR PRINT_INT+2,CS
37      013E  26: C7 06 0020 R 0196 R  MOV     WORD PTR TIMER_INT,OFFSET TIMER_HANDLER
38      0145  26: 8C 0E 0022 R         MOV     WORD PTR TIMER_INT+2,CS
```

Figure 10.1 Print Buffer

```
39   014A   B0 36                      MOV     AL,00110110B
40   014C   E6 43                      OUT     43H,AL
41   014E   B0 00                      MOV     AL,0              ; Speed up the timer by 256
42   0150   E6 40                      OUT     40H,AL
43   0152   B0 01                      MOV     AL,1
44   0154   E6 40                      OUT     40H,AL
45   0156   FB                         STI
46   0157   8D 16 28FD R               LEA     DX,BUFFER_END     ; Mark ending address
47   015B   CD 27                      INT     27H               ; Exit and stay resident
48
49   015D   00             TIMER_COUNT  DB     0
50   015E   01ED R         BUFFER_HEAD  DW     BUFFER_START
51   0160   01ED R         BUFFER_TAIL  DW     BUFFER_START
52
53                         ;----- This routine handles INT 17H BIOS calls
54
55   0162                  PRINT_HANDLER PROC  FAR
56                                       ASSUME CS:CODE,DS:NOTHING,ES:NOTHING
57   0162   0A E4                        OR     AH,AH
58   0164   74 05                        JZ     BUFFER_CHARACTER  ; Is this a char print
59   0166   2E: FF 2E 0103 R             JMP    PRINT_VECTOR      ; No, send to ROM
60   016B                  BUFFER_CHARACTER:
61   016B   FB                           STI
62   016C   53                           PUSH   BX
63   016D   51                           PUSH   CX
64   016E   56                           PUSH   SI
65   016F   2B C9                        SUB    CX,CX             ; Time out counter
66   0171                  PRINT_LOOP:
67   0171   2E: 8B 1E 0160 R             MOV    BX,BUFFER_TAIL    ; Get end of buffer
68   0176   8B F3                        MOV    SI,BX
69   0178   E8 01E2 R                    CALL   ADVANCE_POINTER   ; Move the pointer to next
70   017B   2E: 3B 1E 015E R             CMP    BX,BUFFER_HEAD    ; Is there a place in the buffer
71   0180   74 0E                        JE     BUFFER_FULL       ; No, wait until there is
72   0182   2E: 88 04                    MOV    CS:[SI],AL        ; Yes, store in buffer
73   0185   2E: 89 1E 0160 R             MOV    BUFFER_TAIL,BX    ; New end pointer
74   018A   B4 00                        MOV    AH,0              ; Good return code from INT 17H
75   018C                  PRINT_RETURN:
76   018C   5E                           POP    SI
77   018D   59                           POP    CX
78   018E   5B                           POP    BX
79   018F   CF                           IRET
80   0190                  BUFFER_FULL:
81   0190   E2 DF                        LOOP   PRINT_LOOP        ; Try again
82   0192   B4 01                        MOV    AH,1              ; Took too long, mark error
83   0194   EB F6                        JMP    PRINT_RETURN
84   0196                  PRINT_HANDLER ENDP

85
86                         ;----- This routine gets control 4660 times a second
87
88   0196                  TIMER_HANDLER PROC  FAR
89                                       ASSUME CS:CODE,DS:NOTHING,ES:NOTHING
90   0196   50                           PUSH   AX
91   0197   53                           PUSH   BX
92   0198   2E: 8B 1E 015E R             MOV    BX,BUFFER_HEAD
93   019D   2E: 3B 1E 0160 R             CMP    BX,BUFFER_TAIL    ; Anything in buffer
94   01A2   75 14                        JNZ    TEST_READY        ; Yes, move on
95
96                         ;----- This section handles the timer speedup
97
98   01A4                  TIMER_RETURN:
99   01A4   5B                           POP    BX
100  01A5   2E: FE 06 015D R             INC    TIMER_COUNT       ; Increment the frequency divider
101  01AA   75 06                        JNZ    SKIP_NORMAL
102  01AC   58                           POP    AX
103  01AD   2E: FF 2E 0107 R             JMP    TIMER_VECTOR      ;  Go to the ROM timer routine
104  01B2                  SKIP_NORMAL:
105  01B2   B0 20                        MOV    AL,20H            ; This is the 255 out of 256
106  01B4   E6 20                        OUT    20H,AL            ; Send EOI to interrupt controller
107  01B6   58                           POP    AX
108  01B7   CF                           IRET
109
110                         ;----- Character in buffer, try to print it
111
112  01B8                  TEST_READY:
113  01B8   52                           PUSH   DX
114  01B9   1E                           PUSH   DS
115  01BA   2B D2                        SUB    DX,DX
116  01BC   8E DA                        MOV    DS,DX             ; Establish addressing
117                                       ASSUME DS:ABS0
118  01BE   8B 16 0408 R                 MOV    DX,PRINTER_BASE
119  01C2   42                           INC    DX                ; Point to status port
120  01C3   EC                           IN     AL,DX
121  01C4   A8 80                        TEST   AL,80H            ; Test for printer busy
122  01C6   74 16                        JZ     NO_PRINT
123  01C8   4A                           DEC    DX                ; Point to data port
124  01C9   2E: 8A 07                    MOV    AL,CS:[BX]        ; Get the character to print
125  01CC   E8 01E2 R                    CALL   ADVANCE_POINTER
126  01CF   2E: 89 1E 015E R             MOV    BUFFER_HEAD,BX
127  01D4   EE                           OUT    DX,AL             ; Send character
128  01D5   83 C2 02                     ADD    DX,2              ; Control Port
129  01D8   B0 0D                        MOV    AL,0DH
130  01DA   EE                           OUT    DX,AL             ; Strobe to printer
131  01DB   B0 0C                        MOV    AL,0CH
```

Figure 10.1 *Continued*

```
132    01DD  EE                              OUT      DX,AL
133    01DE                        NO_PRINT:
134    01DE  1F                              POP      DS
135    01DF  5A                              POP      DX
136    01E0  EB C2                           JMP      TIMER_RETURN              ; Exit through timer handler
137    01E2                        TIMER_HANDLER  ENDP
138
139    01E2                        ADVANCE_POINTER PROC    NEAR
140    01E2  43                              INC      BX                       ; Bump the pointer
141    01E3  81 FB 28FD R                    CMP      BX,OFFSET BUFFER_END
142    01E7  75 03                           JNE      ADVANCE_RETURN           ; Test for end of buffer
143    01E9  BB 01ED R                       MOV      BX,OFFSET BUFFER_START    ; Wrap around for buffer
144    01EC                        ADVANCE_RETURN:
145    01EC  C3                              RET
146    01ED                        ADVANCE_POINTER ENDP
147
148    01ED                        BUFFER_START    LABEL    BYTE
149    01ED  2710 [                          DB       10000 DUP(?)
150             ??
151                  ]
152
153    28FD                        BUFFER_END      LABEL    BYTE
154    28FD                        CODE    ENDS
155
156                                            END
```

Figure 10.1 *Continued*

This example program can alleviate the problem. Of course, it doesn't come for free. The program sets aside a section of memory as a print buffer. This memory buffer is always allocated to the print buffer. The DOS subtracts this area from your total system memory. For example, if you have a system with 96K bytes of memory, and set aside 10K bytes as a print buffer with this program, you will no longer be able to run the Macro Assembler. The Macro Assembler needs 96K bytes to execute, and with the print buffer in place, there are only 86K bytes left. Before you use this print buffer, make sure that you have enough memory in your system.

The print buffering works something like this. It replaces the normal PRINT command (INT 17H) with a routine that puts the characters in the buffer instead of sending them to the printer. This part of the program is called the print buffering. A separate part of this program, called the printer output, takes the characters from the buffer and sends them to the printer.

Replacing the ROM BIOS INT 17H is the key to this example. Nearly all application programs use this BIOS function to send characters to the printer. This means that all of the normal print operations will send characters to the print buffering routine rather than to the printer. Specifically for this example, we can TYPE the assembly listing file to the printer using the CTL-PRTSCR keystroke to send the displayed characters to the printer.

When we send an assembly listing to the printer, with the print buffering program in place, the characters go into a memory buffer rather than to the printer. The print buffering adds very little time to the listing process. Once the file has been sent to the screen (and into the print buffer) control returns to DOS. You can stop sending characters to the printer by depressing CTL-PRTSCR again. The listing file is now in the memory buffer, and DOS is ready to continue with other tasks, such as editing or assembling.

Now the second part of the program comes into play. This routine takes characters from the memory buffer and sends them to the printer. The timer interrupt drives this routine. At each timer interrupt, the print output routine also gains control. If there is a character in the buffer, and if the printer is ready, this routine outputs the character to the printer. Thus, characters are taken from the buffer and sent to the printer at a rate the printer can handle. Since this print output routine runs in the "background," you can do other tasks, such as editing or assembling, in the foreground.

Let's look at the program in Figure 10.1 and see how the different components fit together. First, it defines the segment ABS0, which contains the interrupt vectors the program deals with. This example replaces both the print (INT 17H) and the timer (INT 8) interrupts. Also note that ABS0 defines the location of PRINTER_BASE. This location contains the base address for printer 0. This example assumes that all of the printing goes to the system printer.

The CODE segment is the section of the program that remains resident. We have set up the program as a .COM file using ORG 100H. This means that you must use the steps outlined in Chapter 5 to create the .COM file from the linker output. The program uses the memory locations PRINT_VECTOR and TIMER _VECTOR to store the original values of those vectors. Although the program replaces those vector values, it needs to know the original vector during the print output section.

The first part of the CODE segment, beginning at START, is the initialization portion of this program. This section reads the current values of the two interrupt vectors. It stores these addresses in the data areas in the CODE segment. The initialization routine replaces the low memory interrupt vectors with the new values that the print buffering and print output programs use. Notice the CLI instruction that disables interrupts before doing this operation. Since the program is changing the timer interrupt, it can't allow a timer tick during this interval. If a timer interrupt occurred when the program had changed only one of the two words of the timer interrupt vector, the processor would most likely start executing in an unknown location. It's better to disable the interrupts than to take a chance on the system branching to some unknown location.

Before the program reenables the interrupts, it modifies the timer count value. Normally, the timer interrupts about 18 times a second. The printer can print at 80 characters a second. If the printer output program sent a single character every timer tick, the maximum print rate would be 18 characters per second. By speeding up the timer, timer ticks occur more frequently. This allows the program to drive the printer at the full 80 characters per second. This example loads the count value of 256 into the timer. This is 256 times smaller than the normal value. The TIMER_HANDLER routine compensates for this speedup.

The initialization routine exits to DOS using INT 27H. Before exiting, the program sets DX to point just beyond the last byte of the entire program. Notice that we have included all of the programs and the print buffer within this area. According to the INT 27H rules, DOS will not disturb any of this area.

This program does waste some storage. The initialization code executes only once. There is no reason why it should remain in storage. We could optimize the program by taking the section of code from START to INT 27H and moving it to after the BUFFER END label. In that case, when the INT 27H is performed, the initialization code would lie outside the protected region. The next program loaded by DOS (for example, the assembler) would overlay the initialization code. Saving about 90 bytes out of more than 10,000 doesn't seem necessary in this example. But the savings are available if you need them.

Next up is the PRINT_HANDLER routine. Whenever a program does an INT 17H to do an operation with the printer, this routine gains control instead of the ROM BIOS. The first three instructions handle the takeover from ROM BIOS. This routine acts only when a character is to be printed, AH = 0. For any other function, the normal ROM BIOS does the job. Accordingly, the program tests for AH equal to zero. If it isn't, the program does an indirect jump using the saved value of the original print vector. This passes control to the ROM BIOS routine, and it handles the requested function. That means we only have to write code to support the changes we have made.

There are two things to note about this way of handling the print operations. First, it really isn't a good idea to pass on all of the printer functions except AH = 0. If a program initializes the printer (AH = 2) while the print buffering is in action, the ROM BIOS takes over and sends a reset command to the printer. That command cancels the current line that the printer is working on. In most cases, this causes the loss of one or more characters in the printed output. If you want to make this program more foolproof, you should consider handling all of the printer functions.

The second thing to note is the use of the saved print interrupt vector. We could have looked at the BIOS listing in the Technical Reference Manual and found the starting location for the print routine. We could have coded that address directly into the program, just as we set up the other absolute addresses. However, this would have tied our programs to that ROM BIOS address. If IBM ever changed the ROM routines in the BIOS, and in so doing modified the print routine address, the program would no longer work. Of course, if you write this program for your own machine, and never buy a new machine or sell your program to others who might, there won't be a problem. But in general, it's best to avoid using an absolute address if there's an alternative. In this example, the initialization routine can easily use the print interrupt vector to determine the ROM location of the BIOS print routine.

The remainder of the PRINT_HANDLER routine stores the character in the print buffer. The program tests to ensure that there's room in the buffer before storing the character. If the buffer is full, it waits until a place opens up. Since the normal BIOS routine waits until the printer is ready to accept a character, this wait should pose no problems. For safety's sake, the CX register counts loops through the busy path. If the code makes 64K loops and the buffer is still full, there's probably a problem. Just like ROM BIOS, the PRINT_HANDLER returns a time out error in that case.

The example also uses an internal subroutine ADVANCE_POINTER in the print routine. This simple routine makes the print buffer a circular buffer. If the pointer moves past the end of the buffer, the subroutine moves it back to the beginning. This routine is identical to the keyboard buffer routine in the ROM BIOS. Only here, the buffer is 10,000 characters rather than 16.

The TIMER_HANDLER routine does the interesting work in this example. The initialization code connected this routine to the hardware timer interrupt, so it gains control for every timer tick. This routine must handle the normal timer functions such as time of day by compensating for the timer speedup, as well as sending characters to the printer.

The timer routine first tests for characters to print. There's no sense trying to send characters to the printer if there aren't any to send. If there are no characters in the buffer, the program falls through to the label TIMER_RETURN. This section of the routine takes care of the timer speedup.

The TIMER_RETURN label marks the area that handles the normal timer functions. This code increments a single byte value, TIMER COUNT, for each timer interrupt. If that byte is not zero, the routine exits from the interrupt after issuing an End Of Interrupt to the interrupt controller. If the byte is zero, the routine exits by jumping indirectly to the saved TIMER_VECTOR. This gives control to the ROM BIOS routine to handle time of day and diskette motor turn off. We don't have to duplicate those operations in our program. We go to the ROM BIOS only once for every 256 times we execute this timer routine. But since we speeded up the timer by a factor of 256, the ROM BIOS routine still gets control 18.2 times a second. This means that the time of day will be kept correctly, and the diskette motor will turn off at the right time. That's why we chose to speed up the timer by 256, even though a factor of 5 would probably still run the printer at its full speed.

We chose to speed up the timer by 256 because it was simple. If performance is a concern, we should have used the factor of 5. That's because each timer interrupt takes at least 10 microseconds to execute, and even longer if the print buffer contains characters. The time spent handling the timer interrupt gets subtracted from the performance of the other task in the system, like the assembler. At this rate of timer interrupt, you may be able to notice a degradation in the foreground performance. For optimum performance, a number smaller than 256 should be used for the timer speedup.

What happens in the timer routine when there are characters to print? The routine reads the status port to determine if the printer is ready to accept a character. The program uses the base address in the BIOS data area so this routine works with either the stand-alone printer adapter or the port in the monochrome display adapter. If the printer is not ready, the program exits through the TIMER_RETURN label, where it handles the timer functions if necessary. This print output routine does not wait for the printer to become ready if it isn't already. We know that the timer interrupt will bring us back very shortly, and we can try again then. Waiting for printer ready here would tie up the entire system. The net effect would be as if there was no print buffering taking place.

If the printer is ready, the program extracts a character from the print buffer and sends it to the printer. Here again the routine doesn't do all that it should. The ROM BIOS routine tests for error conditions each time a character is sent. We should do likewise in this routine. But what happens if there is a problem? If the print output routine detects a print error, how can it tell the program that was printing the characters. In some cases, the program printing the characters has already finished. The best idea may be to look for error conditions each time the timer routine sends a character to the printer. If an error is found, the PRINT_ HANDLER routine should report the error the next time any program prints a character using INT 17H. This may not be ideal, but it could be the best choice.

Before we leave this example, we should note a problem. There are other routines that modify the timer interrupt rate. BASICA, the advanced BASIC, speeds up the timer in a manner very similar to this example. If you invoke BASICA after setting up this buffered print, the TIMER_HANDLER no longer gets interrupts at the rate it thinks it is. Since the TIMER_HANDLER filters the control going to the ROM BIOS, the time of day runs 256 times too slow. BASICA also initializes the printer, which, as we noted before, interferes with the printing. This means that the buffer printing won't work for all applications. But it does illustrate the use of INT 27H to provide a permanent system function. This example also illustrates the method of resetting the BIOS vectors to hook a new function into existing programs.

HIGH-RAM LOAD

The DOS INT 27H is the preferred method for putting a permanent device driver type of function in the system. It's a convenient way to make a routine permanent. The user can include the program as part of the AUTOEXEC.BAT file, so it can be loaded automatically. You might use this automatic load facility if you have a special I/O device on your system. DOS loads the device driver every time you boot the system. You might even like your own version of the buffered print routine so well that you always want it loaded in the system.

However, the DOS exist and stay resident may not always work. IBM offers three operating systems for the Personal Computer: DOS, which we are using in this text; CP/M-86 by Digital Research; and the UCSD p-System by SofTech Microsystems. In addition to these offered by IBM, there are several independent software developers selling operating systems. If you want to create a device driver that works with all these systems, you'll have to use something other than the DOS method.

Suppose that you have a special printer that you want to sell as an attachment to the IBM Personal Computer. Because of the low cost of the printer, it requires more BIOS control than the IBM Printer. You design the printer and attachment and write the BIOS code to make it work. If you use INT 27H, you can sell this device only to people who use DOS with their Personal Computers. You need a device driver loading method that works for all operating systems.

A method that works for more than just DOS is called high-RAM loading. This method takes over the system immediately following the power-on self-test. We can do this by creating our own diskette to boot from. We'll put our program on a special diskette and put it in the diskette drive at power on time. The bootstrap routine in ROM BIOS loads the device routine from that diskette into the upper end of read/write memory, the high addresses. We can then adjust the memory size variable maintained in the BIOS data area. We'll decrease the available memory by the size of the program loaded into high memory. If we then boot the normal operating system we'll be back to normal operation. All of the IBM operating systems use the BIOS memory size to determine the end of memory. Those systems won't touch the program loaded in high memory. As long as your system follows those same rules, you can use the high-RAM load method.

We'll do an example that illustrates this technique. Figure 10.2 is the assembly listing for two routines. The first routine handles the initialization and boot of the device driver. The second routine is the device driver itself. As you'll see, it's more convenient if we work with the program in two distinct parts.

```
The IBM Personal Computer MACRO Assembler 01-01-83          PAGE    1-1
Figure 10.2(a) Boot routine for RAM Disk

1                                      PAGE    ,132
2                                      TITLE   Figure 10.2(a) Boot routine for RAM Disk
3       0000                  NEW_DISK     SEGMENT
4       0000                  DISK_BIOS    LABEL    FAR
5       0003                       ORG     3
6       0003                  OLD_VECTOR    LABEL    WORD
7       0003                  NEW_DISK     ENDS
8
9       0000          SEGMENT AT 0  ABS0     SEGMENT AT 0
10      004C              ORG     13H*4
11      004C                  DISK_VECTOR   LABEL    WORD
12      0410              ORG     410H
13      0410                  EQUIPMENT     LABEL    WORD
14      0413              ORG     413H
15      0413                  MEMORY_SIZE   LABEL    WORD
16
17      = 00A0                DISK_SIZE     EQU      160
18      7C00                  ORG     7C00H                      ; Load point for boot record
19      7C00                  BOOT_RECORD   LABEL    FAR
20      7C00                  ABS0     ENDS
21      0000                  CODE     SEGMENT
22                            ASSUME  CS:CODE,DS:ABS0
23      7C00                       ORG     7C00H
24      7C00  8C C8          MOV     AX,CS
25      7C02  8E D8          MOV     DS,AX
26      7C04  8E C0          MOV     ES,AX
27      7C06  BE 7C00 R      MOV     SI,OFFSET BOOT_RECORD
28      7C09  BF 7A00 R      MOV     DI,OFFSET BOOT_RECORD-200H ; Move everything down in memory
29      7C0C  B9 0200        MOV     CX,512
30      7C0F  F3/ A4         REP     MOVSB                      ; Move it all
31      7C11  E9 7A14 R      JMP     NEXT_LOCATION-200H
32      7C14                  NEXT_LOCATION:
33      7C14  83 06 0410 R 40  ADD   EQUIPMENT,40H              ; Increment number of drives
34      7C19  A1 0413 R      MOV     AX,MEMORY_SIZE
35      7C1C  2D 00A0        SUB     AX,DISK_SIZE
36      7C1F  A3 0413 R      MOV     MEMORY_SIZE,AX             ; Remove disk space from memory
37      7C22  B1 06          MOV     CL,6
38      7C24  D3 E0          SHL     AX,CL                      ; Multiply by 1024/16
39      7C26  8E C0          MOV     ES,AX                      ; Segment value for new disk
40      7C28  B8 0201        MOV     AX,201H                    ; Read sector into this area
41      7C2B  BB 0000        MOV     BX,0
42      7C2E  B9 0002        MOV     CX,2
43      7C31  BA 0000        MOV     DX,0
44      7C34  CD 13          INT     13H                        ; Do the disk read into new area
45      7C36  72 1A          JC      BOOT_ERROR
46                            ASSUME  ES:NEW_DISK
47      7C38  A1 004C R      MOV     AX,DISK_VECTOR
48      7C3B  26: A3 0003 R  MOV     OLD_VECTOR,AX
49      7C3F  A1 004E R      MOV     AX,DISK_VECTOR+2
50      7C42  26: A3 0005 R  MOV     OLD_VECTOR+2,AX            ; Move the current pointer
51      7C46  C7 06 004C R 0000  MOV DISK_VECTOR,0             ;   to NEW DISK
52      7C4C  8C 06 004E R   MOV     DISK_VECTOR+2,ES           ; Move pointer to new BIOS routine
53      7C50  EB 06          JMP     SHORT REBOOT               ; Read in the next diskette
```

Figure 10.2   (a) Boot Routine for RAM Disk; (b) RAM Disk Diver Routine.

```
54   7C52                      BOOT_ERROR:
55   7C52   BE 7A8F  R              MOV     SI,OFFSET ERROR_MSG-200H      ; Print error message
56   7C55   E8 7C7D  R              CALL    PRINT_MSG
57   7C58                      REBOOT:
58   7C58   BE 7A9C  R              MOV     SI,OFFSET BOOT_MSG-200H       ; Print boot real OS message
59   7C5B   E8 7C7D  R              CALL    PRINT_MSG
60   7C5E                      WAIT_BOOT:
61   7C5E   B4 00                   MOV     AH,0
62   7C60   CD 16                   INT     16H                          ; Wait for keyboard input
63   7C62   3C 20                   CMP     AL,' '                       ; Must be space
64   7C64   75 F8                   JNE     WAIT_BOOT
65   7C66   B8 0201                 MOV     AX,201H
66   7C69   BB 7C00                 MOV     BX,7C00H
67   7C6C   B9 0001                 MOV     CX,1
68   7C6F   BA 0000                 MOV     DX,0
69   7C72   8E C2                   MOV     ES,DX                        ; Boot in the real OS
70   7C74   CD 13                   INT     13H
71   7C76   72 DA                   JC      BOOT_ERROR
72   7C78   EA 7C00 ---- R          JMP     BOOT_RECORD
73
74   7C7D                      PRINT_MSG    PROC    NEAR
75   7C7D   2E: 8A 04               MOV     AL,CS:[SI]                   ; Get the char to print
76   7C80   46                      INC     SI
77   7C81   3C 24                   CMP     AL,'$'                       ; End of message marker
78   7C83   75 01                   JNE     OUTPUT
79   7C85   C3                      RET
80   7C86                      OUTPUT:
81   7C86   B4 0E                   MOV     AH,14
82   7C88   BB 0000                 MOV     BX,0
83   7C8B   CD 10                   INT     10H                          ; Video BIOS print routine
84   7C8D   EB EE                   JMP     PRINT_MSG
85   7C8F   42 6F 6F 74 20 65   ERROR_MSG    DB      'Boot error',10,13,'$'
86          72 72 6F 72 0A 0D
87          24
88   7C9C   49 6E 73 65 72 74   BOOT_MSG     DB      'Insert new boot diskette',10,13
89          20 6E 65 77 20 62
90          6F 6F 74 20 64 69
91          73 6B 65 74 74 65
92          0A 0D
93   7CB6   48 69 74 20 73 70                DB      'Hit space bar to continue',10,13,'$'
94          61 63 65 20 62 61
95          72 20 74 6F 20 63
96          6F 6E 74 69 6E 75
97          65 0A 0D 24
98   7CD2                      PRINT_MSG    ENDP
99   7CD2                      CODE    ENDS
100                                   END
```

The IBM Personal Computer MACRO Assembler 01-01-83   PAGE   1-1
Figure 10.2(b) RAM Disk Diver routine

```
1                                        PAGE    ,132
2                                        TITLE   Figure 10.2(b) RAM Disk Diver routine
3    0000                      CODE    SEGMENT
4                                      ASSUME  CS:CODE
5                              ;--------------------------------------------
6                              ;   This code becomes sector 1, track 0 of
7                              ;   the RAM disk.  Any Reads/Writes to drive
8                              ;   2 are directed here
9                              ;--------------------------------------------
10   0000                      DISK    PROC    FAR
11   = 0140                    DISK_SIZE    EQU     320                  ; Size of diskette in sectors
12   0000   EB 05 90               JMP     START_BIOS
13   0003   ????????          ORIGINAL_VECTOR DD      ?
14
15   0007                      START_BIOS:
16   0007   80 FA 02               CMP     DL,2                         ; Drive 2 Only
17   000A   74 05                  JE      L1
18   000C                      OLD_BIOS:
19   000C   2E: FF 2E 0003 R       JMP     ORIGINAL_VECTOR              ; Jump to ROM routine
20   0011                      L1:
21   0011   80 FC 01               CMP     AH,1
22   0014   76 F6                  JBE     OLD_BIOS
23   0016   80 FC 04               CMP     AH,4
24   0019   72 06                  JB      READ_WRITE                   ; Handle read/write only
25   001B                      OK_RETURN:
26   001B   B4 00                  MOV     AH,0                         ; OK return indicator
27   001D   F8                     CLC                                  ; No error indicator
28   001E   CA 0002                RET     2
29   0021                      READ_WRITE:
30   0021   53                     PUSH    BX
31   0022   51                     PUSH    CX
32   0023   52                     PUSH    DX
33   0024   56                     PUSH    SI
34   0025   57                     PUSH    DI
35   0026   1E                     PUSH    DS                           ; Save all registers
36   0027   06                     PUSH    ES
37
38                              ;----- Calculate transfer address
39
```

Figure 10.2 *Continued*

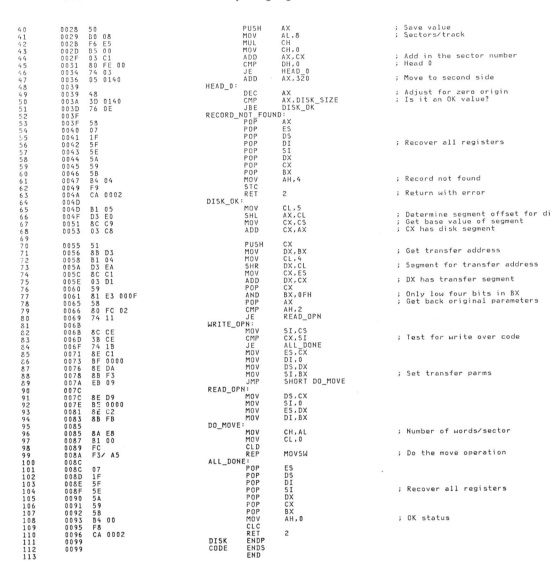

```
40      0028    50                          PUSH    AX                  ; Save value
41      0029    B0 08                       MOV     AL,8                ; Sectors/track
42      002B    F6 E5                       MUL     CH
43      002D    B5 00                       MOV     CH,0
44      002F    03 C1                       ADD     AX,CX               ; Add in the sector number
45      0031    80 FE 00                    CMP     DH,0                ; Head 0
46      0034    74 03                       JE      HEAD_0
47      0036    05 0140                     ADD     AX,320              ; Move to second side
48      0039                        HEAD_0:
49      0039    48                          DEC     AX                  ; Adjust for zero origin
50      003A    3D 0140                     CMP     AX,DISK_SIZE        ; Is it an OK value?
51      003D    76 0E                       JBE     DISK_OK
52      003F                        RECORD_NOT_FOUND:
53      003F    58                          POP     AX
54      0040    07                          POP     ES
55      0041    1F                          POP     DS
56      0042    5F                          POP     DI                  ; Recover all registers
57      0043    5E                          POP     SI
58      0044    5A                          POP     DX
59      0045    59                          POP     CX
60      0046    5B                          POP     BX
61      0047    B4 04                       MOV     AH,4                ; Record not found
62      0049    F9                          STC
63      004A    CA 0002                     RET     2                   ; Return with error
64      004D                        DISK_OK:
65      004D    B1 05                       MOV     CL,5                ; Determine segment offset for di
66      004F    D3 E0                       SHL     AX,CL               ; Get base value of segment
67      0051    8C C9                       MOV     CX,CS
68      0053    03 C8                       ADD     CX,AX               ; CX has disk segment
69
70      0055    51                          PUSH    CX
71      0056    8B D3                       MOV     DX,BX               ; Get transfer address
72      0058    B1 04                       MOV     CL,4
73      005A    D3 EA                       SHR     DX,CL               ; Segment for transfer address
74      005C    8C C1                       MOV     CX,ES
75      005E    03 D1                       ADD     DX,CX               ; DX has transfer segment
76      0060    59                          POP     CX
77      0061    81 E3 000F                  AND     BX,0FH              ; Only low four bits in BX
78      0065    58                          POP     AX                  ; Get back original parameters
79      0066    80 FC 02                    CMP     AH,2
80      0069    74 11                       JE      READ_OPN
81      006B                        WRITE_OPN:
82      006B    8C CE                       MOV     SI,CS
83      006D    3B CE                       CMP     CX,SI               ; Test for write over code
84      006F    74 1B                       JE      ALL_DONE
85      0071    8E C1                       MOV     ES,CX
86      0073    BF 0000                     MOV     DI,0
87      0076    8E DA                       MOV     DS,DX
88      0078    8B F3                       MOV     SI,BX               ; Set transfer parms
89      007A    EB 09                       JMP     SHORT DO_MOVE
90      007C                        READ_OPN:
91      007C    8E D9                       MOV     DS,CX
92      007E    BE 0000                     MOV     SI,0
93      0081    8E C2                       MOV     ES,DX
94      0083    8B FB                       MOV     DI,BX
95      0085                        DO_MOVE:
96      0085    8A E8                       MOV     CH,AL               ; Number of words/sector
97      0087    B1 00                       MOV     CL,0
98      0089    FC                          CLD
99      008A    F3/ A5                      REP     MOVSW               ; Do the move operation
100     008C                        ALL_DONE:
101     008C    07                          POP     ES
102     008D    1F                          POP     DS
103     008E    5F                          POP     DI
104     008F    5E                          POP     SI                  ; Recover all registers
105     0090    5A                          POP     DX
106     0091    59                          POP     CX
107     0092    5B                          POP     BX
108     0093    B4 00                       MOV     AH,0                ; OK status
109     0095    F8                          CLC
110     0096    CA 0002                     RET     2
111     0099                DISK        ENDP
112     0099                CODE        ENDS
113                                     END
```

Figure 10.2 *Continued*

The device driver we'll do in this example is a memory version of a diskette. We'll take 160K bytes of system memory and use it as a diskette rather than as system memory. We chose 160K bytes since it matches the smallest diskette size offered by IBM. Of course, with more memory you can simulate a larger diskette. You can use this RAM disk routine to get outstanding performance from programs that use the diskette extensively. For example, if you put the assembler and an assembly source program on this simulated diskette, the assembly is done in seconds rather than minutes. Some programs may speed up by a factor of 10 or more. The price for this performance is 160K bytes of system memory devoted to diskette simulation. If you have a system with 256K bytes of memory, and use it primarily for editing and assembling, you really need only 96K bytes for the assembler. You can use the other 160K bytes for a RAM disk. Remember that the contents of the RAM disk go away when power is turned off, so be sure to save the contents to a real diskette before quitting.

The first routine in Figure 10.2 is the boot routine. This code resides in sector 1 of track 0 on the boot diskette. We'll explain how to get it there later. When POST completes, it reads the contents of sector 1, track 0 into location 0:7C00H. POST then passes control to the first location in that record. This is the way that the IBM system boots DOS or any operating system into memory. All that we're going to do is boot our own simple system.

The segment NEW_DISK defines a location in the device driver routine, which is the second listing in Figure 10.2. Since the two routines are assembled separately, this segment declaration serves to link the boot routine and the device driver at execution time. Segment ABS0 locates the interrupt vectors that the boot routine replaces. The CODE segment contains the instructions booted in from the diskette. The CODE segment is the only portion of this listing that is placed on the boot diskette.

The first thing the program does is move itself to location 0:7A00H. Later in the initialization process, the routine reboots the system, to load the real operating system. This boot goes to location 0:7C00H. If the initialization routine did not move itself out of the way, it would read the next boot record onto itself during the reboot.

At NEXT_LOCATION, the initialization routine installs the device driver. It modifies the equipment flags to show one more diskette drive than the planar board switches indicated. This fools the real operating system into believing that the RAM disk is part of the hardware. Next, the initialization reduces the MEMORY_SIZE value by the 160K bytes. This is the amount reserved for the simulated diskette. This should keep the operating system from attempting to use the storage allocated to the simulated diskette. The routine also calculates the segment value for this 160K-byte region because it needs to know where to load the device driver. Now that it knows where, the initialization routine reads into the reserved storage the contents of sector 2 of track 0 on the boot diskette. We'll explain how to put the device driver in sector 2 at the same time we place the boot routine into sector 1.

Following the read of the device driver code, the initialization routine modifies the diskette BIOS vector (INT 13H) to point to this new device driver. As in the preceding example, the routine saves the old diskette vector. The new device driver needs that vector to read the real diskettes as opposed to the simulated diskette. Finally, the routine reboots the system. It prompts the user to insert the system diskette, waits for a positive response, and reads in the boot record. (If the routine hadn't moved the program earlier, it would be clobbered right now.) If everything goes well, the routine jumps to the first location of the boot record and lets the real operating system take over.

Before we go further, let's see how to load the boot routine onto the new boot diskette. First, we need a formatted diskette that contains nothing of value. That will become the boot diskette. As the sequence of Figure 10.3 shows, assemble and link the boot routine as normal. Enter the DOS DEBUG program, loading the boot routine. The boot routine loads at offset 7C00H of the code segment set up by DEBUG. We set up the registers to use the ROM BIOS to write a single diskette sector. The three-byte program at location 200H does the job. If the status is OK following the write, the boot record is on the diskette.

To write the device driver to sector 2, you follow the next steps of Figure 10.3. Using the DEBUG commands, we load the RAM disk driver routine. The DEBUG write command places the driver code in relative sector 1 (sector 2 of track 0) of the diskette in drive A:. We could also use this same method to write the boot record on the diskette.

This method of setting up the BIOS call in DEBUG to do a diskette write can also be used for nearly all BIOS functions. If you want to determine just what the BIOS call does, try it using DEBUG. You can set up the registers for the call, and write a simple three-byte program to do the software interrupt and return to DEBUG. This method is also very convenient for testing a device driver routine you may have written.

Back to the RAM disk driver routine in the second part of Figure 10.2. This routine is the device driver for the simulated diskette. Notice that the boot routine stored the original diskette INT 13H vector at offset 3 of this segment. The driver routines uses that vector for any diskette function that isn't handled by the simulated diskette. This routine assumes that the RAM disk is drive 2. The driver routine passes on a request for any other drive to the ROM BIOS, using the saved ORIGINAL_VECTOR. A disk reset request likewise goes to the ROM BIOS. If the function requested for the simulated drive is anything other than a read or write, the diskette simulator does nothing and returns with the status set for OK. The RAM disk doesn't need formatting, and since we have no error checking, there's nothing to verify.

If the requested operation is a read or write, the driver calculates the location in memory of the simulated sector. Anything outside the bounds of the diskette returns a record not found error. The driver code sets the source and destination registers according to the direction of the operation. Finally, a REP MOVSW transfers the data between simulated diskette and the user's buffer. The routine always sets the return status to OK and returns to the calling program.

This example shows how to set up a simulated diskette. However, this example is not ready for production use. To be a general-purpose utility, the program should be modified to work for any simulated drive and not just drive 2. The program could be changed to handle any sector size, although this normally isn't necessary. In fact, if this diskette simulation is used exclusively with DOS, the initialization routine should format the diskette with a directory and File

```
A>MASM BOOT,,,;
The IBM Personal Computer MACRO Assembler
Version 1.00 (C)Copyright IBM Corp 1981

Warning Severe
Errors  Errors
0       0

A>B:LINK BOOT,,,;

IBM Personal Computer Linker
Version 1.10 (C)Copyright IBM Corp 1982

 Warning: No STACK segment

There was 1 error detected.

A>MASM DISK,,,;
The IBM Personal Computer MACRO Assembler
Version 1.00 (C)Copyright IBM Corp 1981

Warning Severe
Errors  Errors
0       0

A>B:LINK DISK,,,;

IBM Personal Computer Linker

Version 1.10 (C)Copyright IBM Corp 1982

 Warning: No STACK segment

There was 1 error detected.

A>B:DEBUG BOOT.EXE
-R

AX=0000  BX=0000  CX=7CD3  DX=0000  SP=0000  BP=0000  SI=0000  DI=0000
DS=06D7  ES=06D7  SS=06E7  CS=06E7  IP=0000   NV UP DI PL NZ NA PO NC
06E7:0000 0000          ADD     [BX+SI],AL                 DS:0000=CD
-U7C00 7C05
06E7:7C00 8CC8          MOV     AX,CS
06E7:7C02 8ED8          MOV     DS,AX
06E7:7C04 8EC0          MOV     ES,AX
-RAX
AX 0000
:301
-RBX
BX 0000
:7C00
-RCX
CX 7CD3
:1
-RDX
DX 0000
:
-RES
ES 06D7
:6E7
-E200
06D7:0200  00.CD   00.13   00.CC        ;*** Insert boot diskette here
-G=100

AX=0000  BX=7C00  CX=0001  DX=0000  SP=0000  BP=0000  SI=0000  DI=0000
DS=06D7  ES=06E7  SS=06E7  CS=06E7  IP=0102   NV UP EI PL NZ NA PE NC
06E7:0102 CC            INT     3
-NDISK.EXE                             ;*** Insert program diskette here
-L
-U0 10
06E7:0000 EB05          JMPS    0007
06E7:0002 90            NOP
06E7:0003 0000          ADD     [BX+SI],AL
06E7:0005 0000          ADD     [BX+SI],AL
06E7:0007 80FA02        CMP     DL,02
06E7:000A 7405          JZ      0011
06E7:000C 2E            SEG     CS
06E7:000D FF2E0300      JMP     L,[0003]  ;*** Insert boot diskette here
-W0 0 1 1
-Q
A>
```

Figure 10.3   Steps for Creating High-RAM Load

Allocation Table (FAT). As the routine stands now, you must "format" drive C: following the boot of DOS. No physical formatting is needed for the simulated diskette, but the DOS FORMAT utility writes the FAT and directory needed for DOS operation.

This routine also stores the device driver program in simulated sector 1 of

Track 0. DOS doesn't use this sector for drive C:, but other systems may. You may have noticed that the simulation code prevents a write to the simulated sector of track 0, so at least it doesn't destroy itself.

In general, the high-RAM loading technique is clumsy. You must boot from two diskettes, which means the operator must do extra diskette handling. The DOS INT 27H is much better, unless you need to address systems other than DOS. Then high-RAM load may be the only method.

ASSEMBLY LANGUAGE SUBROUTINES

Besides permanent device drivers and stand-alone programs, assembly language is often used for subroutines in a large program predominantly written in a high-level language. The high-level language, such as BASIC or Pascal, allows you to quickly and succinctly write a large program. However, these languages may not let you do everything you need to. This is particularly true in the Personal Computer because a good application takes advantage of all the machine capabilities. The high-level language may not let you do a good job. Either the high-level language does not make the function available (calling a BIOS routine, for example) or the overhead of the language may make the application unacceptably slow (doing PEEK and POKE in BASIC to read some specific memory locations).

Fortunately, the high-level languages have mechanisms that allow you to call an assembly language subroutine. You can do the job efficiently and quickly in machine language, and then return to the high-level language for the remainder of the program. We'll do several examples in this section, showing a couple of different methods of including an assembly routine into a high-level language.

BASIC BLOAD ASSEMBLY ROUTINE

The first method adds a machine language program to the BASIC interpreter. The BASIC interpreter is probably the most common method of writing programs for the Personal Computer. The assembly language routine we're going to include in our program is fair-sized, over 100 bytes in length. A program this long is difficult to enter as part of the BASIC program, a method we'll cover in the next example.

The function we're adding to our BASIC program is the capability of sending a graphics screen image to the printer. The IBM includes graphics capabilities. The graphics commands let a program control the individual dots on the printer, much the same as the graphics modes of the color display adapter allows the programmer to control individual pixels. Figure 10.4 summarizes the graphics commands that the example requires. In general, the printer provides the graphics functions through escape sequences. Instead of sending the printer an ASCII character, the program sends an Escape character (ASCII value 27). The values

Command	Action
ESC+"3"+n	Set line feeding to n/216"
ESC+"K"+n1+n2+v1...vk (k = n1 + 256*n2)	Print dot images of v1...vk as 480 dots across the page

Figure 10.4 Graphics Commands to the Printer

following the Escape define a specific action by the printer, rather than characters to print. As you can see from Figure 10.4, there are commands to send bit images to the printer so that it prints a specific dot image.

The program in Figure 10.5 uses these graphics commands to print an image of the 320 × 200 graphics screen on the printer. Every dot on the screen is transferred to the printer. If a screen dot is in the background color, no black dot is sent to the printer. If the dot is in any one of the three foreground colors, the program places a black dot on the paper. This routine does no scaling of the data, so a circle on the screen may come out as an ellipse on the printer. There is no distinction between the three foreground colors. A multicolored picture becomes a confusion of black and white only.

The PRINT_SCREEN routine is a FAR procedure. The CALL from BASIC is a FAR CALL, so the return in this routine must match it. The ESC + "3" + 24 sequence sets the printer line spacing so that one row of dots meets with the following row. The print head has eight wires, each separated by 1/72 inch. Setting the line spacing to 8/72 inch (or 24/216 inch) arranges it so the rows meet. This sequence of code shows the way to send the escape sequences to the printer. The sequence of characters and values is transmitted to the printer just as if they were normal characters to print. The printer handles the rest.

Each pass of the print head across the paper prints eight rows (one for each dot in the printer head) for all 320 columns. At the label NEXT_ROW, the program sends the sequence ESC + "K" + 64 + 1 to the printer. This signifies that the next 320 bytes (64 + 1 × 256) are dot images for the graphics printer. The "K" graphics mode can print a maximum of 480 dots across the printer.

The program uses the BIOS video function to read the dots from the display. It reads eight rows of dots in the current column, gathering those values into a single byte. A "1" means that the video dot is a foreground color and should appear as a dot on the printer. The program continues through the NEXT_COLUMN loop until all 320 columns (which means 320 bytes) have been sent to the printer. The program moves to the next group of eight rows, after moving the printer to the next line by sending a carriage return and line feed (ASCII values 13 and 10). Twenty-five passes by the printer covers all 200 rows. The FAR return goes back to the BASIC interpreter.

The PRINT subroutine is a convenience for the program. This routine sends the byte to the printer, using the ROM BIOS print function. This routine places the register setups necessary for ROM BIOS in a single place. Without the

```
The IBM Personal Computer MACRO Assembler 01-01-83              PAGE    1-1
Figure 10.5 Graphics Print Screen

1                                              PAGE     ,132
2                                              TITLE    Figure 10.5 Graphics Print Screen
3
4     = 001B                            ESC    EQU      27               ; Escape ASCII Character
5
6       0000                            CODE   SEGMENT
7                                              ASSUME   CS:CODE
8       0000                            PRINT_SCREEN  PROC    FAR
9       0000  B0 1B                            MOV      AL,ESC           ; Set up 1/8" spacing
10      0002  E8 0060 R                        CALL     PRINT
11      0005  B0 33                            MOV      AL,'3'
12      0007  E8 0060 R                        CALL     PRINT
13      000A  B0 18                            MOV      AL,24            ;   as 24/216 "
14      000C  E8 0060 R                        CALL     PRINT
15      000F  BA 0000                          MOV      DX,0             ; Row number
16      0012                            NEXT_ROW:
17      0012  B0 1B                            MOV      AL,ESC           ; Send out ESC K
18      0014  E8 0060 R                        CALL     PRINT
19      0017  B0 4B                            MOV      AL,'K'
20      0019  E8 0060 R                        CALL     PRINT
21      001C  B0 40                            MOV      AL,320-256       ; Byte count of 320
22      001E  E8 0060 R                        CALL     PRINT
23      0021  B0 01                            MOV      AL,1
24      0023  E8 0060 R                        CALL     PRINT
25      0026  B9 0000                          MOV      CX,0             ; Column number
26      0029                            NEXT_COLUMN:
27      0029  52                               PUSH     DX               ; Save row number
28      002A  BB 0008                          MOV      BX,8             ; Number of bits to read
29      002D                            NEXT_DOT:
30      002D  D0 E7                            SHL      BH,1             ; Open up least significant bit
31      002F  B4 0D                            MOV      AH,13            ; Read dot
32      0031  CD 10                            INT      10H              ;   at current row and column
33      0033  0A C0                            OR       AL,AL
34      0035  74 03                            JZ       BACKGROUND       ; Test for background color
35      0037  80 CF 01                         OR       BH,1             ; Not background, turn on bit
36      003A                            BACKGROUND:
37      003A  42                               INC      DX               ; Move to next row
38      003B  FE CB                            DEC      BL               ; Decrement row count for this pass
39      003D  75 EE                            JNZ      NEXT_DOT
40      003F  8A C7                            MOV      AL,BH            ; Dots to print
41      0041  E8 0060 R                        CALL     PRINT            ; Send to printer
42      0044  5A                               POP      DX               ; Recover starting row of this pass
43      0045  41                               INC      CX               ; Move to next column
44      0046  81 F9 0140                       CMP      CX,320           ; Last column?
45      004A  75 DD                            JNZ      NEXT_COLUMN
46      004C  B0 0D                            MOV      AL,13            ; Send carriage return and line feed
47      004E  E8 0060 R                        CALL     PRINT
48      0051  B0 0A                            MOV      AL,10
49      0053  E8 0060 R                        CALL     PRINT
50      0056  83 C2 08                         ADD      DX,8             ; Move to next group of rows
51      0059  81 FA 00C8                       CMP      DX,200           ; Have we done last row yet?
52      005D  72 B3                            JB       NEXT_ROW
53      005F  CB                               RET                       ; Return to BASIC
54      0060                            PRINT_SCREEN  ENDP
55
56      0060                            PRINT  PROC     NEAR
57      0060  52                               PUSH     DX
58      0061  B4 00                            MOV      AH,0             ; Print the character
59      0063  BA 0000                          MOV      DX,0             ;   in AL
60      0066  CD 17                            INT      17H
61      0068  5A                               POP      DX
62      0069  C3                               RET
63      006A                            PRINT  ENDP
64      006A                            CODE   ENDS
65                                             END
```

Figure 10.5 Graphics Print Screen

subroutine, the program would have to set AH and DX to zero everywhere the PRINT subroutine is called.

How do we get to this subroutine from BASIC? First, there are two ways to include the program in BASIC. When the BASIC interpreter is running, it uses the remaining system memory, up to a maximum of 64K bytes as a workspace. If your system has more than 96K bytes of storage, there are sections of storage that BASIC can't use. It is best to put the subroutine there. If you don't have extra memory, you can set aside some storage from the BASIC workspace to hold the subroutine. We'll do this example storing the subroutine outside the BASIC workspace. A later example will show a way to include the subroutine in the BASIC variable area.

Figure 10.6 shows the sequence of events that sets up the subroutine for later use. This information is given in Appendix C of the BASIC Reference Manual. Part (a) is for a machine with 96K bytes or more. We assemble the program as normal. When we link the program, we specify the /H option. The linker sets up the .EXE file so that the program loads at the high end of memory rather than at the lowest available location.

To get the subroutine into the BASIC program, we need DEBUG. After loading BASIC while in DEBUG, and noting the registers, we load the assembly language routine. This example was done on a machine with 128K bytes. The CS value of 1FF9H indicates that the program was loaded 70H bytes from the end of memory. Notice that the program is about 6AH bytes long, so that the linker has placed the program at the highest possible location in storage, keeping it on a paragraph boundary. Another thing to note is that the program is code segment relocatable. This means that we can move the program anywhere in memory, as long as it executes with the first instruction at offset 0 in the current code segment. If we were to move this program to another machine with more or less memory, this feature is critical.

We now get the BASIC interpreter running. To do this, we must change the

```
B>A:MASM FIG10-5,,,;
The IBM Personal Computer MACRO Assembler
Version 1.00 (C)Copyright IBM Corp 1981

Warning Severe
Errors  Errors
0       0

B>A:LINK FIG10-5,,,/H;

IBM Personal Computer Linker
Version 1.10 (C)Copyright IBM Corp 1982

 Warning: No STACK segment

There was 1 error detected.

B>A:DEBUG A:BASIC.COM
-R

AX=0000  BX=0000  CX=2B80  DX=0000  SP=FFF0  BP=0000  SI=0000  DI=0000
DS=04B5  ES=04B5  SS=04B5  CS=04B5  IP=0100     NV UP DI PL NZ NA PO NC
04B5:0100 E91329        JMP     2A16
-NFIG10-5.EXE
-L
-R

AX=0000  BX=0000  CX=006A  DX=0000  SP=0000  BP=0000  SI=0000  DI=0000
DS=04B5  ES=04B5  SS=1FF9  CS=1FF9  IP=0000     NV UP DI PL NZ NA PO NC
1FF9:0000 B01B          MOV     AL,1B

-RSS
SS 1FF9
:4B5

-RCS
CS 1FF9
:4B5

-RIP
IP 0000
:100

-G

----- In BASIC Interpreter, enter these commands

DEF SEG = &H1FF9
BSAVE "FIG10-5",0,&H70
```

(a)

Figure 10.6 (a) Creation of BASIC Subroutine; (b) Creation of BASIC Subroutine in 64K Machine.

```
B>A:MASM FIG10-5,,,;
The IBM Personal Computer MACRO Assembler
Version 1.00 (C)Copyright IBM Corp 1981

Warning Severe
Errors  Errors
0       0

B>A:LINK FIG10-5,,,/H;

IBM Personal Computer Linker
Version 1.10 (C)Copyright IBM Corp 1982

 Warning: No STACK segment

There was 1 error detected.

B>A:DEBUG A:BASIC.COM /M:&H8000
-R

AX=0000  BX=0000  CX=2B80  DX=0000  SP=FFF0  BP=0000  SI=0000  DI=0000
DS=04B5  ES=04B5  SS=04B5  CS=04B5  IP=0100   NV UP DI PL NZ NA PO NC
04B5:0100 E91329          JMP     2A16
-NFIG10-5.EXE
-L
-R
AX=0000  BX=0000  CX=006A  DX=0000  SP=0000  BP=0000  SI=0000  DI=0000
DS=04B5  ES=04B5  SS=0FF9  CS=0FF9  IP=0000   NV UP DI PL NZ NA PO NC
0FF9:0000 B01B            MOV     AL,1B

-RSS
SS 0FF9
:4B5

-RCS
CS 0FF9
:4B5

-RIP
IP 0000
:100

-G

----- In BASIC Interpreter, enter these commands

DEF SEG = &H0FF9
BSAVE "FIG10-5",0,&H70
```

(b)

Figure 10.6 *Continued*

registers back as they were after BASIC was loaded. After BASIC is running, we use the DEF SEG statement to locate the subroutine. the BSAVE command places the object code back on the diskette, ready to be reloaded from BASIC with the BLOAD command.

Part (b) of figure 10.6 repeats the actions of part (a), but for a machine with 64K bytes of storage. The difference here is that BASIC can't use the full memory region for its workspace. The /M option on the BASIC command line limits the BASIC workspace and leaves room for the subroutine. We'll need a similar BASIC command when we run the program.

You can also DEBUG your assembly routine while running BASIC. As part of the "G" command that begins execution of BASIC, set a breakpoint in the subroutine. When the breakpoint executes, the BASIC interpreter is suspended and the normal DEBUG register display appears.

Now we're ready to execute the assembly language routine as part of a normal BASIC execution. Once again assuming a 128K-byte system, we execute this sequence of commands.

Enter "BASIC" from the DOS command level.

Enter "SCREEN 1" once the BASIC interpreter is in execution.

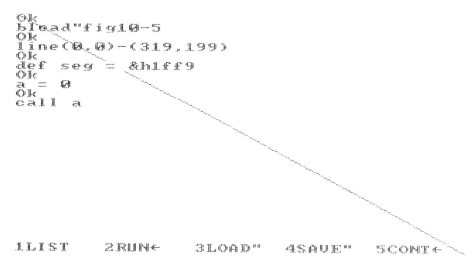

Figure 10.7 Print Screen Output

This gets us into the interpreter and into the 320 × 200 display mode. Figure 10.7 shows the rest of the story. The BLOAD command loads the subroutine into the same memory locations it was saved from. The BLOAD command can contain parameters that load the program into a different location, if desired. The LINE statement gives the graphics print screen routine something to print. To call the subroutine, we use the DEF SEG to set the CS value of the routine. The IP value for the routine goes into a simple variable. The CALL statement does a long call to the defined location. Figure 10.8 is a copy of the actual printer output from the execution of the routine.

If we had a 64K-byte system memory, the program would differ in two areas. BASIC /M:&H8000 would be used to invoke the interpreter, reserving the upper end of memory for our assembly routine. The DEF SEG would point to the location of the routine as we saw in part (b) of Figure 10.6.

EMBEDDED SHORT PROGRAM

The preceding example showed a fairly large assembly program stored in its own object file and loaded into the system memory by the BASIC interpreter. What about the case where the program is very small? It seems like a lot of effort just to load the program in from its own file. Appendix C of the BASIC Reference Manual shows a method of "poking" the machine language program into a storage area outside the BASIC workspace. Instead of that, we'll do an example using a different method.

Figure 10.8 contains the assembly language program that we'll be using. This routine calls the ROM BIOS to scroll the screen. As you can see from the

```
 1                                        PAGE    ,132
 2                                        TITLE   Figure 10.8  Scroll routines for BASIC
 3      0000                      CODE    SEGMENT
 4                                        ASSUME  CS:CODE
 5      0000                      SCROLL  PROC    FAR
 6      0000  55                          PUSH    BP
 7      0001  8B EC                       MOV     BP,SP
 8      0003  8B 76 06                    MOV     SI,[BP+6]       ; Get address of parm
 9      0006  8B 0C                       MOV     CX,[SI]         ; Get the parm
10      0008  0A C9                       OR      CL,CL
11      000A  B7 07                       MOV     BH,7
12      000C  B8 0601                     MOV     AX,601H
13      000F  75 0C                       JNZ     WINDOW1         ; Determine which window
14      0011  B9 0200                     MOV     CX,200H         ; Set window 0
15      0014  BA 1010                     MOV     DX,1010H
16      0017                      DO_SCROLL:
17      0017  CD 10                       INT     10H
18      0019  5D                          POP     BP
19      001A  CA 0002                     RET     2
20      001D                      WINDOW1:
21      001D  B9 0514                     MOV     CX,514H         ; Set window 1
22      0020  BA 1224                     MOV     DX,1224H
23      0023  EB F2                       JMP     DO_SCROLL
24      0025                      SCROLL  ENDP
25      0025                      CODE    ENDS
26                                        END
```

Figure 10.8 Scroll Routines for BASIC

parameters stored in the CX and DX registers, the scroll window represents only a portion of the screen. We'll be using this routine to break up the display into several windows, each of which can be scrolled separately. Since the BASIC language doesn't give us any way to do this, we'll need an assembly language program to do the job.

As you can see from the assembly listing in Figure 10.8, the program uses an input parameter to determine which of the two windows to scroll. The BASIC program passes this parameter to the assembly language routine by the CALL statement. Figure 10.9(a) shows the contents of the stack when BASIC calls the SCROLL subroutine. The CALL statement pushes the address of any argument onto the stack before doing the FAR CALL to the machine language subroutine. The address on the stack is the offset of the argument, relative to the DS register.

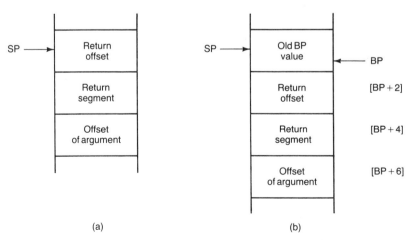

(a)   (b)

Figure 10.9 Stack for Subroutine Call

The first instructions of the SCROLL routine get that address into the SI register, so that the actual value can be loaded into the CX register. Figure 10.9(b) shows the contents of the stack after the SCROLL routine has pushed the BP register on the stack and then moved the contents of SP into BP. Notice that the address of the argument is six bytes into the stack. If the BASIC program had passed more arguments, they would have been pushed onto the stack in a similar fashion before the CALL. Jumping ahead, notice that the return from this subroutine also pops the argument from the stack, using the RET 2 instruction. BASIC expects the subroutine to remove the parameter from the stack before returning.

Based on the value of the argument, the SCROLL routine handles one of two windows on the screen. If the parameter is zero, it scrolls the window defined by (2,0) and (16,16) up by one line. If the parameter is nonzero, the window (5,20) to (18,36) is scrolled up by one line. Only the text in the defined window is moved. All of the rest of the text or data on the screen remains untouched. This windowing is part of the BIOS scroll function. To use it we need only to call the BIOS with the parameters correctly set.

Figure 10.10 is the BASIC language program that uses this SCROLL subroutine. This simple example writes character strings into each of the windows, and then calls the scroll routine to move the text up. This BASIC routine does nothing more than illustrate the use of the scroll windows.

The first thing to notice is the method for loading the machine language program into the system. The character string P$ contains the program. Each of the characters in the string is one byte from the object code in Figure 10.8. This program is entered by reading the assembly listing and typing in the BASIC program. That's one of the reasons why this method should be limited to short programs. It's very easy to make mistakes when entering a program in this fashion.

Once the machine language program is defined in P$, the BASIC program uses the VARPTR function to determine the address of that character string. Since the CALL statement needs the address of the subroutine, we must use VARPTR to find it. Using the information from Appendix C of the BASIC Reference Manual, we can find the address of the character string from the second

```
1 CLS
5 DEFINT A-Z
10 P$=CHR$(&H55)+CHR$(&H8B)+CHR$(&HEC)+CHR$(&H8B)+CHR$(&H76)+CHR$(&H6)
20 P$=P$+CHR$(&H8B)+CHR$(&HC)+CHR$(&HA)+CHR$(&HC9)+CHR$(&HB7)+CHR$(&H7)
30 P$=P$+CHR$(&H8B)+CHR$(&H1)+CHR$(&H6)+CHR$(&H75)+CHR$(&HC)+CHR$(&HB9)
40 P$=P$+CHR$(&H0)+CHR$(&H2)+CHR$(&HBA)+CHR$(&H10)+CHR$(&H10)+CHR$(&HCD)
50 P$=P$+CHR$(&H10)+CHR$(&H5D)+CHR$(&HCA)+CHR$(&H2)
60 P$=P$+CHR$(&H0)+CHR$(&HB9)+CHR$(&H14)
70 P$=P$+CHR$(&H5)+CHR$(&HBA)+CHR$(&H24)+CHR$(&H12)+CHR$(&HEB)+CHR$(&HF2)
100 ENTRY!=(PEEK(VARPTR(P$)+1))+(PEEK(VARPTR(P$)+2))*256
110 IF ENTRY!>32768! THEN ENTRY%=ENTRY!-65536! ELSE ENTRY%=ENTRY!
120 A$="/ 8CDEFGHIJ"
130 L=0:R=1
140 LOCATE 1,1:PRINT "Window Scrolling Example . . ."
200 LOCATE 15,1:PRINT A$;
210 CALL ENTRY%(L)
220 LOCATE 18,21:PRINT A$;
230 CALL ENTRY%(R)
240 A$=RIGHT$(A$,9)+ LEFT$(A$,1)
250 GOTO 200
```

Figure 10.10   BASIC Program for Scroll Windows

and third bytes of the string descriptor. The value returned by VARPTR gives us the address of the string descriptor for P$. The program extracts the string address from the descriptor and stores it in ENTRY!. Since this value can be in the range 0 to 65,536, the routine must convert it into a single word integer in the range −32,768 to 32,767, which it puts in the variable ENTRY%. The remaining lines of the program write the character string into the scroll windows, and then call the SCROLL routine to move the text.

If you run this program, you'll see that the data move independently in the two windows. This technique lets us define two different windows on the screen and move the text in them separately. If we wanted to write a longer program, we could draw lines around each window to really set them off. The use of similar windowing methods can lead to some good-looking programs if you want to display several different text areas.

Before we quit on this program, how do you go about debugging the machine language part of the program? To debug the machine language part, you need to have the DOS DEBUG program ready to go. You can do this by first loading DEBUG and then bringing in BASIC.COM (or BASICA.COM, if your program requires Advanced BASIC). After loading the BASIC program, change the first character of P$ (and consequently, the first byte of the machine language program) to CHR$(&HCC). This is the value for the INT 3 breakpoint interrupt. Now when you execute the BASIC program and it calls the machine language program, the DEBUG program gains control. You can now reset the 0CCH to the original opcode value (in this example, that would be 055H). You can use the facilities of DEBUG to trace your way through the machine language program. Of course, since the assembly language program is nice and short, there won't be much debugging necessary for that routine. In fact, you'll probably find that in most cases the problems are caused typing errors in entering the machine language program in the BASIC character string.

COMPILED HIGH-LEVEL LANGUAGES

The previous examples dealt with an assembly language program used with the BASIC interpreter. The BASIC language that's part of the IBM Personal Computer is an interpreted language. This means that the computer stores the program in a form very similar to the original language. The interpreter does not convert the BASIC language instructions into machine language. Rather, the BASIC interpreter looks at each BASIC instruction during the execution of the BASIC program, and does the necessary steps to accomplish that instruction.

A compiler works differently. The compiler converts the high-level language statements directly into machine language. IBM offers compilers for the Personal Computer for the BASIC, Pascal, FORTRAN, and COBOL languages. The output of the compiler is a machine language program (a file named *.OBJ) that is very similar to the output of the assembler. Running a program written in a compiled high-level language is a two-step process. First the program must be compiled and linked. Then it can be executed. An interpreted program can be executed directly, without the compilation step.

The compiled high-level languages for the Personal Computer are similar to BASIC in that they don't let you do everything with the hardware that you might want to do. In fact, the BASIC interpreter allows the programmer to read and write the I/O ports and memory locations with statements in the program. The other languages don't necessarily even offer this capability. Thus, it may be even more necessary to use assembly language routines as part of your Pascal or FORTRAN program. You may have to if you want to take full advantage of the capabilities of the hardware.

Fortunately, it's very easy to handle assembly language subroutines with a compiled high-level language. That's because the output of the compiler is an object file, ready for linking. The output of the assembler is also an object file. Therefore, you can just link together the high-level language program and the assembler program using the DOS Linker. You don't have to link the programs together during the execution, as you do with the BASIC interpreter.

We'll do a FORTRAN example. Pascal is very similar. The example that we'll do is similar to the example shown in Appendix D of the FORTRAN Compiler Reference Manual. This example combines a FORTRAN main program with an assembly language program that reads the current time of day using the BIOS software interrupt. The assembly routine calls BIOS to determine the time of day and returns the current time to the FORTRAN routine. The main program converts the timer tick value into the current time in hours, minutes, and seconds.

Figure 10.11 contains the FORTRAN main program. This program calls an external subroutine named TIMER with a single parameter A. This variable is a four-byte integer. The value that returns from TIMER is the current time of day, measured as timer ticks since midnight. The FORTRAN program calculates the time in HOURS, MINS, SECS, and HSECS (hundredths of a second) from the number returned by the TIMER routine. Notice how simple it is to multiply and divide numbers in FORTRAN, and compare that to the effort necessary to do the same job in an assembly language program. You can see here that placing all of these operations in FORTRAN made the programming job much simpler. Of particular convenience is the way that the integers are converted into printable characters using the FORTRAN WRITE and FORMAT statements. To do this job in assembly language would take several hundred lines of code. Recall the

```
$STORAGE:4
        INTEGER A,HOURS,MINS,SECS,HSECS
        CALL TIMER(A)
        HOURS=A/65543
        A=A-HOURS*65543
        MINS=A/1092
        A=A-MINS*1092
        SECS=A/18
        HSECS=(100*(A-SECS*18))/18
        WRITE(*,10)HOURS,MINS,SECS,HSECS
   10   FORMAT(1X,'THE TIME IS: ',I2,':',I2,':',I2,'.',I2)
        END
```

Figure 10.11 FORTRAN Program for Time of Day

```
The IBM Personal Computer MACRO Assembler 01-01-83          PAGE    1-1
Figure 10.12  Assembly Routine for FORTRAN Main Program

 1                                      PAGE      ,132
 2                                      TITLE     Figure 10.12  Assembly Routine for FORTRAN Main Program
 3                              FRAME    STRUC
 4      0000  ????             SAVEBP   DW        ?
 5      0002  ????????         SAVERET  DD        ?
 6      0006  ????????         A        DD        ?              ; Pointer to parameter
 7      000A                   FRAME    ENDS
 8
 9      0000                   CODE     SEGMENT   'CODE'
10                             DGROUP   GROUP     DATA
11                                      ASSUME    CS:CODE,DS:DGROUP,ES:DGROUP,SS:DGROUP
12      0000                   TIMER    PROC      FAR
13                                      PUBLIC    TIMER          ; Let linker know where it is
14      0000  55                        PUSH      BP
15      0001  8B EC                     MOV       BP,SP          ; Establish addressing to FRAME
16      0003  B4 00                     MOV       AH,0
17      0005  CD 1A                     INT       1AH            ; Call BIOS for Time of Day
18      0007  C4 5E 06                  LES       BX,[BP]+A      ; Get pointer in ES:BX to parameter
19      000A  26: 89 17                 MOV       ES:[BX],DX     ; Store low part of time
20      000D  26: 89 4F 02              MOV       ES:[BX+2],CX   ; Store high part of time
21      0011  5D                        POP       BP
22      0012  CA 0004                   RET       4              ; Return and pop parm address
23      0015                   TIMER    ENDP
24      0015                   CODE     ENDS
25                                      END
```

Figure 10.12   Assembly Routine for FORTRAN Main Program

example we did with the 8087, where the program converted the floating-point number into an ASCII representation. That program required a considerable number of instructions and the use of an 8087.

Figure 10.12 is the assembly language routine that does the subroutine TIMER. As you can see, this simple program calls the BIOS interrupt to read the time of day and then stores the value in a doubleword location. What we need to examine here is the method in which the parameters are passed from the FORTRAN program to the assembly program.

Figure 10.13 shows you the stack at the time the assembly language program starts executing. Just as with the BASIC interpreter, the FORTRAN program passes the address of the parameter on the stack. However, the FORTRAN and Pascal compilers pass a doubleword pointer to the parameter, rather than just the offset of the parameter. This means that the assembly language program must set

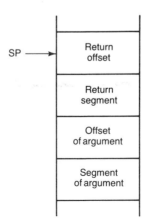

SP →

| Return offset |
| Return segment |
| Offset of argument |
| Segment of argument |

Figure 10.13   Stack for FORTRAN Call

both the segment register and the offset address before it can access the parameter. If there had been more than one parameter, the FORTRAN program would have pushed the address values for the other parameters on the stack before the call.

The TIMER program in Figure 10.12 addresses the stack by pushing the BP register and setting it to the top of the stack. The FRAME structure helps to identify the offsets of the different values on the stack after the program pushes the BP register. The LES BX,[BP]+A instruction gets the address of the parameter into the ES:BX register pair. The program stores the four-byte time-of-day value into the four-byte integer variable using that address.

Notice that the TIMER routine pops the parameter address from the stack as part of the return instruction, just as the BASIC routines. Notice also that this assembly program uses the PUBLIC statement to identify TIMER. That's so that the linker can find this routine and correctly link the assembly program to the FORTRAN program. We didn't need to do that with the BASIC interpreter, because the BASIC program was never linked to the assembly program.

SUMMARY

Assembly language programming is a very powerful tool. It allows the programmer to exercise complete control over the actions of the machine hardware. However, this total control also forces the programmer to handle details that are incidental to the main actions of the program. All of this power sometimes translates into mind-numbing detail.

This chapter has explored some of the ways that you can trade off the power of assembly language programming and the convenience of a high-level language. By properly partitioning the work to be done, the skilled programmer can let the high-level language handle the infinity of details about the programming while the programmer concentrates on the job to be done. Then, when the program requires the additional performance or detailed machine control, the programmer can shift into assembly language. Assembly language lets the programmer do things that either can't be done in the high-level language, or things that would take much too long if the overhead of the high-level language is imposed.

There are two different ways this division of labor between assembly and high-level language can be performed. In one case, you can install a new device driver that allows the programmer to use the standard methods to access a completely new device. We did several examples here, allowing us to buffer the printer and build a memory-based version of a diskette. In the other method, the assembly language program becomes part of the entire program, with explicit calls to the assembly program to do the job when it is needed. Either way, this chapter brought together all the assembly language concepts of the book.

APPENDIX

A

8088
Instruction Set

DATA TRANSFER

MOV = Move:

	7 6 5 4 3 2 1 0	7 6 5 4 3 2 1 0	7 6 5 4 3 2 1 0	
Register/memory to/from register	1 0 0 0 1 0 d w	mod reg r/m		
Immediate to register/memory	1 1 0 0 0 1 1 w	mod 0 0 0 r/m	data	data if w 1
Immediate to register	1 0 1 1 w reg	data	data if w 1	
Memory to accumulator	1 0 1 0 0 0 0 w	addr-low	addr-high	
Accumulator to memory	1 0 1 0 0 0 1 w	addr-low	addr-high	
Register/memory to segment register	1 0 0 0 1 1 1 0	mod 0 reg r/m		
Segment register to register/memory	1 0 0 0 1 1 0 0	mod 0 reg r/m		

PUSH = Push:

Register/memory	1 1 1 1 1 1 1 1	mod 1 1 0 r/m
Register	0 1 0 1 0 reg	
Segment register	0 0 0 reg 1 1 0	

POP = Pop:

Register/memory	1 0 0 0 1 1 1 1	mod 0 0 0 r/m
Register	0 1 0 1 1 reg	
Segment register	0 0 0 reg 1 1 1	

XCHG = Exchange:

Register/memory with register	1 0 0 0 0 1 1 w	mod reg r/m
Register with accumulator	1 0 0 1 0 reg	

IN=Input from:

Fixed port	1 1 1 0 0 1 0 w	port
Variable port	1 1 1 0 1 1 0 w	

OUT = Output to:

Fixed port	1 1 1 0 0 1 1 w	port
Variable port	1 1 1 0 1 1 1 w	
XLAT-Translate byte to AL	1 1 0 1 0 1 1 1	
LEA-Load EA to register	1 0 0 0 1 1 0 1	mod reg r/m
LDS-Load pointer to DS	1 1 0 0 0 1 0 1	mod reg r/m
LES-Load pointer to ES	1 1 0 0 0 1 0 0	mod reg r/m
LAHF-Load AH with flags	1 0 0 1 1 1 1 1	
SAHF=Store AH into flags	1 0 0 1 1 1 1 0	
PUSHF=Push flags	1 0 0 1 1 1 0 0	
POPF=Pop flags	1 0 0 1 1 1 0 1	

ARITHMETIC

ADD = Add:

Reg/memory with register to either	0 0 0 0 0 0 d w	mod reg r/m		
Immediate to register/memory	1 0 0 0 0 0 s w	mod 0 0 0 r/m	data	data if s w 01
Immediate to accumulator	0 0 0 0 0 1 0 w	data	data if w 1	

ADC = Add with carry:

Reg/memory with register to either	0 0 0 1 0 0 d w	mod reg r/m		
Immediate to register/memory	1 0 0 0 0 0 s w	mod 0 1 0 r/m	data	data if s w 01
Immediate to accumulator	0 0 0 1 0 1 0 w	data	data if w 1	

INC = Increment:

Register/memory	1 1 1 1 1 1 1 w	mod 0 0 0 r/m
Register	0 1 0 0 0 reg	
AAA=ASCII adjust for add	0 0 1 1 0 1 1 1	
BAA=Decimal adjust for add	0 0 1 0 0 1 1 1	

SUB = Subtract:

Reg/memory and register to either	0 0 1 0 1 0 d w	mod reg r/m		
Immediate from register/memory	1 0 0 0 0 0 s w	mod 1 0 1 r/m	data	data if s w·01
Immediate from accumulator	0 0 1 0 1 1 0 w	data	data if w 1	

SBB = Subtract with borrow:

Reg/memory and register to either	0 0 0 1 1 0 d w	mod reg r/m		
Immediate from register/memory	1 0 0 0 0 0 s w	mod 0 1 1 r/m	data	data if s w·01
Immediate from accumulator	0 0 0 1 1 1 0 w	data	data if w·1	

DEC Decrement:

	7 6 5 4 3 2 1 0	7 6 5 4 3 2 1 0	7 6 5 4 3 2 1 0	7 6 5 4 3 2 1 0
Register/memory	1 1 1 1 1 1 1 w	mod 0 0 1 r/m		
Register	0 1 0 0 1 reg			
NEG Change sign	1 1 1 1 0 1 1 w	mod 0 1 1 r/m		

CMP Compare:

Register/memory and register	0 0 1 1 1 0 d w	mod reg r/m		
Immediate with register/memory	1 0 0 0 0 0 s w	mod 1 1 1 r/m	data	data if s w 01
Immediate with accumulator	0 0 1 1 1 1 0 w	data	data if w 1	
AAS ASCII adjust for subtract	0 0 1 1 1 1 1 1			
DAS Decimal adjust for subtract	0 0 1 0 1 1 1 1			
MUL Multiply (unsigned)	1 1 1 1 0 1 1 w	mod 1 0 0 r/m		
IMUL Integer multiply (signed)	1 1 1 1 0 1 1 w	mod 1 0 1 r/m		
AAM ASCII adjust for multiply	1 1 0 1 0 1 0 0	0 0 0 0 1 0 1 0		
DIV Divide (unsigned)	1 1 1 1 0 1 1 w	mod 1 1 0 r/m		
IDIV Integer divide (signed)	1 1 1 1 0 1 1 w	mod 1 1 1 r/m		
AAD ASCII adjust for divide	1 1 0 1 0 1 0 1	0 0 0 0 1 0 1 0		
CBW Convert byte to word	1 0 0 1 1 0 0 0			
CWD Convert word to double word	1 0 0 1 1 0 0 1			

LOGIC

NOT Invert	1 1 1 1 0 1 1 w	mod 0 1 0 r/m
SHL/SAL Shift logical/arithmetic left	1 1 0 1 0 0 v w	mod 1 0 0 r/m
SHR Shift logical right	1 1 0 1 0 0 v w	mod 1 0 1 r/m
SAR Shift arithmetic right	1 1 0 1 0 0 v w	mod 1 1 1 r/m
ROL Rotate left	1 1 0 1 0 0 v w	mod 0 0 0 r/m
ROR Rotate right	1 1 0 1 0 0 v w	mod 0 0 1 r/m
RCL Rotate through carry flag left	1 1 0 1 0 0 v w	mod 0 1 0 r/m
RCR Rotate through carry right	1 1 0 1 0 0 v w	mod 0 1 1 r/m

AND And:

Reg/memory and register to either	0 0 1 0 0 0 d w	mod reg r/m		
Immediate to register/memory	1 0 0 0 0 0 0 w	mod 1 0 0 r/m	data	data if w 1
Immediate to accumulator	0 0 1 0 0 1 0 w	data	data if w 1	

TEST   And function to flags, no result:

Register/memory and register	1 0 0 0 0 1 0 w	mod reg r/m		
Immediate data and register/memory	1 1 1 1 0 1 1 w	mod 0 0 0 r/m	data	data if w 1
Immediate data and accumulator	1 0 1 0 1 0 0 w	data	data if w 1	

OR   Or:

Reg/memory and register to either	0 0 0 0 1 0 d w	mod reg r/m		
Immediate to register/memory	1 0 0 0 0 0 0 w	mod 0 0 1 r/m	data	data if w 1
Immediate to accumulator	0 0 0 0 1 1 0 w	data	data if w 1	

XOR   Exclusive or:

Reg/memory and register to either	0 0 1 1 0 0 d w	mod reg r/m		
Immediate to register/memory	1 0 0 0 0 0 0 w	mod 1 1 0 r/m	data	data if w 1
Immediate to accumulator	0 0 1 1 0 1 0 w	data	data if w 1	

STRING MANIPULATION

REP=Repeat	1 1 1 1 0 0 1 z
MOVS=Move byte/word	1 0 1 0 0 1 0 w
CMPS=Compare byte/word	1 0 1 0 0 1 1 w
SCAS=Scan byte/word	1 0 1 0 1 1 1 w
LODS=Load byte/wd to AL/AX	1 0 1 0 1 1 0 w
STOS=Stor byte/wd from AL/A	1 0 1 0 1 0 1 w

CONTROL TRANSFER

CALL = Call:

	7 6 5 4 3 2 1 0	7 6 5 4 3 2 1 0	7 6 5 4 3 2 1 0
Direct within segment	1 1 1 0 1 0 0 0	disp-low	disp-high
Indirect within segment	1 1 1 1 1 1 1 1	mod 0 1 0 r/m	
Direct intersegment	1 0 0 1 1 0 1 0	offset-low	offset-high
		seg-low	seg-high
Indirect intersegment	1 1 1 1 1 1 1 1	mod 0 1 1 r/m	

JMP = Unconditional Jump:

	7 6 5 4 3 2 1 0	7 6 5 4 3 2 1 0	7 6 5 4 3 2 1 0
Direct within segment	1 1 1 0 1 0 0 1	disp-low	disp-high
Direct within segment-short	1 1 1 0 1 0 1 1	disp	
Indirect within segment	1 1 1 1 1 1 1 1	mod 1 0 0 r/m	
Direct intersegment	1 1 1 0 1 0 1 0	offset-low	offset-high
		seg-low	seg-high
Indirect intersegment	1 1 1 1 1 1 1 1	mod 1 0 1 r/m	

RET = Return from CALL:

	7 6 5 4 3 2 1 0	7 6 5 4 3 2 1 0	7 6 5 4 3 2 1 0
Within segment	1 1 0 0 0 0 1 1		
Within seg. adding immed to SP	1 1 0 0 0 0 1 0	data-low	data-high
Intersegment	1 1 0 0 1 0 1 1		
Intersegment, adding immediate to SP	1 1 0 0 1 0 1 0	data-low	data-high

	7 6 5 4 3 2 1 0	7 6 5 4 3 2 1 0
JE/JZ=Jump on equal/zero	0 1 1 1 0 1 0 0	disp
JL/JNGE=Jump on less/not greater or equal	0 1 1 1 1 1 0 0	disp
JLE/JNG=Jump on less or equal/not greater	0 1 1 1 1 1 1 0	disp
JB/JNAE=Jump on below/not above	0 1 1 1 0 0 1 0	disp
JBE/JNA=Jump on below or equal/not above	0 1 1 1 0 1 1 0	disp
JP/JPE=Jump on parity/parity even	0 1 1 1 1 0 1 0	disp
JO=Jump on overflow	0 1 1 1 0 0 0 0	disp
JS=Jump on sign	0 1 1 1 1 0 0 0	disp
JNE/JNZ=Jump on not equal/not zero	0 1 1 1 0 1 0 1	disp
JNL/JGE=Jump on not less/greater or equal	0 1 1 1 1 1 0 1	disp
JNLE/JG=Jump on not less or equal/greater	0 1 1 1 1 1 1 1	disp

	7 6 5 4 3 2 1 0	7 6 5 4 3 2 1 0
JNB/JAE=Jump on not below/above or equal	0 1 1 1 0 0 1 1	disp
JNBE/JA=Jump on not below or equal/above	0 1 1 1 0 1 1 1	disp
JNP/JPO=Jump on not par/par odd	0 1 1 1 1 0 1 1	disp
JNO=Jump on not overflow	0 1 1 1 0 0 0 1	disp
JNS=Jump on not sign	0 1 1 1 1 0 0 1	disp
LOOP Loop CX times	1 1 1 0 0 0 1 0	disp
LOOPZ/LOOPE Loop while zero/equal	1 1 1 0 0 0 0 1	disp
LOOPNZ/LOOPNE Loop while not zero/equal	1 1 1 0 0 0 0 0	disp
JCXZ=Jump on CX zero	1 1 1 0 0 0 1 1	disp

INT Interrupt

	7 6 5 4 3 2 1 0	7 6 5 4 3 2 1 0
Type specified	1 1 0 0 1 1 0 1	type
Type 3	1 1 0 0 1 1 0 0	
INTO=Interrupt on overflow	1 1 0 0 1 1 1 0	
IRET=Interrupt return	1 1 0 0 1 1 1 1	

PROCESSOR CONTROL

	7 6 5 4 3 2 1 0	7 6 5 4 3 2 1 0
CLC Clear carry	1 1 1 1 1 0 0 0	
CMC Complement carry	1 1 1 1 0 1 0 1	
STC Set carry	1 1 1 1 1 0 0 1	
CLD Clear direction	1 1 1 1 1 1 0 0	
STD Set direction	1 1 1 1 1 1 0 1	
CLI Clear interrupt	1 1 1 1 1 0 1 0	
STI Set interrupt	1 1 1 1 1 0 1 1	
HLT Halt	1 1 1 1 0 1 0 0	
WAIT Wait	1 0 0 1 1 0 1 1	
ESC Escape (to external device)	1 1 0 1 1 x x x	mod x x x r/m
LOCK Bus lock prefix	1 1 1 1 0 0 0 0	

Footnotes:

AL = 8-bit accumulator
AX = 16-bit accumulator
CX = Count register
DS = Data segment
ES = Extra segment
Above/below refers to unsigned value.
Greater = more positive;
Less = less positive (more negative) signed values
if d = 1 then "to" reg; if d = 0 then "from" reg
if w = 1 then word instruction; if w = 0 then byte instruction

if mod = 11 then r/m is treated as a REG field
if mod = 00 then DISP = 0*, disp-low and disp-high are absent
if mod = 01 then DISP = disp-low sign-extended to 16-bits, disp-high is absent
if mod = 10 then DISP = disp-high: disp-low
if r/m = 000 then EA = (BX) + (SI) + DISP
if r/m = 001 then EA = (BX) + (DI) + DISP
if r/m = 010 then EA = (BP) + (SI) + DISP
if r/m = 011 then EA = (BP) + (DI) + DISP
if r/m = 100 then EA = (SI) + DISP
if r/m = 101 then EA = (DI) + DISP
if r/m = 110 then EA = (BP) + DISP*
if r/m = 111 then EA = (BX) + DISP
DISP follows 2nd byte of instruction (before data if required)

*except if mod = 00 and r/m = 110 then EA = disp-high: disp-low.

if s:w = 01 then 16 bits of immediate data form the operand.
if s:w = 11 then an immediate data byte is sign extended to
     form the 16-bit operand.
if v = 0 then "count" = 1; if v = 1 then "count" in (CL)
x = don't care
z is used for string primitives for comparison with ZF FLAG.

SEGMENT OVERRIDE PREFIX

0 0 1 reg 1 1 0

REG is assigned according to the following table:

16-Bit (w = 1)	8-Bit (w = 0)	Segment
000 AX	000 AL	00 ES
001 CX	001 CL	01 CS
010 DX	010 DL	10 SS
011 BX	011 BL	11 DS
100 SP	100 AH	
101 BP	101 CH	
110 SI	110 DH	
111 DI	111 BH	

Instructions which reference the flag register file as a 16-bit object use the symbol FLAGS to represent the file:

FLAGS = X:X:X:X:(OF):(DF):(IF):(TF):(SF):(ZF):X:(AF):X:(PF):X:(CF)

APPENDIX

B

8087
Instruction Set

	7 6 5 4 3 2 1 0	7 6 5 4 3 2 1 0	7 6 5 4 3 2 1 0	7 6 5 4 3 2 1 0

Data Transfer

FLD = LOAD

Integer/Real Memory to ST(0)	ESCAPE MF 1	MOD 0 0 0 R/M	(DISP-LO)	(DISP-HI)
Long Integer Memory to ST(0)	ESCAPE 1 1 1	MOD 1 0 1 R/M	(DISP-LO)	(DISP-HI)
Temporary Real Memory to ST(0)	ESCAPE 0 1 1	MOD 1 0 1 R/M	(DISP-LO)	(DISP-HI)
BCD Memory to ST(0)	ESCAPE 1 1 1	MOD 1 0 0 R/M	(DISP-LO)	(DISP-HI)
ST(i) to ST(0)	ESCAPE 0 0 1	1 1 0 0 0 ST(i)		

FST = STORE

ST(0) to Integer/Real Memory	ESCAPE MF 1	MOD 0 1 0 R/M	(DISP-LO)	(DISP-HI)
ST(0) to ST(i)	ESCAPE 1 0 1	1 1 0 1 0 ST(i)		

FSTP = STORE AND POP

ST(0) to Integer/Real Memory	ESCAPE MF 1	MOD 0 1 1 R/M	(DISP-LO)	(DISP-HI)
ST(0) to Long Integer Memory	ESCAPE 1 1 1	MOD 1 1 1 R/M	(DISP-LO)	(DISP-HI)
ST(0) to Temporary Real Memory	ESCAPE 0 1 1	MOD 1 1 1 R/M	(DISP-LO)	(DISP-HI)
ST(0) to BCD Memory	ESCAPE 1 1 1	MOD 1 1 0 R/M	(DISP-LO)	(DISP-HI)
ST(0) to ST(i)	ESCAPE 1 0 1	1 1 0 1 1 ST(i)		

FXCH = Exchange ST(i) and ST(0)

	ESCAPE 0 0 1	1 1 0 0 1 ST(i)		

Comparison

FCOM = Compare

Integer/Real Memory to ST(0)	ESCAPE MF 0	MOD 0 1 0 R/M	(DISP-LO)	(DISP-HI)
ST(i) to ST(0)	ESCAPE 0 0 0	1 1 0 1 0 ST(i)		

FCOMP = Compare and Pop

Integer/Real Memory to ST(0)	ESCAPE MF 0	MOD 0 1 1 R/M	(DISP-LO)	(DISP-HI)
ST(i) to ST(0)	ESCAPE 0 0 0	1 1 0 1 1 ST(i)		

FCOMPP = Compare ST(1) to ST(0) and Pop Twice	ESCAPE 1 1 0	1 1 0 1 1 0 0 1		
FTST = Test ST(0)	ESCAPE 0 0 1	1 1 1 0 0 1 0 0		
FXAM = Examine ST(0)	ESCAPE 0 0 1	1 1 1 0 0 1 0 1		

Arithmetic

Bit positions: 7 6 5 4 3 2 1 0   7 6 5 4 3 2 1 0   7 6 5 4 3 2 1 0   7 6 5 4 3 2 1 0

FADD = Addition

Integer/Real Memory with ST(0)

| ESCAPE MF 0 | MOD 0 0 0 R/M | (DISP-LO) | (DISP-HI) |

ST(i) and ST(0)

| ESCAPE d P 0 | 1 1 0 0 0 ST(i) |

FSUB = Subtraction

Integer/Real Memory with ST(0)

| ESCAPE MF 0 | MOD 1 0 R R/M | (DISP-LO) | (DISP-HI) |

ST(i) and ST(0)

| ESCAPE d P 0 | 1 1 1 0 R R/M |

FMUL = Multiplication

Integer/Real Memory with ST(0)

| ESCAPE MF 0 | MOD 0 0 1 R/M | (DISP-LO) | (DISP-HI) |

ST(i) and ST(0)

| ESCAPE d P 0 | 1 1 0 0 1 R/M |

FDIV = Division

Integer/Real Memory with ST(0)

| ESCAPE MF 0 | MOD 1 1 R R/M | (DISP-LO) | (DISP-HI) |

ST(i) and ST(0)

| ESCAPE d P 0 | 1 1 1 1 R R/M |

FSQRT = Square Root of ST(0)

| ESCAPE 0 0 1 | 1 1 1 1 1 0 1 0 |

FSCALE = Scale ST(0) by ST(1)

| ESCAPE 0 0 1 | 1 1 1 1 1 1 0 1 |

FPREM = Partial Remainder of ST(0) ÷ ST(1)

| ESCAPE 0 0 1 | 1 1 1 1 1 0 0 0 |

FRNDINT = Round ST(0) to Integer

| ESCAPE 0 0 1 | 1 1 1 1 1 1 0 0 |

FXTRACT = Extract Components of ST(0)

| ESCAPE 0 0 1 | 1 1 1 1 0 1 0 0 |

FABS = Absolute Value of ST(0)

| ESCAPE 0 0 1 | 1 1 1 0 0 0 0 1 |

FCHS = Change Sign of ST(0)

| ESCAPE 0 0 1 | 1 1 1 0 0 0 0 0 |

Transcendental

FPTAN = Partial Tangent of ST(0)

| ESCAPE 0 0 1 | 1 1 1 1 0 0 1 0 |

FPATAN = Partial Arctangent of ST(0) ÷ ST(1)

| ESCAPE 0 0 1 | 1 1 1 1 0 0 1 1 |

F2XM1 = $2^{ST(0)} - 1$

| ESCAPE 0 0 1 | 1 1 1 1 0 0 0 0 |

FYL2X = $ST(1) \cdot \log_2 [ST(0)]$

| ESCAPE 0 0 1 | 1 1 1 1 0 0 0 1 |

FYL2XP1 = $ST(1) \cdot \log_2 [ST(0) + 1]$

| ESCAPE 0 0 1 | 1 1 1 1 0 0 0 1 |

Constants

FLDZ = LOAD + 0.0 into ST(0)

| ESCAPE 0 0 1 | 1 1 1 0 1 1 1 0 |

FLD1 = LOAD + 1.0 into ST(0)

| ESCAPE 0 0 1 | 1 1 1 0 1 0 0 0 |

FLDPI = LOAD π into ST(0)

| ESCAPE 0 0 1 | 1 1 1 0 1 0 1 1 |

FLDL2T = LOAD $\log_2 10$ into ST(0)

| ESCAPE 0 0 1 | 1 1 1 0 1 0 0 1 |

FLDL2E = LOAD $\log_2 e$ into ST(0)

| ESCAPE 0 0 1 | 1 1 1 0 1 0 1 0 |

FLDLG2 = LOAD $\log_{10} 2$ into ST(0)

| ESCAPE 0 0 1 | 1 1 1 0 1 1 0 0 |

FLDLN2 = LOAD $\log_e 2$ into ST(0)

| ESCAPE 0 0 1 | 1 1 1 0 1 1 0 1 |

Processor Control

		7 6 5 4 3 2 1 0	7 6 5 4 3 2 1 0	7 6 5 4 3 2 1 0	7 6 5 4 3 2 1 0	7 6 5 4 3 2 1 0
FINIT = Initialize NDP	ESCAPE 0 1 1	1 1 1 0 0 0 1 1			
FENI = Enable Interrupts	ESCAPE 0 1 1	1 1 1 0 0 0 0 0			
FDISI = Disable Interrupts	ESCAPE 0 1 1	1 1 1 0 0 0 0 1			
FLDCW = Load Control Word	ESCAPE 0 0 1	MOD 1 0 1 R/M	(DISP-LO)	(DISP-HI)	
FSTCW = Store Control Word	ESCAPE 0 0 1	MOD 1 1 1 R/M	(DISP-LO)	(DISP-HI)	
FSTSW = Store Status Word	ESCAPE 1 0 1	MOD 1 1 1 R/M	(DISP-LO)	(DISP-HI)	
FCLEX = Clear Exceptions	ESCAPE 0 1 1	1 1 1 0 0 0 1 0			
FSTENV = Store Environment	ESCAPE 0 0 1	MOD 1 1 0 R/M	(DISP-LO)	(DISP-HI)	
FLDENV = Load Environment	ESCAPE 0 0 1	MOD 1 0 0 R/M	(DISP-LO)	(DISP-HI)	
FSAVE = Save State	ESCAPE 1 0 1	MOD 1 1 0 R/M	(DISP-LO)	(DISP-HI)	
FRSTOR = Restore State	ESCAPE 1 0 1	MOD 1 0 0 R/M	(DISP-LO)	(DISP-HI)	
FINCSTP = Increment Stack Pointer	ESCAPE 0 0 1	1 1 1 1 0 1 1 1			
FDECSTP = Decrement Stack Pointer	ESCAPE 0 0 1	1 1 1 1 0 1 1 0			
FFREE = Free ST(i)	ESCAPE 1 0 1	1 1 0 0 0 ST(i)			
FNOP = No Operation	ESCAPE 0 0 1	1 1 0 1 0 0 0 0			
FWAIT = CPU Wait for NDP	1 0 0 1 1 0 1 1				

FOOTNOTES:

if mod = 00 then DISP = 0*, disp-low and disp-high are absent
if mod = 01 then DISP = disp-low sign-extended to 16-bits, disp-high is absent
if mod = 10 then DISP = disp-high; disp-low
if mod = 11 then r/m is treated as an ST(i) field

if r/m = 000 then EA = (BX) + (SI) + DISP
if r/m = 001 then EA = (BX) + (DI) + DISP
if r/m = 010 then EA = (BP) + (SI) + DISP
if r/m = 011 then EA = (BP) + (DI) + DISP
if r/m = 100 then EA = (SI)   + DISP
if r/m = 101 then EA = (DI)   + DISP
if r/m = 110 then EA = (BP) + DISP*
if r/m = 111 then EA = (BX) + DISP

*except if mod = 000 and r/m = 110 then EA = disp-high: disp-low.

MF =   Memory Format
        00 — 32-bit Real
        01 — 32-bit Integer
        10 — 64-bit Real
        11 — 16-bit Integer

ST(0) =   Current stack top
ST(i) = i^{th} register below stack top

d =   Destination
      0 — Destination is ST(0)
      1 — Destination is ST(i)

P =   Pop
      0 — No pop
      1 — Pop ST(0)

R =   Reverse
      0 — Destination (op) Source
      1 — Source (op) Destination

For **FSQRT:** $-0 \le ST(0) \le +\infty$
For **FSCALE:** $-2^{15} \le ST(1) < +2^{15}$ and ST(1) integer
For **F2XM1:** $0 \le ST(0) \le 2^{-1}$
For **FYL2X:** $0 < ST(0) < \infty$
                    $-\infty < ST(1) < +\infty$
For **FYL2XP1:** $0 < |ST(0)| < (2 - \sqrt{2})/2$
                    $-\infty < ST(1) < \infty$
For **FPTAN:** $0 \le ST(0) < \pi/4$
For **FPATAN:** $0 \le ST(0) < ST(1) < +\infty$

Bibliography*

BASIC Reference Manual, IBM (P/N 6025013), Boca Raton, Fl, 1981.

Component Data Catalog, Intel, Santa Clara, CA, 1982.

Disk Operating System Reference Manual, IBM (P/N 6024001), Boca Raton, Fl, 1981.

The 8086 Family User's Manual, Intel, Santa Clara, CA, 1980.

The 8086 Family User's Manual Numerics Supplement, Intel, Santa Clara, CA, 1980.

FORTRAN Compiler Reference Manual, IBM (P/N 6024012), Boca Raton, Fl, 1982.

Guide to Operations, IBM (P/N 6025003), Boca Raton, Fl, 1981.

Macro Assembler Reference Manual, IBM (P/N 6024002), Boca Raton, Fl, 1981.

Technical Reference Manual, IBM (P/N 6025008), Boca Raton, Fl, 1981.

*Note: All of the manuals published by IBM are available at authorized IBM Personal Computer dealers.

Index